Obsessive-Compulsive Disorder

Help for Children and Adolescents

Obsessive-Compulsive Disorder

Help for Children and Adolescents

Mitzi Waltz

Beijing • Cambridge • Farnham • Köln • Paris • Sebastopol • Taipei • Tokyo

Obsessive-Compulsive Disorder: Help for Children and Adolescents
by Mitzi Waltz

Printed in the United States of America.

Published by O'Reilly & Associates, Inc., 101 Morris Street, Sebastopol, CA 95472.

Editor: Linda Lamb

Production Editor: Sarah Jane Shangraw

Cover Design: Edie Freedman

Printing History:

April 2000: First Edition

This book is meant to educate and should not be used as an alternative for professional medical care. Although we have exerted every effort to ensure that the information presented is accurate at the time of publication, there is no guarantee that this information will remain current over time. Appropriate medical professionals should be consulted before adopting any procedures or treatments discussed in this book.

Library of Congress Cataloging-in-Publication Data:

Waltz, Mitzi.
Obsessive-compulsive disorder : help for children and adolescents / Mitzi Waltz.
p. cm. — (Patient-centered guides)
Includes bibliographical references and index.
ISBN 1-56592-758-3 (pbk.)
1. Obsessive-compulsive disorder in children. 2. Obsessive-compulsive disorder in adolescence. I. Title. II. Series.

RJ506.O25 W35 2000
618.92'85227—dc21

99-086990

[M]

For the “ocdteen” list crew

Table of Contents

Foreword

I AM A PSYCHOLOGIST WHO WORKS WITH OCD. I didn't learn much about this disorder in graduate school, but did have a chance to work with some people who have published research and treatment material about OCD. That got me interested, and then I met a couple of people with OCD who needed some help. I decided I ought to learn more about how they could be treated and what worked. I got a chance to attend training with some of the most famous people in the field.

One of my other interests is computers. I have a son who is a certified computer geek. He introduced me to the Internet before most people had heard of it. I started poking around on the Internet looking for ways I could pass on my knowledge, as well as learn from others. When I found email lists, newsgroups and web sites devoted to OCD, I started trying to answer questions, give advice, dispel myths, and comfort the distressed. In the years since, I have learned an incalculable amount and made many friends, most of whom I have never seen or even spoken to. I think I have even helped a few people.

At the 1999 convention of the Obsessive-Compulsive Foundation, I was given an award. It was a total surprise to me. I have been answering question on "Ask the Expert," which is located on the OC Foundation web site. In less than a year I answered over 700 questions there alone. Of the thousands of questions I responded to, none are more poignant than those of frantic, desperate parents who have a child with OCD. When I was asked to write the foreword for this book, I was pleased to accept the task. I see this book as filling an information gap by helping parents understand why their child is suffering and letting them know what they can do.

Not long ago, most professionals believed three myths about OCD that regarded its rarity, its treatment, and its cause. The first myth was that OCD is a rare condition. Since it was believed to be rare, little time was devoted to it in professional training. Most of us practiced for years without recognizing a case. If OCD was rare in adults, it was assumed to be even more unusual in children. A child who refused to go to school, was slow leaving his room, was difficult to put to bed, or who displayed other problematic behaviors would be diagnosed with something else, and her OCD would never be recognized or treated.

For example, a few years ago I joined a group practice with a number of experienced professionals. We had a weekly meeting in which we discussed difficult cases. At one of the first meetings I attended, another psychologist began discussing a child who was refusing to go to school sometimes, and was making a big scene at home about tying her shoes. The psychologist treating the child was having a difficult time, and didn't understand what was going on. I asked if the child had OCD. My colleague replied "I don't know what that would look like in a child." What followed was a little education for an experienced professional. From being someone who "never saw a child with OCD," my colleague has become someone who speaks to me frequently about the new cases she is seeing.

We now know that OCD is not rare—in fact, it is perhaps the fourth most common psychiatric diagnosis. It occurs frequently in children, and begins at very young ages. It is now clearly recognizable in children, and it is not unusual to find children under five years old who have clear cases of OCD. We know that early onset is more common in boys, but it may be seen in both sexes. If you are reading this book because you have a child with OCD or are working with a child who has OCD, you should know that there are millions of others with the same disorder. Sadly, many will not be recognized for years, and even fewer will be given adequate treatment.

The second myth regards treatment for OCD. It has been assumed that treatment of OCD is extremely difficult, and that the treatment of choice would be insight-oriented psychotherapy. Now that research is in, the results are clear: OCD is usually responsive to treatment, but traditional forms of psychotherapy have little to offer. Although much more work has been done on treatment of adults, in recent years studies of treatment of children with OCD have also made it into professional literature.

There are two effective treatments for OCD. The first is cognitive behavioral therapy (CBT), which has been tested and proven effective. Manuals are available for professionals, and this book and others provide information for patients. From the research on adults, we know that this type of treatment is the most powerful. In adults, the benefits of this type of therapy last for years. Research regarding CBT for children is equally encouraging. We have every reason to believe that most children can make major strides in fighting their OCD, and that they can then function as normal, happy, healthy children.

The other treatment that works for OCD is a group of medications that inhibit the reuptake of a brain chemical called serotonin. These drugs, known as selective serotonin reuptake inhibitors (SSRIs or SRIs), have now been used safely in children for a number of years. Drug companies have gone through the expensive and time-consuming effort to prove that these drugs are safe and effective treatments for childhood OCD.

The third, and perhaps most painfully destructive myth, has to do with what causes OCD. Although the experts will still say we don't know for sure what causes OCD, researchers definitely agree that it is a brain disorder. There is evidence for genetic factors, that in some cases may involve a misdirected action of the immune system, and can be described as a malfunction of part of the brain.

What OCD is *not* is the result of poor toilet training, rigid or unloving parenting styles, or sexual or other abuse. It is not the result of some hidden conflict that needs to be explored in endless insight-oriented therapy. I don't know how many parents have written to me about how guilty they feel because their child has OCD. Where did they go wrong? What did they do? The flip side of this problem is that some well-meaning people think the parent of a child with OCD must be doing something wrong, so they want to remove the child or impose other restrictions.

Parents, you can let go of that guilt. This is not a problem you caused, could have predicted, or could have prevented. Even parents who have OCD themselves need to understand that the genetic component does not mean they gave it to their child. The explanations are too complex to address here, but it is important to note that the inherited traits that may lead to development of OCD have both positive and negative aspects. If your child has OCD, you need to accept that fact and get them treatment, not blame yourself for something you cannot control.

When I talk about getting treatment, of course I mean cognitive behavioral therapy and medication. Sadly, the healthcare professionals you meet on an everyday basis may not know this. Many parents are still told things like "It's just a phase," "He'll grow out of it," or "She's just doing that to get attention."

These healthcare professionals may still believe those three old myths. They may not recognize OCD, or, if they do, they may think it is not treatable or not worth treating.

Obviously, both the general public and health professionals still need education about the disorder and its treatment. I hope this book will serve as a step toward getting that.

What happens if childhood OCD is not treated? We don't know for sure, but there is some disturbing data that suggests part of the answer. We know, for example, that OCD is more likely to appear early in boys. We also know that men with OCD are significantly less likely to get married than other men. It's easy to jump to the idea that having OCD as a child impedes social development and leads to an adulthood in which interpersonal relationships are confusing and unmanageable. I have responded to dozens of questions from teens who ask "Do I have OCD?" or "How do I tell my parents?" They often add that they have been told things like "Just stop it," "Why are you being so difficult?" or "You're just doing this to get attention."

Growing up is difficult enough without adding the shame and embarrassment of having horrible anxiety, intrusive thoughts that make you feel like a freak or monster, and compulsive behavioral rituals that lead to isolation or ridicule. This is a tragedy that doesn't have to happen.

If you are dealing with a child with OCD, get help from knowledgeable professionals. If you run across people who believe in the myths I described, keep moving. Know that this disorder can be tamed, and assistance is available. Cognitive behavioral therapy and medication, alone or combined, will dramatically reduce symptoms in most children with OCD. The dismal view of days past has been replaced with a message of great hope.

With loving thanks to all the OCD sufferers who have taught me so much.

—James M. Claiborn, PhD, ABPP

Preface

THIS BOOK IS INTENDED TO BRING TOGETHER all the basic information needed by parents of a child or teenager diagnosed with obsessive-compulsive disorder (OCD). Professionals working with young people who have OCD should also find it useful.

The first two chapters provide a broad overview of OCD, and explain how it is diagnosed. Subsequent chapters cover family issues, treatment options, strategies for dealing with insurance problems and the healthcare system, school, and transition planning for teens with OCD. Appendix A, *Resources*, lists books, web sites, organizations, special diagnostic and treatment centers, and more, to help you find the assistance that your child needs. Appendix B reprints the Children's Yale-Brown Obsessive Compulsive Scale, the most commonly used assessment instrument for young patients.

We've done our best to provide accurate information about resources in the English-speaking world, including North America, the UK, the Republic of Ireland, Australia, and New Zealand. OCD is a universal phenomenon, however, and occurs in all races and nationalities. Readers in other parts of the world may be able to find local resources and current information in languages other than English on the Web; some of the web sites and email discussion groups listed in Appendix A can point you toward resources in your part of the world. Simply because we are writing in the US, some information will be skewed toward American readers. Most, however, will be useful to all.

We present findings from the latest medical research throughout the text. This information is not intended as medical advice. Please consult your physician before starting, stopping, or changing any medical treatment. Some of the health information provided comes from small studies, or is controversial in nature. We encourage readers to carefully examine any claims made by healthcare facilities, pharmaceutical firms, therapists, supplement manufacturers, and others before implementing new treatments.

We also bring you the words of other parents and patients throughout the book. Their quotes are offset from the rest of the text and presented in italics. In many cases their names and other identifying details have been changed at their request.

OCD occurs in both girls and boys, so we've tried to alternate between pronouns when talking about patients.

Acknowledgments

Many teenagers and young adults with OCD, and over twenty parents of children with OCD, took the time to answer questions about their personal experiences. They deserve much of the credit for this book, as their replies guided its structure and contents.

Several experts, including psychologist Dr. Jim Claiborn, who specializes in treating OCD and is a member of the Scientific Advisory Board of the Obsessive-Compulsive Foundation, provided me with information and granted me interviews. A draft of the manuscript was reviewed by Dr. Jim Hatton of the San Diego Regional Program for OCD and Trichotillomania; Dr. Michael Jenike, director of the OCD Institute at McLean Hospital; Dr. John March, director of programs in pediatric anxiety disorders and psychopharmacology at Duke University; Kelly Lister, moderator of the Obsessive-Compulsive and Spectrum Disorders Association's (OCSDA) online discussion group for teens with OCD, and parent of a person with OCD; and Diane Sands, a parent of a person with OCD who is also president of the OCSDA. Their comments and criticisms were invaluable and much appreciated.

The OCSDA and the Obsessive-Compulsive Foundation have been particularly helpful, and are a great source of information and contacts for families and patients. Contacts made through *ocdandparenting*, an Internet mailing list for parents of children with OCD moderated by Louis Harkins; *OCD-L*, a mailing list for people with OCD moderated by Chris Vertullo; OCDA's *ocd-teen* list; and *Sunrise Tourette*, a mailing list moderated by Jackie Aron, have also been essential to this project. I thank everyone who shared their experiences and concerns with me.

The National Alliance for the Mentally Ill has also been an extraordinarily valuable resource. Created by parents, this organization gives voice to families and patients affected by brain disorders like OCD. It works to provide information, help, and hope in the nation's legislature, in the media, online, in its excellent annual conference, and in hundreds of community support groups.

Linda Lamb, Carol Wenmoth, Shawnde Paull, Claire Cloutier, Sarah Jane Shangraw, Edie Freedman, and all of the extraordinarily professional editorial and production staff at O'Reilly & Associates have my utmost respect and admiration, as does my literary agent, Karen Nazor.

I know from personal experience how difficult it can be to care for a child with OCD, and how difficult it is to be a child with this disorder. That's why I have to thank my two children for teaching me a great deal about how OCD has affected their lives. I must also thank my parents for doing a great job of raising me despite my own OCD, which went undiagnosed and untreated until I was 33. Today's treatment options really do work, and they have the power to change lives dramatically. They have definitely changed my family's life for the better, and I hope that the same will be true for yours.

—Mitzi Waltz

If you would like to comment on this book or offer suggestions for future editions, please send email to *guides@oreilly.com*, or write to O'Reilly & Associates, Inc. at 101 Morris St., Sebastopol, California, 95472.

CHAPTER 1

Introduction to OCD

OBSESSIVE-COMPULSIVE DISORDER (OCD) is one of the most common psychiatric problems faced by children. Estimates vary, but as many as 1 in 100 may have OCD. Nevertheless, most people know little about this disorder. As a result, many children are never diagnosed or treated.

This chapter introduces common symptoms of OCD in children and teenagers. It also discusses what causes OCD, and how this disorder is related to other neurological problems in children.

What OCD looks like

Childhood OCD can be a truly debilitating disability, not just a minor problem or a personality quirk. Children with OCD experience extreme anxiety, embarrassment, and sometimes even harassment, because of this disorder. Their OCD symptoms often prevent them from building good relationships, from achieving their best in school, and from having a normal childhood. The effects of this disruption can be painful and lifelong. OCD symptoms manifest in many different ways, as the following anecdotes reveal:

- Steve, a junior in high school, has OCD. He could not be more miserable. He can't leave the house without spending two hours performing useless rituals. Although his family isn't especially religious, his thoughts are consumed with worries about pleasing God or battling the devil. He feels compelled to turn in circles and touch a series of objects just to move from one room of his home to the other.
- Lisa is a 7-year-old with OCD. Her obsession *du jour* is Furbies, talking toys. She literally can't get her mind off these creatures. She has collected eight Furbies, spends her entire day at school making "Furby books," with stories and pictures of life in Furbyville, and the electronic toys are her sole topic of conversation. Lots of kids are crazy about collections or favorite toys, but Lisa's obsession is out of control. Not only

is it worrying her parents and teacher, it's also bothering her, because her friends are starting to avoid her. Now her parents are noticing other unusual behavior in Lisa, including having to arrange her Furbies and other objects in a certain order each night.

- Lenny also suffers from OCD. He carries a box of tissues in his backpack, and uses them to open doors. Under no circumstances will he touch an "unprotected" doorknob. He fakes illness to stay out of gym class, because he's afraid he might catch AIDS from using the locker room with the other boys. An observant teacher might notice that he makes multiple trips to the restroom each day to scrub furiously. His parents already know, of course...his endless showers, multiple handwashings, and germ phobias rule their household.

Steve, Lisa, and Lenny all have undiagnosed obsessive-compulsive disorder, a brain-based biological illness. Like many young people with OCD, their life options are circumscribed by obsessions and compulsions, anxieties and rituals. Although it is usually thought of as an adult problem, OCD affects between 1 and 5 percent of American teenagers, some of whom had an onset of symptoms as early as the toddler years. About 22 percent of adults with OCD report that their symptoms began before age 15, and the actual number is probably higher.

The good news is that OCD is very treatable. With prompt, consistent intervention, Steve, Lenny, Lisa, and most young people with OCD can wrest back control of their lives.

Although OCD is a physical illness, each person's symptoms are somewhat unique. The way OCD is expressed in a particular person sometimes has its roots in life experiences; for example, a child with OCD who experiences the traumatic death of a friend or relative may develop excessive worries related to death or disease. The experience does not cause OCD, but it does affect the development of that particular obsession.

However, there is often no known link between symptoms and experiences at all. Many OCD-related behaviors seem to be over-amplified versions of perfectly normal human behaviors, mostly small, automatic things that we all do, from grooming our hair to protecting ourselves against dirt and disease.

In fact, researchers note that all animals have certain basic behaviors that seem built-in rather than learned. Pet owners know that some animals get carried away with these automatic behaviors, such as dogs that chew their skin raw, or cats that instinctively insist on sharpening their claws on the couch despite reprimands. OCD researchers theorize that in people with OCD, one or more automatic thought or behavior circuits has developed a "tape loop" of sorts—and the latest information on brain function indicates that they're right.

Psychiatrists sometimes categorize patients who have certain common OCD behaviors as "counters," "cleaners," "checkers," and "hoarders." Most of the troubling symptoms reported by children with OCD fall into one or more of these four common categories. Put simply, counters are those who have a compulsion to count and recount their own steps, passing cars, the letters in each word they read, and so on. Cleaners carry out rituals that center around cleansing their bodies or their environment. Checkers feel compelled to check and double-check the status of things (for example, whether doors are locked, if the stove is off, or whether they are annoying people). Hoarders must get and save certain items.

Another fairly common OCD behavior is scrupulosity, the compulsive repetition of rituals that have a religious or ethical nature.

Most people with OCD have both obsessions and compulsions, and they're usually intertwined, with obsessions driving compulsive behaviors. For example, cleaning compulsions are usually driven by obsessions with germs, disease, or other forms of contamination. However, some people appear to obsess mostly on topics, while others mostly feel compelled to repeat tic-like behaviors, including complex patterns of counting, touching, or moving, that have no intrinsic meaning.

According to most researchers, males are more likely to develop OCD in childhood or adolescence, while girls are more likely to have their first symptoms after age 20. However, the incidence of OCD is about equal in adult men and women, and it could be that female children and adolescents with OCD are less likely to be screened for the disorder or appropriately diagnosed. For example, a girl who is overly concerned with her eating habits, extremely fastidious, and socially withdrawn may be considered less unusual than a boy with these characteristics. Some disorders that are closely related to OCD are diagnosed much more frequently in girls (see "Special subtypes" later in this chapter). These disorders may represent variants that, if included in the totals, would bring childhood OCD numbers closer in line with those for adults.

Common symptoms

Almost everyone occasionally experiences the fears, thoughts, feelings, and behaviors that the following list outlines. This is especially true for children, who go through phases of refusing certain foods, insisting on reading *Goodnight Moon* before bed every night for months, or worrying too much about looking cool.

When a child or teenager has OCD, however, these common fears and behaviors may be repeated, unfounded, extreme, or unstoppable. When the obsessive behavior or compulsive behavior is interrupted, the child or teenager doesn't just feel silly—they feel very upset, angry, fearful, perhaps even physically ill.

The following list of symptoms is by no means complete, especially where children are concerned. If you think a child or patient might have OCD, and if he or she has some of these symptoms, you should talk to a medical professional. You can find the official criteria for diagnosing OCD and information about getting a diagnosis in Chapter 2, *Diagnosis*; and a standard questionnaire for measuring the severity of childhood OCD, the Children's Yale-Brown Obsessive Compulsive Scale (CY-BOCS), is reprinted in Appendix B of this book.

Symptoms frequently seen in children and teens with OCD are as follows:

- Excessively cleaning hands, body, teeth, clothing, or items in the environment. These actions are usually driven by fear of contamination or illness.
- Fear of getting a terrible illness. Common worries include AIDS, cancer, and infectious diseases. The person may compulsively research or talk about his worries, ask for unnecessary medical tests, or seek constant reassurance that he is not sick.
- Fear of contracting germs from "contaminated" surfaces, places, or people. The person may take extreme steps to avoid suspect areas and people.
- Fear of "contaminating" surfaces, places, other people, or oneself by bodily waste or secretions, dirt, toxic chemicals, or undefined sources. The person may take extreme steps to avoid contaminating areas and people.

- Fear of causing a fire, car accident, or other catastrophe without noticing, or fear that something the person has left undone may cause such an event. This can lead to checking compulsions, such as repeatedly making sure the stove is off, or making sure no accident victims' bodies have been left in the street the person just drove on.
- Having unwanted, intrusive thoughts or mental images of sexual behavior, of acting contrary to one's religious beliefs, or of doing violence to oneself or others. These thoughts may be accompanied by the fear that the person might actually act on the intrusive thoughts. Usually, the person will exhibit compulsive behaviors designed to ward off that possibility or make amends for evil thoughts.
- Having obsessions about appearance, weight, hair, and clothing. The result may be compulsive dieting or eating, repetitive weighing, and spending hours to get hair or clothing "just right."
- Having symmetry obsessions. The person may feel compelled to constantly readjust clothing or other items to be in perfect symmetry or to fit with a number obsession (everything in pairs or threes, for example). The person may compulsively order objects, or straighten and align items with each other.
- Performing eating rituals. The person may exhibit obsessions about how food is prepared or served (for example, insisting that food items on a plate must not touch, or weighing each portion), or how it is eaten. For example, the person may cut food into specific-sized bites, chew each bite a certain number of times, or refuse certain perfectly edible foods because they are "contaminated" or otherwise "inedible." Teens commonly disguise eating rituals with talk about diets, "allergies" (in the absence of actual allergies), or other semi-plausible explanations.
- Performing bedtime rituals. Nighttime fears usually drive these compulsive patterns which may include ordering objects, insisting on certain exchanges of words before bed, or saying specific prayers to prevent danger.
- Compulsively saving useless objects, such as food wrappers or bottle caps.
- Excessively hoarding useful objects, such as old magazines or food. This behavior is usually driven by a fear of accidentally throwing away something important.

- Endlessly repeating routine activities for no reason, such as going through or opening a door, often requiring a certain number of repetitions, or repetition until it "feels right."
- Performing repetitive, non-functional, tic-like behaviors, such as tapping fingers, blinking, staring, touching people or objects a certain number of times, or turning around.
- Asking the same questions over and over. Some children will also expect the same answer each time, or the ritual is not complete.
- Erasing and rewriting letters, words, or phrases to make written work "perfect." This may be done so often that the paper is rubbed away by the eraser. If the child can't meet his own standards of perfection, he may throw the paper away.
- Persistently holding a belief that certain numbers are "lucky" or "unlucky." Many children with OCD rely a great deal on magical thinking and superstitions like this.
- Excessively checking and rechecking work for mistakes, such as when balancing a checkbook or doing math homework.
- Exhibiting extreme slowness in carrying out even the most routine activities. Rituals and compulsions can cause the slowness, as the child attempts to do things perfectly or in a certain order.
- Repeatedly asking a trusted person if you have committed an unwanted act.
- Experiencing, and often acting on, an overpowering need to tell another person something or to confess something.
- Ruminating, or endlessly thinking over all possibilities to the point of being unable to make decisions or take action.
- Constantly making and revising lists of things owned, things wanted, or things to do.
- Experiencing hypersensitivity to smells, sounds, textures, or touch. Sensory issues often become tied to obsessions, as in the case of a child who avoids the school lunchroom because the sound of someone chewing food from across the room makes her feel ill.

Unique childhood symptoms

The symptoms listed in the previous section are almost identical to those of adults with OCD. There are a few symptoms that are somewhat unique to children, or that may stand out even more in children than they do in adults. These include:

- Separation anxiety (see "Early warning signs," later in this chapter).
- School phobia.
- Social phobia that extends to selective mutism—refusing to speak in some situations. (This condition is sometimes called elective mutism.)
- Extreme versions of common childhood fears, such as fear of monsters under the bed or in the closet.
- Being "hooked" on topics, or even people, easily.
- Extreme inflexibility and insistence on getting their way. These children balk, to put it mildly, when their expected routine is interrupted.
- Attempts to exert extreme control over their environment. Some children with OCD spend as much time as possible in "safe" spaces, such as a closet or small playhouse, as a way to shut out the rest of the world.
- High levels of secretiveness.
- Persistent, near-paranoid feelings of being watched or followed, with resulting anxiety.
- Temper tantrums that occur long after the toddler years and that may be long, severe, and unexpected. Tantrums may occur when a child's obsession (for example, an obsession with purchasing a certain item for a collection) is interrupted.

Many adults with OCD have feelings that are similar to these, but because they have had more life experiences, they're usually able to get past them, or at least to avoid situations in which these feelings are triggered. Adults are more able to control their environment; they choose their own home or apartment, they decide whether or not to see scary movies, and they can prepare their own "poison-free" meals. Children cannot control most of their daily environment and activities, and this can make OCD-related obsessions and resulting anxieties even stronger.

Another difference between adults and children with OCD is that older patients can usually give a reason for their unusual behaviors. They act as they do to prevent something bad from happening, as if performing their rituals can magically stave off doubts and anxieties that plague them. Their compulsive behaviors are usually connected to dealing with specific fears, such as disease or death. They know that these fears and behaviors are not reasonable, and they try to disguise them.

Young children with OCD may not be able to put their fears into words—they just know they must do these things without always being able to understand why. "I just have to," may be the best explanation they can come up with. And because they are too young to have much insight into other people's behaviors and thoughts, they may not be aware that they have a problem. In fact, children are much more likely to be very open about their fears, obsessions, and compulsions than are adults, and may make little or no effort to hide them. However, obsessions and compulsions that center around death and sexuality tend to be so disturbing that even young children may try to hide them.

That's why diagnosis of OCD depends on observation by parents, other caregivers, and medical professionals, as well as on self-reported symptoms—especially with young children.

Early warning signs

When adults and teens with OCD look back, they may recognize the first glimmerings of the illness in early childhood. One of the most striking behaviors shared by many children who have or later develop OCD is separation anxiety—extreme fear of being separated from their mother or other caregiver. Parents describe their children with OCD as having been clingy and fussy right from the start, long before anything as recognizable as OCD emerged. They may be shy children, less likely to seek out and play with others than their siblings or other children their age.

Many families report insistence on consistency and routine. Most young children like predictability, but these children wanted the same order of activities every night before bed, for example, and were very agitated when their routines were disrupted. Such children may develop fixations, such as wearing only pink clothing or refusing any foods not served on a special plate, at a very early age.

Some children who are described by their parents as picky eaters (or just plain picky about everything from broccoli to toys to TV) are later diagnosed with OCD. They may seem uncomfortable in their clothes and easily irritated, symptoms that are probably related to sensory integration problems (see Chapter 4, *Therapeutic Interventions*), which seem to be very common in these children.

Most children with OCD develop fairly normally physically, but there may be subtle signs of problems if you take a closer look. Quite a few parents say that their child with OCD was clumsier than his or her siblings and crawled, walked, and talked a little later or differently. Recent research has corroborated these reports, finding a higher rate of "soft" neurological signs in children with OCD.[1] Some children with OCD also seem to have immune-system problems from infancy, such as frequent and severe ear infections, unusual reactions to minor childhood illnesses or immunizations, and allergies. These are all signs of subtle brain differences that affect early childhood development and general health. They're not the kind of major developmental problems that cause parents and doctors to take immediate notice, however.

Of course, many children who later develop OCD have no early warning signs at all.

Special subtypes

Not all of the experts agree, but there are a few disorders that resemble OCD so closely that some researchers think they are just special versions of it. One of the most common of these is trichotillomania: compulsive hair-pulling. "Trich" is more common in girls than in boys, and people who have it may pull hair from their heads or any other body area. The behavior isn't quite automatic enough to be an unconscious tic, and for most people it's preceded by an irresistible urge, perhaps accompanied by an uncomfortable or prickly physical sensation. People with trich say they feel compelled to pull, and they may feel further compelled to perform even more complex behaviors, like tying knots in the pulled hair.

Another closely related problem is body dysmorphic disorder (BDD), along with its close relatives anorexia and bulimia. These problems also affect girls more frequently than boys. People with body dysmorphic disorder have a persistent and unfounded belief that they are ugly. They are obsessed with improving (or simply hiding) their appearance to the extent that some may repeatedly pursue unneeded cosmetic surgery, exercise compulsively, or follow dangerous diets.

It's the latter problem that can develop into eating disorders, along with the "picky eating" obsessions seen so often in children with OCD. Girls and boys with anorexia or bulimia are obsessed with food: eating it, not eating it, the number of fat grams and calories in it, and how it affects them. They may feel compelled to diet, to binge, or to purge. Eating disorders have long been believed to have their roots in childhood abuse or societal problems such as pressure on young girls to be thin. As we've seen, life experiences can influence how OCD develops in a particular person, but it doesn't cause the disorder. This may hold true for eating disorders as well.

There are compelling reasons to believe that for many people with trichotillomania, body dysmorphic disorder, anorexia, or bulimia, their symptoms arise from the same brain differences that cause OCD. These conditions are rampant in people with OCD—far, far more common than they are in the general population. Those who have been diagnosed with both OCD and one of these problems usually say that the compulsions and obsessions feel pretty much the same, whether it's an obsession with thinness or with the proper order of objects on a shelf.

Some researchers feel that other disorders, such as kleptomania (compulsive stealing), compulsive gambling, pyromania (strong fascination with fire and/or compulsive fire-setting), and substance abuse disorders are related to OCD. All of these conditions will be defined and discussed further in Chapter 2.

Long-term consequences

Living or working with a child who has OCD can be exasperating. As adults, we want the world to make sense, and OCD just doesn't. As difficult as life is for those who care for children with OCD, the inner experience of this disorder is much worse.

Raegan, 18 years old, talks about her experience with the disorder:

> *I had just about every symptom of OCD. I had to take four showers a day because I had a terrible fear of germs. I checked everything around me, from clocks to ovens. I couldn't even do simple things like watch a television show because obsessive thoughts were always with me. My mind was the worst thing for me to live with. Doctors have told me that they are surprised that I survived this hellish lifestyle.*

OCD symptoms take time away from family, friends, school, and fun. If other kids catch a child exhibiting some kind of "weird" behavior, they may tease or ostracize her. Parents are not always understanding, and extended family members who don't know about or believe in the diagnosis may be even less so.

Teenagers who have had OCD since childhood frequently describe feelings of confusion, powerlessness, shame, embarrassment, and even rage toward those who have belittled and misunderstood them. They are acutely sensitive to what others think of them, even when they pretend not to care. Many have internalized the labels applied to them over the years—bad, crazy, lazy, stupid, strange, sick, and all the rest—developing a poor self-image that feeds depression and apathy.

Difficult relationships in the family can lead to withdrawn or oppositional behavior in teens with OCD, especially if they don't feel that their parents are on their side. For their own part, parents are stressed out by trying to walk the fine line between supporting their child's needs and refusing to facilitate OCD behaviors. All parents fail sometimes, falling to one side or the other. Kids sometimes use these momentary failures as a way to manufacture even more misery.

When OCD keeps kids out of school and away from participation in community activities, they lose out on opportunities to advance academically, learn appropriate social skills, and make friends. Many young adults with OCD find they are not ready for the schoolwork demands and social freedom of college—not to mention complex adult relationships—because their academic and social skills are still at the junior-high level. They've been so busy simply trying to hold things together that they've missed whole chunks of their education and development.

John, father of 14-year-old Tori, talks about the difficult consequences of her illness:

> *Tori has not been able to attend school for the past two years. The regular school system is a very difficult place for a child with OCD, especially when OCD is accompanied by Asperger's syndrome. Tori placed high academic goals on herself, but these perfectionist goals were unrealistic when she had attention and written work difficulties. The social aspect of school became intolerable as she reached higher grades.*

Tori cannot interact physically with her younger brother because of contamination fears. She has lost contact with any of her past friends: even extended family have little patience for her obsessional interests.

As a result of missed opportunities, adults with OCD are less likely to have satisfying relationships, less likely to be employed, and more likely to be employed in low-paid, menial jobs than are others in their age group. Some subsist on disability payments or are cared for by spouses or relatives. Serious problems are more likely to occur in adulthood when OCD has gone undiagnosed and untreated for many years, particularly when symptoms emerged during childhood. Without reliable medical help and support from family, friends, and schools, people with OCD may develop poor coping strategies, such as substance abuse or social withdrawal, that force them further into isolation and despair.

Parents and helping professionals can't make everything turn out perfectly for kids with OCD, but they can make a sincere effort to remember that successful treatment gives consideration to the whole child, not just the child's OCD. Knocking out symptoms with therapy and/or medications is a start, but it doesn't recover lost time or build new skills—it just makes this hard work possible. Parents and professionals also need to remember that building a strong sense of self-worth, good coping skills, and solid medical knowledge about OCD will go far to help kids cope with this baffling disorder, no matter what symptoms it throws at them in later years.

OCD and other disorders

Many experts feel that OCD is more eloquently described as a spectrum disorder, one of several identifiable neurological problems that affect thought and behavior. It's certainly true that many children diagnosed with OCD also turn out to have other brain-based disorders, particularly Attention Deficit Disorder (ADD) or Attention Deficit Hyperactivity Disorder (ADHD).

Besides ADD and ADHD, conditions that occur more often in people with OCD than in the general population include:

- **Tourette's syndrome and other tic disorders.** Tic disorders appear to originate in the same part of the brain as OCD, and about half of those diagnosed with Tourette's syndrome also have obsessive-compulsive disorder. There appears to be a strong genetic link between Tourette's and OCD.

- **Autistic spectrum disorders.** This category includes autism, Asperger's syndrome, and pervasive developmental disorder—not otherwise specified (PDD-NOS). There appears to be a strong genetic link between these conditions and OCD.
- **Anxiety disorders.** On close examination, problems such as social phobias or panic attacks sometimes simply turn out to be manifestations of underlying OCD.
- **Mood disorders.** These disorders include depression and manic depression (bipolar disorder).
- **Learning disabilities.** Specific learning disabilities are dyslexia and dysgraphia.

If a child is diagnosed with OCD *and* another disorder, such as depression, it is called a "comorbid disorder."

Some children with OCD don't have one of these other disorders in its full-blown, clinical form, but share certain symptoms and traits that may respond to treatments usually used for these disorders. If your child has puzzling symptoms or traits that don't seem to fit within the confines of OCD, looking at the criteria of one of these other conditions may shed some light on the problem and indicate treatment possibilities. When you read the next section, "What causes OCD?," these relationships will become even clearer.

If you'd like to know more about the relationship of OCD, obsessive-compulsive symptoms, and other childhood psychiatric disorders, Dr. Mark Riddle of Johns Hopkins University has made his slide show, "OCD-Related Psychiatric Disorders in Children and Adolescents," available on the Web at *http://www.wpic.pitt.edu/ocd/riddle/sld001.htm.* Comorbid disorders associated with OCD are also defined and discussed in greater detail in Chapter 2.

What causes OCD?

OCD originates in the brain. This tight-knit bundle of nerves buzzes with activity all day and night, responding to messages relayed from nerves that stretch into every part of the body.

The human brain is still the most complicated computer on the planet. Although it is prewired during fetal development, it has the ability to grow, change, and learn throughout a lifetime of experiences.

As noted earlier in this chapter, many of the repetitive thoughts and behaviors associated with OCD are very basic, essential functions. One of the brain's most important basic duties is checking the environment for dangers, giving an advance warning of potential problems, and keeping a database of what we learn in the process. In the jungle or in traffic, this nearly unconscious business of checking, doubting, and comparing what we see with past experiences can be a lifesaver.

When you can't turn that same circuit off, however, you have OCD.

Brain differences

Only in recent years have we been able to see inside a working brain. Although we can't yet use it to diagnose OCD, advanced brain-scanning technology has allowed researchers to literally watch circuits misfiring inside the brains of people who have OCD.

What they've discovered is that the brains of people with OCD use incredible amounts of energy compared to those of people without the disorder. Their neural pathways are firing on all pistons as they worry, worry, worry away.

Figure 1-1 shows a general diagram of the brain, while Figure 1-2 shows the areas of the brain involved in OCD.

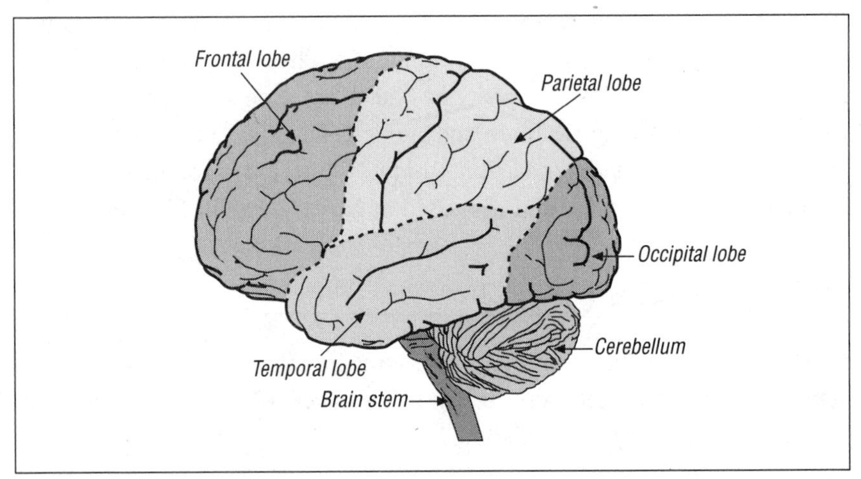

Figure 1-1. Parts of the brain

Specific areas of the brain are also especially active, or act differently. Perhaps the most prominent of these areas are the basal ganglia, a small group

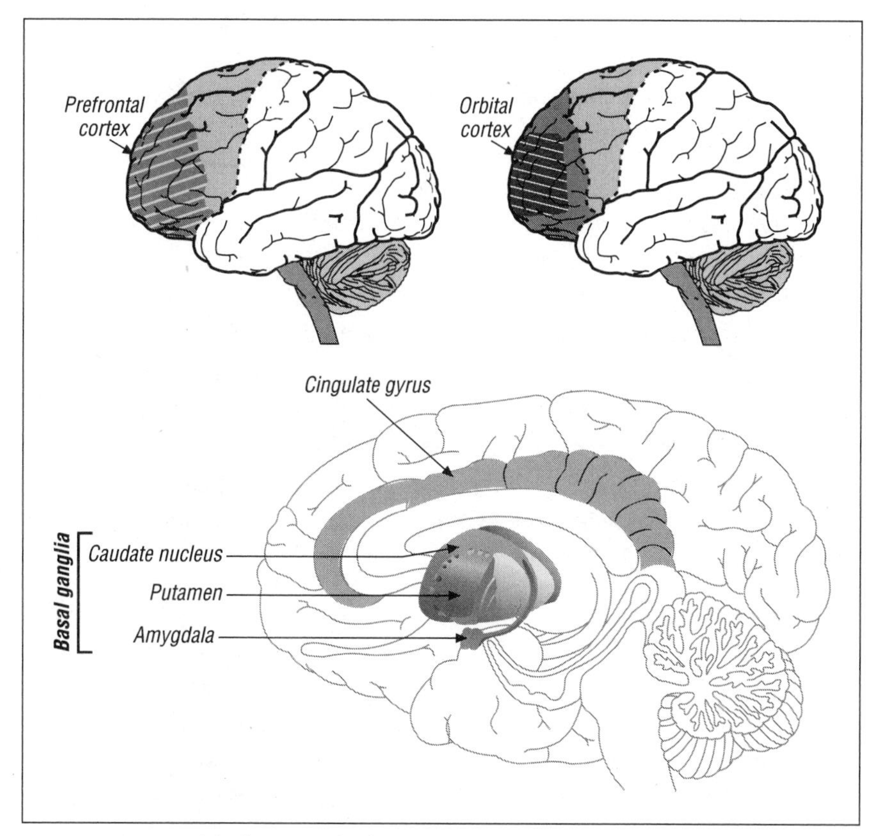

Figure 1-2. Parts of the brain involved in OCD

of affiliated structures in the very center of the brain. The basal ganglia include the putamen, the caudate nucleus, and the amygdala. These structures have jobs with importance that is out of proportion to their size. They're in charge of controlling built-in, practically unconscious movements, such as raising your hands to fend off an oncoming object. They also control impulsiveness and inhibition in general. The amygdala is specifically involved in controlling fear and rage.

Also involved in OCD is the orbital cortex. This region of the brain is right behind your eyes. It's part of the foremost layer of the brain, the prefrontal cortex, which in turn is part of the brain's frontal lobe. Its job is to tell you whether you should believe what you see, hear, or feel: in other words, it's the seat of your doubting and checking circuit. A great deal of "higher-level" thinking goes on in this area of the brain. It seems to be where we make moral judgments, not just practical ones, based on what we have learned to believe. Brain images of people with OCD show extra activity occurring in the orbital cortex. The orbital cortex communicates very directly with the basal ganglia, giving the basal ganglia the information they need to call up an appropriate automatic response.

The cingulate gyrus lies between the orbital cortex and the basal ganglia. When the hair pricks up on the back of your neck because someone is following you, this is the part of your brain that has gone on alert. It takes danger signs processed by the orbital cortex and translates them into fear and dread, emotions that are actually caused by a sudden rush of chemicals that heighten your awareness and make you ready for rapid response. These automatic warnings can save you from harm, but when they're erroneously activated in OCD, they cause senseless anxiety. These erroneous messages keep on rolling until they reach the basal ganglia, which may then cook up some illogical way to relieve the mysterious anxiety—an automatic behavior that turns into a ritual or compulsion, perhaps.

It seems obvious that a difference in brain function anywhere along this winding path could lead to OCD, and in fact, obsessive-compulsive symptoms are seen in some people who suffer an injury to these parts of the brain. Damage to or differences in the basal ganglia appears to be the deciding factor though, because without its permission to have that repetitive thought or do that repetitive behavior, the whole aberrant process fizzles out pretty quickly.

Most researchers suspect that if you can calm down the over-activity in the basal ganglia, the cingulate gyrus and the orbital cortex will eventually fall into line, and thought and behavior processes will become more normal. And in fact, that's just what both medication and cognitive behavioral therapy—the two treatments recommended for OCD—appear to do. You can even see the difference in basal ganglia activity levels by comparing pre- and post-treatment brain scans. These treatments don't just cover up the problem or help patients learn to cope better, they make real and lasting changes in brain activity and brain chemistry.

Of course this theory applies only when the brain's structure is relatively sound (minor abnormalities are actually pretty normal—there's great variation between individual brains, and the organ seems to route around minor damage most of the time). It is rare, but serious brain malformations or damage occasionally cause obsessive-compulsive symptoms. For example, uncontrolled seizure activity in a part of the temporal lobe called the limbic system has been known to cause obsessiveness, and religious fixations in particular. If there is any reason to believe that your child or patient has suffered a serious head injury, or if problems in other physical or mental functions indicate larger problems, it's a good idea to take a closer look at the brain's general state of health. An EEG can check for seizure activity, and brain imaging can find structural problems.

The brain function differences seen in OCD are much like those observed in brain scans of people with related disorders, such as ADHD. For example, MRI scans of people with ADHD have uncovered significant loss of normal right/left asymmetry in the caudate nucleus, a smaller right globus pallidus, a smaller right anterior frontal region, a smaller cerebellum, and reversal of normal lateral ventricular asymmetry, among other differences.[2] In patients with bipolar disorders (manic depression), differences in the prefrontal and anterior paralimbic areas of the brain are found,[3] as is an enlarged caudate nucleus.[4]

Neurotransmitter differences

All parts of the brain are made up of cells called neurons and glial cells. The neurons are the brain's internal communication centers, but they don't trade messages directly. Instead, they use a complicated sequence of electrical and chemical messengers.

Neurons have a central cell body with long "arms" called *axons*, and smaller tentacle-like structures called *dendrites*. (See Figure 1-3.) Inside a neuron, all the messages are sent via electrical impulses. Where two neurons meet to swap information, however, a small space between them called the *synaptic cleft* remains. Their electrical impulses must be translated into chemicals called *neurotransmitters* to cross the synaptic cleft, after which they are translated into electrical signals on the other side. (See Figure 1-4.)

Most of us are at least somewhat familiar with the chemicals known as hormones. These chemicals, which include estrogen and testosterone, are special neurotransmitters that carry information about reproduction-related development and activity between the brain and the body. They're not single-minded compounds, either—estrogen, for example, affects such diverse functions as ovulation, mood, and water retention.

There are dozens of such chemicals relaying information between parts of the human brain, the central nervous system (CNS), and other parts of the

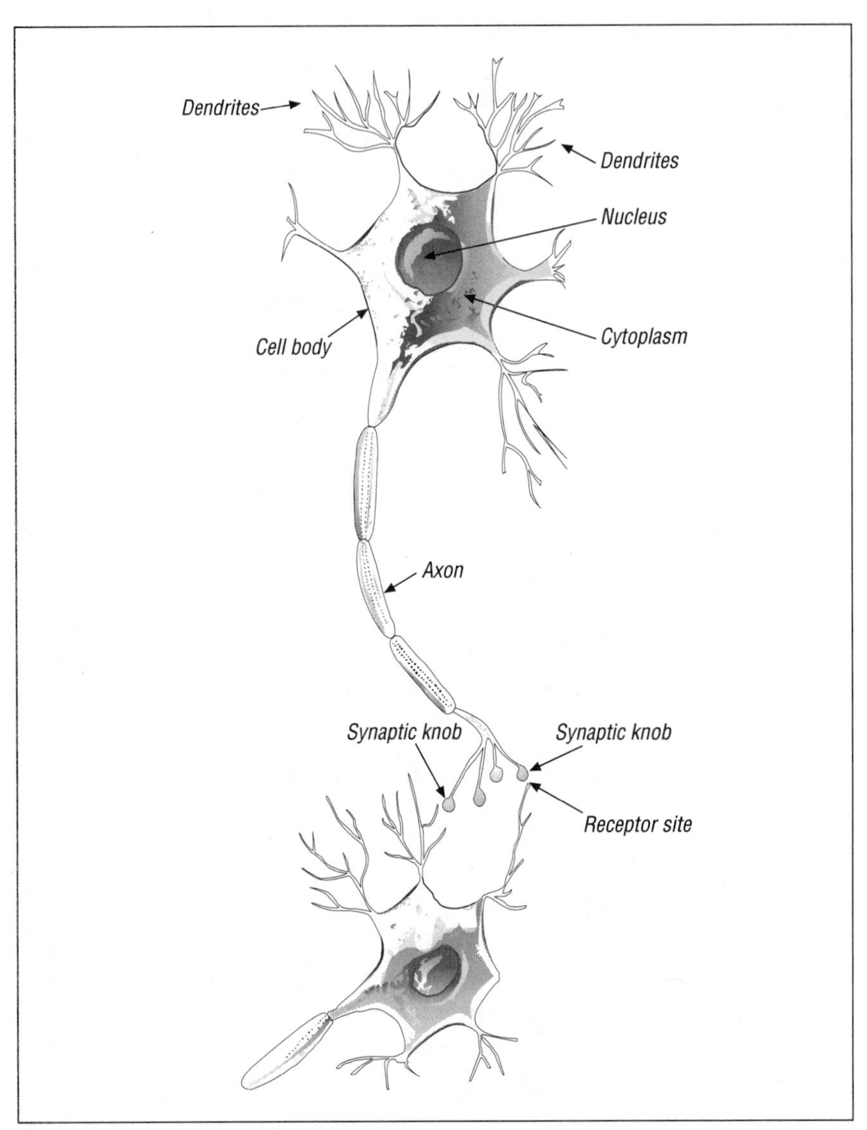

Figure 1-3. The structure of a neuron

body, such as the gastrointestinal system. They're all site-specific chemicals, which means they can be absorbed only by certain cells in certain places. This ensures that the right kinds of messages get through. The chemicals are also used and absorbed differently in various areas of the body, and sometimes turned into other chemicals.

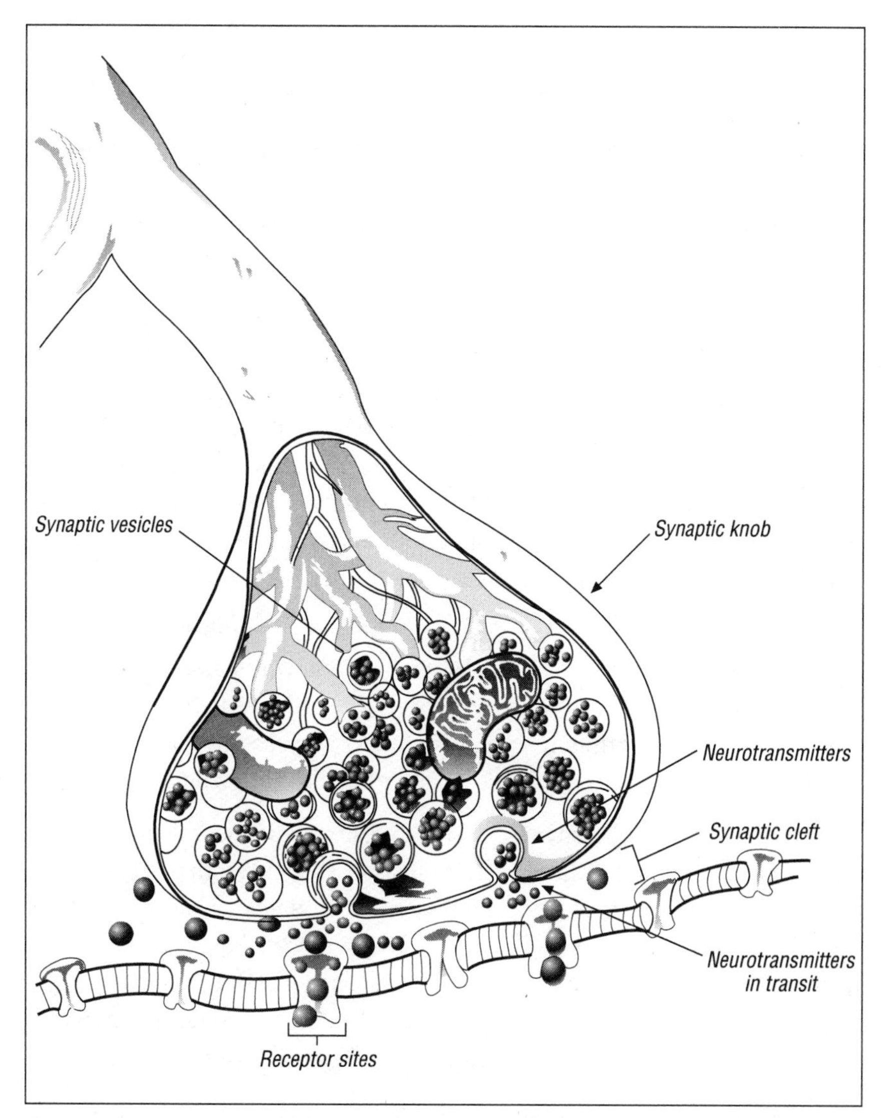

Figure 1-4. Neurotransmitters crossing the synaptic cleft

Neurotransmitters that appear to be strongly involved in obsessive-compulsive disorders include:

- **Serotonin**. Serotonin, also called 5-hydroxytryptamine or 5-HT, controls sleep, mood, some types of sensory perception, body-temperature regulation, and appetite. It affects the rate at which hormones are released, and has something to do with inflammation.

- **Dopamine.** Dopamine, sometimes abbreviated as DA, helps control body movements and thought patterns, and also regulates hormone release.
- **Norepinephrine.** Norepinephrine is used by both the central nervous system and the peripheral sympathetic nervous system (the nerves that communicate with the rest of the body). It governs arousal, the "fight or flight" response, anxiety, and memory.

Medications that change how much of certain hormones and neurotransmitters are produced, or how these chemicals are absorbed in the brain, produce changes in symptoms—that's one of the clues that has let researchers know which neurotransmitters have something to do with OCD. All of the medications known to be effective in treating OCD affect the serotonin system. Serotonin, in turn, affects the production and use of dopamine and norepinephrine. They're all interconnected, and a subtle change in chemistry appears to be capable of starting a cascade effect—for better or worse.

Physical activity, exercise, diet, vitamins, and herbal supplements can also affect neurotransmitters. That's one of the reasons why parents and professionals need to be as careful about choosing alternative treatments as they would be about prescription drugs. For more information about nonpharmaceutical treatments for OCD, see Chapter 6, *Other Interventions*.

Cognitive behavioral therapy also seems to cause actual neurological change over a period of time. There is some reason to believe that stressful life events can cause a change in neurotransmitter production that may kick off episodes of OCD. For example, OCD clinics report that they often have many calls from new patients after a serious earthquake. Perhaps the initial response to the quake and the protracted anxiety experienced during the aftershocks "trips the circuits" in those whose brains are vulnerable to OCD.

Many people don't care for the idea that so much about behavior and even personality seems to be bound up in chemical and electrical processes, but that is what science seems to be telling us. For example, the DSM-IV has a diagnostic category for obsessive-compulsive personality disorder (OCPD) as well as for OCD. OCPD is defined as a "difficult" personality style characterized by extreme rigidity and a controlling attitude. For years, psychologists believed that while OCD was an obvious biological disorder, OCPD was learned behavior.

Well, they're now reconsidering, because when people diagnosed with both OCD and OCPD take effective OCD medication, their OCPD characteristics also start to disappear. It looks more and more like much of what we think of as personality is really just chemicals in action.[5]

Genetic differences

Normally, humans inherit 46 chromosomes: 22 pairs of non-sex chromosomes and 2 sex chromosomes (2 X chromosomes for women; an X and a Y for men). Each chromosome is comprised of uncounted bits of code called genes. Your genes "program" everything about how you will develop, from the curl of your hair to your vulnerability to ragweed allergies.

Some genes are dominant, which means you only need to inherit one copy of the gene to express the trait for which it codes. The gene that codes for brown eyes is dominant, for example. Other genes (those that code for blue eyes, for example) are recessive, so you need two copies of the gene to express its respective trait.

As of this writing, scientists around the world are working feverishly to decode the mysteries of the human genetic code. The Human Genome Project is an ongoing effort to make a "map" of the whole human genotype, matching each spot on a gene with its purpose. For now, most of what we know about the genetic code has been learned by studying what happens when a gene is missing (deleted), changed (mutated), or duplicated. That's why genetic studies of people with disorders closely related to OCD are providing clues, and why knowledge about certain rare, genetic disorders that feature obsessive-compulsive symptoms may also help.

One thing geneticists already know is that OCD is not going to be an easy puzzle to solve. It's definitely not caused by a single, dominant gene, because a difference that easy to spot would be seen even on primitive chromosome tests. It's almost surely what is called a multigenic disorder: a problem caused by several genes working together. Some of these genes may be recessive, some dominant. There might even be more than one genetic combination that causes OCD or certain subtypes of OCD (such as the immune-system-linked variant discussed in the section "Immune-system differences," later in this chapter). Or, it may be caused by different combinations of genes in men and women.

The genetic differences could be causing differences in brain structure, neurotransmitter production or use, the immune system, metabolism, or any combination of these and other factors. They may cause OCD directly, or simply make a person more susceptible to developing OCD in response to environmental factors, such as infectious disease.

So far, no OCD-linked genes have been identified positively, although several studies are underway. The serotonin transporter gene, also known as HTT, is considered a top contender. The HTT gene codes for a protein that lets serotonin be re-absorbed by nerve cells after its release.[6] Located on chromosome 17, a difference found in a bit of code known as the HTT promoter gene may be the key. This gene turns the HTT gene on or off—or makes it work at lowered capacity.

A 1997 study found that men with a less-active version of a gene that codes for an enzyme called catechol-O-methyltransferase (COMT) are six times more likely to have OCD than men without it. This gene is located on chromosome 22 in an area where researchers already know that some people with OCD or schizophrenia are prone to have deletions (missing bits of genetic material). The COMT enzyme inactivates dopamine and related neurotransmitters. The researchers didn't find the same difference in women with OCD, but noted that estrogen negates COMT anyway, so that probably isn't important.[7]

Incidentally, researchers working on OCD genetic studies are especially interested in families in which more than one member has OCD. Participating usually requires nothing more than a blood sample or two and a diagnostic work-up. There is no charge to participants, and in some cases you may be provided with transportation, housing, and meals if you need to travel to the study site. Please contact the Obsessive-Compulsive Foundation (see Appendix A, *Resources*) for more information about studies in your area.

In the absence of definitive data about genes in OCD, researchers are looking at what is known about closely related disorders, especially Tourette's syndrome and autistic spectrum disorders. Table 1-1 shows some of the genes that researchers believe may link to OCD.

The latest genetic model for Tourette's syndrome is a mixed model, with both recessive and dominant genes involved. Researchers believe that along with this combination, a single additive major gene is necessary for

Tourette's to develop. They have theorized that this as-yet-unidentified gene occurs in about 1 in 100 people—about the same rate as the prevalence of adult OCD—but the combination of other genes that allows it to be expressed as Tourette's is probably more rare. Most researchers believe OCD may be an alternative expression of the same basic genotype. The wild card is environmental factors, such as life experiences and infections. These factors seem to govern the severity of Tourette's and/or OCD symptoms.[8]

More genetic research has identified other "suspicious" sites on chromosomes of people with Tourette's syndrome, but so far research is still in its formative stages.

The genetics of autism have not been studied for long, but over the past few years a concentrated effort at identifying multiple sites has begun to bear fruit. A 1997 study found that autistic children tend to have a shortened version of the HTT promoter gene.[9] This, and a second HTT difference seen in some people with autism, has also been linked to bipolar disorders.[10]

In 1997, one group of genetic researchers announced that the first of three to five genes believed to cause most autistic spectrum disorders had been tentatively located on chromosomes 7 and 16.[11] This is of particular interest to OCD researchers, because a rare genetic disease called tuberous sclerosis is also linked to chromosome 16.

Tuberous sclerosis can be caused by two different genetic defects (the other occurs on chromosome 9). Only one of these genes is necessary to cause the condition, although other unknown genetic factors may determine who develops the disorder. People with tuberous sclerosis may develop neurological problems that resemble OCD or autism. Recent studies have shown that the severity of these features, including obsessive-compulsive behaviors, correlate with the number and size of tubers (benign tumors) growing in the patient's temporal lobes.[12]

Some people with autism have duplications of genes on chromosome 15 in the region 15q11-q13, as do people with the rare genetic disorders Angelman syndrome and Prader-Willi syndrome, and some people with communication disorders. The symptoms of both Angelman syndrome and Prader-Willi syndrome include obsessive-compulsive or autistic traits. This region on chromosome 15 contains three genes that code for the neurotransmitter gamma-aminobutyric acid (GABA), which is already a well-known player in anxiety disorders. It prevents cells from firing, inhibiting normal nerve responses.

Another research team has noted that several genes with possible links to autism are near genes that code for immune-system function. For example, the C4B gene on chromosome 6 codes for complement C4 protein, which works with the antibody immunoglobulin A to fight viruses. Many people with autism have a form of the C4B gene that produces no protein.

Many of the genetic differences noted in Table 1-1 have been found in only a few patients, and may represent unique conditions rather than clues about the causes of OCD and related disorders.

Table 1-1. Some Suspicious Genes in OCD and Related Disorders

Chromosomes with "Suspect" Genes	OCD	Tourette's Syndrome	Autistic Spectrum Disorders	Other Linked Disorders
1				
2		D2S1790		Dyslexia (DYX3)
3				Tuberous sclerosis (possible subtype)
5		Dopamine receptor 1 gene, 5q31-34	5q22.1 subband Monosomy on short arm of chromosome Duplication of 15q11-13 region	
6		D6S477	Complement C4 protein gene, C4B Partial trisomy 6p	
7		translocation with 18		
8		D8S257		
9			9q34	Tuberous sclerosis
11		D11S933 Dopamine receptor 2 gene, 11q22-23		Alcoholism, ADHD, schizophrenia (Dopamine receptor 2 gene, 11q22-23)
12				Tuberous sclerosis (possible subtype)
13				
14		D14S1003		

Table 1-1. Some Suspicious Genes in OCD and Related Disorders (continued)

Chromosomes with "Suspect" Genes	OCD	Tourette's Syndrome	Autistic Spectrum Disorders	Other Linked Disorders
15			GABA receptor genes, 15q11-q13 Partial trisomy 15	Angelman syndrome, Prader-Willi syndrome, communication disorders (GABA receptor genes, 15q11-q13) Anxiety disorders
16			Trisomy or partial trisomy 16	
17	HTT promoter gene	HTT gene	HTT promoter gene Trisomy 17 (very rare)	Affective disorders/ depression, anxiety disorders (HTT promoter gene)
18		Translocation with 7		
20		D20S1085		
21		D21S1252		
22	COMT gene			Anxiety disorders
X and Y	HRAS (part of the G protein secondary messenger system)	X-linked gene affecting monomine oxidase (MAO) receptors	Fragile sites on X chromosome (Fragile X) Rett syndrome (MECP2) HRAS (part of the G protein secondary messenger system) Region between the DXS453 and DXS1001 markers, specifically at DXS287 and DXS424	Substance abuse (X-linked gene affecting MAO receptors)

For today's parents and professionals, genetic studies are an interesting sideline but they don't yet have practical value. There is no genetic test for OCD at this time, nor is there any "gene therapy" in the works.

Parents often want to know if they can predict whether their next child will also have OCD. It's known that there is an increased likelihood of OCD in siblings of those with OCD, and that parents with OCD are more likely to have a child with OCD. There is no way to predict whether the disorder will occur in a particular child, however. Since there is reasonable hope for effectively treating this disorder, it's unlikely that a genetic counselor would advise parents who desire more children not to try to conceive.

Immune-system differences

All this talk about genetic differences brings us to a current hot topic in OCD research: the possibility that immune-system differences may be at the root of at least some cases of OCD.

One thing that still divides "mental" illness from "physical" illness in the minds of both patients and doctors is that diagnosing mental illness is a very subjective process. You can take a blood test for hepatitis, and you can get a biopsy for cancer, but mental illness is all about observing symptoms and making a judgment call. So imagine the excitement that swept the medical research community when the first biological marker for a mental illness became known in late 1996.

Dr. Susan Swedo and a team of doctors working with the National Institutes for Mental Health, a federally funded research organization, were looking at children who developed obsessive-compulsive symptoms after an illness known as rheumatic fever. Rheumatic fever is a serious complication of infection with the Group A beta-hemolytic streptococcus (GABHS) bacteria—the same type of strep that causes strep throat and many childhood ear infections. Children who get rheumatic fever often develop a movement disorder called Sydenham's chorea, which is characterized by twisting, writhing movements of the hands and legs, facial grimacing, obsessions, over-emotional behavior, anxiety, and compulsions. Because rheumatic fever can also damage the heart and cause other serious health problems, no one had really given much thought to the mental health implications of these unusual symptoms. But Dr. Swedo's team took a closer look, and found an unusual protein in the blood of most rheumatic fever patients who developed these extra symptoms. They called this protein D8/17. Then the team took a look at a group of children with OCD and/or Tourette's syndrome.

Parents had been telling doctors for years that their child with OCD and/or Tourette's had a sudden onset of the illness, or that their symptoms took a sudden turn for the worse, not long after a bout with strep throat. They had also wondered aloud why some children with these disorders (and, it should be noted, some with ADD/ADHD or autistic spectrum disorders) suffered from so many more serious ear infections than their siblings or other children the same age.

Cindy, mother of 10-year-old Brett, tells a common story about strep and OCD:

> *Brett started with ear infections at 3 months old and has continued with them until he was diagnosed with OCD last year. He had monthly infections, even with tubes, twice. He also has quite a few medication allergies. I never thought about when the ear infections stopped and the OCD increased, and am not sure there is a connection to that.*

Questions like Cindy's went unanswered until Dr. Swedo's team announced its preliminary findings: 85 percent of children with OCD or Tourette's syndrome who seemed to react to strep infection also had the same D8/17 blood protein as children who developed Sydenham's chorea after getting rheumatic fever.[13] Another study of children with OCD and/or tics found that 100 percent had the D8/17 marker.[14]

It took some digging, but Swedo eventually announced to the astounded medical community that the D8/17 marker indicates an immune system gone slightly haywire. The body has created antibodies to the strep bacteria, just as it should, but those antibodies are attacking the basal ganglia in the brain as well. It's that attack on the body's own tissue—an autoimmune reaction—that causes the unusual movements in children with Sydenham's chorea, and the tics and obsessive-compulsive symptoms seen in this subgroup of children with OCD and/or Tourette's syndrome.[15]

A formal study has not been done in children with ADD/ADHD, but one small study of children with autism found the blood marker as well.[16] Much more research needs to be done, but one thing is certain: for some—but not all—patients, there is a link between a malfunctioning immune system and the appearance and severity of their OCD symptoms. Dr. Swedo has named this disorder Pediatric Autoimmune Neuropsychiatric Disorders Associated with Streptococcal infections, or PANDAS.

Currently, there's no commercial version of the blood test that Dr. Swedo's team used in its study, but some children with OCD who had sudden onset after a strep infection, or repeated flares in response to strep, have been diagnosed with PANDAS simply by observation. They have been given treatments that seem to help. Chapter 5, *Medical Interventions*, has more information about these new treatment ideas.

Interestingly, strep may not be the only offender. Many different types of infections may have an adverse affect on the brains of some people with immune-system-linked OCD. In fact, a link between obsessive-compulsive symptoms and brain infections (encephalitis) has been known since at least the 1930s.

What doesn't cause OCD

Although parents pass on chromosomes to their children, and chromosomes have lately been implicated in OCD, parents can no more control this part of their genetic contribution than they can control the hair or skin color of their offspring. No parent *wants* to pass on the genes for OCD, so there's no reason to feel guilty about it. Thankfully, it is not a deadly genetic disorder. There are even some who would argue that the genes for OCD probably carry some powerful benefits as well—otherwise, why would the disorder be so common? Perhaps the genes for perseverance, attention to detail, and moral conscientiousness, if there are such things, are also part of this genetic package.

Even the most rotten, mean, and downright abusive parents can't cause OCD in a child. Many adults with OCD went through years of painful psychoanalysis back in the bad old days, when mental illness was still thought to be caused by overbearing moms and "Raging Bull" dads. We've since figured out that those "bad parents," who supposedly caused biological mental illnesses, were probably suffering from undiagnosed, untreated mental illnesses themselves.

Indeed, many adults with OCD report that one of their parents met the criteria for OCD or one of its cousins, like OCPD or social phobia, but never got help. This certainly did not make life any easier for their children. Today parents with psychiatric illness shouldn't suffer. By getting treatment, they can do their children a great service—for those children who happen to share their diagnosis and those who do not.

In summary, bad parenting can't cause OCD, but it doesn't help. In fact, parents of children with OCD usually have to rethink everything they thought they knew about being a good parent, because these kids challenge all the traditional rules. Parents do need some special skills to cope well with these unique kids and their symptoms. (See Chapter 3, *Living with OCD*, for more information about parenting problems and solutions for families coping with OCD.)

If you are the parent of a teenager with OCD and you've been struggling all these years in ways that don't mesh with the current advice, don't feel bad—you didn't cause the disorder by making mistakes, and it's never too late to make positive changes. Like every other parent in this club, you've been coping as best as you can. Hopefully this book will help you turn the situation around, bring relief to your child, and lower your own stress level.

CHAPTER 2

Diagnosis

A PRECISE DIAGNOSIS IS A NECESSARY FIRST STEP along the road to helping your child. However, the road to diagnosis is marked by a number of hazards. This chapter discusses choosing a doctor, getting a referral, and navigating the diagnostic process. It outlines the current medical criteria for obsessive-compulsive disorder in adults and children, and covers subtypes of OCD and related disorders, including eating disorders, body dysmorphic disorder, hypochondria, and more.

It also includes brief sections on other psychiatric disorders that occur more often in people with OCD, such as ADD/ADHD, Tourette's syndrome, autistic spectrum disorders, and other anxiety and panic disorders.

Getting started

When you're worried about your child, all you want to do is find an expert who can tell you exactly what's wrong, and how to help. Unfortunately, when it comes to neurological problems in children, that's not easy to do.

Kelly, mother of 8-year-old Amanda, talks about the hard road to diagnosis and treatment:

> *At age 2, I took Amanda in to her pediatrician. Of course, this was all just a stage and I was a worried mom. At age 3, I knew it wasn't a stage and tried to find help again. This time I was able to see a child psychologist. Amanda went through about six months of play/talk therapy.*
>
> *During this time she got much worse. The doctors never saw any of her OCD, she would just sit there during her therapy. Their take on the situation was that children who are 3 years old do not have OCD. It must be bad parenting or abuse. I asked if she could possibly be put on medication. I was told by the head of the department—the head psychiatrist—that he was now sure Amanda was being abused, because no parent would want their 3-year-old put on medication. I called him an idiot and walked out.*

There is a woeful lack of knowledge about OCD among the professionals to whom most parents look first for help—pediatricians, teachers, school counselors, and even many child psychologists and psychiatrists. If you feel that OCD is a distinct possibility, it's best to have your child evaluated by a doctor who specializes in this disorder, and who has worked with many patients your child's age. For some families, this may mean traveling to the nearest large city, but it will be worth it if you access the right person.

Cheri, mother of two daughters with OCD and Tourette's syndrome, talks about the perils of relying on the wrong doctor:

> *In the very beginning we saw a child psychologist for our 8-year-old—not a very good one, I might add—who was all over the map with what might be wrong. After twelve or so sessions, she said, "Well, I think she must have been sexually abused at some point." I knew then that we were getting nowhere. I was a stay-at-home mom and she never left my side. There was a lot I did not know, but that was one thing I did know! Then when the 3-year-old started to show signs of tics, I brought this to our new pediatrician. He's the one who then suspected Tourette's in both girls and sent us to a neurologist. They both also have OCD with contamination fears.*

Starting points for identifying an expert include:

- National OCD organizations and their local chapters.
- Specialty clinics where OCD and related disorders, such as anxiety disorders and Tourette's syndrome, are the focus of their daily work. These professionals and centers can help you get—or rule out—an OCD diagnosis for your child with the least amount of runaround. They can also prepare a detailed report about the diagnosis, including a list of your child's current symptoms, and concrete suggestions for how to help. Even if you can't come back to the center for medication management and therapy, this report can help you get what your child needs from a local practitioner.
- Internet discussion groups like *ocdandparenting* or *OCD-L*. We'll talk more about the value of support groups, both traditional and online, in Chapter 3, but the best time to make first contact with these groups is when you are still in search of a diagnosis and help. You can avoid dead ends, unqualified doctors, and much heartache by tapping into these resources right away. Even if it turns out that your child's problems are due to another condition, you'll be glad to have found out so quickly.

- The psychiatry or neurology department of a nearby medical school. Many medical schools have excellent clinics staffed by both experienced doctors and residents who are learning the ropes. Some of the foremost experts in child and adolescent OCD are affiliated with university programs. These doctors are often (but not always!) aware of the latest research findings and treatments.

A list of OCD organizations and clinics is included in Appendix A, *Resources*, as are several university-affiliated programs with special expertise in OCD. If you don't see a nearby facility listed, call the large hospitals or universities located in your area. They should be able to point you toward a qualified professional, but be sure to talk to this new doctor before making an appointment.

Your very best bet is a board certified child psychiatrist who has a working relationship with a good hospital, preferably one affiliated with a university medical school. "Board certified" means that the doctor has completed a very rigorous training program, has already practiced child psychiatry for some years, and meets the highest qualifications in the field as set by an official board of peers. Of course, the best doctors are also the busiest. Make sure you have a second-best choice in the wings, just in case.

Once you have identified the experts, call them to make sure they are currently taking new patients. Ask specifically if they see OCD patients who are your child's age. You may also want to ask if they have worked with your health plan or HMO before. Usually, insurance regulations or the rules of your national health plan govern how you go about accessing a specialist. We'll discuss problems that frequently occur, and provide ideas for dealing with them, in Chapter 7, *Insurance Issues*.

Consultation appointment

Now that you know whom your child should eventually see, you have to go back to square one. Usually, you must put the diagnostic process in motion by requesting a consultation appointment with your child's pediatrician, primary care physician, or general practitioner. This kind of appointment is a little different from the typical "height check, weight check, immunization booster, your throat looks fine" visit. In fact, it may take place in a meeting room or office rather than in an examination room. It should also be longer in length: a half hour at least, preferably an hour.

Accurate, detailed records are the most important thing parents can contribute at this appointment. These should include the usual "baby book" milestones (first step, first word, etc.) as well as notes about anything unusual that parents have observed. Areas the pediatrician is likely to ask about include patient and family medical history, the child's relationships with family members and peers, and the child's play patterns and interests.

Your doctor will want to know a lot of details about your family's mental health history. Take the time to ask older relatives what they know. In the past, most people with OCD were never officially diagnosed, but may be described by those who remember them as anxious, paranoid, phobic, nervous, picky, overly rigid, etc. You may get some surprises at this stage of the game, such as tales of a grandparent's secret trips to the hospital or sanitarium. On the other hand, some people are very reluctant to tell the truth about mental illness in the family. You may need to go so far as sleuthing through medical records or diaries in the attic, checking public records to see if family members were institutionalized or imprisoned for behavior that could have been due to OCD, or questioning doctors who may have known older family members well. Physicians are duty-bound not to give you personal information about living persons, but they can generally be more forthcoming about deceased patients. Once you have this family history in hand, you might want to put it in very simple "family tree" form for your physician, as shown in Figure 2-1.

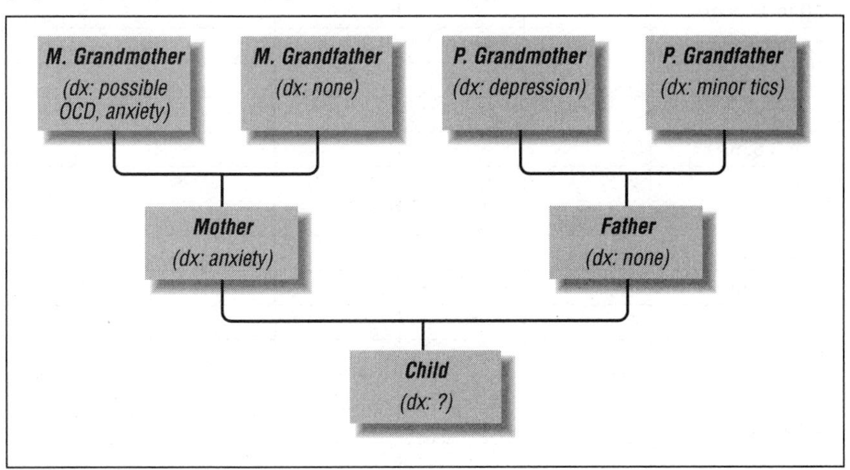

Figure 2-1. Sample family tree

Keeping a daily diary is also an excellent way to prepare for the consultation appointment. Many families have learned a great deal during this process.

Use your diary to record diet, activities, behavior, symptoms of physical illness, and medications each day for a period of two weeks or more, with the time and duration of activities and behaviors noted. Not only can this diary provide a very complete picture of the child to a professional, it can also help identify patterns. Some families have identified food allergies this way, or have found data they needed to create the most beneficial daily routine for their child. If you can, use a calendar, personal diaries, medical notes, notes and checkmarks from school report cards, and your own recollections to create a rough chart of your child's obsessions and compulsions over the past year or so. Table 2-1 is a sample diary page.

Table 2-1. Sample Daily Diary

Time	Diet	Activities	Behavior	Health	Medications
12 to 1 a.m.					
1 to 2 a.m.					
2 to 3 a.m.					
3 to 4 a.m.					
4 to 5 a.m.					
5 to 6 a.m.					
6 to 7 a.m.					
7 to 8 a.m.					
8 to 9 a.m.					
9 to 10 a.m.					
10 to 11 a.m.					
11 to 12 p.m.					
12 to 1 p.m.					
1 to 2 p.m.					
2 to 3 p.m.					
3 to 4 p.m.					
4 to 5 p.m.					
5 to 6 p.m.					
6 to 7 p.m.					
7 to 8 p.m.					
8 to 9 p.m.					
9 to 10 p.m.					
10 to 11 p.m.					
11 to 12 a.m.					
Summary:					

If an article or book does a better job of describing what you're worried about, don't hesitate to bring it along. You would be surprised at how many people have diagnosed themselves or a loved one by reading something.

For instance, 17-year-old Emma found a magazine article very helpful:

> *When I was suffering from it, the counselor I saw was most concerned, but she didn't have the knowledge to diagnose me with OCD or anything else. I read about OCD in a magazine, then went to a psychologist, and he made an official diagnosis.*

If your child has seen other doctors, you must sign releases to have her medical records transferred to the pediatrician before the consultation, and to the specialist later on. School records that would be helpful can also be transferred if a signed release is on file. Transfers always seem to take longer than you would expect, so take care of releases early, and make sure the records were actually sent and received. Alternatively, if you have your own copies of these records (and you should), you may photocopy and deliver them yourself.

Parents should also summarize their concerns in writing. The records already mentioned can help you gather your thoughts. You don't have to be an eloquent writer to express your worries. You can jot down a simple numbered list rather than writing whole paragraphs if you prefer. It may help to compare your child to his or her siblings, or to other children in the day-care center or school. Be sure to include specific information about obsessions and compulsions, unusual behaviors, or problems that you think might be OCD-related. Also list any behaviors—such as suicide threats or attempts, aggressive behavior, self-mutilation, sudden onset of school phobia or other fears, anxiety or panic attacks, and possible substance abuse—about which you want to make sure the pediatrician knows. Some parents send their summary of concerns to the doctor in advance; others prefer to use it as an agenda for discussion during the consultation.

Cindy, mother of 10-year-old Brett, first found help from a regular MD:

> *Looking back now, I see there have always been symptoms, but until last summer, when he refused to swim and needed constant reassurance about the weather, he was able to function "normally." So we had never really sought help. It just so happens I work for a medical office and was expressing some of my frustrations to a physician, and he suggested OCD might be the cause.*

You might also want to talk to a nurse or physician's assistant who works closely with the pediatrician. In large medical practices and HMOs, nurses and assistants play an important part in the organization. They can be allies for parents who need referrals to specialists, or even just a listening ear. If you are lucky enough to find a knowledgeable and sympathetic nurse, his or her input can help greatly, even if it's just because of comments made during office chitchat with the doctor.

If possible, your information and your child's complete medical file should be available to the pediatrician at least a week before the consultation appointment. You should request that the doctor review the file before the meeting. You want to ensure that your child's case is fresh in your doctor's mind at the consultation appointment.

When you arrive for the consultation, bring any additional records you have gathered, copies of your earlier letter (just in case it never reached the doctor), your summary of concerns, and a list of any questions you want to ask. We suggest bringing a small notebook or tape recorder as well, so you can keep a record of the discussion. If your child tends to be difficult to manage, bring a bag of toys or books that are likely to help keep him occupied.

Remember, the goal of this visit is not to get a diagnosis, but to get a referral to an expert who has the knowledge to diagnose OCD. Your documentation should help you make a case for this referral. The doctor's notes from this meeting will also be placed in your child's file, and should help the expert get a head start on diagnosis.

Unfortunately, getting a referral is sometimes difficult, especially in those HMOs that financially punish participating doctors for referring patients to specialists. If your doctor seems reluctant to refer your child, and perhaps suggests a "wait and see" approach, use your best judgment on how to proceed. Possible strategies include:

- Agreeing to observe your child's symptoms for a specific period of time (six weeks, for example), and making an appointment to return then with further notes.
- Strongly attempting to persuade your doctor to approve the referral. This is when your documentation can be most useful for reiterating the reasons why this referral is needed.

- Asking your doctor for a written refusal to refer. This ploy may get you the referral itself, and if not, it will give you a document you can use in an appeal.
- Appealing your doctor's decision to an appeals board through your HMO or insurance company.
- Seeking a second opinion from another primary care provider.
- Making a direct appointment with the expert you want to see. You will probably have to pay for this appointment yourself. However, if your child is then diagnosed with OCD, you may be able to appeal the charge to the appeals board of your HMO or insurance company.

Under no circumstances should you agree to wait for an undefined period of time if your child's symptoms are causing significant distress.

Evaluation appointment

When you see an OCD expert, bring copies of the same records to your child's evaluation appointment. This appointment is, hopefully, when the actual diagnosis will be made.

Every doctor has a different way of going about things, but you're likely to encounter some standardized OCD symptom questionnaires; psychiatric, neurological, and/or IQ testing; and the usual patient and parent interview. Your supporting documentation will prove invaluable in moving this process along, especially if you can get your expert to look it over in advance. After the evaluation is over, you should be given information—not just a diagnostic label, but information about your child's specific challenges and needs, and how to address them.

Defining OCD

The next several sections are devoted to explaining how the experts get and use the information they need to diagnose OCD.

DSM-IV

In the US, the handbook for diagnosing mental health disorders is the fourth version of the *Diagnostic and Statistical Manual of Mental Disorders*, better known as the DSM-IV. This book was written by a committee chosen by the

American Psychiatric Association. The DSM-IV makes an effort to divide all known forms of mental illness into general categories—for example, OCD appears in the larger Anxiety Disorders category—and to define commonly accepted criteria for making each specific diagnosis.

Families, patients, and non-psychiatrists need to know what psychiatric professionals are already well aware of: the DSM-IV is a guide, not holy writ. It is updated approximately once each decade, and at the rate that neurobiological knowledge has accumulated in the past few years, much of this otherwise very valuable book is out of date. That said, the DSM-IV does provide a rough guide, and its diagnostic codes are necessary for insurance claims, entry to various therapy programs, and many other purposes.

The following excerpt is the section of the DSM-IV that pertains to diagnosing an individual with OCD.

DSM-IV 300.3: Obsessive-Compulsive Disorder

- Criteria A. The person exhibits obsessions and/or compulsions.

  Obsessions are indicated by the following symptoms:

  - Recurrent and persistent thoughts, impulses, or images that are experienced, at some time during the disturbance, as intrusive and inappropriate, and that cause marked anxiety or distress.
  - The thoughts, impulses, or images are not simply excessive worries about real-life problems.
  - The person attempts to ignore or suppress such thoughts, impulses, or images, or to neutralize them with some other thought or action.
  - The person recognizes that the obsessional thoughts, impulses, or images are a product of his or her own mind (and which are not imposed from without, as in thought insertion).

  Compulsions are indicated by the following symptoms:

  - Repetitive behaviors (e.g., hand washing, ordering, checking) or mental acts (e.g., praying, counting, repeating words silently) that the person feels driven to perform in response to an obsession or according to rules that must be applied rigidly.
  - The behaviors or mental acts are aimed at preventing some dreaded event or situation; however, these behaviors or mental acts either are not connected in a realistic way with what they are designed to neutralize or prevent, or are clearly excessive.

- Criteria B. At some point during the course of the disorder, the person has recognized that the obsessions or compulsions are excessive or unreasonable.
- Criteria C. The obsessions or compulsions cause marked distress, are time consuming (take more than one hour a day), or significantly interfere with the person's normal routine, occupational/academic functioning, or usual social activities or relationships.
- Criteria D. If another Axis I disorder is present, the content of the obsessions or compulsions is not restricted to it (e.g., preoccupation with food in the presence of an Eating Disorder; hair pulling in the presence of Trichotillomania; concern with appearance in the presence of Body Dysmorphic Disorder; preoccupation with drugs in the presence of a Substance Use Disorder; preoccupation with having a serious illness in the presence of Hypochondriasis; preoccupation with sexual urges or fantasies in the presence of a Paraphilia; or guilty ruminations in the presence of major Depressive Disorder).
- Criteria E. The disturbance is not due to the direct physiologic effects of a substance (e.g., drug abuse, medication) or a general medical condition.

  Specify if: With Poor Insight. If, for most of the time during the current episode, the person does not recognize that the obsessions and compulsions are excessive or unreasonable.

[Taken by permission from *Diagnostic and Statistical Manual of Mental Disorders, Fourth Edition*, copyright © American Psychiatric Association, 1994.]

International classification

In Europe, Africa, and Asia, the diagnostic guide used most frequently is Revision 10 of the World Health Organization's *International Classification of Diseases* (ICD-10). The ICD-10 Classification of Mental and Behavioral Disorders lists OCD under the following codes:

- F42. Obsessive-compulsive disorder.

  For a definite diagnosis, obsessional symptoms or compulsive acts, or both, must be present on most days for at least two successive weeks and be a source of distress or interference with activities. The obsessional symptoms should have the following characteristics:

  a. They must be recognized as the individual's own thoughts or impulses;

b. There must be at least one thought or act that is still resisted unsuccessfully, even though others may be present that the sufferer no longer resists;

c. The thought of carrying out the act must not in itself be pleasurable (simple relief of tension or anxiety is not regarded as pleasure in this sense);

d. The thoughts, images, or impulses must be unpleasantly repetitive.

- F42.0. Predominantly obsessional thoughts or ruminations.
- F42.1. Predominantly compulsive acts (obsessional rituals).
- F42.2. Mixed obsessional thoughts and acts.
- F42.8. Other obsessive-compulsive disorders.
- F42.9. Obsessive-compulsive disorder, unspecified.

Note: The ICD definition also states that obsessional symptoms in persons with schizophrenia, Tourette's, or organic mental disorder should be regarded as part of these conditions rather than a separate psychiatric condition.

[Taken by permission from ICD-10, copyright © World Health Organization, 1992.]

The Axis system

The American Psychiatric Association also uses a special system to rate the patient in five areas of function, each of which it calls an "axis"—a center about which something (in this case, psychiatric and behavioral symptoms) revolves. Each axis is considered individually, and then graphed as a separate part of the diagnosis. The axes are:

- **Axis I**. Major psychiatric disorders, such as obsessive-compulsive disorder or schizophrenia.
- **Axis II**. Personality disorders (ingrained personality traits that cause the patient difficulty in life), mental retardation, or developmental delay.
- **Axis III**. Physical disorders that can affect thought or behavior, such as epilepsy.
- **Axis IV**. Stresses in the patient's life, such as being the victim of child abuse.
- **Axis V**. Level of function described on a scale of 0 (minimal function) to 100 (perfect function).

Any disorders listed on Axes I, II, and III will be classified using the DSM-IV.

Items listed on Axis IV come from interviews with the patient and/or his parents.

The "score" listed on Axis V is based on everything the doctor has learned during the diagnostic process. It is a subjective measure of how well the patient is able to handle everyday life at home and at school, and of how well the patient is able to handle stressful situations. You may see an axis chart on your child's diagnostic report, mental health evaluation, or treatment plan.

Other diagnostic tools

Getting to diagnosis isn't as simple as just opening the DSM-IV or the ICD-10 and finding a match, of course. Doctors use a combination of symptom checklists, parent and patient interviews, and patient histories to make an accurate call about the presence and severity of OCD.

There are several symptom checklists in use for adults, including the Florida Obsessive-Compulsive Inventory (FOCI) and the University of Hamburg Obsession-Compulsion Inventory Screening Form. Some of these checklists are available on the Web: see Appendix A for more information.

The Yale-Brown Obsessive Compulsive Scale (Y-BOCS) is considered the gold standard of OCD checklists. It doesn't diagnose OCD, but it does provide an easy way to rate the severity of a patient's obsessive-compulsive symptoms, and its detailed questions are helpful to professionals as they try to get the patient to describe symptoms that they may be reluctant to talk about.

Teenagers may find that the regular Y-BOCS meets their needs, but a special version called the CY-BOCS has been developed for use with children. This instrument has proven to be very accurate.[1] CY-BOCS appears in its entirety in Appendix B, *Children's Yale-Brown Obsessive Compulsive Scale*.

Y-BOCS and CY-BOCS also give doctors a way to measure the efficiency of treatment: if a patient retakes the test and gets a lower score, that means symptoms are becoming less severe. The average drop in patients in a good cognitive behavioral therapy program is 6 to 7 YBOCS points.

Interviews

The Y-BOCS and CY-BOCS are helpful tools, but they aren't used in isolation. Diagnosticians interview the patient, and in the case of children, the child's parents or caregivers, in order to get a complete picture of the disorder. Questions asked usually revolve around whether the child met the usual developmental milestones (crawling, walking, talking, etc.) in a timely manner, when unusual behaviors first emerged, and any special factors (such as adoption, abuse, or family breakup) that might have a bearing on diagnosis or treatment.

With young children, the diagnostician may use techniques of play therapy to elicit answers about the child's symptoms. Puppets, stuffed toys, or action figures can help break down communication roadblocks with children.

Because OCD can be an inherited disorder, many diagnosticians also take a family psychiatric history. This process is most important in families in which OCD tends to emerge before adulthood, because researchers have found that the genetic links are strongest for early-onset OCD.[2,3,4]

Behavioral, psychiatric, and neuropsychiatric tests

Some of these tests are highly clinical instruments that are used to distinguish disorders with similar symptoms (such as OCD and generalized anxiety disorder), or to diagnose coexisting disorders like ADHD (psychiatrists usually use the term "comorbid disorders" to describe these). Others are more subjective, and are used by teachers and other non-physicians to rank behavior problems or uncover emotional difficulties.

Like the Rorschach Blot interpretation test, which is rarely used anymore, tests for emotional disturbance that ask patients to draw and interpret what they've drawn are highly subjective. These so-called projective tests have little use in diagnosing OCD, but are sometimes administered anyway, especially in school settings.

No test should ever be used as the sole means of diagnosing or measuring emotional disturbance. Following is a list of tests sometimes used to help the diagnostic team get more information about a child:

- **Aberrant Behavior Checklist (ABC).** One of the most popular behavioral checklists, the ABC also has a good reputation for accuracy. Versions are available for children and adults. Scores are expressed as scales in the areas of irritability and agitation, lethargy and social withdrawal, stereotypic behavior, hyperactivity and noncompliance, and inappropriate speech.

- **Achenbach Child Behavior Checklist (CBC).** The CBC is available in versions for girls and boys of various ages. Six different inventories are used, including a parent report, teacher report, youth report (if practical), and structured direct observation report. The test looks at the child's behaviors in several areas, including withdrawal, anxiety, etc. The results are classified as clinically significant or normal.
- **Attention Deficit Disorders Evaluation Scale.** Versions of this questionnaire about behaviors linked with ADD/ADHD are available for parents to fill out at home or in a clinical setting, as well as for direct use with older children and adults. Scores are expressed as a scale.
- **Behavior Assessment System for Children (BASC).** This set of tests includes a Teacher Rating Scale, Parent Rating Scale, and Self-Report of Personality. The BASC attempts to measure both problem and adaptive behaviors, as well as behaviors linked to ADD/ADHD. Scores are expressed as a scale keyed to a norm.
- **Conner's Rating Scales (CRS).** Parent and Teacher versions are available for this scale-based test, which is intended to uncover behaviors linked to ADD/ADHD, conduct disorders, learning disabilities, psychosomatic complaints, and anxiety, among other conditions. Scores are plotted graphically.
- **Draw-a-Person.** This is a projective psychological screening procedure in which the patient is asked to draw three human figures: a man, a woman, and himself. The drawing is then rated on a scale, with differences in ratings according to gender and age. Ratings are subjective interpretations, not objective measures.
- **House-Tree-Person Projective Drawing Technique.** In this projective test, the patient is asked to draw a house, a tree, and a person, and then is asked a series of questions about these drawings. Sometimes these drawings are separate, sometimes they are done on a single page. Ratings are subjective interpretations, not objective measures.
- **Kinetic Family Drawing System for Family and School.** In this projective test, the patient draws her family or classmates doing something. The patient is then asked questions about what's going on in the drawing. Ratings are subjective interpretations, not objective measures.

- **Luria-Nebraska Neuropsychological Battery (LNNB)/Luria-Nebraska Neuropsychological Battery, Children's Revision (LNNB-CR).** The LNNB-CR contains 11 scales with a total of 149 test items, that are intended to measure motor skills, rhythm, tactile response, visual ability, receptive speech, expressive language, writing, reading, arithmetic, memory, and intelligence. Each test item is scored on a scale, and a total scale for all items is also derived. The adult LNNB also tests the maturation level of the frontal lobe tertiary zones.
- **Multidimensional Anxiety Scale for Children (MASC).** This instrument has 39 items covering physical anxiety, social anxiety, harm avoidance, and separation anxiety. Results are expressed as a scale.
- **Pediatric Symptom Checklist (PSC).** A simple questionnaire about behavioral symptoms, the PSC is commonly used as a screening tool by pediatricians. Score is expressed as a scale.
- **Psychiatric Assessment Schedule for Adults with Developmental Disability (PAS-ADD).** Used primarily in the UK, this is a self-reporting questionnaire used to assess psychiatric state in people with developmental delay, learning disability, neurobiological disorders, or senility, among other conditions. Score is expressed as a scale.
- **Reitan-Indiana Neuropsychological Test Battery for Children (RINTBC)/ Halstead-Reitan Neuropsychological Test Battery for Children (HNTBC)/ Reitan-Indiana Neuropsychological Test Battery (RINTB).** These may be the most widely used neuropsychological tests, and are intended to reveal signs of brain damage. The RINTBC contains the following tests: Category, Tactile Performance, Finger Oscillation, Sensory-Perceptual Measures, Aphasia Screening, Grip Strength, Lateral Dominance Examination, Color Form, Progressive Figures, Matching Pictures, Target, Individual Performance, and Marching. The HNTBC adds the Seashore Rhythm Test, Speech Sounds Perception, Finger-Tip Number Writing Perception, and Trail-Making, but omits some other tests. The RINTB is very similar. Results are usually expressed as a scale (the Neuropsychological Deficit Scale or the Halstead Impairment Index). Additional information about right-left dominance or performance patterns may also be derived.
- **Vineland Adaptive Behavior Scales.** These tests measure personal and social skills from birth to adulthood, using a semi-structured interview with a parent or caregiver. Versions are available for children of all ages.

Social and behavioral maturity in four major areas—communication, daily living skills, socialization, and motor skills—is assessed. Responses are rated on a 100-point scale for each area, and a composite score is also provided. Scores can be translated into developmental or mental ages.

Intelligence, developmental, and academic tests

Some school and medical programs require IQ testing for all incoming youth. Don't let these tests or scores give you too much worry: repeated studies have shown that children's IQs can and do change when they are measured differently, or when the child is taught differently and then re-tested. Children with certain OCD behaviors may find these tests especially difficult. For example, they may have to choose between numbered multiple choice answers, but the right answer is their "unlucky" number, or they may go over and over answers in their head and become unable to give a straight answer.

Most IQ tests also carry some cultural, racial, language, and/or gender bias, although testing companies are certainly trying to create better tests. However, because these biases have inappropriately placed non-handicapped students from ethnic minorities into special education classes in the past, it is no longer legal to use IQ tests alone as an evaluation tool in US schools.

As a result of this misuse, IQ testing has been supplanted in some school districts and programs by tests that measure adaptive behavior, which can be loosely described as how well and how quickly a person can come up with a solution to a problem and carry it out. These tests provide more realistic measures of "intelligence" as most people think of it, as opposed to measures of cultural knowledge.

Developmental tests rank the individual's development against the norm, often resulting in a "mental age" or "developmental age" score. Some of the tests listed in the "Behavior, psychiatric, and neuropsychiatric tests" section later in this chapter also chart a patient's developmental stages.

Academic testing is a must during the special education evaluation process. It's also used to provide clues about undiscovered learning disabilities in older patients, to design transition programs for teenagers, and to design adult learning programs. Some clinicians like to compare the results of these three types of tests, a practice that provides a picture of actual achievement against the background of supposed innate capability.

Sometimes a local, state, or national academic test is used instead of one of the commercial tests listed to rate a child by grade level.

IQ tests in use today include:

- **Adaptive Behavior Inventory for Children (ABIC).** This standardized measure of adaptive behavior uses a questionnaire format, with a parent or caregiver providing the answers. It includes subtests called Family, Community, Peer Relations, Nonacademic School Roles, Earner/Consumer, and Self-Maintenance. Used with the WISC-III IQ test and a special grading scale, ABIC is part of the System of Multicultural Pluralistic Assessment used by some districts to make more sensitive assessments of racial minority children. Results are expressed on a scale.
- **Battelle Developmental Inventory.** This test ranks a child's self-adaptive skills (self-feeding, dressing, etc.) as a percentage of his chronological age. The score may be expressed as a percentage, such as "between 40 percent and 55 percent of his/her chronological age," or as a single-number standard deviation.
- **Cattell Scales.** This test rates the person's developmental level. The score is expressed as a Mental Age (MA).
- **Children's Memory Scale (CMS).** The CMS test is intended to provide a complete picture of a child's or adolescent's cognitive ability, and is often used with children who have acquired or innate neurological problems. Areas screened in six subtests include verbal and visual memory; short-delay and long-delay memory; recall, recognition, and working memory; learning characteristics; and attentional functions. The test rates skills in all areas, and links them to an IQ score.
- **Developmental Assessment Screening Inventory II (DASI-II).** This screening and assessment tool for preschool children does not rely heavily on verbal or language-based skills. Its scores rate the patient's developmental level.
- **Developmental Profile II.** This developmental skill inventory is for children up to 9 years old (or older people whose developmental levels fall within that range), and is based on an interview with a parent or other caregiver. It covers physical, self-help, social-emotional, communication, and academic skills. Scores are provided as an individual profile depicting the functional developmental age level in each area.

- **Kaufman Assessment Battery for Children (Kaufman-ABC).** A nonverbal IQ test, the Kaufman-ABC measures cognitive intellectual abilities in children aged two-and-a-half to twelve. It's one of the best tests for use with non-verbal children without significant fine-motor problems. Scaled scores are provided for overall ability (the Mental Processing Composite) and for Simultaneous and Sequential Processing.
- **Learning Potential Assessment Device (LPAD).** This test of cognitive function uses different assumptions from some of the other IQ tests, and was designed for use primarily with learning disabled or developmentally disabled children. It provides several scaled scores, with interesting ideas about interpreting and using them.
- **Leiter International Performance Scale, Revised (Leiter-R).** This nonverbal IQ test has puzzle-type problems only covering the areas of visual, spatial, and, in a few cases, language-based reasoning. It produces scaled results.
- **Peabody Developmental and Motor Scales (PDMS).** These tests use activities, such as threading beads or catching a ball, to gauge the level of physical development, motor capabilities, and coordination. They can be used to test large groups of children. Scores are expressed on a scale interpreted as an age level, so raw numbers may be followed by notations like "below age level by five percentiles" or "above age level."
- **Peabody Individual Achievement Test (PIAT).** These short tests measure performance in reading, writing, spelling, and math. Scores are expressed as a grade level.
- **Stanford-Binet Intelligence Test, Fourth Edition (S-B IV).** An intelligence test sometimes used with young or nonverbal children, although not preferred by most clinicians. The score is expressed as an IQ number or a scale.
- **Test of Nonverbal Intelligence 3 (TONI-3).** This short, nonverbal IQ test for children over 5 presents a series of increasingly difficult problem-solving tasks, such as locating the missing part of a figure. The score is expressed as an IQ number or age equivalent.
- **Vineland Adaptive Behavior Scales.** A standardized measure of adaptive behavior, the Vineland scale tests problem-solving and cognitive skills. Scores are presented as a scale, IQ-style number, or age equivalent.

- Weschler Preschool and Primary Scale of Intelligence (WPPSI), Weschler Intelligence Scale for Children, Revised (WISC-R), Weschler Intelligence Scale for Children, Third Edition (WISC-III), Weschler Adult Intelligence Scale (WAIS-R). All of the Weschler Scales are intelligence tests that use age-appropriate word-based activities and mechanical, puzzle-like activities to test problem-solving skills. They return scores for verbal IQ and performance IQ, which may be broken down into several categories.
- Wide Range of Assessment Test, Revision 3 (WRAT 3). This standardized test determines academic level in reading, writing, spelling, and math. Scores are expressed as raw numbers or grade-level equivalents.
- Woodcock-Johnson Psycho-Educational Battery, Revised (WJPEB-R, WJ-R). An individual test of educational achievement in reading, writing, spelling, and math, the WJ-R has many subtests that can be given as a group or separately. Standard scores that compare the test-taker against US norms, and that can also be expressed as an age or grade-level equivalency, are derived. One popular subtest, the Scales of Independent Behavior, Revised (SIB-R/Woodcock-Johnson Battery, Part IV) is a standardized measure of adaptive behavior. SIB-R scores are raw numbers similar to IQ scores, but may be shown as a grade or age equivalent.

Medical tests

In some cases, your doctor may want to do a medical workup for PANDAS or other disorders that can include elements of obsessive-compulsive behavior. PANDAS is most often suspected if there is a sudden onset of OCD in a child, or if you can document that previous episodes of strep throat or ear infections were followed by obsessive-compulsive symptoms.

A commercial test for the B lymphocyte antigen D8/17 associated with PANDAS, and with Sydenham's chorea, is not available as of this writing. Accordingly, PANDAS is not an easy diagnosis to make. If it appears to be a possibility, a strep titer (blood test) may be done to measure the level of strep antibodies in the blood. If an abnormally high strep titre is associated with sudden onset or worsening of OCD symptoms, it may indicate PANDAS, especially if elevated strep titres and symptomatic behavior match up more than once. A strep throat swab or other strep culture can only show that strep bacteria are present, not the unusual level of immune-system activity that leads to PANDAS. Often the strep titre in children with PANDAS will be sky-high even with a negative throat swab test.

If choreiform movements (twisting, writhing, tic-like movements, usually of the extremities) are present, the doctor may also want to look at Sydenham's chorea itself as a possibility.

Screening for specific OCD subtypes and variants (see "OCD subtypes and variants," later in this chapter), and for comorbid disorders, may also be undertaken. The psychiatric tests listed previously may be used, along with the same family history and interview tools used to diagnose OCD. Some OCD subtypes and related disorders involve behavior that your child may be intensely embarrassed about, and may attempt to hide. Don't be surprised if your child admits some months or years later that he or she has an eating disorder or another OCD-linked problem that she denied in earlier interviews. Familiarize yourself with the signs of self-injurious behaviors (such as cutting), eating disorders and, for teenagers, substance abuse disorders in particular. Your sharp eyes may spot a problem before it becomes too serious.

In fact, many clinicians believe that any child with obsessive-compulsive symptoms should be carefully and regularly screened for self-injurious behaviors and eating disorders. These compulsive behaviors have the potential to become deadly, and are much harder to treat when they have become ingrained after years of practice. Scars, marks, or bruises from self-injurious behavior are usually found on areas of the arms, legs, or chest that are normally hidden by clothing, but can be spotted during a physical. Screening for anorexia and bulimia involves a physical exam and medical history to check for signs, such as severe weight loss, obvious malnutrition, disturbed electrolyte levels, cessation of menstruation, edema (water retention), and damage to the teeth and/or throat from repeated vomiting.

OCD subtypes and variants

Everyone with OCD is a unique case, although certain symptoms are so common that they're considered "classic." Your child may have some unusual symptoms or additional difficulties that require special intervention. Some symptoms may fall into one of the categories listed as a heading within this section.

There is controversy over the relationship between some of the categories and OCD. For example, while scrupulosity is one of those "classic" OCD symptoms, not all clinicians agree that hypochondria is a subtype of OCD, despite its obvious similarities. Eating disorders and self-injurious behavior are sometimes, but possibly not always, related to OCD. The same caveat applies to impulse disorders.

There are still some, for example, who argue for a purely psychological explanation for self-injurious behavior, including some of the most prominent writers to cover the topic. There is an unfortunate rift between the medical and psychological research wings that, while it is slowly being bridged, still prevents many on both sides of the divide from seeing the whole picture.

Today the majority of medical researchers with expertise in OCD feel that in many cases, if not all, the symptoms described in the following sections can be thought of as existing on a single continuum: obsessive-compulsive spectrum disorders. In some cases they may be different manifestations of the same underlying problem. In others, they may represent attempts to gain control over anxieties raised by OCD. Most people with OCD have symptoms that wax and wane over time, and may have a wide variety of different problems over the years even though certain symptoms are more prominent than others.

Beth-Anne, who is 15 years old, has dealt with symptoms across the spectrum:

> *Counting, touching, over-thinking, I have trichotillomania. Everything must be in perfect condition. Having OCD interferes with school in many ways. . .I re-read sentences, paragraphs, etc. several times. Sorting, being tidy. I have a fear of smelling bad. Symmetry, unwanted repetitive thoughts. I often become depressed.*

Scrupulosity

One form of OCD has been recognized and treated longer than any other: obsessive-compulsive behavior that centers on religious or ethical issues. Known as scrupulosity, this type of OCD has been recognized by spiritual advisors in the Catholic and Jewish faiths for well over 1,000 years. Sufferers torture themselves with religious doubts, obsessions, and rituals that go well beyond what normal or even devout practice calls for.

Today, both clinicians and religious authorities recognize the signs of scrupulosity in the lives of some early Christian saints and mystics, some of whom also had symptoms of eating disorders and other OCD-related difficulties. They are also visible in the characteristics of several prominent religious figures from the past few centuries. Eminent people such as Reformation leader Martin Luther and Redemptorist Community founder St. Alphonsus Liguori suffered under the yoke of scrupulosity. For example, Liguori's tendency toward rumination caused him to consider whether to accept an appointment as bishop for over a year, consulting various "experts" all the while. He also became severely depressed and physically ill many times as a result of OCD; at one point he had a mental and physical breakdown so severe that he was granted Last Rites.

Paradoxically, the fruits of his scrupulosity were so admired that in 1950, Pope Pius XII declared Liguori the official patron saint of moralists (scholars who compose and interpret rules of moral doctrine for Catholics) and confessors.[5] In a way, he became the patron of those with OCD as well: Liguori knew the disorder so intimately that his words are still used in this definition of scrupulosity, found in the modern *Catholic Encyclopedia*:

> *Scrupulosity is. . . a condition in which one influenced by trifling reasons, and without any solid foundation, is often afraid that sin lies where it really does not. This anxiety may be entertained not only with regard to what is to be done presently, but also with regard to what has been done. The idea sometimes obtaining that scrupulosity is in itself a spiritual benefit of some sort, is, of course, a great error. The providence of God permits it and can gather good from it as from other forms of evil. That apart, however, it is a bad habit doing harm, sometimes grievously, to body and soul. Indeed, persisted in with the obstinacy characteristic of persons who suffer from this malady, it may entail the most lamentable consequences. The judgment is seriously warped, the moral power tired out in futile combat, and then not infrequently the scrupulous person makes shipwreck of salvation either on the Scylla of despair or the Charybdis of unheeding indulgence in vice.*

Note that Liguori, writing in the eighteenth century, stressed that scrupulosity is a disease: it would be another 200 years before medical science recognized what a person with unwanted, tormenting religious obsessions and compulsions instinctively knew.

Today, scrupulosity is known to occur in people of all religious faiths, as well as in persons whose ethics are not informed by religious belief. As for treatment, most clinicians agree with what Ligouri recommended 200 years ago: that the patient submit completely to the moral judgment of a single, trustworthy authority—one priest, minister, rabbi, shaman, or secular advisor. This person should direct the patient's spiritual and ethical course, and will need to set ever-increasing limits on how often the person can approach him or her with new questions in order to help improve the patient's symptoms. This is the earliest known form of cognitive behavioral therapy, and it definitely works.

Of course, medication and garden-variety cognitive behavioral therapy has proven just as useful for those with scrupulosity as it has for counters, checkers, cleaners, and others with OCD. But due to the nature of the specific worries, the involvement of a spiritual or ethical authority in cases of scrupulosity usually gets the best results.

Hoarding

If your child is a pack rat, this problem may also be related to his or her OCD. Inability to throw away items, even seemingly useless things like food wrappers, is a fairly common OCD subtype. The core problem seems to be false ideas about the importance of possessions. People with OCD may fear that if they throw something out, something bad will happen. Hoarders tend to be people who ruminate over every decision in their lives, not only about things they collect. Their inability to make quick value judgments makes it hard for them to part with things that might be useful, or that have taken on special significance. They are perfectionistic in the extreme, and fearful of accidentally throwing out something important.[6]

Hoarding does respond to cognitive behavioral therapy techniques and medication, especially if the behavior is caught and treated early in life.

Toileting troubles

Gaining control over bowels and bladder is an important developmental milestone. The fact that toileting problems are very common in children with OCD is a measure of how seriously this disorder can affect child development. Unfortunately, this is not a topic that most people care to discuss, so many families never find out that their child's toileting traumas are related to OCD.

Judy, mother of 14-year-old Dave, tells about a typical OCD-related toileting problem:

> *My son experienced bowel problems when younger—since he could not use public restrooms, he would "hold it" until he got home. He is now chronically constipated.*

Many children with OCD do not develop bowel or bladder control until a much later age than usual. Others experience episodes of soiling (encopresis), daytime wetting (enuresis), or bedwetting that appear to be OCD-related. Sometimes, as in Dave's case, contamination issues keep a child out of the bathroom. Other children develop a compulsion—sometimes, but not always, related to fears of being contaminated by their own bodily wastes—to hold their feces or urine as long as possible, with accidents occurring when they've waited too long.

Others become obsessed with toileting, sitting on the toilet for hours "just in case," or worrying too much about the frequency or appearance of their bodily wastes.

Children with contamination issues often have an abnormal distaste for normal toileting functions. They may develop elaborate rituals around toileting, including changing their clothing or showering every time they use the bathroom, coating all surfaces with antibacterial spray, even wearing disposable gloves when wiping themselves. Toilet paper disappears at an astounding rate, as these children try to ensure that they are absolutely clean after a bowel movement.

Carmel, mother of Madison, tells about her daughter's embarrassing difficulties with enuresis:

> *Our 19-year-old daughter experienced bladder accidents that had to be connected with OCD. We first thought it was related to Prozac, then several medications later, we knew it had to be OCD related. We have since decided that it had to do with the rituals she had to do before she sat down on the toilet, which she put off until the last minute, thus causing frequent accidents. Sometimes she soiled her bed and just continued to lay in it. She has said that she seemed to have no muscle control. She has for the most part stopped having "accidents"; they only happen rarely. It was an extremely tough part of learning to deal with OCD. It really kept her down.*

Encopresis and enuresis are not only embarrassing and unhygienic, they can also cause medical problems. Children who compulsively hold their urine can develop an extended bladder, poor bladder muscle control, and cystitis, from irritation caused by concentrated urine. Urinary tract infections are also a common result, especially in children who wet or soil themselves but do not change their clothes. Children who attempt to hold their bowels can also end up with sphincter muscle problems or constipation.

Under no circumstances should a child with OCD be punished or shamed for these problems: treatment and understanding are the key. Cognitive behavioral therapy can be very effective, and medication helps, too.

Eating disorders

If all you know about eating disorders is what you've read in the popular press or sensationalistic books, you may be surprised to learn that most cases of anorexia and bulimia are not caused by our society's fanatical obsession with thinness. True, social factors always influence OCD symptoms: they play an equally important role in the development of scrupulosity, and hypochondria, for example, as they do in the development of eating disorders.

But eating disorders are nothing new. In fact, they have a strong link to scrupulosity. There are a number of documented instances in which Christian mystics developed an aversion to all food except the communion wafer, or starved themselves as penance for imagined sins...and also had the telltale obsessions and compulsions of scrupulosity. Indeed, these mystics, like many young people today who develop anorexia and/or bulimia, believed that eating was an immoral act. To them, the immorality lay in greed and physicality; today, the immorality is tied to erroneous ideas that link virtue and class status to a thin body. The effect—and the underlying cause—is the same.

Anorexia and bulimia also are not strictly diseases of young, thinness-obsessed women; in fact, the majority of deaths attributed to anorexia nervosa occur in people over the age of 65, particularly men.[7]

An entire industry has emerged that encourages people with eating disorders to blame their parents, ignoring current neurobiological research. Psychological interpretations are still the norm in many eating disorder treatment centers, and can cause great damage to families. Children with eating disorders are often encouraged to enter intensive psychotherapy for a period of years, during which they may be further encouraged to give the name "abuse" to parental imperfections, such as divorce, communication difficulties, mental or physical illness, pushiness, or adherence to outdated ideas about women's social roles, or even to "remember" abuse that may never have happened. This business of setting blame cuts the patient off from his or her family, which instead could have been the child's most effective ally in treatment.

In some cases of anorexia and bulimia there is a link to serious physical abuse or sexual abuse, in which case-extended therapy and removing the young patient from danger can be essential. The important thing is for parents to know that if they've done things wrong in raising their child, they are in great company—no family is perfect. The important thing for helping professionals to know is that except in clear-cut cases of physical or sexual abuse, the family must be part of the treatment team for success to occur. These patients, like most children with obsessive-compulsive behaviors, have great difficulty forming supportive social relationships. Removing them from the most important and long-lasting relationship they have is usually counterproductive. In fact, therapy that involves parents and siblings can be very helpful for people with eating disorders. Group therapy has also shown promise for older patients.

Eating disorders are seen far more often in people with diagnosed OCD than in the general population, and the vast majority of people with eating disorders also have other OCD symptoms.[8] Other clues point toward genetic and functional links between OCD and eating disorders. The two occur more frequently not only in the same individuals, but in the same families. A link between an autoimmune reaction to strep infection has been found in some cases of sudden-onset anorexia, just as in the PANDAS variant of OCD.[9] The genetic disorder Prader-Willi syndrome includes both obsessive-compulsive symptoms and compulsive eating. And perhaps most compellingly, eating disorders usually respond to the very same medications and therapy techniques that work for OCD. (Some binge eaters and bulimics have also found relief from opiate-blocker medications.)

Eating disorders include anorexia nervosa, bulimia nervosa, pica, and compulsive (binge) eating. Anorexia is self-starvation, the deliberate limiting of food intake. Many people with anorexia not only avoid eating, they use laxatives or self-induced vomiting to rapidly eliminate what little food they do eat. This practice also characterizes bulimia, in which eating binges are followed by purging via laxatives or vomiting. Pica is the compulsive practice of eating non-food items. Compulsive or binge eating is considered pathological if the person overeats not because they enjoy food, but because they feel an unwanted compulsion to do so.

Beyond the area of diagnosable eating disorders, OCD is frequently associated with food, eating, and weight. Judy tells about a common eating problem in children with OCD:

> *My 14-year-old son has an eating disorder caused by OCD: he finds most foods to be "nasty" (he has mostly contamination-type OCD) and therefore won't eat them. Textures, appearances, imaginary imperfections, etc. I took him to an eating disorders clinic, but they would not treat him, saying OCD is not an eating disorder per se, and he wouldn't fit into their treatment.*

Sixteen-year-old Michael also has trouble with eating:

> *If I don't wash my hands, I can't eat the little piece of part of the food that I touch. So I have to hide it. I throw it on the floor or put it in my pocket so people don't look at me. I would like to rid myself of some of my food obsessions and fears.*

Because eating disorders can quickly become a life-threatening medical problem, therapy is not enough. Immediate medical intervention is a must, as about 150 people die from anorexia every year, and many more do permanent damage to their teeth and internal organs.

Sadly, there are activities and professions in which eating disorders are not only common, but almost acceptable, at least to others within these closed societies. They include athletics, particularly girl's gymnastics, dance—especially ballet, acting, and modeling. Parents of children with OCD may want to gently steer them clear of these areas of endeavor, simply because these children are likely to be more receptive to the siren song of extreme diets and unrealistic physical ideals that can lead to eating disorders in those with obsessive-compulsive tendencies.

Hypochondria

Up to 60 percent of people seeking medical care from doctors have no discernible cause for their supposed illness. For years, doctors have dismissed the most persistent of them as "hypochondriacs," but it has recently come to light that most cases of hypochondria are simply a disease-obsessed variant of OCD, and that the condition can be treated with SSRI medications and cognitive behavioral therapy.[10]

Hypochondria is currently classified as a somatoform disorder, a psychiatric condition in which inner anxieties emerge as physical feelings. However, this definition is becoming more controversial. There was no scientific research on hypochondria until 1993, but as study results emerge, it is looking more and more like a subset of OCD.

Some people with OCD have single-issue medical obsessions, with fears about getting or transmitting AIDS or cancer especially prevalent (in years past, tuberculosis was a primary worry). Others try to pin their symptoms on various disorders in turn. Minor symptoms are misinterpreted and cause high levels of anxiety, which in turn produce further physical symptoms.

Kim, mother of 16-year-old Lindsey, says her medical obsessions have been maddening:

> *Lindsey has worried about her health ever since she was little. Even at age 5 she would ask us if she was going to die from this or that. When she turned 12 she got freaked out about AIDS, and that became her big OCD thing. She worried that surfaces, places (like the doctor's office), or people would give her AIDS. Last year she started getting AIDS tests. As far as we know she has never had sex, and she has never used any kind of drugs, but she is in mortal fear that she will get it. And one test wasn't enough, she thought maybe the lab made a mistake and got a second one at another clinic. It was negative too, but she still worries.*

People with hypochondria can be hard to treat with medication. They often have an irrational fear of prescription medications, and are likely to notice even the most minor side effects. Many strongly resent the implication that they have a mental illness rather than a physical disease.

Cognitive behavioral therapy has proven to be effective, especially if it can be coupled with medication. Patients with hypochondria may also benefit from a tactic similar to the one used for scrupulosity: choosing a single medical advisor, drawing up a concrete healthcare plan that includes common-sense limits on appointments, tests, and consultation calls, and agreeing to defer to the judgment of this doctor in all medical matters.

Trichotillomania

Trichotillomania is one of the most common OCD-linked disorders: compulsively pulling out one's own hair. People with trichotillomania usually pull hair from their heads, but may also pull from any other area of the body. Most pull in response to an anticipatory "tingle," itch, or sensory cue. Some also tie knots in, roll, or save the hair that they pull.

The behavior is not health threatening, but it can cause bald patches or even complete hair removal, leading to embarrassment and discomfort. Skin irritation is also common with repeated pulling.

"Trich" responds well to the same medications and therapeutic techniques used for OCD. While they are in treatment, people with trichotillomania may want to look into techniques for covering up their handiwork, including wigs, hats, and hair extensions that can cover bald areas on the scalp.

Body dysmorphic disorder

Body dysmorphic disorder (BDD) is an obsession with imagined ugliness or deformity. The late-stage anorexic's insistence that he or she is still "fat" represents a similar kind of thinking.

People with BDD may be obsessed with individual physical features, or with the whole package. They may feel compelled to conduct elaborate grooming and dressing rituals to get their appearance "just right," and still avoid mirrors. Some adults with BDD pursue unnecessary cosmetic surgery; others hide away from society for fear their appearance will offend others. Some are fixated on imagined body odor rather than appearance.[11]

Recent research indicates that BDD is equally common in men and women, co-occurs frequently with eating disorders, impulse disorders, and OCD, and responds to the same medications and therapeutic techniques as does OCD. One study has found that about 12 percent of adults with OCD also meet the criteria for BDD.[12]

Self-injurious behavior

The most common forms of self-injurious behavior (SIB) in people with OCD are also the most minor: skin picking and scab picking. As in trichotillomania, people who pick at their skin or at scabs usually say they are responding to a premonitory sensation: an itch, a tingle, or a feeling of tightness or "wrongness."

Skin- and scab-picking can cause scarring, especially in people who are prone to keloids, and it can also make the patient more susceptible to infection through the broken skin. Parents whose young children are prone to this behavior may be able to use bandages to discourage it, although medication and cognitive behavioral therapy are the most effective treatments.

There are many other forms of SIB, including cutting, burning, the use of caustic chemicals, head-banging, deliberate breaking of bones, and even self-strangulation. There's also some bad information out there about this disorder. In some cases, childhood abuse may set off this particular symptom because it encourages the patient to make a link between pain and mental escape. Abused children learn to be stoic during episodes of abuse to reduce the physical and emotional pain. That does not mean that if a patient is a cutter, he or she has been abused. There has been little realistic research into the link between SIB and OCD, but doctors who understand OCD as a biological disorder feel that it can be just another type of compulsion, although it has more serious repercussions for the patient than checking or counting rituals.

Laurie, a 19-year-old with OCD, finds her SIB experience hard to explain:

> *I was not an extreme self-mutilator. I used to use my fingernails to break the skin between my fingers. I would then force blood to ooze out. The pain of doing it did hurt, unlike what some people think. It was the feeling of power after doing it that was the high. It was something I could control, like people with eating disorders do with food. I don't know why I stopped, only I am very glad I did.*

Self-injurious behavior is described by patients as more addictive than other compulsive behaviors. While SIB creates intense sensations, many who self-injure say their acts are not especially painful. Some do achieve a sort of temporary high that may be even stronger than those experienced by people who compulsively shoplift, gamble, eat, or have sex; but the majority seem to feel a heightened sense of awareness or "reality," and a numbing effect that also deadens psychological pain. Research is preliminary, but both these paradoxical responses and the addictive quality of SIB may be caused by the release of endorphins, the body's natural opiates, in response to pain. One clue is the effectiveness of the opiate-blocker drug naltrexone (ReVia) in at least some patients with SIB.

One quality that many people who self-injure have in common is the ability to dissociate (see "Depersonalization disorder," in the next section).

Self-injurious behavior as experienced by people with OCD is usually done in private and kept hidden. It's not done for attention, and it's not an attempt at suicide, although if a patient is dissociating when they self-injure, serious injury or death is a possibility. Tattooing and piercing are social behaviors, not SIB. Forms of masochism in which self-mutilation is linked to sexual pleasure are usually also not SIB, although masochism can become a compulsive behavior.

Depersonalization disorder

Depersonalization is a form of dissociation: the ability to somehow step out of the reality that the rest of us share. People with depersonalization disorder may feel detached from their bodies, or have unusual sensory experiences in their bodies.

Margie, a 35-year-old woman whose OCD symptoms date back to age 6, describes one such episode:

> *I would be sitting in my second-grade classroom, often counting the holes in the ceiling tiles, which was one of my compulsions then, when everything would just go strange. I felt like I was cut off from the rest of the room by a curtain or something, and everything was fuzzy. If the teacher was talking, it was like the grown-ups in the "Charlie Brown" cartoons: "wonk-wonk, wonk-wonk, wonk-wonk." I couldn't understand a word. You can imagine how scary this was! I never told anyone about these experiences.*

It appears that some people have an inborn ability to dissociate, and that women are more capable of it than men (evolutionarily speaking, it's an ability that could have been quite useful during childbirth without pain medication or preparation). In some cultures, the ability to dissociate is considered a gift, and such people are revered. However, those who experience depersonalization in the modern world rarely see it as a benefit—it can be quite frightening.

Migraine, seizure disorders, and hallucinogenic drugs can cause similar symptoms. People with self-injurious behaviors often describe themselves as being in a depersonalized, altered state when they self-injure, as do some people who suffer from impulse disorders, particularly pyromania.

More serious forms of dissociation are also seen. For example, dissociation is the key finding in cases of dissociative identity disorder, previously known as multiple personality disorder.

Impulse disorders

Impulse disorders are most simply defined as problems that occur when one's impulses are not overridden, allowing a person to commit harmful or unwanted acts. The category includes pyromania, kleptomania, pathological gambling, compulsive shopping, and more. Trichotillomania is technically considered an impulse disorder.

This is a complex category, and while some people with impulse disorder have OCD or OCD-like symptoms, the majority of them probably do not. These behaviors, like self-injurious behavior, can be somewhat rewarding in their own right. People with OCD who have impulse disorders usually experience these behaviors as unwanted, and are guilt-ridden afterwards.

Because having a compulsion to set fires is serious business, and one that is likely to have strong personal and legal consequences, pyromania deserves special mention.

Manuel, now 30 years old and diagnosed with OCD, comes forth about his fire-setting compulsions:

> *I had a problem "playing" with fire while growing up. I almost burned down two houses and my first job. Not good!*

Fire-setting compulsions are seen more often in patients under the age of 21 than in older people with OCD, and seem to be much more common in boys than in girls. Although the DSM-IV definition of pyromania would seem to rule out this diagnosis for someone who also has OCD, it may be used anyway. Most juvenile fire-setters do not have OCD. The majority could be described as antisocial and aggressive instead.

Impulse disorders are usually treated with cognitive behavioral therapy, particularly exposure and response techniques. Medication also helps some patients. Others have found group therapy useful.

Substance abuse and other addictions

Many people do not feel comfortable thinking of substance abuse as an illness, although the idea of alcoholism as a disease is gaining wider acceptance. Certainly, not everyone who uses or abuses alcohol or drugs is responding to a genetic compulsion—but it's equally possible that some are. Substance abuse is also not an uncommon strategy for dealing with the unpleasant symptoms of mental illness.

The combination of both mental illness and substance abuse is called dual diagnosis, and there are some special programs available to treat both problems simultaneously. There is strong evidence that even if a patient gets great results from OCD treatment, the OCD is likely to return if the substance abuse disorder is not also treated. Likewise, reducing OCD symptoms can contribute to more successful substance abuse treatment in dual-diagnosis patients.[13]

In her paper, "Challenges in Assessing Substance Use Patterns in Persons with Comorbid Mental and Addictive Disorders,"[14] dual-diagnosis researcher Kate Carey states:

> *Substance use assessment is applicable to all persons in treatment for mental disorders. Use of illicit drugs or alcohol is more common than abuse, and information about use patterns may be desired to determine risk for medication-drug interactions and other health concerns. Finally, substance use assessment should play a central role in the treatment of comorbid disorders. It serves as the basis for treatment planning and as a point of departure for outcome assessment.*

Alcohol and drugs are now known to have complex effects on the neurotransmitter system, effects that can feel even stronger and seemingly more desirable to people whose neurotransmitter system is out of balance. If unchecked, substance abuse follows the same course as other disease: it can go through primary, progressive, and fatal stages. Some estimates indicate that at least half of all adult patients with a mental illness also have a substance abuse problem.[15]

The lifetime prevalence of alcohol abuse and dependence in people with OCD is currently estimated at 24.6 percent. A higher risk can be expected if the picture is complicated by the presence of other neurological disorders, particularly ADHD or bipolar disorders. There do not seem to be current statistics available on the prevalence of drug abuse among people with OCD, but studies indicate that for some people, the onset of anxiety disorders is associated with the use of drugs, particularly cocaine.[16]

Paraphilias

No research seems to have been done on sexual compulsions known as paraphilias (sadism, masochism, fetishes, pedophilia, etc.) and OCD, although both sexual obsessions and compulsions are reported by people with OCD. Perhaps the greatest difference between these two groups is that, as with impulse disorders, for people with OCD, these are guilt-producing compulsions. Intrusive thoughts about these behaviors are probably fairly common in people with OCD, but acting on them is probably not.

Personality disorders

The DSM-IV category known as the personality disorders is increasingly controversial. These ten "personality styles" are defined as learned behaviors that, while not mental illnesses per se, can have a negative effect on a person's life and the people around him. The controversy occurs because some personality disorders are poorly defined and are considered to be pejorative labels—especially borderline personality disorder. There's also the idea that medication tends to help people with personality disorders and should not be able to help with learned behaviors.

In fact, it was obsessive-compulsive personality disorder, commonly abbreviated as OCPD, that made the connection clear. When people diagnosed with both OCD and OCPD were given medications for OCD symptoms, the rigidity and compulsiveness that characterize OCPD also began to disappear.

Now many professionals are thinking of the personality disorders as mild, subclinical versions of major mental disorders—with the possible exception of antisocial personality disorder, the medical diagnosis for a sociopath. Very briefly defined, the personality disorders are divided and defined this way:

- Cluster A
  - **Paranoid.** Distrustful, suspicious of others and their motives.
  - **Schizoid.** Has very limited social and emotional range.
  - **Schizotypal.** Has limited social and emotional range coupled with unusual thought and behavior patterns.
- Cluster B
  - **Antisocial.** Unconcerned about rules, laws, or the rights of others; often violent, aggressive, destructive. The adult version of ODD or Conduct Disorder. Also called sociopathic or psychopathic personality.

- **Borderline.** Has unstable relationships, values, self-image, and emotions; reckless and impulsive; episodes of aggressive or highly emotional behavior.
- **Histrionic.** Attention-seeking, highly emotional.
- **Narcissistic.** Self-absorbed, self-important, demanding, limited understanding of other peoples' perspectives.

- Cluster C
  - **Avoidant.** Feels inadequate, overly sensitive to criticism, avoids social interaction.
  - **Dependent.** Overly dependent on others for approval or care, clinging and submissive.
  - **Obsessive-compulsive.** Overly controlled (and controlling), orderly, and perfectionistic.

Whether the personality disorders are discrete entities or shadows of larger problems, personality problems that drive others away are certainly something one should help children avoid through consistent parenting, providing early medical intervention, teaching good coping skills, ensuring that kids have access to special education resources as needed, and providing personal, family, community, and therapeutic support, and medications.

Besides OCPD, a personality disorder diagnosis that is sometimes given by mistake to young women with OCD is borderline personality disorder. This disorder is characterized by great difficulty in maintaining interpersonal relationships, sudden shifts in mood and affect, and insecurity. Some critics say it has taken the place of Freud's own favorite, "hysteria," as a catch-all diagnosis for women whose behavior is considered aberrant.

Some women with borderline personality disorder may have biologically-based deficits in understanding social cues, as seen in OCD and autistic spectrum disorders, leading to a weak sense of self and of reality. In particular, there seems to be a subgroup of women diagnosed with borderline personality disorder who better meet the criteria for Asperger's syndrome, a form of high-functioning autism that is sometimes comorbid with OCD. Women in Western culture are supposed to do much of the emotional work in relationships, but such women are singularly ill equipped for the task. They misread others, lack information about what is "normal" in friendship and romantic relationships, and may be repeatedly abused by men during their search for a stable caretaker. Many have no female friends, as they find it difficult to handle the more subtle shadings of interpersonal relationships among women. They tend to make a man their "everything," and play dramatic games to test the relationship's security.

Social skills work and cognitive behavioral therapy should be able to help, especially if these tendencies are caught early. Parents can encourage positive relationships and skill-building, and limit their own willingness to be manipulated.

Comorbid disorders

If a patient's biggest difficulties are with OCD, but he or she also has ADHD, OCD would be called the primary diagnosis and ADHD the secondary diagnosis. Together they would be comorbid diagnoses.

Conditions that occur more frequently in people who are also diagnosed with OCD include: ADD/ADHD, Tourette's syndrome and tic disorders, autistic spectrum disorders, other anxiety disorders, depression and manic depression, and certain rare conditions.

ADD/ADHD

To fit the DSM-IV criteria for ADHD, some hyperactive, inattentive, or impulsive symptoms must appear before the age of 7; symptoms must be present in two or more settings (such as at school and at home); and the symptoms must cause real difficulty for the child. The official ADHD criteria also state that symptoms must not be due to another mental disorder, including OCD. This "either/or" position is controversial with some clinicians.

To meet the criteria for ADHD, item 1 or 2 must be true:

1. Six or more of the following symptoms must be present, persisting for at least six months, occurring frequently, and occurring to a degree inconsistent with the child's developmental level:

    a. Fails to pay attention to details, makes careless mistakes in schoolwork or other activities

    b. Difficulty sustaining attention in schoolwork, chores, or play activities

c. Does not seem to listen when spoken to directly

d. Failure to follow instructions, does not finish schoolwork or chores (not due to deliberate oppositional behavior or failure to understand instructions)

e. Difficulty organizing tasks and activities

f. Avoids, dislikes, or is reluctant to try tasks that require sustained mental effort, such as homework

g. Loses things needed for tasks or activities, such as toys, homework assignments, or books

h. Easily distracted by noise or other external stimuli

i. Forgetful in daily activities

2. Six or more of the following symptoms of hyperactivity/impulsivity must be present, persisting for at least six months, and to a degree that is inconsistent with developmental level:

   a. Fidgets with hands or feet, squirms in seat

   b. Can't seem to remain seated in the classroom or other places where it is expected

   c. Runs and climbs excessively in inappropriate situations and places (in adolescents, this can be subjective feelings of restlessness)

   d. Difficulty playing quietly

   e. Physically very active—acts as if "driven by a motor"

   f. Talks excessively

   g. Blurts out answers before questions have been completed, or out of turn

   h. Can't seem to wait for turn in play or at school

   i. Interrupts or intrudes on others by butting into conversations or games, invading others' personal space, etc.

Based on the preceding criteria, the DSM-IV separates ADHD into four categories:

- **ADHD, Predominantly Inattentive Type** (314.00). Child meets the criteria in section 1, but not in section 2. This is what's commonly called ADD: attention deficit without marked hyperactivity.
- **ADHD, Predominantly Hyperactive-Impulsive Type** (314.01). Child meets the criteria in section 2, but not in section 1.
- **ADHD, Combined Type** (314.01). Child meets the criteria in both section 1 and section 2.
- ADHD NOS (314.9). Child has prominent symptoms of hyperactivity/impulsivity and/or attention deficit, but doesn't meet all of the required criteria for any of the other three types. This diagnosis is sometimes used when the child has another primary condition, such as bipolar disorder, but also has symptoms of ADHD that are not fully explained by that disorder. NOS stands for "not otherwise specified."

Tourette's syndrome and tic disorders

Tourette's syndrome is characterized by repetitive, largely involuntary muscle movements known as tics. When the movements involve the muscles of the mouth and produce sounds, they are called vocal tics; when they affect other body parts, they are called motor tics. For a diagnosis of Tourette's, both types must be present for over six months. If only one type is present, a diagnosis of tic disorder may be made.

Typical motor tics include repetitive eye blinking, facial twitches, tapping, spinning, "cracking" certain joints compulsively, straightening clothes and objects, and making complex combinations of physical movements. Typical vocal tics include snorting, shrieking, grunting, whistling, making animal sounds, and compulsively repeating words or phrases. The famous symptom of blurting out obscene or derogatory words is experienced by about 10 percent of all people with Tourette's, and is usually a transitory symptom. Tics tend to wax and wane over time, much like obsessions and compulsions.

At least half of all patients diagnosed with Tourette's also have OCD. In families where Tourette's occurs, women frequently have OCD while men are more likely to have Tourette's, leading scientists to believe that the two disorders may be different expressions of the same genotype. In people who have Tourette's, physical tics sometimes diminish by middle age, but "mental tics" (obsessive thoughts, such as a need to repeat certain words mentally) tend to stick around for life.

Autistic spectrum disorders

The autistic spectrum ranges from autistic disorder to Asperger's syndrome, with atypical and unspecified pervasive developmental disorders in the middle. Obsessive-compulsive behavior is common in people with autism, and is considered to be part of the diagnostic criteria for these disorders. Although the common perception is that people with autism cannot talk or relate to others, many people with an autistic spectrum disorder can do both—although their ability to maintain social relationships tends to be limited.

One form of autism that is frequently confused with OCD, or that may occur with it, is Asperger's syndrome. Asperger's is characterized by narrow areas of interest and a self-centered way of looking at the world. People with Asperger's are rarely retarded; they are often quite intelligent. However, social skills just don't come naturally to them at all, and they do not read social cues well. They don't have noticeable language delays; in fact, many are very early talkers and early readers (a symptom known as *hyperlexia*). Most do have speech differences, most noticeably a tendency to lecture endlessly on topics of special interest like a pedantic "Little Professor."

Asperger's is characterized by strong interests in a limited number of subjects or activities, interests that become full-fledged obsessions. Many people with Asperger's are highly successful in technology careers, such as computer programming and engineering, that both minimize contact with other people and make use of their special interests. Others find their progress hampered by social difficulties, or by comorbid conditions like OCD or depression, which are fairly common in this group.

People with autistic spectrum disorders tend to have topic fixations more than any other type of obsessions.

Other anxiety disorders

Anxiety disorders are common enough that almost everyone knows someone who suffers from one. They include panic disorders, generalized anxiety disorder, post-traumatic stress syndrome, and extreme phobias of all sorts, from claustrophobia (fear of being in small, enclosed places) to arachnophobia (fear of spiders). Basically put, anxiety disorders involve an extreme reaction to certain situations or stimuli, as the body puts its "fight or flight" system in motion for no good reason.

Depression and manic depression

Unipolar, or "simple," depression is just that: depressed mood that lasts longer than two weeks, and is not due to another medical condition, the side effects of medication, or normal reaction to a major life event (such as grieving after a parent's death). It is the most common form of depression. Most people with unipolar depression have periods of feeling normal, including feeling happy.

Some people with OCD develop situational depression as a reaction to their debilitating symptoms.

Bipolar I disorder was formerly known as manic depression. People with Bipolar I swing into depression cyclically, and have had at least one manic episode. Some have also had hypomanic episodes. Hypomania is an abnormally elevated, expansive mood with such signs as hyperactivity, irritability, fast speech, and rapid-fire thinking. Mania takes these symptoms to the next level, in which the patient's thoughts and actions are out of control altogether.

Bipolar II disorder is defined as recurrent depression with hypomania, but not mania or mixed states. People with Bipolar II also tend to be more *emotionally labile* (moody) in between actual mood swings.

Bipolar disorders can complicate OCD treatment, because most antidepressants can cause manic episodes. Patients with bipolar disorder need to be on a working dose of a mood stabilizer before trying an antidepressant.

Raegan, age 18, tells about one such incident:

> *During the early years of my OCD, I wasn't a bad-tempered child, though I kept to myself and avoided being with people. However in the fall of 1997, my first doctor put me on a large dose of Paxil. The large amount caused me to have angry outbursts over simple things. My mom took me to another doctor after that, and this doctor took me off the high amount of Paxil right away. My anger stopped when my medicine was lowered.*

Cyclothymic disorder, another bipolar disorder, is described in children as a chronic mood disturbance lasting for at least a year. Both depressed and hypomanic moods are present, but there are no major depressive, manic, or mixed episodes. The patient must have gone without a period of normal mood for more than two months during the year. The cycles and moods are not as severe as those seen in Bipolar II. Seasonal Affective Disorder ("winter blues") is a form of cyclothymic disorder.

Rare conditions

If a person with obsessive-compulsive behaviors also has physical anomalies, mental retardation, or other unusual finding, a physician may want to consider one of the following rare explanations.

Cornelia de Lange syndrome

Cornelia de Lange syndrome is a very rare genetic disorder with hallmarks of: developmental delays; a small head that may also be short and wide, a small and broad pug nose; thick, arched eyebrows that grow together; and long eyelashes that curl. Many other physical differences may be present, including malformations of major organ systems, webbed toes, and unusual hormone activity.

People with this disorder are usually, but not always, mentally retarded. Like people with autism, they often have stereotypic behaviors (mouthing of hands and objects is especially common). They may also have perseverations (obsessions) and self-injurious behaviors.

Prader-Willi syndrome

Prader-Willi syndrome is a genetic disorder believed to be caused by a mutation on chromosome 15. It sometimes occurs with autism or includes autistic-like features. Its most prominent symptom is an obsession with food and compulsive eating. Sexual characteristics may be underdeveloped, as are muscles. Most people with Prader-Willi syndrome are mildly retarded, and have speech and movement problems. Temper tantrums, skin picking, and sleep difficulties are also frequently seen.

Medication does not seem to help this population very much. It's likely that an associated metabolic disorder governs how food is absorbed and whether the stomach feels full, but no one has yet discovered how to address the problem. Special diets and behavior modification can be useful for maintaining health and improving performance at school and in the community.

Rett syndrome

Rett syndrome has recently been linked to a gene known as MeCP2, which is located on the X chromosome. The disorder is not obvious at birth, but usually appears between the ages of 6 and 18 months. The torso and limbs may shake, the gait is wobbly and rigid, and breathing seems difficult, as does eating.

Children with Rett syndrome are always female; recent research indicates that males who inherit the Rett gene die before or shortly after birth. They tend to grow slowly and be short, and to have a small head (*microencephaly*). There is always retardation, generally ranging from severe to profound. About 80 percent of girls with Rett Syndrome also have epilepsy.

Girls affected by Rett syndrome wring their hands repetitively. They frequently have obsessions and compulsions. While they may start out with social phobia, this tends to lift by the gradeschool years.

Some girls diagnosed with Rett syndrome do recover some abilities that were lost. This is rare, however, and may represent a milder subtype. A 1997 study published in *European Child and Adolescent Psychiatry* described seven girls of Italian descent and one of East Indian heritage who fit this profile. The researchers noted that despite regaining many abilities, including making major improvements in speech and socialization, these children retained many autistic features. Some of the more severe symptoms associated with Rett syndrome, including seizures and microcephaly, were much more rare in this group.

Williams syndrome

Williams syndrome is a rare genetic disorder characterized by mild mental retardation. Many people with Williams syndrome exhibit autistic or OCD behaviors, including hypersensitivity to sounds, extreme food likes and dislikes, and preservation. They usually have developmental, gross-motor, and language delays.

These sociable, often quite animated people have cardiovascular abnormalities, high blood pressure, and elevated calcium levels, as well as unique facial features that can be described as "pixie-like," including almond-shaped eyes, perfect oval ears, a broad mouth with full lips, and a narrow face with a small chin.

Tuberous sclerosis

Tuberous sclerosis is a relatively rare disorder (affecting about 1 in 6,000 people) that affects the brain, the skin, the eyes, and other organs of the body with varying degrees of severity. As many as half of all children diagnosed with tuberous sclerosis have autistic features, most have epilepsy, and many are mentally retarded. Tuberous sclerosis can be caused by two different genetic defects, one on chromosome 9 and one on chromosome 16. A defect need occur on only one of these genes to cause the condition, although other unknown genetic factors may determine who develops the disorder.

The link between tuberous sclerosis and autistic symptoms, including obsessive-compulsive behaviors, may be physical rather than genetic. A 1997 study published in the medical journal *Lancet* stated that when the brains of patients with both tuberous sclerosis and a diagnosis of either autism or atypical pervasive developmental disorder were imaged, tubers (a tumor-like growth characteristic of tuberous sclerosis) were found in the temporal lobes. These patients also had more tubers in their brains in general than did patients without autistic features.[17]

What to do with a diagnosis

When you finally have all the information you need about your child's challenges, where do you go from there? There are no therapies currently available that cure the underlying genetic or neurological causes of OCD, although medical treatments that may control symptoms of the PANDAS variant are being developed. Instead, OCD is attacked in two complementary ways: with medication that affects the serotonin system involved in OCD, and with cognitive behavioral therapy that helps the patient use the power of his or her mind to resist and reduce obsessions and compulsions.

Chapter 4, *Therapeutic Interventions*, will explore cognitive behavioral therapy and other helpful therapies. Chapter 5, *Medical Interventions*, will explain medication options.

Families may also want to pursue other avenues that may help their children, including learning new parenting techniques (see Chapter 3, *Living with OCD*), using sensory integration therapy to reduce OCD triggers, complementing their medical and psychiatric efforts with alternative health concepts (see Chapter 6, *Other Interventions*), and using the special education system to ensure that their child receives an education despite his or her symptoms (see Chapter 8, *School and Transition*).

CHAPTER 3

Living with OCD

THIS CHAPTER WILL DISCUSS the effects childhood-onset obsessive-compulsive disorder has on patients and their families. Topics include common problems, learning more effective parenting techniques, and building community support systems that provide the best possible environment for a child or adolescent with OCD.

Turbulent times

OCD turns family life upside down. Parents of children with OCD frequently report that their child's obsessions and compulsions rule the household, with parents and siblings caught up in following or facilitating rituals that the child dictates. They feel forced to prepare special meals, follow specific cleaning procedures, and go along with odd behaviors just to keep the peace.

Cheryl, mother of 9-year-old Jenny, explains:

> *Unless you live with a child with OCD, you could never understand what a family goes through. It is like taking the child you once knew and replacing her with a stranger. Sometimes we are afraid to say anything to her in fear it would set her off into another rage.*

Mary, mother of 13-year-old Ryan, agrees:

> *The most stressful part has been losing the freedom to go out and do things as a family. Our son has become a prisoner to OCD and to our house. Rage behaviors started recently as the OCD has gotten worse. It is definitely connected to the OCD, especially when cognitive behavioral therapy has been questioned or interrupted. It has been devastating.*

The result of giving in to your child's demands may be a temporary calm, but these accommodations can cause harm in the long run. First, parents and siblings feel natural resentment at having to carry out a child's instructions, especially if the demands are unreasonable. Second, the more obsessive-compulsive behaviors are permitted, the more they are reinforced.

Mornings, bedtimes, and meal times are often especially problematic. Many parents interviewed for this book reported that their child with OCD had bedtime rituals, and sometimes morning rituals, that "had" to be performed. Of course, this is true for many young children, who will go to school or to sleep only after they've had the customary hug, cup of cocoa, or story. But when rituals take more than a few minutes to perform, they start to interfere with normal life.

Children with OCD experience extreme frustration when these rituals are interrupted, just as they do when other compulsive behaviors, such as washing or counting, are cut short. In some this causes rage, in others frustration or withdrawal. This can be very confusing and demoralizing for parents.

Meals are often also the scene of OCD-related conflicts. Children with OCD may severely restrict their own diets, refusing to eat the foods their families have prepared. Some have unreasonable fears of germs or contamination that prevent them from eating with the rest of the family, or from using the same plates and utensils. Others have a heightened sensitivity to sound that amplifies other people's chewing noises. Some children fear that others will hear and be disgusted with their chewing sounds.

During these times, as with other daily turbulence, parents may feel like they are walking on eggshells. They know that if they completely refuse to acquiesce, the fallout will affect everyone in the household. Using cognitive behavioral therapy techniques is the only way to gradually reduce the number, frequency, and severity of ritual behaviors.

Parents can't always expect a child with OCD to act logically when presented with limits on ritual behavior. Although limit-setting by parents can play an important role in decreasing rituals, especially with younger patients, the child must commit to these limits for the process to continue. Chapter 4, *Therapeutic Interventions*, provides specifics on how to introduce cognitive behavioral techniques—including exposure and response prevention—into your child's daily routine.

As you carry out these slow exercises to reduce compulsive behavior, keep in mind that your child is probably experiencing far greater inner pain than he is showing; this may help you hold on to patience. Young people with OCD are rarely forthcoming about how terrible they feel, but their distress is intense.

Emma, age 17, explains how OCD affects her inner life:

> *The most stressful part has been loneliness—not understanding what's happening, and not being able to resist compulsions. The terror of the obsessions was unbearable. My parents don't understand. My mum sometimes tries; my dad couldn't care less. My boyfriend doesn't understand why I am so self-conscious, which frustrates him.*

Sixteen-year-old Elizabeth says coping with her OCD symptoms is extremely difficult:

> *My relationship with my mom has become more strained because she doesn't understand what is really going on in my head. She thinks that by reminding me not to do my rituals that I just won't. She doesn't understand that OCD is not like a bad habit; it's like a demon crawling in the back of your mind. Nothing you can do will really make it go away; it will always prowl.*

Thinking about thinking

Some of the most persistent problems of children and adolescents with OCD involve types of thinking that are irrational and difficult for others to understand. When young people learn to recognize and name these "thought errors," they can avoid making a scene, getting embarrassed, and getting in trouble. The longer these off-kilter thought patterns continue, the more likely they are to become ingrained, lifelong habits. These habits of thought contribute to development of the hard-to-treat personality disorders that bedevil some adults with OCD. Once you can label and dissect an irrational thought, however, you take away a little of its power.

Shana, age 20, tells about how thought errors bother her:

> *My primary behaviors at the moment are obsessive and intrusive thoughts, but over the years I have been a checker, counter, washer, and many others. Being able to tell if my thoughts are because of OCD or not has been the hardest part. Trying to distinguish between obsessions and reality is very difficult.*

Problematic thought styles include:

- **Magical thinking.** The belief that by doing some sort of ritual, one can avoid harm to himself or others. The ritual may or may not be connected with the perceived harm, and sufferers tend to keep their rituals secret. Children are not always sure what harm the ritual is fending off; they may simply report knowing that "something bad will happen" if they don't touch each slat of the fence or make sure their footsteps end on an even number. Others may come to feel that ritual behavior will bring about some positive event. This type of thinking is central to OCD, particularly for children.
- **Personalization.** A form of magical thinking characterized by feeling as if you are the center of the universe, and that you cause events for good or ill that truly have little or nothing to do with you. For example, a child might believe that writing or seeing the number seven could make his mother ill, and start performing ritual behaviors to prevent this harm from occurring.
- **Catastrophizing.** Seeing only the worst possible outcome in everything. For example, your child might think that because she failed her algebra test she will get an F for the semester, everyone will know she's stupid, the teacher will hate her, you will ground her, and moreover, she'll never get into college. . .and on and on. No matter what soothing words or solutions you try to apply, she'll insist that there's no remedy.
- **Minimization.** Another side of catastrophizing is minimizing your own good qualities, or refusing to see the good (or bad) qualities of other people or situations. People who minimize may be accused of wearing rose-colored glasses, or of wearing blinders that allow them to see only the worst. If a person fails to meet the minimizer's high expectations in one way—for example, by being dishonest on a single occasion—the minimizer will suddenly write the person off forever, refusing to see any good characteristics that may exist.
- **Leaps in logic.** Making seemingly logic-based statements, even though the process that led to the idea was missing obvious steps—i.e., jumping to conclusions, often negative ones. One special type of logical leap is assuming that you know what someone else is thinking. For instance, a teenager might assume that everyone at school hates her, or that anyone who is whispering is talking about her. Another common error is the "mind reader mistake"—assuming that other people will naturally

know what you are thinking, leading to great misunderstandings when they don't seem to grasp what you're talking about or doing.

- **"All or nothing" thinking.** Being unable to see shades of gray in everyday life can lead to major misperceptions and even despair. A person who thinks only in black-and-white terms can't comprehend small successes. He's either an abject failure or a complete success, never simply on his way to doing better. This is a common expression of the perfectionism seen in some young people with OCD, especially when it comes to moral issues.
- **Paranoia.** In its extreme forms, paranoia slides into the realm of delusion. Many people with OCD experience transient feelings of paranoia because of personalizing events, catastrophizing, or making leaps in logic. A teen with mildly paranoid thoughts might feel that everyone at school is watching and judging him, when in fact he's barely on their radar screen.

Not only are these thought styles in error, they're intensely uncomfortable to the person who uses them—or should we say, suffers from them, because no one would deliberately choose to have these anxiety-producing thoughts. When these thoughts emerge in words and deeds, the damage can be even worse. Expressing such ideas alienates friends and family, and can lead to teasing, ostracism, and severe misunderstandings.

Young children in particular don't have much of a frame of reference when it comes to thinking styles. They may well assume that everyone thinks this way! Older children and teens are usually more self-aware, and they may try hard to keep their "weird" thoughts under wraps. That's an exhausting use of mental energy, and makes the sufferer feel terribly alienated.

The rigidity that these problematic thought patterns have in common may come partly from life experiences. Many clinicians suspect that because people with OCD often deal with illogical waves of emotion and activity, they try to impose strict structures on their thoughts and beliefs to compensate. It's easy to get carried away with this, though, especially for children who don't have a lifetime of "normal" thinking to compare these thought patterns to.

Because these thought styles have at least some chemical basis, however, medication may also help. For more information about medications, see Chapter 5, *Medical Interventions*.

Cognitive behavioral therapy is used specifically to help people identify erroneous thinking and mistaken beliefs about themselves and the world. We'll talk more about cognitive therapy in Chapter 4, but the following basic techniques used by cognitive therapists can be used independently of a comprehensive therapeutic program:

- Listen to what your child says she is thinking and feeling—really listen. You might even want to take notes. Don't interrupt or make a value judgment on the thoughts your child is expressing while you're in active listening mode.
- Ask questions about the thoughts expressed. See if you can help your child express the logic (or discover the lack of it) behind his statements. It can be hard to do, but try to avoid evaluating his words yourself. What you're trying to do is not so much to tell him the "right" way to think, but to help him discover his own thought errors, and to help him learn ways to correct or avoid these mistakes in the future.

Knowing the formal rules of logic can be extraordinarily helpful to someone with OCD, especially for children whose behavior tends to be very rule-based. These rules are taught in speech classes and sometimes in writing classes, used on debate teams, and can also be learned from books. They'll help your child know when others are trying to fool her, and also give her some clues for recognizing when her own brain is playing illogical tricks. However, these rules can sometimes be misused by people with OCD to justify their behavior. It's important to teach children how to recognize overvalued ideas, and to explain how the laws of probability interact with "pure" logic.

Kids with a visual bent may benefit from diagramming their thoughts using boxes and lines, or using "if-then" statements. This technique can help people see how flexible most situations and problems are, with many possible choices, solutions, and end results. Choose Your Own Adventure books which let readers drive the story by making choices for the characters, can help explain this concept. You can also ask, "What do you think made him do that?" and "What if?" questions about the thoughts and choices of characters in a child's favorite book or movie.

Whether verbal, written, or drawn representations work best for your child, the goal is for him to judge the accuracy of his own thinking and be able to toss out thoughts that are illogical. This is an empowering skill for young people with OCD, giving them increased mastery over the brain's error messages.

Discipline

Discipline is difficult when a child has any type of mental or neurological illness. Not only do the old rules not always apply, but you have to be flexible about behaviors that are due to your child's illness. Because OCD symptoms wax and wane, this is particularly hard to do if you want to maintain consistency in your disciplinary style.

Punishing your child for performing rituals or for talking about her obsessions will not work. That doesn't mean her behavior and endless rumination must be allowed to go unchecked. It's okay for adults to set limits, but those limits must be grounded in reality to be workable. You may, for example, be able to help your child limit talking about his obsessions to a certain part of the day. You may be able to bend on some items while you work on more pressing issues through therapy.

Proactive measures

The best strategy is to be proactive. Use preventative measures like consistent medical care and daily structure to reduce the opportunity for problem behaviors. Make and apply consistent rules. . .but be able to bend them when it is truly needed due to your child's illness.

When your child is well, discuss measures you should take when he is not able to help acting out, and when his compulsions are most severe. Set up a system of signals he can use to let you and his teachers know when he needs extra assistance. These signals can help you gracefully remove him from a situation, such as a Little League game or classroom, before things get out of hand.

Set up a safe place at school and at home where he can take a self-imposed "time-out" when stress starts to build up too high. At school, this may be a resource room, a quiet office, or the library. At home, it may be your child's room or a cushy living room chair. When you're out in the community, your car can become a refuge, or you can search out a public restroom, restaurant booth, or park bench. Most people prefer a feeling of being safely enclosed when they're on the verge of losing it. Some kids find that full-body pressure seems to calm the storm, and may benefit from being held by a parent, swaddled tightly in a blanket, or lying under a mattress, heavy blanket, or sofa cushions.

Your child's physician may be able to prescribe a tranquilizer or other medication for use "as needed" during emergencies. Make sure you thoroughly discuss when, how, and how often this medication can be used—emergency medication is only safe when you follow appropriate procedures. If you don't have emergency medication available, an over-the-counter antihistamine like Benedryl can sometimes help temporarily calm a raging, sleepless, anxiety-plagued child. Obviously, you don't want to make this a regular practice, and you must make sure it's okay to use it with any regular medications your child takes.

Positive discipline

Most parents and school behavior experts have found that positive consequences are more effective than negative consequences for keeping kids with OCD on track. Many behavioral classrooms use a "token economy" to encourage improvement. Each positive action merits a star or other mark on a chart, or a physical token such as a poker chip or paper chit. When a certain number of stars, chips, chits, or other tokens have been collected, a reward is earned. Classroom rewards may include computer time, playtime, having lunch with the teacher, or small items like stickers or nifty pencils.

You can adapt the token economy system for use at home, tying an allowance, event, special time with parents or siblings, or other desired reward to earning a certain number of tokens. Try not to set the bar too high, of course. Start out with easily achievable goals and small rewards, and work up from there. Try not to take away tokens for negative behavior—just firmly refuse to give tokens for anything but positive, desirable behavior. Many families use the token system not only to reinforce rules, but as part of rewarding progress in cognitive behavioral therapy.

Children shouldn't expect a treat for every good deed, of course. Your goal should be to eventually make a hug, smile, or positive statement about the behavior reward enough. . .and, in the long term, to make the inner feelings your child gets from behaving well and helping others to be a sufficient incentive.

Giving rewards for good behavior goes against the grain for many parents. It may help to remember that kids with OCD don't always get good feelings from good behavior. In fact, controlling their own behavior and complying with requests can be anxiety-producing, even almost painful. By adding a tangible incentive, you're chipping away at a disordered nervous system that has previously been reinforcing the wrong behavior and may even have been working against the desired behavior.

Be sure to "catch your child being good" whenever you can. Too often, discipline stresses and even reinforces bad behavior by giving it more attention than the positive things children and teenagers do. Be more lavish with your praise (when warranted) than you are with your disapproval and anger.

Sometimes parents need to take a self-imposed time-out. We've all had those days when a long string of minor misbehavior and stress adds up to a major blow-out over some little thing, like a ball thrown in the house or a spilled soda pop. Use the same stress-busting techniques that you encourage your child to use, whether it's deep breathing and counting to ten, or going to your room for five minutes. Your example is probably the best teaching tool you have.

Pick your battles

Many parents have found Ross Greene's excellent book *The Explosive Child: A New Approach for Understanding and Parenting Easily Frustrated, Chronically Inflexible Children* to be very helpful. Greene encourages parents and teachers to employ what he calls the basket system: use the mental device of several baskets to sort your rules in order of importance. Rules and chores that go in Basket A are the essentials. The rest go in Baskets B, C, and so on, in order of descending importance. Greene stresses the need to pick your battles carefully when dealing with a child who is oppositional, has tantrums or rages easily, or has out-of-proportion reactions to small disagreements or requests. This is good advice, especially when your child is experiencing severe OCD symptoms.

This discipline model works well with cognitive behavioral therapy. One of the first things therapists may do with your child is identify which obsessions and compulsions she wants to reduce first. Helping your child resist these impulses and carry out assigned exposure and response-prevention exercises can be a Basket A item, while other OCD issues are put aside in other baskets to work on later. Taking the pressure off your child in this way can help him move forward slowly but surely, without the extra anxiety produced by feeling that he has to change everything about his behavior at once.

And although your child's compulsive behaviors may be annoying and should not be over-accommodated, educate yourself well about what she can and cannot control.

Another good resource for discipline ideas is a video called "Bending the Rules," available from the Southern California chapter of the Tourette's Syndrome Association (TSA). Some children with Tourette's syndrome also have episodes of hard-to-handle behavior, including uncontrollable rages, like those seen in some children with OCD. The national TSA also has a well-written pamphlet available about neurologically caused rages. Ordering information for these and some other helpful materials on behavior are listed in Appendix A, *Resources*.

You can expect some disparity between your child's behavior at home and at school. Many kids with OCD hold it together at school, but fall apart at home. By adding some accommodations at school that take the pressure off a bit, you may be able to achieve a happy medium. Until then, do your best to keep after-school time, weekends, and vacations structured for low stress.

When you do apply consequences for misbehavior, willful or otherwise, make sure they fit the description of "natural and logical consequences." Children with OCD tend to have a passion for fairness that can escalate into yet another battle if the punishment does not fit the crime. Parent Effectiveness Training (PET) and similar programs for helping parents of non-disabled children improve their discipline strategies won't fit your needs entirely, but they can help you learn more about identifying natural and logical consequences. These programs are widely available through social service agencies, religious institutions, and private training centers.

Seek out support

When things get really tough, don't try to go it alone. Many parents have a hard time managing their child's behavior without getting physical. Almost every parent of a child with OCD has crossed the line sometime, and felt tempted to do so many more times. Reach out for help to increase your repertoire of techniques through consultation with a behavior expert, or with parenting training that is geared toward working with mentally ill children. You should be able to access help through your school district, a government mental health agency, a hospital with a psychiatric care department, or private programs.

Disciplining teenagers is especially difficult, even under the best of circumstances. The techniques that worked when your child was younger may seem babyish now, and physical control is tougher when your child is larger. Keep applying proactive measures to protect your child, family, and community as best you can. Don't be afraid to call in reinforcements: the parents of your child's friends, your neighbors, teachers and other school personnel, mental health professionals, or even the juvenile authorities if your teen's behavior is bringing him into conflict with the law.

Also try to build a personal support system made up of friends and family members, an online or in-person support group, or even a telephone crisis line for parents. Having someone to talk to can really help you keep up the struggle without resorting to violence. See the section "Support and advocacy" later in this chapter for more specifics.

When stress strikes

Stress is an unavoidable part of modern life. Unfortunately, kids with OCD often are unable to take it in stride. When there's time to prepare for a potentially stressful situation, such as the first day of school or a scheduled hospital admission, proactive planning and rehearsal should reduce the event's impact. Providing information, role-playing the upcoming situation, and answering your child's questions can help. For example, a child with OCD who is moving to a new school may benefit from touring the school while it is empty, meeting teachers and other personnel, and meeting one or more of her classmates in advance. Some children like to talk, write, draw, or read about impending events that worry them.

You may be able to set some event-related therapy goals in concert with your child's therapist. Temporary medication changes can also be used, with your doctor's approval and guidance.

Unexpected stress, such as a death in the family or natural disaster, is more troublesome. It's hard to prepare for the unpredictable. With most children it's possible to talk in general terms about everything from earthquakes to old age, but children with OCD often become excessively fearful as a result of even the simplest reference to touchy topics such as illness, death, or injury. These are areas for which your child's therapist may offer suggestions carefully tailored to his needs. Some children with OCD are able to approach these difficult subjects through books or films, even when they can't muster the courage to talk about them openly.

Regardless of the source, you can expect stress to impact your child's obsessive-compulsive symptoms. We all produce certain brain chemicals in response to stress, and as noted in Chapter 1, *Introduction to OCD*, these neurotransmitters simply act differently in people with OCD.

Socialization

The social world is fraught with problems for young people with OCD. Their unusual behaviors can make them social pariahs or the targets of bullying. Some suffer from social phobia (another anxiety disorder) in addition to OCD. This condition can often be addressed with the same medications and therapies used to treat OCD. The feelings of fear and anxiety that accompany obsessive-compulsive symptoms have a strong impact on the ability to socialize.

E. J., age 19, explains how OCD and depression have affected her social life:

> *Social problems were much more difficult for me than anything else. It's very hard to relate to my peers when I have so many stray thoughts and worries going through my head. Although most friends who knew about the diagnosis tried to be very supportive, most did not understand enough about OCD to be helpful. I have been hurt many times by the comments and well-meaning actions of my friends.*
>
> *I don't know whether it is better to tell friends or to keep the OCD a secret. Either way, it is very uncomfortable. People tend to see me as weak or unable to take care of myself when they know about my OCD. But if they don't know, then I have to try to be someone else when I'm around them, and I spend all my energy trying to hide the OCD, so I have no energy left to have a friendship.*
>
> *My friendships have been devastated since the onset of OCD—I have been reduced to having just a few close friends (the ones who are usually understanding about the way I act and who are supportive). When something goes wrong in one of those relationships, it is very traumatic for me. It is almost impossible to maintain a close friendship when my OCD is bad.*

Younger children and some teens with OCD can benefit from explicit training in social skills. Usually delivered in a group setting, social skills instruction covers topics like how to have a conversation, how to play well with others, etiquette and proper behavior, and sometimes, personal grooming issues. The group may be made up of children or teens who all have OCD or a related disorder, youths with a variety of disabilities, or a mix of youths with and without special needs. These groups may be available in schools or through mental health clinics. Others are set up by psychiatrists, or are part of group therapy programs or formal mental health support groups for kids.

Usually, parents need to be more involved in the social life of a child with OCD than they might be for a child without OCD. These children have a greater need for supervision, guidance, and advice in negotiating social difficulties. Careful planning and parental supervision—e.g., setting up play dates and other social situations—can help young children achieve greater social success. You can have a lot of say about who your young child associates with. Socializing with one or more peers who have positive outlooks and similar interests can have long-term benefits for a child with psychiatric challenges. You may need to talk openly with the parents of your child's friends to help them understand his needs, and to make plans for what to do if any problems crop up during your child's visits to their homes.

One-to-one situations or structured groups like scouting, Campfire, religious youth groups, or activity clubs tend to be more comfortable than just "hanging out" for kids with OCD. These children may, however, have a hard time feeling comfortable in such groups if they lack special supports. Most religious denominations and national youth organizations have disability accommodation specialists, but often they are not as familiar with mental illness as they are with physical disability.

Most children and teens center their social life on school, but this isn't always possible for those with OCD. If necessary, help your child find outlets for safe social activities outside of school. Community theater groups, activity-based clubs, service or activist organizations, sports leagues, or an after-school job are just some of the possibilities that can become a positive focus.

Amy, age 16, echoes the sentiments of many teens with OCD:

> *Sports serve as an outlet for me, and without them, I don't know where I would be. I play five sports year-round.*

Parents should act as "emotion coaches" with their children who have OCD, helping them recognize and manage their own emotions more effectively. You can help your child label the feelings and behaviors that cause him social distress, and think up strategies for dealing with these difficulties (there are posters and books available for working on emotion awareness with young children or those with severe social deficits). A child who withdraws from social contact can be helped out of her shell with ideas and advice that help her gradually ease back into friendships and social activities. A teenager whose social abilities have become more fragile due to the worsening of obsessive-compulsive symptoms may function better in short visits with one close friend.

Perhaps the two greatest social skills you can help your child develop are a sense of humor and flexibility. These will help him weather life's setbacks better than he would with only good manners and conversation skills.

OCD and sexuality

OCD can affect all areas of development. One that is frequently overlooked in young patients is sexuality. Teens with OCD are as likely to have sex-related symptoms as are adults with OCD. These obsessions and compulsions are usually intensely uncomfortable. Among the sex-related symptoms reported are:

- Invasive, unwanted sexual thoughts
- Invasive thoughts that disrupt normal romantic or sexual activity
- Intense feelings of disgust about sex, sexuality, or physicality, often leading to avoidance of contact with potential partners
- Contamination fears that prevent teens from engaging in what would otherwise be appropriate romantic or sexual conduct, such as hugging, holding hands, or kissing
- Obsessions centered around being homosexual or deviant when one is not
- Obsessing within romantic or sexual relationships, frightening away potential partners
- Compulsive masturbation (this also occurs in younger children)

Of all the symptoms that can occur in teens, sexual obsessions and compulsions may be the most difficult for patients to talk about. The teen who has invasive sexual thoughts may think of himself as a "pervert," and undertake elaborate rituals to avoid having such thoughts.

Although "sex addiction" is sometimes defined as compulsive behavior, there is no evidence linking it to OCD. The same can be said for specific types of sexuality, including sexual practices that some may perceive as deviant. The only unusual sexual practice that might be slightly more common in people with OCD is fetishism (becoming sexually aroused by certain objects or clothing, such as high-heeled shoes), because of the unusual sensory experiences reported by some people with OCD, but there is no clinical evidence for this speculation as of yet.

In fact, many teens with OCD are profoundly afraid of their sexuality. They often describe themselves as shy, "backwards," and inexperienced. For parents, this might seem like a blessing in a time when teenage sex bears many risks, including unwanted pregnancy, sexually transmitted diseases, and AIDS. But while sexual activity may be something we would like our children to avoid, sexual development is an important part of adulthood. Young people need to gain self-confidence, knowledge, and the ability to navigate this difficult area of life. If feelings of fear and disgust are attached to sexuality in these formative years, it can have a strong, negative impact on adult relationships, including marriage.

Youth with OCD may be intensely uncomfortable discussing these symptoms with their parents. If you are concerned that your child may be bothered by sex-related symptoms, you might want to broach the idea privately with her therapist, and allow the therapist to raise the issue at an appropriate time.

Parents should also ensure that their child with OCD has adequate information about sex, sexuality, and sex-related risks. Fears that become obsessions are often fed by misinformation. We also need to carefully assess what messages we send to our children about this essential human activity. We can stress sexual morality and responsibility without sowing the seeds of fear and disgust—and we can let our kids know that we will be nonjudgmental when talking with them about this topic.

Safety matters

Suicide is the third leading cause of death among US teens, and the suicide rate has climbed continuously since 1952. . .a sobering reminder of how stressful modern adolescence can be. Obsessive-compulsive disorder subjects your child to additional stresses, and to a higher risk of clinical depression. Thoughts of suicide are relatively common in people with OCD, particularly during the teenage years, but sometimes even in early childhood.

The American Psychiatric Association warns parents to be on the lookout for warning signs of suicide, including:

- Withdrawal from friends and family
- Inability to concentrate
- Talk of suicide
- Dramatic changes in personal appearance
- Loss of interest in favorite activities
- Expressions of hopelessness or excessive guilt
- Self-destructive behavior (such as reckless driving, drug abuse, and promiscuity)
- Preoccupation with death
- Giving away favorite possessions
- Suddenly "cheering up" after a deep depression (the new mood may mean a plan for suicide has been made, causing the person to feel relieved)

Never ignore the warning signs of suicide. Many people who try to kill themselves give advance notice, although it may be encoded in behavior or visual messages. Be open to the nonverbal messages your child may be sending you, and if your suspicions are aroused, *act*. Don't be afraid to come right out and ask if suicide is on his mind. Be careful not to be judgmental. Young people don't want to feel suicidal; these thoughts and feelings come unbidden, either as a result of brain chemistry or in response to difficult life circumstances. Your willingness to listen without blaming increases the chance that your child will be open about suicidal thoughts.

Information and advance planning are your best allies in preventing youth suicide. If your child has already threatened to attempt suicide, or has attempted suicide, here are several resources that can get you in touch with immediate help:

- **The National Alliance for the Mentally Ill.** NAMI is the largest support group for people with mental illness in the US. Its national information line or web site can help you find local resources right away. You can reach NAMI at (703) 524-7600 and *http://www.nami.org/*.
- **National Suicide Prevention Hotline** (US). Call (800) 999-9999 to get information about the closest suicide prevention hotline.
- **Suicide Awareness/Voices of Education** (SA/VE). You can visit SA/VE online at *http://www.save.org/*.
- **Suicide Information and Education Center** (SIEC). SIEC maintains a list of suicide prevention hotlines and services in the US and Canada at *http://www.siec.ca/crisis.html*.
- **Befrienders International Online.** Befrienders maintains a list of crisis and suicide counseling centers throughout the world at *http://www.befrienders.org/centre.html*.

Every parent whose child has OCD should prepare in advance to deal with a suicide crisis, just in case. Many young people with OCD do consider suicide at some time, although not all will make a serious attempt. When and if the moment comes, the prepared parent can concentrate all his energy on helping his child, rather than frantically searching for resources.

A suicide crisis is not something about which to keep quiet, or to handle discreetly at home. Successful suicide attempts mean death, and unsuccessful ones can cause permanent injury or brain damage. Because some teenagers make half-hearted "cry for help" suicide attempts in response to breaking up with a boyfriend or similar minor tragedies, emergency room personnel are not always as sympathetic as they should be. To protect your child from callous treatment or a premature release, you need to have a hospital admission plan set up in advance.

The most helpful person for putting this plan in place is your child's psychiatrist. Set up a private session to talk about local mental health facilities. Most psychiatrists have had to commit a patient from time to time, and almost all have worked with local facilities or members of their staffs. They can usually tell you which hospitals have the best ward for children or teens, and which staff person you should talk to in advance.

A county or provincial mental health professional or social worker may also have information about local resources, and parents in local support groups can tell you about their experiences as well.

Make an appointment to visit the best facility, or the top two or three, in advance. If possible, meet the program's director. Find out about the admissions process—where you go in case of a crisis, who you can call if you need help getting your child to the facility, and what the criteria for admission are. Tell the appropriate staff a little about your child and the concerns that have led you to check out their program. (Evaluating hospital programs is discussed in greater detail in Chapter 5.)

Lack of information is one of the biggest problems families face when their child needs emergency mental health care. Transferring paper medical files and even computerized files seems to take forever, and sometimes the documents that do arrive are incomplete. You may want to provide the facility you would use in a crisis with an advance copy of your child's basic medical and mental health history, a list of medications used currently and in the past, and your insurance data, just in case. Alternatively, make a copy of this information and store it where you can grab it en route to the facility.

In larger cities, there may be a crisis triage center for mental health admissions. This is usually a separate area of a hospital. If a suicide attempt that caused injury has been made, including an attempted drug overdose, you would go to the emergency room first. If no physical harm has occurred, but your child is in a dangerous mental state, you may be able to go to the crisis triage center instead. Here she can be evaluated by professionals, given emergency medications if needed, and directed to an inpatient or day treatment facility.

John, father of 14-year-old Tori (diagnosed OCD and Asperger's syndrome), has used local emergency facilities for immediate help:

> *The hospital emergency center has been used many times for Tori's protection and for a way to deal with situations that have gotten out of hand. It is a form of behavioral consequence if our daughter chooses to let her reactions go astray.*

In areas without a special intake center, you can call ahead to the emergency room and let the staff know if there are special security needs or medications that should be on hand when you arrive. In some areas you may be able to take your child directly to a mental health facility, such as a county mental hospital, for immediate evaluation. Be sure to call first, as some facilities will turn you away unless the staff feels it is a matter of life or death. Others don't have good assessment facilities on site, and you'll only end up waiting or being redirected.

Of course, your insurance company, HMO, and public health policies can have a lot to do with how you go about accessing emergency mental health care. We'll look at these more closely in Chapter 7, *Insurance Issues*.

Preventative measures

Another important step you can take to prevent youth suicide is to remove implements of self-destruction from your home, particularly guns. A gun is a terribly final choice, and it is the weapon used in more than half of all suicides. Usually when a child or teenager shoots himself, he found the gun in his own home. If you own guns, or if members of your extended family own guns, get rid of them. Locking them up is not enough to stop a person who is determined to kill himself.

If your gun is needed for your job as a police officer, soldier, or security guard, store it securely at the station house, base, or company headquarters.

If you currently keep a gun in the home for protection against criminals, get a burglar alarm, security bars, panic button, or guard dog instead.

Don't assume that your child would never use a gun. Today, suicidal girls are almost as likely as boys to use a gun—and boys who choose guns are often the quiet, gentle types you would not expect to do so.

Talk to the parents of your child's friends, her baby-sitters, and others whose homes she may go to, about their guns. Most conscientious people will comply with your request to keep weapons out of their home for your child's sake or, at the very least, securely lock up any firearms they own. If someone resists, you can mention the legal liability involved in leaving firearms within reach of children, especially when one has been warned about a person with suicidal impulses. If that doesn't work, you'll just have to make that home off-limits to your child.

Guns aren't the only danger, of course. You may need to have a lock installed on your kitchen knife drawer, get rid of hunting knives and sharp tools, and ensure that there are no hoses around that would fit over your car's exhaust pipe. Some families have had to take very stringent measures during a suicide crisis, from removing closet bars to taking the door off their child's room. Some have had to bar windows from the outside and add keyed interior locks to keep a suicidal child from running. Nonetheless, suicidal individuals will try to find a means of self-harm, from using a light fixture to hang themselves to slicing their arms with glass from a broken window. Constant supervision is the key to preventing the suicide of a determined patient, and it is best to seek hospitalization if things reach this level.

You most certainly should lock up medications—and not just prescription medications. Aspirin and Tylenol are used very frequently in suicide attempts. Both of them are potentially fatal in large doses (in fact, Tylenol is one of the medications used most often in successful attempts). Use a daily pill reminder box to measure any family member's daily medications in advance, and keep the original bottles in a securely locked medicine chest. A heavy-duty cash box, available at most office supply stores, is a portable substitute. If you happen to have a safe in your home for important papers, you might also use that to store medications.

Handling self-injurious behavior

As discussed in Chapter 2, *Diagnosis*, self-injurious behavior (SIB) is more common in people with OCD than in the general population. Compulsive self-injury is one of the hardest symptoms with which patients and parents alike must cope. It's important to be accepting about the person and even the behavior, although this is difficult for many parents and professionals. A child with SIB will continue to hide the problem and avoid help unless she feels safe talking to you about it.

Many medical people don't understand SIB, and some actually do more harm than good when they work with patients who self-injure. Some doctors still try to psychoanalyze patients with SIB, assuming that it always arises from some secret trauma. For a person with OCD, this approach can be more harmful than getting no treatment at all. It essentially blames the patient, and does nothing to assuage the actual feelings and impulses that cause repetitive self-injury. If your child needs help with SIB, look for a psychiatrist who has expertise in this area and understands the need to help the patient gradually decrease the frequency and intensity of these behaviors.

Both medication and cognitive behavioral therapy can be effective interventions for SIB. Young patients report that setting up physical barriers to SIB is also sometimes effective, especially for skin and scalp picking, fingernail chewing, and compulsive hair pulling (trichotillomania).

Emergency care, if needed, should be provided with respect. People with SIB often report that they are treated with derision in the ER, even refused treatment or given stitches without the use of painkillers. This is not acceptable. Accompany your child to the ER or urgent care clinic and insist that those helping your child act professionally, as you have a right to expect. If SIB is a persistent problem, you and/or your child's therapist may want to meet with an administrator to set up an advance plan for working with your child. Treating SIB as a chronic health problem rather than a personal failing can salvage your child's self-esteem and ensure that he will come to you if treatment is needed.

Substance abuse and dependency

When a person first tries drugs or alcohol, there's still time to stop. She needs to think about the reasons why she has chosen to try alcohol or drugs, such as feeling self-conscious in social situations or because of an inability to handle peer pressure. You can help your child identify other activities that might have positive effects, such as improving her social skills, and learning to use humor to break the ice or defuse insults. You can also help identify ways to avoid temptation, including choosing a different peer group or steering her friends toward something other than bong hits and beer bashes. These are issues that can be discussed with a parent or a counselor.

Most teens will attend a wild party or two out of curiosity or boredom, if nothing else. You may be able to prevent them from harm even when they've made a bad choice. Many families have drawn up a contract with their children, promising that they will retrieve them from a dangerous situation at any hour, with no lecture to follow. Let them know that while they may make some poor judgment calls, you're available to come to their rescue.

You may also need to actively help kids whose peers are fixated on drinking and drugs to find other ways to spend their time. This negative aspect of youth culture isn't just a big-city phenomenon, by the way—small towns and rural areas, which may lack activities and places to go, can have extraordinarily high rates of drinking and drug use among teens. The drug and alcohol problems of suburban youth are often covered up, but they exist and can be aggravated by lack of supervision after school, access to cash, and easy mobility.

Substance use becomes abuse when it continues despite negative consequences or occurs in situations (such as driving) that are dangerous. Abuse can develop into substance dependency if unchecked. Signs of substance dependency include a growing tolerance to the substance, use of the substance to stave off ill effects of not having it, spending more and more time using or trying to get the substance, and continuing to use the substance despite the physical, social, and emotional problems that it causes.

Symptoms of drug and alcohol use can include:

- Deterioration of school performance
- Defiant behavior and attitude
- Withdrawal
- Missing alcohol, prescription drugs, or money in home, at work, or at school
- Unexplained mood swings
- Unexplained physical complaints
- Changes in eating habits
- Changes in sleep pattern, difficulty waking
- Odor of gasoline or other household products on body, clothing, or personal items
- Presence of paint on face or hands
- Alcohol on breath, or new use of strong breath deodorizers under suspicious circumstances
- Slurred speech
- Staggering, loss of balance
- Dilated (enlarged) or "pinned" (very small) pupils
- Presence of drug paraphernalia (pipes, rolling papers, syringes, etc.) or drug residues (powders, seeds, plant matter, burnt spoons or tin foil) in child's pockets, purse, backpack, room, or locker
- Blatant advocacy of drug or alcohol use, such as wearing shirts or jewelry bearing pro-drug slogans or the logos of alcohol manufacturers

Reliable statistics on substance abuse and dependency in people with OCD are not available, but most experts agree that they are higher than rates seen in the general population. Some patients may try substances to blunt their painful symptoms, particularly social anxiety and intrusive thoughts. This strategy may succeed temporarily. Coupled with the compulsivity that is part and parcel of OCD, this momentary relief can start patients on a rapid downward spiral.

As with suicide, accidents, and SIB, the best approach to substance abuse is prevention. First, take a look at your own example. . .if you find that drugs or alcohol have become important coping strategies for you, be sure to seek immediate treatment. Talk to your child about responsible use of alcohol for adults: for example, a glass of wine with a special meal, or a cold beer on a hot day at the ball game. Point out examples of inappropriate or excessive use, from street alcoholics to news stories about young people in trouble due to drug use or drunken driving. You really don't have to preach, just provide a good example and accurate information to counteract the messages your child will receive from ads, pop culture, and peers.

Despite your best efforts, substance use may continue and escalate. When a patient has both OCD and a problem with substance abuse or dependency, he is said to be a "dual diagnosis" patient. Experts in treating children and teenagers with a dual diagnosis say that appropriate psychiatric medication and therapy, education about their psychiatric condition and the dangers of drug and alcohol abuse, and close monitoring are essential for success.

Although some sources recommend treating the substance abuse first—often because drugs and alcohol can have severe interactions with the medication used to treat OCD—both really need to be addressed at once. Obviously, a person who is not sober is unable to adhere to the lifestyle changes, medication regime, and therapy appointments needed to hold back OCD symptoms. At the same time, some people with OCD drink or use drugs to self-medicate their symptoms, or (to put it another way) use their anxieties as an excuse for getting high.

Drug treatment programs, including inpatient "detox" centers, are becoming more knowledgeable about working with dual diagnosis patients. If your child will be going to a drug treatment program, make sure that its clinical staff is fully aware of the implications of OCD, and that appropriate medication and therapy for OCD symptoms will be available as part of the overall program. The earlier a drug or alcohol abuser seeks effective treatment, the more likely he is to achieve complete freedom from substance abuse, and to avoid actual dependency.

If your child is drug- or alcohol-dependent, treatment may begin with an inpatient detox center. These centers say that about a month is needed to break an addiction's physical grasp, and it takes a year of sobriety before an addict can honestly feel mentally comfortable without his substance of abuse.

Many alcoholics and drug addicts use self-help resources like Alcoholics Anonymous (AA) and Narcotics Anonymous (NA) to get and stay sober. In these programs, people attend regular meetings to talk about their addiction problems and offer each other support. Former substance abusers who have come clean sponsor newcomers, making themselves available for personal support when temptation strikes. Generally speaking, these "12-step programs" are an excellent resource for drug and alcohol users in recovery.

There are also adjunct groups for the families of addicts. Family support groups can really help you make it through this difficult period. These groups are helpful even if your child is not involved in a 12-step program or other drug and alcohol treatment. You'll learn many strategies for helping your child on the road to recovery, and for ensuring that family dynamics, such as codependency, aren't contributing to the problem.

The only drawback of 12-step programs is that a few former addicts are against using prescription medications for brain disorders, seeing them as simply a legal substitute for street drugs or alcohol. This is *not* an official policy of AA or NA, by the way. To make sure a particular 12-step group doesn't have this orientation, talk to one of the group's long-term members.

Of course, abuse of prescription drugs is a concern for people with a history of drug or alcohol abuse, and particularly for those who have been addicted. Many programs use some variation on directly observed therapy—having patients take their prescribed medication in front of the doctor each day, and possibly checking to make sure it hasn't been hidden in the hand or mouth for later use. Ask the professionals working with your child about how to handle this issue at home and at school.

Maintaining your equilibrium

A parent who is stressed to the point of burn-out has little chance of effectively parenting a difficult child. You've got to mobilize your inner and outer resources to protect your own peace of mind. That includes taking care of your physical health with regular checkups, eating right and exercising. It also means caring for your own mental health. You need a personal safety net just as much as your child does. A caring therapist, a family social worker who keeps your needs in the picture, and supportive family members can make a big difference.

It's uncomfortable for many of us to consider, but the genetic nature of OCD dictates that many parents of children with OCD also have the disorder, or must deal with less severe versions of obsessive-compulsive symptoms. It's not at all uncommon for a parent to be diagnosed after their child.

Even if you're leery of medication or therapy based on past experiences, it's very important to do as much as you can to help yourself. Think of the analogy of airplane oxygen masks: Parents are instructed to first put their own oxygen mask in place, then ensure that their child's oxygen mask is working properly. If your physical or mental health falls by the wayside, you won't be available to help your child.

Respite care is one resource that can be very helpful, especially for single parents and families with more than one affected member. Respite care providers are baby-sitters with extra training in working with the mentally or physically disabled. They can take your child for a few hours, or even a few days, allowing you time to take care of other tasks, attend to your own health needs (such as a scheduled operation that may require a few days in bed), reacquaint yourself with your spouse, or even take a short vacation.

Respite care has been very hard to access in the past, but that's changing. Talk to your county or provincial mental health department, and to local support and advocacy groups for the disabled, for information about respite resources in your area. If there is not a NAMI chapter or similar group for the families of people with mental illness in your area, groups like the ARC (formerly known as the Association of Retarded Citizens), United Cerebral Palsy, Easter Seals, and Samaritans may know where to send you. Respite services may be available at no or low cost through a charitable group, or through government mental health services.

Unfortunately, respite care services are limited. There is a shortage of respite providers, and there are even fewer with special training in working with the mentally ill. This is an essential need for families, though. If formal respite services are not available in your area, see if you can work out an arrangement with another family whose child has OCD or a related disorder, or with a family member who's able to tackle the job.

Another thing you can do to maintain your sanity is keep careful records. Nothing gives parents more headaches than school systems and medical facilities that can't seem to keep track of information on medications given, treatments tried, and classroom strategies that worked or flopped. If you can keep your medical and school information neatly filed, you'll find that a major stress in your life will almost disappear. It's not easy, but it's really worth the trouble.

Finally, find ways to let yourself relax—even just for a few minutes while your child is sleeping. Prayer, meditation, yoga, or just a nice hot bath with a favorite novel can do wonders for your spirit. Without these stolen moments of peace, it's hard to find the energy to keep up the hard work of raising a child with OCD.

Support and advocacy

No family can handle OCD well on its own. Besides the many professionals who can help, there are also families who have walked this road before. Their advice, support, and friendship can be a precious gift in your life. When you join a good support group for families coping with OCD, you'll gain shoulders to lean on, people you can call in a crisis, and a source of the latest information on services, health care, education, local doctors, and opportunities for your child. You'll meet parents just like yourself. You'll have people in your life for whom you don't have to put up a brave front.

Another kind of helpful group concentrates on advocacy for mentally ill people and their families. In the US, NAMI is the biggest of these, with chapters in almost every part of the country. These groups work to improve services, medical treatment, and schools, and change the laws that affect people with mental illness. Many also have a support group component, especially in rural areas, where support and advocacy goes hand in hand. OCD-specific organizations include the OC Foundation (OCF) and the Obsessive-Compulsive and Spectrum Disorders Association (OCSDA). See Appendix A for more information.

Support and advocacy groups also give people who are living with mental problems and their families a way to give something back to the community, and to lift up those who are faced with a new diagnosis.

John, father of Tori, recommends these options:

> *We, as new parents, knew nothing about OCD. We have attended hospital-run workshops and training sessions; these help give direction. We have also attended parent support groups. Meeting other families and sharing stories and resources is helpful.*

A new kind of support group has arrived with the advent of the Internet: online support communities for people with mental or neurological disorders and their families. The great thing about these online groups is that they're available 24 hours a day. You can "log in" whenever it's convenient for you—late at night, when the kids are at school, or on your lunch break at work. All you need is a computer and an Internet account, either through a local Internet service provider or through a major commercial service like America Online or Europe Online.

The OCSDA-sponsored mailing list *ocdandparenting* (*http://www.onelist.com/subscribe/ocdandparenting*) is probably the only online support group specifically for parents of children with OCD. Participants range from parents of newly diagnosed children to "old hands," who can provide excellent advice. There are also doctors and therapists among the subscribers.

Chris, mother of 7-year-old Kelsey, relates her *ocdandparenting* experience:

> *The* ocdandparenting *list has been a lifeline for me! We have no family close by, and quickly realized there were really no friends we felt we could call on in the depths of despair. I don't know if I'd have made it through without the empathy, kindness, wise experience, and advice of many on that list.*

Online support groups can be helpful for kids, too. The *ocdteen* group, also sponsored by OCSDA (send e-mail to *kelly@ocsda.org* for information about subscribing) brings together several hundred teenagers and young adults to chat about symptoms, medications, school problems, and other issues.

Patty, age 17, is an *ocdteen* subscriber:

> *Honestly, I don't really have anybody in the "real" world. I'd feel horrible burdening "mentally healthy" people with my problem. What's more, they wouldn't really understand what I go through. However, I am on ocdteen, and that has been extremely beneficial. It's wonderful to know that you are not totally alone after all. It is there where I meet people who go*

through the same things I do. It may sound a bit cheesy, but we are here for each other.

You do have to be careful about online medical advice—it's no substitute for getting local medical care. But these groups can help parents and patients learn as much as possible about these disorders, and about dealing with associated behaviors, school problems, and family issues.

A list of OCD-related online support groups, discussion forums, and web sites is included in Appendix A.

Wishful thinking

Parents who have experienced years of worry, fear, and pain due to a child's illness may think that hope will be lost somewhere along the way. Most parents know what kind of resources would be most useful for themselves and their child, but they despair of ever finding them. Their wishes can be powerful, though, because if enough families wish out loud (and then add their shoulders to the wheel) these resources might become a reality.

Several parents, when asked about their hopes, dreams, and wishes for their children, responded:

As Tori's father, I hope she will be able to deal with other people, to cope with commitments and responsibilities in a relationship with a partner. I would provide highly competent intensive care and treatment programs, within a center or the patient's home, for those who need it.

• • • • •

My hope is that my 10-year-old son can lead a normal life. . .go to college, have a family and be happy. I hope we are giving him the skills to understand OCD and how he has to deal with it daily to survive. My husband also has OCD, and he still leads a productive life.

We try to look at OCD as a positive thing, too. A person with OCD is sensitive to others, can be very creative and very successful. So we try to point out that if you have to have something wrong with you, OCD can be a good thing to have. It's just a matter of getting control of it and making it work for you.

• • • • •

I'm hopeful for my daughter these days. After seeing how well and quickly CBT (cognitive behavioral therapy) worked for OCD and is working for social phobia, I believe Kelsey can be whomever she wants to be when she grows up! I think kids' brains are malleable and they can change if they want to.

If I could, I'd train a slew of good OCD CBT therapists and send them nationwide so that everyone with OCD could easily find someone who could help. Then I'd take on the insurance companies so that they would understand that by paying for CBT, instead of just reimbursing for psychiatry and medications, they'd be saving themselves lots of money in the long run.

• • • • •

As the mother of a 10-year-old daughter with OCD, I would devote big bucks to research about more medical interventions for OCD, as I am convinced that in the future we will be able to determine the exact chemical problem in the brain that causes OCD, and then treat it.

What do children with OCD wish for themselves? Here are some of their responses:

I'm 16. I hope my OCD stays the same or does not get any worse.

• • • • •

Now that I'm 19, I hope that I will "grow out of" some of the worries I have. In order to go into the career that I want, some of my OCD symptoms will have to get somewhat better and stay better. I have made a lot of improvement in a short period of time. I just hope I keep the gains I have made.

I would especially try to make people aware of the attitudes that they hold unknowingly toward people with OCD. I would help people to see that we are just as valuable and capable as anyone else. I would make them see that I don't need sympathy or need to be taken care of. I just want to be respected as a friend and an equal.

• • • • •

As a teenage girl with OCD, I hope I will be able to pursue my goals and achieve them.

• • • • •

I wish I could make it just disappear.

CHAPTER 4

Therapeutic Interventions

THE FIRST TREATMENT CONSIDERED for children with OCD is cognitive behavioral therapy (CBT), either on its own or with medication to reduce the anxiety involved in carrying out CBT exercises. This chapter will explain what CBT is and how it can help. It will also take a look at other kinds of therapy that may or may not be useful.

Cognitive behavioral therapy

When someone says, "you need some therapy," the first picture that comes into most peoples' minds is one of lying on a leather couch in a wood-paneled office while a fellow with a suspicious resemblance to Sigmund Freud asks questions about your dreams. This image from a Woody Allen film doesn't look at all like the type of therapy recommended for treating OCD, although both images are founded on building a relationship of trust between patient and professional.

That relationship may be more important to success than anything else, especially with young patients who experience excessive guilt and doubt over their OCD symptoms. Without a basis of trust, it's hard to even get started.

Patty, age 17, explains:

> *I go to a therapist, but it hasn't helped much yet. Of course, I've only been going for a few months, and the lack of progress is partly my fault due to my hesitancy to "open up."*

Patty's therapist is, evidently, not doing CBT. Instead of probing dreams and childhood experiences for repressed emotions and Oedipal conflicts, cognitive behavioral therapy concentrates on the here and now. It's an intensely practical kind of help that gives patients tools they can use to stop anxiety-producing thoughts and conquer their compulsions.

The basic concept of CBT is simple: by changing your behavior, you can eventually change how you think and feel. That's the reverse of what many people would expect. Old-fashioned psychotherapy worked the other way, exploring thoughts and emotions and assuming that changing them could change the patient's behavior. CBT usually works fairly quickly, and it relies mostly on action, not insight. That makes it easier for children to use, even very young children, and more practical for people whose thought processes are disordered due to mental illness.

Kathy, mother of 5-year-old Kel, tells about her successes with CBT:

> *Kel has done well at learning to recognize OCD thoughts and compulsions and "boss" them back. After several therapists told me my daughter was too young for CBT exposure and response prevention exercises, I bought John March's manual on doing CBT therapy, and tried some of the exercises with her myself. From the onset she railed against "stupid" OCD that tried to trick her that something was scary when she knew it wasn't. That seemed a good enough basis to me to at least give CBT a try—it seemed there was little to lose.*
>
> *One concession I made to her age: making a hierarchy of fears was almost impossible, so we settled on working on whatever OCD thing is bothering her the most and she most wants gone. If it's a biggie, we break it into small do-able parts, a mini-hierarchy. We reward her efforts with toys, trips to Discovery Zone, etc., to motivate her through the work. She's had great successes and feels more in control, and her self-esteem is so much higher than it was before we started.*
>
> *I will say that when we first started, it seemed we were chipping away at an iceberg, more of an exercise than anything of practical value, but then Kel just "got it," and it seemed that almost overnight a big chunk of OCD just slid away. I would recommend these techniques to anyone.*

Mark's story

To give you an inside view of CBT, let's introduce a hypothetical 16-year-old patient, Mark, and his new therapist, Dr. Jones. Mark has just been diagnosed with OCD by a school psychologist, who suggested that he pursue therapy at a local mental health clinic. He has a number of obsessions and compulsions, some noticeable to others, some strictly internal. All of them cause him anxiety, but some are definitely more troubling than others.

At their first meeting, Mark, his parents, and Dr. Jones chat fairly informally about what OCD is and how it is affecting Mark's life. Mark decides that he feels fairly comfortable with this therapist, who has an easy-going, nonjudgmental manner. For one thing, Dr. Jones has seen other people his age with the same need to repeat prayers to prevent harm from coming to others—Mark had thought he might be the only one, or that the doctor might call him a religious fanatic. Dr. Jones reassures him that in people with OCD, this compulsion is common.

Mark goes to the second session alone. After talking for a while, he feels comfortable enough to reveal that he is also repeating the prayers to counteract unwanted sexual thoughts. Dr. Jones doesn't delve deeply into the contents of those thoughts. "That's not very important," he says, which surprises Mark. "Everybody has strange thoughts about sex sometimes," he adds, "What's different about people with OCD is that they pay attention to them and feel more guilt about them, which causes them to keep coming back, and brings on more anxiety. If only you could convince yourself that the thoughts are not important, they wouldn't make you upset—and you wouldn't feel the need to do anything about them at all." This makes sense to Mark, although he isn't totally convinced that it will be so simple as just ignoring the thoughts.

Now Dr. Jones asks Mark to make a list of what symptoms he would like to work on. Here's a short version of Mark's list:

- Intrusive sexual thoughts/compulsion to say prayers to counteract these thoughts
- Obsession with causing harm to family by thinking evil thoughts/compulsion to say prayers to counteract these thoughts
- Obsession with symmetry/compulsion to adjust clothes, hair, etc.
- Compulsion to crack knuckles three times when stressed out

Mark decides that while others may be bothered by his knuckle cracking and clothes adjusting, the symptoms causing him the most distress are his sexual and "evil" thoughts, and the repetition of prayers to drive them away. Dr. Jones agrees that this is a sensible place to start. They decide to set to work on the first symptom right away, and get to the others in order.

Before the session ends, they have turned Mark's list of symptoms into a list of goals. When Mark looks at his list later that week, he feels discouraged.

There are so many things on it! He has tried to handle his obsessions and compulsions before on his own, and failed. He comes to the third session feeling a little overwhelmed. Dr. Jones responds by asking Mark what happens now when he tries to make his sexual thoughts go away by repeating his prayers. "They go away for a minute, but as soon as I stop, they're back, and sometimes they're worse," Mark says. "I feel like I would need to pray all the time to make them stop for good."

Dr. Jones assures him that there is nothing wrong with praying for religious reasons, but gently notes that his strategy of using repetitive prayers to make unwanted thoughts go away is not working. They only distract his attention for a few minutes, and the thoughts are getting worse, not better. Now he introduces one of the basic concepts in CBT: habituation. If Mark can accept these thoughts and let them happen, Dr. Jones promises, he will find that the consequences he fears (in this case, acting on his sexual thoughts) will not occur. He will get used to having the thoughts, and they will lose their power to make him feel anxious and want to repeat his prayers. This won't work if you turn all your attention to the thoughts, waiting for them to go away, he notes. The trick is to go on with your everyday activities, while telling yourself that the thoughts are meaningless and will not do him or others harm.

He tells Mark about a technique called exposure and response prevention, often abbreviated E&RP. It means exposing yourself to the very thing that causes fear and anxiety, and using all your strength to simply accept the experience instead of relying on compulsions to counteract it or experiencing a panic attack.

When Dr. Jones says that changing your behavior can actually change your thoughts and feelings, Mark doesn't get it at first. Then the therapist offers an example that makes sense. "Remember your first day of high school, and how nervous you were?" he asks. "You probably didn't know where any of your classes were, and you felt lost and nervous." Mark nods in response—this is one experience that almost everyone has in common.

"The first day you were really stressed out," Dr. Jones continues. "You thought you'd never be able to find your way around. You could have hidden in the library and avoided the whole problem of getting lost. That's like what you're doing with these unwanted thoughts—you don't want them, so you try to avoid them by saying prayers. Instead, you changed your behavior by forcing yourself to find your classes and figure the place out. By the end of the first week you really had gotten lost a few times, but eventually you found your way to where you were supposed to be. Before long you knew where the lunchroom, the office, and your locker were, too. Some other things about school might still make you feel anxious, but you had walked around the place enough times that it felt familiar. You probably haven't worried about getting lost on your way to class in ages, because you exposed yourself to the thing that worried you and worked out a solution. You didn't let anxiety keep you from doing what you needed to do."

Mark is still nervous, but he's willing to try. He has heard of people who have phobias, like a fear of flying, doing something similar. At first, asks Dr. Jones, just see how long you can resist your minor compulsions, like adjusting your clothes. "Time it with your watch, and let me know," he says. "Exposing yourself to these unwanted thoughts, letting yourself feel uncomfortable for a while, is a lot like tackling a new school—change how you react to the problem, and soon it won't bother you as much," he says, smiling.

Mark calls Dr. Jones' office later. He can wait to adjust his clothes for over 30 minutes, but when he tried the same technique with his praying compulsion, the best he was able to do is wait for about a minute. "I feel like I'm going to explode if I wait any longer," he says. "I get so nervous that I start shaking. This is not going to work!"

Dr. Jones says being able to wait a minute to perform a compulsion that carries a lot of anxiety is actually pretty good, and the increased anxious feelings are normal. "You're doing something really hard here, Mark," he says. "It's not going to be easy. But if you keep trying, you'll find that you can wait longer and longer."

He suggests that Mark continue exposing himself to resisting his minor compulsions for a half an hour for a couple of weeks, just to prove that he can quickly gain mastery over these. He reminds Mark about something they discussed in their last session—the idea that Mark should remind himself that OCD sent these thoughts, he didn't ask for them. It's easier to send them away if you accept that they don't represent things you really want to happen, but instead represent your unreasonable fears, Dr. Jones notes. "Boss them back, tell them to get lost—and then forget about them," he says.

Well, it's not quite that easy, of course. A miracle doesn't happen that week, or the next, or even the next. During their next few sessions, Dr. Jones teaches Mark some simple techniques for dealing with the anxiety that comes up during his E&RP exercises, and continues to remind Mark that the thoughts are due to OCD, and are really not something to worry about.

As his CBT skills get better, Mark also works hard to "boss back" his unwanted sexual thoughts every time they occur. He resists the compulsion to pray them away, despite the anxiety they bring. With continued practice, Mark finds that he can wait two minutes, then three, then five. Indeed, the longer he waits, the more he simply accepts the existence of his intrusive sexual thoughts and reminds himself that they are, in his words, "stupid brain blips," the less they bother him. They don't happen as often, he doesn't get as anxious, and his need to repeat prayers diminishes. Around his seventh session with Dr. Jones, Mark is able to happily report: "This CBT stuff really *does* work!"

With that insight, and with a new set of tools for fighting anxiety, obsessions, and compulsions that he has gained, Mark is now able to work on applying the same techniques to his other symptoms.

Although Dr. Jones and Mark meet alone, the therapist also meets with the whole family twice during the next three months to talk about CBT techniques and how his parents and sister can best help Mark. He explains about exposure and response prevention exercises, the idea of "bossing back" OCD, and things Mark might try to reduce his generally high level of stress and anxiety. They talk about how OCD affects thinking, discussing the "thought errors" introduced in Chapter 3, *Living with OCD*. Mark is doing so well with CBT alone that medication probably isn't needed, says Dr. Jones, but he tells the family a little about medication options in case his symptoms ever become worse.

After just a few months, Mark starts meeting with Dr. Jones monthly for a sort of check-up, instead of weekly. If any new symptoms are occurring, they brainstorm exercises that might help diminish them. Mark has a good grasp on CBT by now, both from his sessions with Dr. Jones and from some books the therapist recommended. He feels able to apply the knowledge he has gained to pretty much any kind of obsession or compulsion. Yes, he still has OCD, but at this point he sees it as more of a minor annoyance or personality quirk than a disabling problem.

At the end of the year, he has his last session with Dr. Jones. "Call me if you run into trouble with anything," the therapist says as they part ways. And Mark knows that if he needs to, he can.

Empowering the patient

Perhaps the most important thing that Mark gained in his sessions with Dr. Jones was not the specific techniques of CBT, but a sense of power over his OCD. Although the disorder is difficult to handle, it's not impossible once you have the tools. These tried-and-true techniques have worked for thousands of other people with OCD. They are just as effective with children and teenagers as with adults—in fact, they may work even better with younger patients, who haven't yet developed a repertoire of bad responses to obsessions and compulsions.

The cognitive part of CBT helps patients learn that their brain is sending them error messages, and how to recognize and respond to these errors in ways that are more functional. Although the focus is not on gaining insight into one's deepest psyche, the patient does gain insight into the nature of OCD itself and the thought errors it creates. They come to understand OCD as an illness, not an intrinsic part of their psyche that can't be changed. They learn to test the false realities that OCD-related thinking presents. Therapists may work to help patients challenge the rationality of their own thought patterns, showing them where they are in error and introducing more realistic ways of seeing the world. More frequently, they simply encourage patients to test out their own faulty hypotheses: If they don't wash their hands four times, will their father *really* become ill? If they take the escalator, will they *really* fall over the side? This side of CBT is also known as cognitive restructuring.

The behavioral part of CBT involves changing behaviors by learning specific techniques, such as exposure and response prevention, relaxation, and anxiety prevention. This is also known as self-instructional training, problem-solving therapy, or stress inoculation.

Tailoring CBT to fit symptoms

CBT techniques can work with any obsession or compulsion. Most common OCD symptoms, such as counting, checking, and contamination fears, respond very well to exposure and response prevention techniques.

Therapists, parents, and patients can work together to set up situations in which the patient will expose herself to a feared situation, use new techniques for facing the anxiety that comes with this exposure, and refuse to carry out compulsive behaviors.

For example, if a child fears falling down the stairs and is using avoidance of stairs to reduce her anxiety, an E&RP exercise might start with standing at the foot of the stairs, progress to walking up and then down the first steps, and progress from there until the child can handle the whole staircase without excess anxiety. Each step can be repeated until the anxiety level decreases enough to be tolerable. It's important to take "baby steps" with E&RP, and to reassure the patient that she needn't erase the symptom all at once or immediately. She may need to experience anxiety reduction over a period of time to really believe this tactic will work.

A person with contamination fears would do CBT exercises that involve exposing himself to "contaminated" places, surfaces, or people in small doses, working through the anxiety that occurs while resisting the impulse to wash his hands or carry out other compulsions, and seeing that the feared outcome does not happen.

This approach has worked well for 11-year-old Kristen, according to her mother, Debby:

> *Kristen has had cognitive behavioral therapy for her contamination fears. Every fear that she had, such as cigarettes, poisonous berries, raw meat, and gasoline, did respond very well to this. She has never developed a fear back to these. Her psychologist was very well trained in this area, and he was also very inventive and creative.*

A person who has checking compulsions could gradually fight the impulse to make sure the door is locked, starting with waiting for a minute, and building up from there.

A person who hoards useless items because she fears throwing away something valuable could set up a plan to throw away one bag of hoarded items each day, or even just one item each day, starting with items that she is least worried might be important. As she continues to work toward throwing away things she has attached more importance to, she usually finds that the expected high anxiety never materializes because of her earlier success. She might have to work through this part of the process at a slower rate, but she can work with her therapist to make sure she does at least some work toward her goal each day. Meanwhile, she can work on the mental exercise of revaluing the useless items—seeing them as simply old newspapers or magazines, for example, not as essentials.

Although CBT techniques have proved effective for all kinds of OCD symptoms, it's true that some are harder to handle than others. The most difficult to manage, according to experienced therapists, are compulsions that have an automatic, tic-like quality, such as hair pulling (trichotillomania) or tapping. A CBT variation known as habit reversal is usually used for these.

Habit reversal starts with becoming aware of the behavior and when it occurs. With young children, this may require observation and a verbal reminder by the parent; older kids can use a journal or checklist to track when and how the need to do the behavior occurs.

As the patient becomes more attuned to when she does the behavior, she will be encouraged to look for triggers. In the example of trichotillomania, hair pulling may be a response to noticeable stress, boredom, or a physical sensation. A patient may have just one trigger, or there may be several.

Next, the therapist will ask the patient to look at the whole sequence that leads to the behavior. For instance, a person with trichotillomania may start pulling hair due to an odd physical sensation on the scalp, and the first movement may be an almost absent-minded movement of the hand to the head. The person may then touch and stroke various hairs until she finds the one that "feels right" to pull. The behavior may end there, or it may continue to involve pulling out many hairs, perhaps from the eyebrows or other parts of the body as well. And once the patient knows what all the steps in the process are, she can use CBT techniques to stop the process at any point along the line.

The eventual goal is for her to recognize the sensation on her scalp that usually leads to pulling out hair, and respond to it differently. She can experiment with different responses to the situation that compete with, and therefore prevent, hair pulling. For instance, she might respond to the sensation by brushing her hair, squeezing a rubber ball with the hand she usually uses to pull, or pressing her hands together. You don't want to turn the response into yet another compulsion, of course, just to short-circuit the hair-pulling compulsion. For that reason, the patient may want to come up with multiple responses she can try. Probably some will be effective, while others are not.

As anxiety rises due to resisting the compulsion, the patient can use relaxation techniques to fight back.

It's important to note that while CBT can help patients who have tic-like compulsions, it is not effective for preventing actual tics. Tics are less voluntary in nature than compulsions. Patients can't identify why they occur or what the rationale behind them is. People who have both OCD and a tic disorder, such as Tourette's syndrome, explain that tics simply "feel different" from compulsions. They are more like an automatic response to a deep physical sensation, not a reaction to a thought or fear.

CBT techniques can often help people with tics cope better with the anxiety they cause, however, and can sometimes be used to temporarily suppress an impending tic in a situation when it would be especially unwelcome, without the usual buildup of severe anxiety and discomfort. Tics cannot be suppressed forever, though—this use of relaxation and anxiety prevention techniques is strictly a temporary coping mechanism.

"Pure obsessions"—obsessive thoughts that cause anxiety but do not result in compulsive behaviors—are also sometimes difficult to treat with CBT.

One technique that works for some patients is called "thought stopping": identifying the thoughts and when they occur, and substituting another thought for them. For example, if a patient experiences excessive obsessive thoughts about a particular topic, he could decide that after a few minutes of thinking about that topic he will turn his attention to something else. If anxiety occurs when he tries to change the subject of his thoughts, he can use anxiety prevention techniques to deal with it.

Trying to never think about the topic at all is likely to actually reinforce the problem, and thought stopping doesn't work for all patients. People who have an autistic spectrum disorder in addition to OCD, for example, tend to find this technique ineffective.

Another method that sometimes works for obsessive thoughts, especially when they take the form of obsessive worries rather than topic obsessions, is setting aside a period of "worry time" and working toward confining those thoughts to that time. The patient might decide that at 5 p.m. he will allow himself 20 minutes to worry about things, and that he will use CBT techniques to boss back his intrusive thoughts the rest of the time.

You can also use exposure and response prevention techniques with obsessive worries and intrusive thoughts. In this case, the exposure would be thinking, in complete and possibly even gory detail, about the end result that you fear. For example, if a patient worries constantly that her father will die in a plane crash whenever he is on a business trip, she can try imaging what would realistically happen should that actually occur. She can think about how she would feel if it happened, and how her life would change. She can think about the funeral, and how her mother would act. These thoughts will naturally be quite horrifying at first—but it's trying to prevent thinking them, that has caused the worry and anxiety. Patients report that this technique, while very stressful, really does work. They are eventually able to confront and accept their fears, and the worries lose their power. This technique is sometimes called flooding.

If full exposure to the fearful scenario is too difficult, the patient may start with exposure to a partial scenario. Therapists note that recording an audiotape about the fear and listening to it repeatedly is often very helpful. This form of flooding helps the patient externalize the obsession and takes away some of its power to cause anxiety, as does reading about the obsession as a form of deliberate exposure.

Exposure and response prevention is especially powerful for dealing with intrusive violent or sexual thoughts. Devaluing the thoughts is an important part of the process—realizing that such thoughts are common and that they do not mean you are on your way to becoming a serial killer, a rapist, a sexual deviant, or whatever it is that the content of your thoughts causes you to fear. Therapists may actually encourage such patients to see how many books are available that cover the topic they are trying not to think about (the answer is "lots," because so many people are curious about violence and sex). They may ask patients to talk about or write down what they fear they might do, and then talk about whether this is a realistic fear based on the patient's actual actions and desires. All of these processes are intended to help the patient see that the intrusive thoughts are, as Mark put it earlier, "stupid brain blips." The thoughts themselves are normal; it's the act of obsessing about what they mean that makes them keep coming back, and causes anxiety.

Remember, some patients may experience such excessive anxiety that their best efforts at CBT are ineffective. Others may find that CBT works for some kinds of symptoms, but not for others. These are the situations where medication for OCD may be recommended, and very useful indeed.

CBT at home

Cognitive behavioral therapy takes place for the most part in the patient's everyday life, not in the therapist's office. The first attempts at applying CBT techniques to your child's OCD symptoms may occur with the therapist, but after that, exercises will be occurring in your home, at school, and in the community—wherever the symptoms intrude on your child's life. The younger the patient, the more closely parents will be involved in the CBT process.

Glynnis and George, parents of 10-year-old Nancy, have been part of the therapy team from the beginning:

> *Both of us have been involved with Nancy's therapy. Either her father or I, sometimes both of us, sit in on her sessions. The family approach has helped us tremendously in helping her at home and functioning better as a family. She sees a clinical psychologist who uses CBT, including exposure and response prevention.*

In fact, parents and older patients who are unable to find a therapist with experience using CBT to treat OCD can use self-help guides, such as those listed in Appendix A, *Resources*, to design their own exercises. This isn't the ideal way to go about it, of course, but it's better than going without this very effective treatment.

Your child's therapist should train you and your child in how to apply the techniques of CBT. You'll also need to know how to assess their effectiveness, what kinds of changes you might try if an exercise doesn't seem to work, and how to use relaxation and anxiety prevention techniques.

With younger children, you'll probably also want to discuss ideas about motivation. Teenagers have enough insight to understand that OCD prevents them from enjoying themselves, gets in the way of relationships, and sometimes causes embarrassing situations. They are usually just as motivated as adults to make it go away. The younger a child is when OCD appears, however, the less likely it is that he has insight into the problem. That means that successfully working through an E&RP exercise may not be its own reward: you may have to add external motivators for doing CBT homework. As Kel's mother noted earlier in this chapter, earning a special trip is one such motivator. Others may include toys, treats, video rentals, special activities at home with a parent or friend, or extra privileges, like getting to stay up half an hour later. You know best what motivates your child, and your child's therapist may be able to think of some possibilities as well.

Some parents report that humor helps defuse frightening thoughts. Patients who are trying to expose themselves to scary possibilities can allow their minds to take them from realistic consequences into the world of completely ridiculous consequences. For example, a 17-year-old who is afraid of driving the family car could imagine driving through town while using the vehicle as a "bumper car." There are realistic things to worry about while driving, but chances are the sorts of things a teenager with OCD is worried about—accidentally hitting a pedestrian with the car and not noticing, for example—are as unlikely as the silliest scenario he could imagine.

Although therapists may study for a long time to become very good at designing CBT programs, parents who don't have access to an experienced therapist need not worry. Trying these techniques themselves will not harm their child, even if they don't do a very good job of using CBT concepts. The worst thing that could happen is the exercises won't work. Of course, parents who have to "wing it" should take care to use good resource material and think any CBT exercises through before trying to use them with their child. Although poorly designed exercises in themselves are not harmful, failure could turn your child off to the whole idea of CBT.

Treating scrupulosity and hypochondria

Scrupulosity and hypochondria are two subtypes of OCD that sometimes make both patients and therapists uncomfortable about using straight CBT techniques.

In the case of scrupulosity, patients fear that if they don't pay attention to their obsessions and carry out their compulsions, they may pay truly severe consequences, displeasing God being chief among them. By permitting "forbidden" thoughts, as in the case of Mark earlier in this chapter, they may technically be breaking a religious law.

In the case of hypochondria, patients usually do not believe that they have a mental disorder, or they believe that a medical condition is at least part of the problem. Their physical symptoms are very real. They fear that if they ignore these symptoms by seeking psychiatric help only, they could become sicker and perhaps even die.

Both scrupulosity and hypochondria are primarily doubt-based types of OCD: they may have consulted spiritual and medical texts and experts hundreds of times to find out if their fears were valid, but they are never reassured. Simply hearing from a therapist that everything will be fine is not going to be enough.

The treatment of these two conditions works best when there is a team approach. In addition to the patient himself, his therapist, and his family, the team should include a trustworthy expert who is willing to commit to long-term treatment that may be very challenging. For scrupulosity, that would be a spiritual or moral advisor; for hypochondria, a knowledgeable primary care physician.

The patient must agree to work through CBT exercises with the added support of advice from this single expert during a regular, but gradually decreasing, schedule of appointments. This is the hardest part for patients, who feel compelled to seek reassurance and advice repeatedly. It's important for the patient to know that while useless reassurance will gradually be discouraged, a regular program of spiritual or medical counsel will continue indefinitely.

These patients will probably put relaxation and anxiety prevention techniques to the test frequently. Many with these symptoms have found that medication for OCD gives them the extra edge they need to work through this very difficult process, which forces them to reexamine everything they think they know about their spiritual or physical nature.

Play therapy

As discussed earlier in this chapter, very young children with OCD can have a hard time understanding why they should change, even if some of their symptoms cause them distress. They don't have any other kind of life experience to which to compare their own.

Play therapy is a special technique for communicating with young children that can be used to educate them about OCD and about CBT. Play therapists use toys and games to engage the child's attention and subtlety teach them what they need to know. Sometimes a child will talk to a toy when she won't talk to a strange adult, or can use toys to enact her fears when she doesn't have adequate words to express them.

Play therapy is not a substitute for CBT for children with OCD, but it can be a valuable adjunct. It can also be used to do directed work on social skills with children, using toys to model different situations and brainstorm how to handle them. This is an especially good method for young children with social phobia or school phobia.

Traditional psychotherapy

If OCD-like behavior is very specific and limited to a discrete topic or area of life, patients may want to explore the roots of these symptoms in therapy. For example, a patient with body dysmorphic disorder may want to understand more about why these particular symptoms affect her. Although the root cause of OCD is a chemical imbalance, the specific symptoms that a person develops may be rooted in life experiences.

Increased self-understanding cannot cure OCD, but it can help patients feel more comfortable with themselves. This reduces anxiety, which can certainly be helpful.

Traditional psychotherapy alone is not recommended as a treatment for OCD, however. In fact, simply discussing your fears and worries without gaining tools to combat them can actually increase the severity of OCD symptoms in many patients.

Group therapy

In most psychiatric clinics, group therapy consists of patients with a similar diagnosis discussing their problems with the help of a trained mediator or therapist. This type of group therapy is not a treatment for OCD, but a related model that might be called group supportive therapy. Group supportive therapy for OCD brings patients together to learn and apply new CBT techniques, encourage each other, discuss difficult symptoms, and talk about how they are working on them. Patients can tell each other about what has worked or not worked for them, while the therapists are available to provide expert information and lead group exercises.

A therapeutic model sponsored by the Obsessive-Compulsive Foundation, Giving Obsessive-compulsives Another Lifestyle (G.O.A.L.), combines the professional guidance of group therapy with aspects of a support group. G.O.A.L. groups are available in some urban areas. A G.O.A.L. meeting has three parts: discussion of an OCD-related topic chosen by the group, working on developing personal CBT goals within smaller breakout groups, and informal socializing with other people who have OCD. You can learn more about the G.O.A.L. concept at the OCF web site (*http://www.ocfoundation.org/*), or by ordering the G.O.A.L. video (listed in Appendix A) from the OCF.

Milieu therapy

In residential or day treatment programs for children with mental health issues, milieu therapy may be the basis for the program. This concept assumes that all aspects of interaction among residents and between residents and staff have the possibility of being therapeutic. As a result, almost every aspect of the daily schedule and interpersonal relations may be scrutinized for what lesson it teaches.

It's a great idea, but as with any program designed to benefit a large group, it may not always produce the hoped-for results. Children with OCD often need very personalized plans to succeed in intensive treatment programs. Parents can work with staffers and the patient to come up with ideas that fit the milieu therapy concept, and that also take the patient's special needs into account.

Living for today

Due to their built-in propensity for doubting, people with OCD doubt their self-worth, find it hard to trust others, and even doubt the veracity of their memories and thoughts. The greatest lesson one can learn from using CBT techniques to ferret out thought errors may be that people are healthiest when living in the present. There's no way to change the past, there's no way to predict or control the future, and we have to simply accept our lack of control. Like the old song says, "Que sera, sera" (what will be, will be).

On the other hand, right now we can influence what's going on in our environment and in our own minds. Enjoying the things we do have control over, making the most of today's opportunities, has to be enough. When young people with OCD begin to grasp this basic truth, it lifts away a terrible burden of feeling responsible for things that they can't help, opening a path to healing.

CHAPTER 5

Medical Interventions

THERE ARE NOW SEVERAL HIGHLY EFFECTIVE MEDICATIONS available for treating OCD. This chapter will cover all of the options, with special attention to the physiology and responses of children and adolescents. Special sections will cover diagnosis and treatment of pediatric autoimmune disorders associated with strep (PANDAS), a variant of OCD that is modulated by bacterial infection, and other special OCD subtypes and symptoms. This chapter also discusses inpatient treatment programs for children with OCD, including how to evaluate a hospital or treatment center's psychiatric program.

Before you consider medication

Medication is not the first option to consider when treating childhood-onset OCD. Cognitive behavioral therapy, the main topic in Chapter 4, *Therapeutic Interventions*, is considered the top treatment and should almost always be tried, either alone or in concert with medication. Unfortunately, many families do not have access to a therapist who knows how to use CBT techniques for OCD. You can use books like this one, and the detailed guides listed in Appendix A, *Resources*, to devise your own CBT program for your child.

You may find that some psychiatrists, especially those affiliated with managed care groups, see their primary role as prescribers and managers of medication. Today's psychiatric medications are truly marvelous and have brought new hope to millions diagnosed with OCD and other mental health conditions. If your doctor suggests medication for your child, don't be afraid to consider it, especially if your child's OCD symptoms are so severe that even basic CBT exercises are too anxiety-provoking.

The role of medication in OCD is not curing the disorder; it merely reduces the anxiety, fear, depression, and inertia that prevent people from tackling their obsessions and compulsions. Results are not sudden. In time, the right medication makes the patient feel as though a burden has been lifted. Some symptoms may actually disappear; others will simply become more manageable. The patient can work through CBT exercises that would have been far too difficult before, relieving her OCD symptoms even more.

For some patients, medication is a temporary measure. Others find that even with the regular application of CBT techniques, their OCD symptoms return in force if they stop taking their medication. This is not a sign of personal weakness, and it's nothing about which to be ashamed or worried. Most people with a chronic health condition, such as asthma, take some sort of medication throughout their lives. If your child needs to take medication on a long-term basis, he is part of a very large club.

General tips about medication

OCD symptoms are too different in each person for there to really be a medication "for OCD." The drugs prescribed for OCD are all slightly different from one another, although all of them are also antidepressants—medications used to treat clinical depression. They include Anafranil, which is in a family of medications called the tricyclic antidepressants; as well as the entire drug family known as the selective serotonin reuptake inhibitors (SSRIs). The SSRIs are Celexa, Luvox, Paxil, Prozac, and Zoloft.

Anafranil was the first medication approved specifically to treat OCD. It reduces obsessions and compulsions by blocking absorption of the neurotransmitters norepinephrine and serotonin at adrenergic nerve terminals, and works against the hormone acetylcholine, resulting in an increase of monoamine transmission in the brain and other effects. Today Anafranil is rarely the first choice for treating OCD, particularly for children, because it carries a higher risk of side effects than the SSRIs. However, it is highly effective for many patients, and is still widely used. None of the other tricyclic antidepressants are FDA-approved for use against OCD, but they are occasionally effective for patients who have not responded well to other choices (see the section "Strategies for treatment-resistant OCD" later in this chapter for more information).

While the SSRIs all inhibit the reuptake (absorption) of serotonin at certain nerve terminals, each member of the SSRI family has unique qualities and actions. For example, Celexa, Paxil, and Luvox tend to be sedating, while Prozac and Zoloft tend to be energizing. For this reason, doctors may want to try Celexa, Paxil, or Luvox for a child who has OCD and anxiety or hyperactivity; while Prozac or Zoloft might be indicated for a child with OCD and depression or fatigue. These qualities can be particularly important to remember when the SSRIs are combined with other medications. For instance, combining a sedating SSRI with a neuroleptic can sometimes produce an exponential increase in sedation.

Cherie, mother of 15-year-old Kacie and 9-year-old Colleen, compares Anafranil and an SSRI:

> *We first tried Anafranil with Kacie, who was then 8, but she began throwing up within an hour of the first dose. We then switched to Prozac, and it has worked beautifully for both kids.*

Each person's body chemistry is different, and some people have unusual responses to certain medications, for good or ill. Criteria that doctors may consider when choosing a medication for OCD include the patient's past responses to medications; her general state of health, especially if it might be worsened by a known side effect; medications she takes for another health condition; good or bad responses to a medication experienced by immediate family members; and the doctor's clinical experience with and knowledge of a specific drug. For a patient who is believed to be at risk for suicide, doctors may want to avoid medications that are potentially deadly in doses equal or less than the amount in a single prescription bottle, or in combination with alcohol. With a patient who has a history of substance abuse, doctors may avoid medications with a high potential for abuse or addiction, such as the benzodiazepine tranquilizers.

Glynnis, mother of 10-year-old Nancy, reports that a family medication response helped her doctor find a good match:

> *Nancy is taking Prozac. Her dosage had to be raised twice. The doctor felt she would respond well because I take Prozac for depression, as does my mother. She has had no adverse reactions; however, Nancy did gain a significant amount of weight.*

In some cases doctors are also bound by HMO regulations that limit them to prescribing only approved drugs from a list called a formulary. These restrictions can be circumvented, but it may require your physician to document the reason for using an off-formulary drug. You may have to pay more if your child is prescribed an off-formulary medication.

The use of medications to treat conditions for which they have not been FDA-approved is rarely an issue. Known as "off-label" use, this is a common practice.

It's best to have patients drive medication choices if possible, especially when a person has more than one medical challenge to cope with. Doctors should start by assessing symptoms, and medicate for those that are the most bothersome. They should ask patients directly which symptoms they can live with, and which they can't.

Your doctor should always explain medication choices and changes to you and, when practical, to your child. This information helps patients to be better-informed healthcare consumers, and increases the likelihood of compliance. It also increases the likelihood that the medication will actually help, since belief in drug effectiveness is estimated to account for about 30 percent of any benefit experienced from medication.

As for selecting the correct dose, even though there are guidelines available, it's more of an art than a science. Doctors who are unfamiliar with a medication usually start with the manufacturer's recommendations, according to the patient's weight and/or age. Differences in individual metabolism, and the use of other medications (including vitamins and herbal supplements) at the same time can make a lot of difference in what the optimal dose for your child should be.

When it comes to children, there is one dosage rule that should almost always be followed: start low, and go slow. If a patient is given too high a starting dose, or if medications are increased to the full therapeutic dose over just a few days, difficult side effects are far more likely to occur. Gradual *titration* (increase in dosage) over a period of weeks can make all the difference, although patients will be even less likely to see positive effects in short order. The only exception to this rule occurs in cases where OCD is severely disabling—for example, when OCD symptoms are preventing a person from eating or are confining her to home—it may be worth starting with a higher dose level despite the risk.

This is a point that doctors should always make clear to patients and their parents: although occasionally a patient will report dramatic results in just a week or so, the medications used to treat OCD normally take between six and twelve weeks to have a noticeable therapeutic effect. The changes can be so gradual that patients may complain that the drug is not working, only to realize after a few more weeks of use that certain obsessive-compulsive symptoms have dropped away somewhere along the line. It's rare for there to be a moment when you say, "My gosh, it's working!" Instead, there's a gradual decrease in both anxiety and in specific symptoms, coupled with a greater ability to manage symptoms and take things in stride.

To ensure that you see a medication's true effects, only one drug at a time should be started, added, or increased, if possible. You shouldn't make major dietary changes or start taking an herbal remedy, vitamin, or supplement at the same time as starting a new medication. Otherwise, it's hard to identify the culprit, should a benefit or side effect occur.

Some patients do seem to need more than one psychiatric medication to obtain relief from OCD, and others will need to mix OCD medications with drugs for treating other health conditions. This practice is known as polypharmacy. Done with careful supervision and adequate professional knowledge, it can bring help to even the most complex patient. Done haphazardly, it can be dangerous.

For people with OCD, there are a few areas of special concern. One involves mixing two or more medications that affect the neurotransmitter serotonin. You may get more than just an additive effect from combining, because some medications *potentiate* (increase the potency of) others by leaps and bounds. Knowledgeable doctors can use the potentiation effect to their advantage, using one drug to boost the effect of another without raising its dose so high that side effects occur. If this effect is unexpected, however, side effects can occur, including serotonin syndrome (see the section "Major medication side effects" later in this chapter).

On the other hand, one medication can negate the effects of another drug, preventing it from being effective.

These factors mean that even if your child's first experience with a medication was negative or not helpful, you shouldn't write it off completely. In a different dose or combination, that same drug might work well.

Another hazard involves mixing any medication with one of the monoamine oxidase inhibitors (MAOIs). These older antidepressants, which inhibit the metabolization of the neurotransmitters serotonin, norepinephrine, and dopamine, are rarely prescribed to children or teens in the US. They have unpleasant and even life-threatening interactions with many other drugs, including common over-the-counter medications. People taking MAOIs must also follow a special diet, because these medications interact with natural compounds found in many foods. The list of proscribed foods includes chocolate, aged cheeses, beer, and more. If your child must take an MAOI, check for warning labels on everything, and familiarize yourself thoroughly with the dietary restrictions.

Here are some more important dos and don'ts:

- Do not start or stop taking any prescription medication on your own.
- Follow indications for dose amount, dosage time, and other instructions ("take with food", etc.) exactly.
- Be sure to tell both your physician and pharmacist about all other prescription medications your child takes.
- Inform your physician and pharmacist about over-the-counter (OTC) drugs your child takes. Aspirin, ibuprofen, decongestants, OTC asthma inhalers, Alka-Seltzer and similar medications, and cough syrup are just some of the common substances that can cause dangerous side effects when mixed with prescription drugs.
- Inform your doctor about your child's use or suspected use of alcohol, tobacco, any illegal drugs, and any supplements or vitamins other than a regular daily multivitamin.
- If your doctor is unsure about how a medication might interact with an herbal remedy or supplement, you may need to help her find more information. Most doctors are not well informed about the chemical action of nutritional supplements or herbal medicines, but many are willing to work with you on these matters.
- If you suspect that your child has been given the wrong medication or the wrong dosage, call your pharmacist right away. Such errors do occur, and your pharmacist should be able to either reassure you or fix the problem.

- If your teenage or adult child is pregnant or breastfeeding, or if she could become pregnant, ask your physician or pharmacist about any side effects specifically related to reproduction and nursing.
- If your teenage or adult child is actively trying to father a child, you may also want to ask about male reproductive side effects.

Even if you think your child is too young for the information, it's important to start educating her as soon as possible about possible interaction hazards, and side effects that should be reported. Some kids find out the hard way, and their distress could have been avoided.

Elizabeth, age 16, has learned from her mixture mistake:

> *I am currently taking 150 mg of Zoloft every day, and the two main side effects I've had are insomnia and sweating excessively. To prevent bigger problems, my main suggestion is don't mix alcohol with your prescription drugs for OCD. It often makes your symptoms go nuts, and you may begin to have anxiety attacks. It's best to just stay away.*

Special drug formulas

It doesn't help that drugs often come in one size only. Even the least powerful pill may be too much for some patients to start with, especially for young children. Surprisingly, many doctors are unaware of options that can help. These include:

- A number of psychiatric medications, including Prozac, Risperdal, and Haldol, are available in liquid form. Liquids can be measured out in tiny doses and increased very gradually. Incidentally, liquid medications can be easily administered to children who refuse pills. You may even be able to mix them with food or drinks (check with your pharmacist first).
- Some medications can be broken into fractions. Pill splitters are available at most pharmacies for just this purpose. Make sure it's okay to split a medication before you go this route, however: time-release medications and some pills with special coatings will not work properly when broken. Generally speaking, if the pill is scored down the middle, you can split it. If it isn't, ask your pharmacist, or call the manufacturer's customer hotline.
- Some pills that are too small to split can be crushed and divided into equal parts. Again, ask your pharmacist before doing this, as it's difficult

to get precise doses with crushed pills. Tiny mortar and pestle sets can be found at health food or cookware shops. You can buy empty gel caps to put the powder in, or you may be able to mix it into food or drink.

Some medications come in patch form. Tempting though it may be, don't try cutting these patches to get a smaller dose or to move up to a larger dose gradually. Doing so will keep the medication from being absorbed properly. Many patches need to be securely covered to deliver the full dose. If the patch comes with overlays that don't work well, as is the case with clonidine, try using the transparent, waterproof dressing Tegaderm, or the large, decorated Nexcare "Tattoos" bandages. You can guess which option younger kids would prefer. Patches should be placed on a padded, non-bony part of the body that doesn't flex too much. Many teens and adults prefer the upper arm area; children are more likely to leave them alone if you place them on an inaccessible area of the back.

Compounding pharmacies make medications to order in their own lab. For example, they can make a liquid version of a prescription normally available in tablet form only. These pharmacies are especially helpful to individuals with allergy problems. Many pills and syrups contain common allergens, including eggs, soy, corn, and dyes. If a hypoallergenic version isn't available from the manufacturer, seek out a compounding pharmacy. If there isn't one where you live, several allow patients with valid prescriptions to order over the phone, by mail, or via the Internet. Just use a search engine like AltaVista (*http://www.altavista.com*) or Lycos (*http://www.lycos.com*) to search for the term "compounding pharmacy." As always with Internet-based or mail-order businesses, check references before you pay for goods or services.

Follow any instructions about eating or drinking before, with, or after your medication. Also, avoid taking medications with grapefruit juice—it may sound nutty, but grapefruit juice can prevent the breakdown of certain medications.

Keep an eye out for unusual symptoms, and let your physician know about your concerns right away. Most people remember to do this when they first start taking a drug, but forget about it after they've had the same prescription for a long time. Vigilance is especially important when using newer medications. The FDA and similar government bodies in Canada and Europe require studies showing new medications are effective and safe in the short term. Long-term studies are expensive, and because they're not required, they are rarely done. In other words, with any medication introduced in the past ten or twenty years, real-life patients are the long-term study subjects.

Prescription notes

You may see some odd initials on your child's prescriptions or pill bottles. Most of them stand for Latin words, so they are hard to figure out on your own. Table 5-1 lists some of the most common abbreviations used by doctors and pharmacists, and the corresponding meaning.

Table 5-1. Common Prescription Abbreviations

Abbreviation	**Meaning**
ac	Take before meals (*ante cibum*)
bid	Take twice a day (*bis in die*)
gtt	Drops (*guttae*)
mg	Milligrams, a measure of the active ingredient
pc	Take after meals (*post cibum*)
po	Take by mouth (*per os*)
prn	Take as needed (*pro re nata*)
qd	Take once a day (*quaque die*)
qh	Take every hour (*quaque hora*)
qid	Take four times a day (*quater in die*)
q[number]h	Take every [number] of hours
tid	Take three times a day (*ter in die*)
ut dict.	Take as directed (*ut dictum*)

In the US, most pharmacies also use colored stickers and letter codes to let you know about medication side effects and risks. If the picture or wording doesn't make sense to you, ask your pharmacist to explain its meaning.

Blood tests and EKGs

Some medications for OCD and related disorders, such as clomipramine, require monitoring via blood levels. These tests check physical functions or make sure the medication has reached its therapeutic level. They are especially helpful when patients are taking more than one drug, since the drugs may be affecting each other, and for ensuring safety when patients seem to need a higher-than-normal dose.

Blood test results will include a number indicating how much of the medication is found in the blood, or numbers indicating other health markers. Your doctor compares these levels to the patient's own normal level as found on a pre-medication blood test, to a norm, or to a chart of therapeutic blood levels (amounts of the medication that have been found to be effective in patients of various sizes and ages). Be sure to find out how your child's current blood level compares to his therapeutic blood level or normal blood level when these tests are done. A physician's assistant or nurse can help you understand what the test results mean.

Try to learn how to read and understand these figures yourself—many times observant parents have caught mistakes that could have been dangerous. Typical problems include blood assessed with the wrong blood test, misinterpreted levels, and getting someone else's paperwork.

Blood tests may frighten your child at first. The sample taken is small, of course. Good *phlebotomists* (blood-draw specialists) do not cause bruising or more than a twinge of pain when they do their job, unless the patient bruises very easily or has a low pain threshold. If this is the case, let the phlebotomist know—she may have a better way to obtain the sample. Numbing ointments, such as EMLA cream, can help.

Patients who do not have regular access to quality lab facilities, such as those living in remote areas, may have a very difficult time keeping up with regularly scheduled blood draws. Talk to your healthcare provider about alternative ways to handle the need for monthly testing, such as having a visiting home-health nurse do the blood draw in your home and then mail the vial to a lab for testing.

In some cases, liver or heart function should be tested before your child starts taking a particular drug. Liver function is assessed with a blood test that checks the level of certain enzymes, while heart function is usually assayed with a regular blood pressure test, a physical exam, and an electrocardiogram (EKG).

The EKG can be done in the doctor's office, and since it uses wires that stick on the chest with an adhesive patch or gooey substance, it doesn't hurt at all. You just have to lie still, but that's not always an easy task for kids. The wires are attached to a mechanical device that looks something like a seismograph, or to a computer. The EKG machine will spit out a graph of the heart rate and any other cardiac activity it picks up. Your doctor can read this graph to find any problems with or changes in heart function.

Although blood level tests are usually used to ensure the patient's safety, they are sometimes done to ensure that the patient (usually a teenager or young adult) is taking his medication. A special blood test is used to diagnose PANDAS (see the section "Strep-linked OCD" for more information).

Minor medication side effects

The medications used to treat OCD are relatively mild at recommended doses. They are sometimes associated with a few minor side effects, however. Most patients will experience one or more of these at some time. The problem usually goes away on its own after a few weeks. Sometimes these side effects are bothersome enough to force a change in medications, however.

John, father of 14-year-old Tori, tells her side-effect story:

> *Luvox helped for a while, but she developed severe tremors, and it was affecting her vision. Tori put forth great energy towards not letting anyone know she had tremors. This behavior, I believe, is due to her shame of having OCD—she doesn't want anyone to know. The danger was that she was hiding a potential health problem while taking medication that had side effects. She is now very fearful of trying any medication.*

Commonly reported side effects associated with medications for OCD include:

- **Behavior changes.** Sometimes called behavioral side effects (BSEs), these are said to occur in as many as half of all children taking antidepressants for OCD.[1] They can include increased hyperactivity and abnormally elevated mood, provocative and uninhibited behavior, and in a few cases, aggression. These changes are usually mild, and may fade in time or respond to lowering the dose slightly. If behavior changes are more severe or long lasting, they may signal an underlying tendency toward bipolar disorder (manic depression). If so, the patient may need to stop taking the medication and use cognitive behavioral therapy only for OCD; or a physician may start the patient on a mood stabilizer, such as lithium or Depakote, and add an OCD medication again later.
- **Dry mouth.** This side effect, caused by slightly decreased saliva production, comes from the secondary action of these drugs on the neurotransmitter acetylcholine. Usually it's a minor annoyance, but it can

contribute to tooth decay, especially in children who wear braces, and it can also exacerbate compulsive behaviors that involve the teeth, such as tooth-grinding. Drinking plenty of water to relieve the sensation of dryness, brushing the teeth frequently, and using a fluoride mouthwash should also help. Sugarless mints or gum sometimes improve comfort by increasing saliva production. In extreme cases, patients may want to use nighttime mouth guards to prevent tooth damage from grinding, or a doctor may recommend a special moistening spray.

- **Nausea.** This side effect emanates mostly from the action of these medications on serotonin receptors in the gastrointestinal tract. It usually goes away after a few weeks. In the meantime, changes in diet and eating small, frequent meals can relieve symptoms. Check with your doctor before using an over-the-counter stomach remedy.
- **Weight gain or loss.** The effect of these drugs on serotonin extends to the inner feeling of having eaten enough food. Patients report increased or decreased appetite, and ensuing weight gain or loss. Anafranil is probably the worst offender for weight gain among OCD drugs; weight gain is also frequent with neuroleptics. These symptoms are best addressed by dietary changes and, for weight gain, regular exercise. Some clinicians think these drugs may also reset the metabolism, because some patients on controlled diets still gain weight. In these cases, adjustments to dose or adding another medication to treat this side effect may be tried. Stimulants are the most commonly used medications to offset weight gain, although some clinicians report success from using low doses (25 to 50 micrograms per day) of the thyroid hormone Cytomel. Patients with eating disorders need to be especially careful about medications that cause appetite changes.
- **Sexual side effects.** These medications all tend to dampen sexual impulses and lower sensitivity to sexual stimulation, including the ability to achieve erection or orgasm. Obviously, this is more of a problem for adults, but it's one that parents should be aware of as their teenager nears adulthood. Strategies include lowering the medication dose; adding a second medication, such as Effexor, Wellbutrin, BuSpar, or Edronax, that raises sexual response in some patients; using Viagra; trying herbal remedies, such as Gingko biloba or yohimbe, that may affect sexual response; or working on sensitization techniques with a professional sex therapist.

Although doctors call these side effects "minor" because they usually don't endanger health, patients may consider them quite major. If these or other minor side effects really bother your child or teenager, don't let your doctor brush off the problem.

Several young people with OCD, with ages ranging from 16 to 19, share stories about their experiences with their side effects of particular medications:

> *I'm currently on Luvox, which has helped somewhat, but causes me to feel very drowsy.*

• • • • •

> *I took up to 300 mg of Luvox, but I couldn't stand the side effects. Prozac made me either depressed or very happy, so I discontinued use. With Anafranil, I discontinued use because of an allergic reaction. Paxil in combination with 150 mg of Luvox gives me pretty good results with depression, but no change in OCD symptoms.*

• • • • •

> *Prozac at 40 mg is moderately effective for me, with some side effects—agitation, sleeplessness, headaches, possibly tics. I have not discontinued medication despite these.*

• • • • •

> *Paxil helped somewhat, but it eventually stopped working. I discontinued it due to dry mouth. Zoloft and Paxil (when I tried it again) both made me very nauseated. I had severe stomachaches. I don't know what caused that to happen.*

• • • • •

> *Zoloft, Prozac, Dexedrine, Luvox, and clonidine all helped to a certain extent, but then their effects went away. Zoloft and Luvox made me gain a lot of weight. Zoloft made me aggressive. After about two years on Dexedrine, beginning when I was 14, I developed tics.*

Major medication side effects

Except for serotonin syndrome, which is rare, dangerous side effects are not usually associated with the medications used to treat OCD. However, a few patients have unusual reactions to antidepressants, and some take medications for OCD along with neuroleptics, tranquilizers, and antiseizure drugs, all of which are more commonly associated with major side effects.

Of course, you should call your physician immediately if your child ever experiences seizures, heart palpitations, blood in his urine or stool, or other symptoms that seem medically serious in nature. If your doctor is not available on short notice, report to an emergency room. These symptoms may be related to medication, or they may signify another health condition that needs attention.

The side effects listed below are signs of serious trouble, and a few are life threatening. They always warrant immediate medical help. Serious side effects related specifically to psychiatric medications include:

- **Akasthisia.** An intense internal sensation of physical restlessness, "itchiness," and jumpiness—a need to move constantly. A person with akasthisia will look and feel uncomfortable if she tries to be still.
- **Bradyphrenia.** Slowed thought processes.
- **Dystonia.** Muscle rigidity and uncontrollable muscle spasms. This is associated primarily with neuroleptic medications.
- **Encephalopathic syndrome.** Symptoms are similar to those of neuroleptic malignant syndrome (see entry later in this list), of which it may be a variant. Usually associated with lithium toxicity.
- **Extrapyramidal side effects** (EPS). Physical symptoms that include tremor, slurred speech, akathisia (motor restlessness), dystonia (muscle rigidity), anxiety, distress, paranoia, and bradyphrenia (slowed thought processes). Associated primarily with neuroleptics.
- **Hyperkinesia.** Excessive motor activity, the physical expression of akathisia. In children this can mimic common hyperactivity, but the movements may seem both driven and purposeless.
- **Neuroleptic malignant syndrome** (NMS). Rigid muscle movements, fever, irregular pulse and heartbeat, rapid heartbeat, irregular blood pressure, heavy sweating, and strange states of mind characterize this potentially fatal condition. Discontinue the medication immediately and call your doctor if these symptoms occur. In extreme cases, the patient may need emergency care at a hospital. Physicians should report episodes of NMS to the Neuroleptic Malignant Syndrome Information Service (*http://www.nmsis.org/*), which has set up a registry to help researchers reduce the incidence of this problem. NMS is associated primarily with neuroleptics, although it may occur with tricyclic antidepressants or other medications.

- **Oculogyric crisis.** A patient in the throes of oculogyric crisis has a frozen upward gaze, often a very strange-looking facial expression and eye movements, and has contorted facial and neck muscles.
- **Orthostatic hypotension.** Dangerously low blood pressure caused by alpha-adrenergic blockade. Associated primarily with the neuroleptics. Some children who take SSRIs experience dizziness when they stand up suddenly, which is a mild and harmless form of orthostatic hypotension.
- **Parkinsonian symptoms.** These mimic the neurological disorder Parkinson's disease, hence the name. They include a feeling of cognitive slowing, muscle and joint stiffness, tremor, and unusually stiff and unstable gait. Associated primarily with the neuroleptics.
- **Seizures.** Most of the medications used to treat OCD lower patients' susceptibility to seizures. This effect is rarely a problem, but it is something patients and parents should be aware of, especially if there is a family history of seizure disorders. Other than convulsions, which are easy to recognize, mild seizures can mimic fainting spells, dizziness, depersonalization, short-term memory loss, and musical or olfactory intrusions. The last two are like song or smell obsessions, but respond to anti-seizure medications instead of drugs for OCD. Higher seizure risks are seen with Anafranil and Effexor in particular, less frequently with the SSRIs.
- **Serotonin syndrome.** When the brain is bombarded with too much serotonin (for example, from combining two antidepressants), patients may experience shivers, headaches, diarrhea, profuse sweating, confusion, and akathisia. If this happens, stop taking antidepressants immediately and see your doctor without delay. In extreme cases, serotonin syndrome can be fatal. That's why patients taking prescription antidepressants should also avoid "natural" antidepressants, such as St. John's wort.
- **Tardive dyskinesia (TD).** A drug-induced movement disorder characterized by twisting motions of the hands and feet, and smacking or chewing movements of the mouth. Rippling movements of the tongue muscles are considered an early warning sign. Discontinue the medication immediately and call your doctor if these symptoms occur. Between 20 and 30 percent of long-term users of the older neuroleptic drugs, such as Haldol and Thorazine, eventually develop this disorder.

The atypical neuroleptics seem far less likely to cause TD, and patients who do get TD have usually taken very large doses over many years. Very few cases of TD have been associated with tricyclic antidepressants and various mood stabilizers.

Some physicians recommend that people who take drugs that carry a risk for TD also take vitamin E supplements, which appear to stave off the disorder in some people.

If TD is caught early, it may reverse itself once the medication is stopped.

For those who are already affected by TD, only one medication is currently known to help: Nitoman (tetrabenezine, TDZ), also marketed under the name Regulin. This drug depletes dopamine in nerve endings, and so it may interact with other drugs that affect dopamine production or use. Nitoman is available in Canada, Norway, Sweden, Japan, and the UK. In the US, it can only be obtained through compassionate use programs or via special mail order arrangements. Nitoman sometimes causes depression as a side effect, so patients with affective disorders should use it with caution.

These are serious and painful side effects, the kind that understandably make patients want to stop taking their medicine. Careful medication choice and dosage adjustment should reduce them, and complimentary adjustments to diet, vitamins, supplements, and relaxation techniques may also help.

Raegan, age 18, had a very negative first experience with Paxil, which was addressed with a simple dose change:

> *I first tried Zoloft, but it didn't help me at all. Then I went on Paxil. My first doctor put me on too much, and it caused me to have angry outbursts. My new doctor put me on a lower amount of Paxil. I am now on that same small amount of Paxil, along with a small amount of Adderall, and these drugs have helped me amazingly.*

Discontinuing medication

Sometimes a doctor will ask that all medication be withdrawn for a while in order to give her a baseline look at which symptoms are being caused by the disorder and which are due to over-, under-, or mis-medication. This process can be exceptionally trying for patients and families if it is not managed well. There are very few medications that can be stopped cold without causing distress—with some, such as clonidine, this can even be life-threatening.

Gradually tapering off to a lower dose and then to none is almost always the best approach. Patients should be carefully monitored for signs of trouble. In some cases (such as for discontinuing benzodiazepine tranquilizer use after several years), medication withdrawal may need to take place in a hospital setting or under extra-careful home supervision.

Ask your doctor if there are any symptoms you might expect during the withdrawal period. He might be able to recommend over-the-counter or dietary remedies for likely problems, such as diarrhea or nausea. Decide in advance on non-medication strategies for dealing with problems that may occur as drugs are tapered off.

Although the SSRIs are not addictive, some patients do report nausea and other unpleasant symptoms when they stop taking one of these medications. Doctors report that these seeming withdrawal symptoms can be held at bay by titrating up the dose of a new medication while the old one is being tapered off, or using a low dose of a different SSRI during the withdrawal period. Over-the-counter remedies, if approved by your physician, may also be helpful for countering symptoms such as nausea or fatigue during medication changes.

Dr. Jim Hatton explains the pitfalls of discontinuing medication without careful planning:

> *It is also important to carefully consider all the possibilities before discontinuing a medication, or one runs the risk of prematurely deciding that "Medication X doesn't work for me," when it might have worked, or side effects could have been managed, if it was administered in a different way or in a different combination. This can lead to the self-fulfilling prophecy of that medication never working.*

Medications for OCD

The list of medications approved by the US Food and Drug Administration specifically for treating OCD is short. Of these, only Anafranil, Luvox, and Zoloft have earned formal approval for use in children aged 8 (for Luvox), 10 (for Anafranil), or older. Clinical experience indicates that other drugs are also effective for some people with OCD, and these are listed here with their FDA-approved cousins.

Some people find that their OCD symptoms remit when they take the medication Effexor (see the section "Anti-anxiety medications," later in this chapter), which is usually prescribed for anxiety. Effexor actually has a very similar chemical profile to Anafranil, but no hard data is available regarding its usefulness for OCD.

We have listed commonly reported side effects and certain rare but especially dangerous side effects only. See the sections "Minor medication side effects" and "Major medication side effects" earlier in this chapter for more information about what these terms mean, and how to handle side effects when they do occur.

Less common and rare side effects may be associated with any medication, and your child may experience side effects that no one else has ever had. If you see unusual symptoms after your child takes medicine, or after combining more than one medication, call your doctor right away. You may also want to consult the drug reference sheet packaged with your medication for more detailed data.

The information in this chapter was taken from the *Physician's Desk Reference*, pharmaceutical company literature, and other reputable sources. The dosage guidelines for children come from the Obsessive-Compulsive Foundation's publication "OCD Medication: Children—What Parents Should Know."[2] Data should be accurate as of this writing, but new information may emerge. Check out any medications your child takes using a detailed drug reference book, such as those listed in Appendix A, to make sure you are aware of all possible side effects and interactions.

The National Alliance for the Mentally Ill (NAMI) is one of the best resources for information on new drugs for neurological disorders. Its web site (*http://www.nami.org/*) often features "consumer reviews" of new drugs, and previews of new medications that are undergoing clinical trials. Another good resource is the Child Psychopharmacology Information Service, which maintains medication guides at *http://www.psychiatry.wisc.edu/cpis.htm*, and can be reached by phone at (608) 827-2470.

Anafranil

Generic name: clomipramine hydrochloride

Use: OCD and obsessive-compulsive behavior, depression, panic disorder, chronic pain, eating disorders, severe PMS. Sometimes prescribed to treat herpes lesions or arthritis, indicating that it may also have antiviral or anti-inflammatory qualities.

Normal dose range for children: 25 to 250 mg per day (FDA-approved for use in children with OCD age 10 and older).

Action, if known: Tricyclic antidepressant. Blocks norepinephrine and serotonin use, works against the hormone acetylcholine. Has weak antihistamine properties.

Side effects: Sedation, tremor, dry mouth, light sensitivity, mood swings in people with bipolar disorders, weight gain. Lowers the seizure threshold.

Known interaction hazards: Alcohol, MAOIs, blood pressure medications (including clonidine and Tenex), thyroid medication. Potentiated by estrogen, bicarbonate of soda (as in Alka-Seltzer and other OTC remedies), acetazolamide, procainamide, and quinidine. Cimetadine, methylphenidate, Thorazine and similar drugs (neuroleptics), oral contraceptives, nicotine (including cigarettes), charcoal tablets, and estrogen may interfere with Anafranil's action in the body.

Tips: Take with food if stomach upset occurs. Take bulk of dose at bedtime to reduce sedation, if so directed.

Celexa

Generic name: citalopram

Use: Depression. Some doctors are, however, experimenting with this relatively new (to the US) SSRI as an OCD medication.

Normal dose range for children: 20 to 60 milligrams per day (not yet FDA-approved for treating OCD in children, although clinical experience indicates it is effective for some patients).

Action, if known: SSRI. Increases the amount of active serotonin in the brain. Usually has a calming and/or sedating effect.

Side effects: Dry mouth, insomnia or restless sleep, increased sweating, nausea. Reportedly less likely to cause sexual dysfunction than other SSRIs. Lowers the seizure threshold. Can cause mood swings in people with bipolar disorders.

Known interaction hazards: Alcohol. Never take Celexa with an MAOI or soon after stopping an MAOI. Use with caution if you take a drug that affects the liver, such as ketoconazole or the macrolides.

Tips: People with liver or kidney disease should be monitored regularly while taking Celexa.

Luvox

Generic name: fluvoxamine maleate

Use: OCD, social phobia, depression.

Normal dose range for children: 25 to 250 milligrams per day (FDA-approved for use in children with OCD ages 8 and older).

Action, if known: SSRI. Increases the amount of active serotonin in the brain. Usually has a calming and/or sedating effect.

Side effects: Headache, insomnia, sleepiness, nervousness, nausea, dry mouth, diarrhea or constipation, sexual dysfunction. Lowers the seizure threshold. Can cause mood swings in people with bipolar disorders.

Known interaction hazards: Never take with an MAOI or soon after stopping an MAOI. Potentiated by tricyclic antidepressants and lithium. Potentiates many medications, including clozapine, diltiazem, methadone, some beta-blockers and antihistamines, Haldol and other neuroleptics.

Tips: Avoid taking this drug if you have liver disease. Cigarette smoking may make Luvox less effective. Luvox does not bind to protein in the body, unlike the other SSRIs, and may have a very different effect in some people.

Paxil, Seroxat

Generic name: paroxetine hydrochloride

Use: OCD, panic disorder, social phobia, depression.

Normal dose range for children: 10 to 30 milligrams per day (not yet FDA-approved for use in children with OCD, although clinical experience indicates it is effective for some patients).

Action, if known: SSRI. Increases the amount of active serotonin in the brain. Usually has a calming and/or sedating effect.

Side effects: Headache, insomnia or restless sleep, dizziness, tremor, nausea, weakness, sexual dysfunction, dry mouth. Lowers the seizure threshold. Can cause mood swings in people with bipolar disorders.

Known interaction hazards: Alcohol. Never take the drug with an MAOI or soon after stopping an MAOI. Potentiates warfarin, theophylline, paroxetine, procyclidine. Changes how digoxin and phenytoin act in the body.

Tips: People with liver or kidney disease should be monitored regularly while taking Paxil. This medication has a short life in the body, so missed doses may be more likely to cause side effects.

Prozac

Generic name: fluoxetine hydrochloride

Use: OCD, depression. Sometimes also used to treat eating disorders, ADHD, narcolepsy, migraine/chronic headache, Tourette's syndrome, social phobia.

Normal dose range for children: 5 to 60 milligrams per day. Prozac is not yet FDA-approved for use in children with OCD, although studies indicate that it is effective.

Action, if known: SSRI. Increases the amount of active serotonin in the brain. Usually has an energizing effect.

Side effects: Headache, insomnia or restless sleep, dizziness, tremor, nausea, weakness, sexual dysfunction, dry mouth, itchy skin and/or rash. May cause change in appetite and weight. Lowers the seizure threshold. Can cause mood swings, especially manic episodes, in people with bipolar disorders.

Known interaction hazards: Alcohol and all other CNS depressants. Never take Prozac with an MAOI or soon after stopping an MAOI. Do not take OTC or prescription cold or allergy remedies containing cyproheptadine or dextromethorphan. Potentiated by tricyclic antidepressants. Potentiates lithium, phenytoin, neuroleptic drugs, carbamazepine, and cyclosporine. Reduces effectiveness of BuSpar.

Tips: Prozac has a long life in your body. People with liver or kidney disease should be monitored while taking Prozac.

Zoloft

Generic name: sertraline hydrochloride

Use: OCD, obsessive-compulsive behavior, panic disorder, depression.

Normal dose range for children: 50 to 150 milligrams per day (FDA-approved for use in children with OCD).

Action, if known: SSRI. Increases the amount of active serotonin in the brain. Has an energizing quality.

Side effects: Dry mouth, headache, tremor, diarrhea, nausea, sexual dysfunction. May cause mood swings, especially manic episodes, in people with bipolar disorders. Lowers the seizure threshold.

Known interaction hazards: Alcohol and all other CNS depressants. Never take Zoloft with an MAOI or soon after stopping an MAOI. Potentiates benzodiazepine drugs and warfarin. Potentiated by cimetadine.

Tips: People with epilepsy, bipolar disorders, liver disease, or kidney disease should be carefully monitored if they take Zoloft. May affect therapeutic level of lithium.

Strategies for treatment-resistant OCD

For patients who do not seem to respond to any of the SSRIs or to Anafranil, there are other treatment possibilities.[3] Before declaring a medication a failure, parents should make sure that a trial of at least twelve weeks was attempted, and that the dose was adequate for the child's size and symptom severity.

Studies have shown that medication almost always works best when paired with cognitive behavioral therapy, so if you have not yet tried this approach, you should. Some patients will respond to CBT alone, with no need for drugs.

Doctors may experiment with medication combinations, often leveraging on the ability of one drug to potentiate another, as with the combination of Anafranil and Luvox. Patients with a comorbid tic disorder may want to try augmenting an SSRI or Anafranil with an atypical neuroleptic.

As a last-ditch effort, doctors may do a trial of an MAOI antidepressant, although this approach is rarely recommended for children. The other tricyclic antidepressants, although not specifically approved for treating OCD, have also helped some patients.

The next step might be looking at alternative causes for the obsessive-compulsive symptoms: an autistic spectrum disorder, one of the rare genetic disorders listed in Chapter 2, *Diagnosis,* a head trauma, or an infectious cause, such as PANDAS. The presence of one of these conditions could suggest a different course of treatment.

If none of these approaches works, two other alternatives may be available. A very small number of patients with severe OCD have found relief by undergoing brain surgery. One technique that has shown some promise recently involves microsurgery that destroys tissue in the orbitofrontal cortex of the brain.[4] For obvious reasons, brain surgery is reserved for extreme cases that do not respond to any other type of medical or therapeutic treatment.

A new treatment, transcranial magnetic stimulation (TMS), is currently being tested. Although it is not yet commercially available, patients might be able to access this treatment by signing up for a research study.

Electroconvulsive therapy (also known as ECT, or electroshock therapy) is not recommended for treatment-resistant OCD, although it is often very effective for treatment-resistant depression.

Medications for OCD-linked rage

Unexplained rage is a difficult problem for some children and teens with OCD. It is more common in patients who have additional disorders, such as ADHD, Tourette's syndrome, or impulse control disorders, such as intermittent explosive disorder. Rages (which resemble super temper tantrums) may emerge from the difficult combination of frustration due to obsessions and compulsions coupled with extreme impulsivity. Sometimes the patient knows what causes the rage to erupt; other times it seems to come out of the blue. Clinicians who have worked with such children sometimes describe their rages as neurological storms that have a seizure-like quality to them.

Some patients who have rages experience a reduction in this symptom once OCD is well controlled; others[5] may need to add a second medication. This medication will be an antiseizure medication or a neuroleptic, sometimes in a much lower dose than would be used to treat a seizure disorder or psychosis.

Physicians have tried a wide variety of drugs to treat neurologically-induced rages. The first two possibilities on many physicians' lists, Catapres and Tenex, were originally developed to treat high blood pressure.

Catapres

Generic name: clonidine

Use: High blood pressure, ADD/ADHD, tics/Tourette's syndrome, extreme impulsivity, migraine, drug and alcohol withdrawal aid, ulcerative colitis, childhood growth delay.

Action, if known: Stimulates alpha-adrenergic receptors in brain to widen blood vessels, stimulates similar receptors throughout the body.

Side effects: Dry mouth, dizziness, constipation, sedation, unusually vivid or disturbing dreams, weight gain.

Known interaction hazards: Could interact with other medications for blood pressure.

Tips: Do not use if you have heart trouble, disease of the blood vessels in the brain, or chronic kidney failure. The time-release clonidine patch is far less sedating than the pills. You can become tolerant of clonidine, requiring a higher dose. Have regular eye exams, as clonidine can affect the retina.

Tenex

Generic name: guanfacine

Use: High blood pressure, migraines, extreme nausea, heroin withdrawal aid, ADHD/ADD, tic disorders/Tourette's syndrome.

Action, if known: Stimulates CNS to widen blood vessels, and has other as yet unknown effects.

Side effects: Sleepiness, changes in blood pressure or heart rate, nausea.

Known interaction hazards: Alcohol and other CNS depressants. May be counteracted by stimulants such as Ritalin and many OTC drugs; by estrogen and oral contraceptives; and by indomethacin, ibuprofen, and non-steroidal anti-inflammatory drugs.

Tips: If you take another medication that lowers blood pressure, your doctor will need to adjust your Tenex dose accordingly to prevent problems. Most people take Tenex at bedtime due to its sedating effect.

Beth-Anne, age 14 (diagnosed OCD and trichotillomania), has found Tenex effective:

> *I am taking Tenex for anger—I tend to get very angry if people say or do something hurtful but don't explain why, when an ignorant person slanders people with mental disorders, and when somebody says something about my rituals or hair pulling.*

• • • • •

If Catapres or Tenex is not effective, doctors may want to try a mood stabilizer. Lithium is the most commonly used of these; most of the others were originally developed to treat seizure disorders. This class of medications includes the following medications.

Depakene

Generic name: valproic acid

Use: Seizure disorders, bipolar disorders, migraine, panic disorder, rages/aggression.

Action, if known: Antispasmodic. Increases the levels of gamma-aminobutyric acid (GABA) in the brain, and increases its absorption. Also stabilizes brain membranes.

Side effects: Nausea, sedation, depression, psychosis, aggression, hyperactivity, changes in blood platelet function.

Known interaction hazards: Do not take with milk, and do not use charcoal tablets when taking Depakene. Be careful with alcohol, and with any medication that has a tranquilizing or depressant effect. Side effects may increase if you use anticoagulants, including aspirin, non-steroidal anti-inflammatory drugs, erythromycin, chlorpromazine, cimetadine, or felbamate.

Tips: Watch out for increased bruising or bleeding, an indicator of blood platelet problems. Regular liver tests are a must. Do not crush or chew tablets. Starting with a very small dose and titrating up slowly can often help patients avoid even the common side effects. The related drug Depakote has recently been linked to polycystic ovaries in female patients. The symptoms of this problem include irregular periods and unexplained weight gain.

Depakote, Depakote Sprinkles

Generic name: divalproex sodium (valproic acid plus sodium valproate)

Use: Seizure disorders, bipolar disorders, migraine, panic disorder, rages/aggression.

Action, if known: Antispasmodic. Increases the levels of gamma-aminobutyric acid (GABA) in the brain, and increases its absorption. Also stabilizes brain membranes.

Side effects: Nausea, sedation (this usually passes after a few days), depression, psychosis, aggression, hyperactivity, changes in blood platelet function, hair loss.

Known interaction hazards: Do not take with milk, and do not use charcoal tablets when taking Depakote. Be careful with alcohol, and with any medication that has a tranquilizing or depressant effect. Side effects may increase if you use anticoagulants, including aspirin, non-steroidal anti-inflammatory drugs, erythromycin, chlorpromazine, cimetadine, or felbamate.

Tips: Watch out for increased bruising or bleeding, an indicator of blood platelet problems. Regular liver tests are a must. Therapeutic level tests can be misleading with Depakote: actual therapeutic levels may be higher (or perhaps lower) than published charts indicate. Do not crush or chew tablets. Starting with a very small dose and titrating it up slowly can often help patients avoid even the common side effects. For adults, hair loss can be avoided by taking 50 mg of zinc daily; some patients also take .025 mg of selenium to boost zinc's effect. Talk to your doctor about appropriate doses for your child's age and weight. Depakote has recently been linked to polycystic ovaries in female patients. The symptoms of this problem include irregular periods and unexplained weight gain.

Lithium (Eskalith, Lithane, Lithobid, Lithonate, Lithotabs)

Generic name: lithium carbonate, lithium citrate

Use: Bipolar disorders, mood regulation, manic psychosis, PMS, eating disorders, thyroid problems, aggression.

Action, if known: Regulates circuits within the brain, possibly by affecting the enzyme inositol monophosphatase. Phosphoinositide signals are believed to be important for controlling the body's circadian rhythms.

Side effects: Hand tremor, excessive thirst and urination, nausea (this should pass), diarrhea, blurred vision. Any of these side effects occurring over a long period of time can be a sign of toxicity. Call your doctor if they persist.

Known interaction hazards: Potentiates neuroleptics; danger of encephalopathic syndrome. Counteracted by acetazolamide and by theophylline drugs, such as those used for allergies or asthma.

Tips: Before starting lithium, have kidney function, thyroid, blood salts, and blood cell counts checked. Lithium users must have heart function, kidney function, thyroid function, and therapeutic level monitored regularly. Lithium can be toxic in doses that are not much higher than the therapeutic dose. If you are allergic to tartrazine dyes, ask your pharmacist if these are used in your lithium product. If side effects are a problem, the slow-release Lithobid version may be more tolerable. People who have diabetes or a family history of diabetes should be very careful with lithium, which may affect the pancreas.

Neurontin

Generic name: gabapentin

Use: Seizure disorders, especially those that do not respond to other drugs, anxiety, panic, bipolar disorders, rage/aggression.

Action, if known: Antispasmodic. Appears to act by binding a specific protein found only on neurons in the CNS. May increase the GABA content of some brain regions.

Side effects: Blurred vision, dizziness, clumsiness, drowsiness, swaying, eye-rolling.

Known interaction hazards: Alcohol and all other CNS depressants, including tranquilizers, OTC medications for colds and allergies, OTC sleep aids, anesthetics, and narcotics. Antacids may counteract the effects of Neurontin.

Tips: Titrate dose very slowly to avoid side effects. People with kidney disease should be carefully monitored while taking Neurontin. Corn is used as a filler in the usual formulation of this drug, causing allergic reactions in some. Recent parent reports indicate that Neurontin can cause mania in some patients, especially younger patients. This can be offset by adding another medication, or by changing the dose of Neurontin or other medications used with it. Others report that Neurontin made their psoriasis worse. A new drug under development called Pregabolin is based on Neurontin, but with fewer side effects.

Tegretol

Generic name: carmazepine

Use: Seizure disorders, nerve pain, bipolar disorders, rage/aggression, aid to drug withdrawal, restless leg syndrome, Sydenham's chorea, and similar disorders in children.

Action, if known: Antispasmodic. Appears to work by reducing polysynaptic responses, and has other as yet unknown effects.

Side effects: Sleepiness, dizziness, nausea, unusual moods or behavior, headache, water retention. May cause low white blood cell count. Call your doctor right away if you have flu-like symptoms or other unusual reactions while taking this drug.

Known interaction hazards: Never take with an MAOI (MAO, or monoamine oxidase inhibitor). Tegretol is often used in combination with other antispasmodics or lithium, but the dose of Tegretol and drugs used with it must be very carefully adjusted. Tegretol is potentiated by numerous prescription and OTC medications, including many antibiotics, antidepressants, and cimetadine. It also counteracts or changes the effect of many drugs, including Haldol, theophyllin, and acetaminophen. Because these interactions can be very serious, discuss all medications you take—including all OTC remedies—with your doctor before beginning to use Tegretol.

Tips: You should have a white blood cell count done before taking Tegretol, and be monitored thereafter. Do not take the drug if you have a history of bone marrow depression. Tegretol can be fatal at fairly low doses, so all patients taking this drug should be carefully monitored, particularly since it interacts with so many other medications.

• • • • •

Because of the potential for side effects, the last group of choices for treating rage behaviors are the neuroleptics. These drugs are listed in the section "Medications for tics," later in this chapter.

Anti-anxiety medications

Anxiety is an important component of OCD itself, and many people with OCD also suffer from other anxiety disorders, such as panic attacks. These symptoms are often relieved by taking an SSRI, but in more severe cases, the patient may be prescribed an anti-anxiety medication.

Depending on the person's needs, these medications may be taken daily or on an "as-needed" basis. Most of them do have a potential for addiction and abuse, so parents will want to be careful about their use and storage. Some are not FDA-approved for use by children, and generally speaking, their use should be avoided unless other strategies are ineffective. Anti-anxiety medications include the following.

Ativan

Generic name: lorazepam

Use: Anti-anxiety, panic disorder, PMS, irritable bowel syndrome. May also be used in acute mania to induce sleep and stabilize the patient; some doctors prefer Ativan to the neuroleptics commonly used for this purpose.

Action, if known: Benzodiazepine. Slows CNS activity.

Side effects: Sleepiness (this usually passes after a week), lethargy, confusion, headache, slurred speech, tremor. Addictive; withdrawal may be difficult.

Known interaction hazards: Alcohol, all tranquilizers (including OTC sleep aids), narcotics, MAOIs, antihistamines (including OTC allergy and cold remedies), and antidepressants. Potentiated by cimetadine, SSRIs, Depakene, disulfiram, isoniazid, ketoconazole, metoprolol, probenecid, propoxyphene, propranalol, rifampin, and oral contraceptives. Potentiates digoxin and phenytoin, and decreases the effect of L-dopa.

Tips: If you smoke, take theophylline, or use antacids, it may be less effective.

BuSpar

Generic name: buspirone

Use: Anxiety, decreasing emotional lability or mood swings, ADHD, PMS.

Action, if known: Non-benzodiazepine tranquilizer. Enhances serotonin transmission, blocks dopamine receptors, increases metabolism of norepinephrine in the brain.

Side effects: Dizziness, nausea, headache, fatigue, jitteriness, tremor, sore muscles, heart palpitations, sweating, possible liver or kidney damage, tardive dyskensia-like movements or tics.

Known interaction hazards: Do not use with MAOIs. Potentiates Haldol and possibly other neuroleptics. Can cause liver inflammation when used with Desyrel. May have other side effects when used with antidepressants or similar drugs. Prolongs the effectiveness of SSRIs, and is sometimes prescribed for this specific purpose.

Tips: Side effects are a frequent problem with BuSpar, especially when taken in combination with other medications, including OTC remedies. The BuSpar patch may be better tolerated and smoother-acting than the pill, especially for treatment of ADHD or mood swings. It has been tested with good results in children for treatment of ADHD without the same "rebound" effect as Ritalin, and for treating anxiety and irritability in children with neurological disorders. Many physicians like to prescribe BuSpar because it doesn't carry the addiction risk of the benzodiazepines.

Centrax

Generic name: prazepam

Use: Anti-anxiety, muscle spasm, seizures, panic disorder, irritable bowel syndrome.

Action, if known: Benzodiazepine. Slows CNS activity.

Side effects: Sleepiness (this usually passes after a week), lethargy, confusion, headache, slurred speech, tremor. Addictive; withdrawal may be difficult.

Known interaction hazards: Alcohol, all tranquilizers (including OTC sleep aids), narcotics, MAOIs, antihistamines (including OTC allergy and cold remedies), antidepressants. Potentiated by cimetadine, SSRIs, Depakene, disulfiram, isoniazid, ketoconazole, metoprolol, probenecid, propoxyphene, propranalol, rifampin, and oral contraceptives. Potentiates digoxin and phenytoin, and decreases the effect of L-dopa.

Tips: Many people should not take Centrax, including people with severe depression, lung disease, liver or kidney disease, sleep apnea, alcoholism, or psychosis. Intended for short-term use. If you smoke, take theophylline drugs, or use antacids, Centrax may be less effective.

Effexor, Effexor XR

Generic name: venlafaxine

Use: Depression, especially depression with anxiety.

Action, if known: Antidepressant. Limits absorption of at least three neurotransmitters: serotonin, norepinephrine, and dopamine.

Side effects: Blurred vision, sedation, dry mouth, dizziness, tremor, nausea, sexual dysfunction, insomnia. Anecdotal evidence indicates that it may cause mood swings in people with diagnosed or undiagnosed bipolar disorders.

Known interaction hazards: Do not take with MAOIs.

Tips: Take with food.

Klonopin

Generic name: clonazepam

Use: Seizure disorders, panic attacks, anxiety, restless leg syndrome, mania.

Action, if known: Benzodiazepine tranquilizer with an antispasmodic action.

Side effects: Sleepiness, lethargy, confusion, headache, slurred speech, tremor. Addictive; withdrawal may be difficult.

Known interaction hazards: Avoid CNS depressants, including alcohol, narcotics, and other tranquilizers (including OTC sleep aids). Also potentiated by antihistamines, MAOIs, tricyclic antidepressants like Anafranil, oral contraceptives, other seizure medications, and possibly SSRIs. Do not take with valproic acid. Phenobarbital and phenytoin work against Klonopin. Its effectiveness may also be decreased by smoking and antacids. Klonopin may work against digoxin and levodopa.

Tips: Klonopin usually works best when taken between meals, but you can take it with food if it causes nausea on an empty stomach.

Librium

Generic name: chlordiazepoxide

Use: Anxiety, panic attacks, irritable bowel syndrome.

Action, if known: Benzodiazepine. Slows CNS activity.

Side effects: Sedation (this should pass), depression, stupor, headache, tremor, dry mouth, sexual dysfunction. Addictive; withdrawal may be difficult.

Known interaction hazards: Avoid other CNS depressants, including alcohol, narcotics, tranquilizers (including OTC sleep aids), MAOIs, antidepressants, and both prescription and OTC antihistamines. Do not take with antacids. Potentiates digoxin and phenytoin, and reduces the potency of L-dopa.

Tips: Many people should not take Librium, including people with severe depression, lung disease, liver or kidney disease, sleep apnea, alcoholism, or psychosis. Intended for short-term use. Smoking may reduce the effectiveness of Librium.

Serax

Generic name: oxazepam

Use: Anxiety, muscle spasm, seizures, panic disorder, irritable bowel syndrome.

Action, if known: Benzodiazepine tranquilizer. Slows CNS activity.

Side effects: Sleepiness (this usually passes after a week), lethargy, confusion, headache, slurred speech, tremor. Addictive; withdrawal may be difficult.

Known interaction hazards: Alcohol, all tranquilizers (including OTC sleep aids), narcotics, MAOIs, antihistamines (including OTC allergy and cold remedies), antidepressants. Potentiated by cimetadine, disulfiram, SSRIs, Depakene, isoniazid, ketoconazole, metoprolol, probenecid, propoxyphene, propranalol, rifampin, and oral contraceptives. Potentiates digoxin and phenytoin, and decreases the effect of L-dopa.

Tips: Many people should not take Serax, including people with severe depression, lung disease, liver or kidney disease, sleep apnea, alcoholism, or psychosis. Intended for short-term use. If you smoke, take theophylline drugs, or use antacids, Serax may be less effective.

Tranxene

Generic name: clorazepate

Use: Anxiety, panic disorder, irritable bowel syndrome.

Action, if known: Benzodiazepine tranquilizer. Slows CNS activity.

Side effects: Drowsiness (this should pass), confusion, tremor, dizziness, depression. Addiction danger; withdrawal may be uncomfortable.

Known interaction hazards: Do not take with antacids. Alcohol and other CNS depressants, tranquilizers (including OTC sleep aids), narcotics, barbiturates, MAOIs, antihistamines (including cold and allergy medications), and antidepressants all interact negatively with Tranxene. This drug potentiates digoxin and phenytoin. Potentiated by cimetadine, disulfiram, fluoxetine, isoniazid, ketoconazole, metoprolol, probenecid, propoxyphene, propranolol, rifampin, and Depakote/Depakene.

Tips: You should not take Tranxene if you have lung, liver, or kidney disease, psychosis, or depression. Intended for short-term use. Smoking may interfere with the action of Tranxene.

Valium

Generic name: diazepam

Use: Anxiety, muscle spasm, seizures, panic disorder, irritable bowel syndrome.

Action, if known: Benzodiazepine tranquilizer. Slows CNS activity.

Side effects: Sleepiness (this usually passes after a week), lethargy, confusion, headache, slurred speech, tremor. Addictive; withdrawal may be difficult.

Known interaction hazards: Alcohol, all tranquilizers (including OTC sleep aids), narcotics, MAOIs, antihistamines (including OTC allergy and cold remedies), antidepressants. Potentiated by cimetadine, SSRIs, Depakote/Depakene, disulfiram, isoniazid, ketoconazole, metoprolol, probenecid, propoxyphene, propranalol, rifampin, and oral contraceptives. Potentiates digoxin and phenytoin, and decreases the effect of L-dopa.

Tips: Many people should not take Valium, including people with severe depression, lung disease, liver or kidney disease, sleep apnea, alcoholism, or psychosis. Intended for short-term use. If you smoke, take theophylline drugs, or use antacids, Valium may be less effective.

Xanax

Generic name: alprazolam

Use: Anti-anxiety, panic disorder, PMS, irritable bowel syndrome.

Action, if known: Benzodiazepine tranquilizer. Slows CNS activity.

Side effects: Sleepiness (this usually passes after a week), lethargy, confusion, headache, slurred speech, tremor. Addictive; withdrawal may be difficult.

Known interaction hazards: Do not use with alcohol, tranquilizers of any kind (including over-the-counter sleep aids), MAOIs, antihistamines (including OTC allergy and cold medicines), or antidepressants, unless under strict medical supervision.

Tips: Many people should not take Xanax, including people with severe depression, sleep apnea, liver or kidney disease, lung disease, alcoholism, or psychosis.

Medications for tics

Many people with OCD also have tic disorders, including Tourette's syndrome. Tics do not respond to cognitive behavioral therapy, but medicating for tics should be done only when they bother the patient or cause physical discomfort.

In other cases, such as when a tic is distracting others in the classroom, it's best to use non-medication strategies. For example, a child with an occasional vocal tic could be given a special hall pass that allows him to leave the room in advance of an outburst. Children with tics should not be punished for their involuntary behaviors. They can learn coping strategies, including methods for disguising, camouflaging, and delaying tics, that give them increased power over the disorder. It's also important to educate their teachers, fellow students, and school administrators to prevent teasing and inappropriate reactions.

When medication is needed, many doctors first try Catapres or Tenex (see the section "Medications for OCD-linked rage," earlier in this chapter).

If these milder medications are not helpful, the next step may be one of the atypical neuroleptics. These include the following medications.

Clozaril

Generic name: clozapine

Use: Schizophrenia.

Action, if known: Atypical neuroleptic. Works against the hormone acetylcholine, other actions unknown.

Side effects: Sedation, fever (this usually passes), changes in blood pressure or heartbeat, overproduction of saliva, tremor. Major dangers include agranulocytosis (a serious blood condition), seizures, neuroleptic malignant syndrome (NMS), tardive dyskinesia.

Known interaction hazards: Alcohol, CNS system depressants, drugs for high blood pressure, tricyclic antidepressants, and similar drugs should be avoided or used with caution. Danger of NMS increases when used with lithium.

Tips: Weekly blood tests are required. Women, people with low white blood-cell counts, and some people of Ashkenazi Jewish descent have a higher risk of agranulocytosis when taking this drug. People with heart disease, glaucoma, prostate trouble, or liver or kidney disease should be monitored carefully. Smoking cigarettes can affect how quickly your body uses Clozaril.

Risperdal

Generic name: risperidone

Use: Psychosis, schizophrenia, rage/aggression.

Action, if known: Atypical neuroleptic. Affects serotonin and dopamine, raises level of the hormone prolactin.

Side effects: Sedation, headache, runny nose, anxiety, insomnia. Weight gain, especially in children. Danger of neuroleptic malignant syndrome (NMS), tardive dyskinesia.

Known interaction hazards: Decreases action of L-dopa. Interacts with carbamazepine and clozapine. May potentiate, or be potentiated by, SSRIs.

Tips: You should have an EKG before starting Risperdal, and regular heart monitoring while taking it. In some patients, Risperdal (and possibly other atypical neuroleptics) may increase obsessive-compulsive symptoms.

Seroquel

Generic name: quetiapine

Use: Psychosis, rage/aggression.

Action, if known: Atypical neuroleptic. Believed to increase availability of serotonin and dopamine at specific receptors in the brain.

Side effects: Drowsiness, dizziness, sedation, agitation, nausea, changes in appetite, weight gain or loss, sexual dysfunction. Lowers seizure threshold. Danger of neuroleptic malignant syndrome (NMS), extrapyramidal side effects, and tardive dyskinesia.

Known interaction hazards: Avoid alcohol and all CNS depressants, including tranquilizers, sedatives, OTC sleep aids, and narcotics. Potentiated to a high degree by phenytoin. May interfere with the effects of drugs for high blood pressure. May be potentiated by other drugs, including ketoconazole, erythromycin, clarithromycin, diltiazem, verapamil, and nefazodone.

Tips: Avoid extreme heat while taking this drug. People with liver or kidney problems, heart disease, thyroid problems, or low blood pressure should be monitored while taking Seroquel.

Zeldox

Generic name: ziprasidone

Use: Psychosis, rage/aggression.

Action, if known: Atypical neuroleptic.

Side effects: Drowsiness, dizziness, nausea, lightheadedness.

Known interaction hazards: Not yet known, but probably similar to those of other atypical neuroleptics.

Tips: Regular heart monitoring is advised when taking Zeldox. This is a very new drug that is not yet approved for use in the US. According to some doctors, this medication is less likely to cause rapid weight gain than the other atypical neuroleptics.

Zyprexa

Generic name: olanzapine

Use: Psychosis, rage/aggression, tics; also used in cases of hard-to-treat OCD, depression (usually with an antidepressant), or bipolar disorders (usually with a mood stabilizer).

Action, if known: Atypical neuroleptic. Blocks uptake of dopamine and serotonin at certain receptors, and may have other actions.

Side effects: Headache, agitation, dry mouth, hostility, disinhibition, insomnia, slurred speech, neuroleptic malignant syndrome (NMS), tardive dyskinesia, dizziness, seizures.

Known interaction hazards: Alcohol. Potentiated by carbamazepine; potentiates medications for high blood pressure (such as clonidine and Tenex).

Tips: Avoid extreme heat. If you smoke, you may need to take Zyprexa more frequently.

• • • • •

If the atypical neuroleptics do not work and the tics are very difficult for the child to cope with, doctors may try one of the older neuroleptics, despite their high potential for side effects. This group of drugs includes the following medications.

Etrafon, Trilafon, Triavil

Generic name: amitriptyline/perphenazine (Trilafon includes perphenazine only)

Use: Depression, panic disorder, chronic pain, eating disorders, severe PMS.

Action, if known: Neuroleptic with qualities similar to those of a tricyclic antidepressant. Blocks norepinephrine and serotonin use, works against the hormone acetylcholine.

Side effects: Sedation, tremor, seizures, dry mouth, light sensitivity, mood swings in people with bipolar disorders. Danger of tardive dyskinesia, extrapyramidal side effects, neuroleptic malignant syndrome.

Known interaction hazards: Alcohol, MAOIs, blood pressure medications (including clonidine and Tenex), and thyroid medication. Potentiated by estrogen, bicarbonate of soda (as in Alka-Seltzer and other OTC remedies), acetazolamide, procainamide, and quinidine. Cimetadine, methylphenidate, Thorazine and similar drugs, oral contraceptives, nicotine (including cigarettes), charcoal tablets, and estrogen may interfere with Etrafon's action in the body.

Tips: Avoid extreme heat when taking this drug. Not recommended for use in people with severe depression, lung disease, severe asthma, or liver disease. Take with food if upset stomach occurs.

Haldol, Haldol Decanoate

Generic name: haloperidol

Use: Psychosis, tics/Tourette's syndrome, schizophrenia.

Action, if known: Affects the hypothalamus gland in the brain, which in turn affects metabolism, body temperature, alertness, muscle tone, and hormone production.

Side effects: Lowers seizure threshold. Sedation, jaundice (this should pass), anemia, changes in blood pressure or heartbeat, dizziness.

Known interaction hazards: Avoid alcohol and other CNS depressants, narcotics, and tranquilizers (including OTC sleep aids). Potentiated by lithium, causing a greater risk of encephalopathic syndrome. Potentiates tricyclic antidepressants. Anticholinergic medications may make Haldol less effective. Risk of tardive dyskinesia.

Tips: Do not take if you have low blood pressure, Parkinson's disease, or diseases of the blood, kidneys, or liver.

Loxipax, Loxitane

Generic name: loxapine

Use: Psychosis.

Action, if known: Blocks or changes the use of dopamine in several areas of the brain.

Side effects: May suppress the gag or cough reflex. Sedation, depression, light sensitivity, jaundice (this should pass), anemia, changes in blood pressure or heartbeat, dry mouth. Lowers the seizure threshold. Danger of tardive dyskinesia.

Known interaction hazards: Alcohol, any tranquilizer or CNS depressant (including OTC sleep aids), antacids, lithium, and tricyclic antidepressants.

Tips: The drugs Motipress and Motival contain both loxapine and the anti-anxiety medication nortriptyline.

Mellaril

Generic name: thioridazine hydrochloride

Use: Psychosis, depression with anxiety, aggression.

Action, if known: Phenothiazine neuroleptic. Affects the hypothalamus gland in the brain, which in turn affects metabolism, body temperature, alertness, muscle tone, and hormone production.

Side effects: May suppress the gag or cough reflex. Sedation, depression, light sensitivity, jaundice (this should pass), anemia, changes in blood pressure or heartbeat, dry mouth. Lowers the seizure threshold. Danger of tardive dyskinesia.

Known interaction hazards: Alcohol, any tranquilizer or CNS depressant (including OTC sleep aids), antacids, lithium, tricyclic antidepressants. Loses effectiveness when you eat or drink items containing caffeine.

Tips: Avoid extreme heat when taking Mellaril. Do not take if you have blood, liver, kidney, or heart disease, low blood pressure, or Parkinson's disease. Take with food or juice if upset stomach occurs.

Moban

Generic name: molindone

Use: Psychosis.

Action, if known: Moban is a neuroleptic.

Side effects: Drowsiness, sedation, depression, nausea, dry mouth. Risk of tardive dyskinesia.

Known interaction hazards: Alcohol and all other CNS depressants, tranquilizers (including OTC sleep aids), barbiturates, anesthetics, tricyclic antidepressants, and lithium. Moban may have negative interactions with many other medications, including other neuroleptics, Asendin, and Cylert.

Tips: People with liver disease or Parkinson's disease should not take Moban.

Navane

Generic name: thiothixene

Use: Psychosis.

Action, if known: Thiothixene neuroleptic. Affects the hypothalamus gland in the brain, which in turn affects metabolism, body temperature, alertness, muscle tone, and hormone production.

Side effects: Sedation, depression, light sensitivity, jaundice (this should pass), anemia, changes in blood pressure or heartbeat. Danger of tardive dyskinesia.

Known interaction hazards: Alcohol, any tranquilizer or CNS depressant (including OTC sleep aids), antacids, lithium, and tricyclic antidepressants. Do not combine with propranolol. Effect may be reduced by use of anticholinergic medications.

Tips: Avoid extreme heat when taking Navane. Do not take if you have blood, liver, kidney, or heart disease, low blood pressure, or Parkinson's disease. Take with food or juice if upset stomach occurs.

Orap

Generic name: diphenylbutylpiperdine, pimozide

Use: Psychosis, severe tics/Tourette's syndrome, schizophrenia.

Action, if known: Neuroleptic. Affects the amount and action of dopamine in the brain.

Side effects: Extrapyramidal side effects, such as restlessness and unusual movements. Risk of tardive dyskinesia, neuroleptic malignant syndrome (NMS).

Known interaction hazards: Alcohol, other CNS depressants, and tranquilizers (including OTC sleep aids). Taking other neuroleptics increases your risk for tardive dyskinesia, NMS and extrapyramidal side effects. Do not take antihistamines (including OTC cold and allergy remedies) or anticholinergic drugs. Taking tricyclic antidepressants and many other medications with heart effects can increase your risk for heart problems with Orap. Your doctor may need to adjust dosages of other medications you take, especially antiseizure drugs.

Tips: You should have an EKG before starting Orap, and regular heart monitoring while taking it. Orap is considered more risky than some other old-line neuroleptics, not to mention the atypical neuroleptics. Make sure you have exhausted your other options first.

Prolixin, Prolixin Decanoate

Generic name: fluphenazine

Use: Psychosis.

Action, if known: Phenothiazine neuroleptic. Affects the hypothalamus gland in the brain, which in turn affects metabolism, body temperature, alertness, muscle tone, and hormone production.

Side effects: May suppress the gag or cough reflex. Sedation, depression, light sensitivity, jaundice (this should pass), anemia, changes in blood pressure or heartbeat. Danger of tardive dyskinesia.

Known interaction hazards: Alcohol, any tranquilizer or CNS depressant (including OTC sleep aids), antacids, lithium, and tricyclic antidepressants. Loses effectiveness when you eat or drink items containing caffeine.

Tips: Avoid extreme heat when taking Prolixin. Do not take if you have blood, liver, kidney, or heart disease, low blood pressure, or Parkinson's disease. Take with food or juice if upset stomach occurs.

Serentil

Generic name: mesoridazine

Use: Psychosis.

Action, if known: Serentil is a neuroleptic.

Side effects: Drowsiness, dizziness, sedation, agitation, nausea, changes in appetite, weight gain or loss, sexual dysfunction. Lowers seizure threshold. Risk of tardive dyskinesia and extrapyramidal side effects.

Known interaction hazards: Avoid alcohol and all CNS depressants, including tranquilizers, sedatives, OTC sleep aids, and narcotics. Potentiates atropine, phosphorus insecticides, and quinidine.

Tips: Avoid extreme heat while taking this drug. Have regular blood tests and eye exams while taking Serentil. Not recommended for people with severe depression, bone marrow depression, liver or heart disease. Those with high blood pressure should be carefully monitored while taking Serentil.

Stelazine, Vesprin

Generic name: trifluoperazine

Action, if known: Phenothiazine neuroleptic. Affects the hypothalamus gland in the brain, which in turn affects metabolism, body temperature, alertness, muscle tone, and hormone production. Blocks dopamine receptors in the mesolimbic system, increasing turnover of dopamine.

Side effects: May suppress the gag or cough reflex. Sedation, depression, light sensitivity, jaundice (this should pass), anemia, changes in blood pressure or heartbeat. Danger of tardive dyskinesia.

Known interaction hazards: Alcohol, any tranquilizer or CNS depressant (including OTC sleep aids), antacids, lithium, and tricyclic antidepressants. Loses effectiveness when you eat or drink items containing caffeine.

Tips: Avoid extreme heat when taking Stelazine. You may want to supplement the drug with vitamin E, which may protect against tardive dyskinesia. Do not take if you have blood, liver, kidney, or heart disease, low blood pressure, or Parkinson's disease. If you have thyroid problems, use with extreme caution. Take with food or juice if upset stomach occurs.

Thorazine

Generic name: chlorpromazine

Use: Psychosis, schizophrenia.

Action, if known: Phenothiazine neuroleptic. Affects the hypothalamus gland in the brain, which in turn affects metabolism, body temperature, alertness, muscle tone, and hormone production. Interferes with the action of dopamine in the basal ganglia, mesolimbic area, and medulla. Anticholinergic.

Side effects: May suppress the gag or cough reflex. Sedation, depression, light sensitivity, jaundice (this should pass), anemia, changes in blood pressure or heartbeat, dry mouth. Lowers the seizure threshold. Danger of tardive dyskinesia.

Known interaction hazards: Alcohol, any tranquilizer or CNS depressant (including OTC sleep aids), antacids, lithium, and tricyclic antidepressants. Loses effectiveness when you eat or drink items containing caffeine.

Tips: Avoid extreme heat when taking Thorazine. Do not take if you have blood, liver, kidney, or heart disease, low blood pressure, Reye's syndrome, or Parkinson's disease. Take with food or juice if upset stomach occurs.

Strep-linked OCD

If your child has a sudden onset or exacerbation of OCD and/or tics, your doctor may want to consider the possibility of Pediatric Autoimmune Neuropsychiatric Disorders Associated with Streptococcal infections (PANDAS), especially if your child has a recently had a strep infection. A family history of rheumatic fever could also indicate a connection. PANDAS is a subtype of OCD related to an unusual reaction to infection with group A beta-hemolytic streptococcus bacteria. This type of strep is very common, causing strep throat and many childhood ear infections.

The strep bacteria itself is not the culprit in PANDAS—that honor goes to the strep antibodies produced by the patient's own immune system. These misguided antibodies go on the warpath not only against the strep bacteria, but also against the basal ganglia of the brain, causing inflammation that produces obsessions, compulsions, and tics.

The strep infection that started it all may have already cleared the body by the time symptoms become evident, so the usual throat swab test for strep may not be helpful. Also, in many children with PANDAS, the initial strep infection was asymptomatic (without the usual strep throat or ear infection symptoms). Instead, a PANDAS diagnosis relies on the presence of abnormally high numbers of strep antibodies coupled with OCD symptoms and/or tics.

The Antistreptolysin 0 (ASO) and Anti DNase B tests can be used to count strep antibodies. These are blood tests that return numbers called strep titres. Normal ASO results are 200 or below. An Anti DNase B result that is two or three times the normal amount would be cause for concern.

The simplest treatment for PANDAS is prophylactic antibiotics, usually amoxicillin or Augmentin (amoxicillin/clavulanate). The antibiotics are given to prevent reinfection with strep, not to treat PANDAS itself. If strep infection does not recur, the theory goes, neither will PANDAS symptoms.

Of course, taking antibiotics on a long-term basis is not without problems. It can make life-threatening infections more likely and harder to treat, and gastrointestinal problems tend to occur as antibiotics kill off the gut bacteria that aid us in digestion. The latter can be preserved and replenished through the use of "probiotics," such as yogurt with live cultures.

One treatment that attacks existing strep antibodies is intravenous gamma-globulin (IVIG). This substance can be given via an intravenous drip. Studies at the National Institutes of Mental Health (NIMH) have shown that IVIG is highly effective for treating PANDAS. It does not cure the disorder permanently, but it should end the current outbreak.

On the other hand, all IV procedures do have risks, particularly infection at the site of IV insertion. IVIG itself is a blood product derived from multiple donors, which means there is a remote possibility that those who receive it could also receive an unknown virus. It is screened for known bacteria and viruses, of course. IVIG is used to treat many medical conditions, and it is in short supply. That can make it hard to get and expensive. So far most of the patients who have gotten IVIG treatment for PANDAS have been enrolled in research trials.

Plasmapheresis is another option that is effective at removing strep antibodies from the blood. Plasmapheresis is similar to dialysis in that blood is removed, treated, and then returned to the patient. Like IVIG, plasmapheresis carries some minor dangers, is expensive, and currently is rarely available to patients with PANDAS outside of research settings.

Some physicians have also experimented with immunosuppression to treat PANDAS.

Dr. Susan Swedo's team at NIMH has designed a test for the presence of D8/17, a blood protein that may be a marker for susceptibility to PANDAS and rheumatic fever, but this test is not commercially available as of this writing. Interestingly, the D8/17 marker is also found in many people with autism.

OCD and other illness

So much of everyday illness—stomach troubles, headaches, and other aches and pains—is related to stress and anxiety, that it shouldn't surprise anyone that kids with OCD tend to be sick a lot. It's not strictly psychosomatic, either; stress and anxiety both suppress the immune system, leaving people more open to infection. The serotonin imbalance involved in OCD could be the cause of some stomach complaints and headaches. Hormonal imbalances in some patients add to the stew, as do loss of sleep and disordered eating habits.

When your kids drive you crazy with repeated health complaints, make sure that you listen to what they have to say. It's unlikely that they are suffering from yet another serious disease, but any symptom that causes pain and suffering deserves attention and care. It could be a somatic obsession, hypochondria, or amplification of minor aches and complaints due to OCD, in which case your child's psychiatrist should be able to offer advice. On the other hand, it could be something that deserves medical attention. If it's simply a normal health problem that you can treat at home, such as constipation or an upset stomach, remember to check over-the-counter medications with your doctor first.

It's entirely possible that infectious agents other than strep cause OCD in a fashion very similar to strep and PANDAS. The herpes viruses are possible culprits. It's well known that when these common viruses are contracted, they remain in the body, dormant until stress or another illness sets them off again. This viral family includes herpes simplex 1 (HHV-1, the cause of cold sores), herpes simplex 2 (HHV-2, the cause of genital herpes), herpes zoster (HHV-3, the cause of chickenpox and shingles), and a host of lesser-known cousins. Some of the human herpes viruses can infect the brain; others have been recently associated with the presence of autoantibodies to myelin basic protein (MBP), a type of brain tissue.[6] This is an area in which much research needs to be done.

In the meantime, if your child has a sudden onset or large-scale exacerbation of OCD symptoms, and he has recently had a herpes virus infection, you might want to ask your physician to do a serum antibody titre. If the results look serious, antiviral medication might be indicated.

Medical care for eating disorders

As discussed in Chapter 2, eating disorders and food-related symptoms are not uncommon in childhood OCD. Therapy and medication can help with milder symptoms, but actual eating disorders require special medical intervention.

This can be problematic because many eating disorders clinics are oriented toward a psychological model, in which development of these problems is believed to be solely a result of childhood abuse or family pathology. National organizations for people with OCD may be able to help you find a program that understands anorexia, bulimia, binge eating, and pica (compulsive consumption of non-food items) as manifestations of OCD, or your child's psychiatrist may be able to help an existing program tailor its services to fit your child.

When your child has a serious eating disorder, permanent injury to the heart, kidneys, liver, bowel, bones and teeth, and even death, are possibilities. Medically-based treatment programs start with a full physical assessment, with a particular focus on electrolyte levels. An imbalance in these chemicals (sodium, calcium, potassium, and magnesium) in the body's fluids can harm the heart. If an electrolyte imbalance is found, electrolyte solutions (and sometimes blood plasma, since electrolyte solutions administered intravenously dilute the blood and affect its ability to clot) may be administered orally or through an IV. If ulcers are found, treatment may include antibacterial medications to eradicate *H. pylori*, a bacteria that is usually part of the problem, as well as a special diet while the ulcer heals. For young women, dietary support—and sometimes hormone supplements—may be needed to address menstrual problems caused by malnutrition and/or over-exercising.

Next, a nutritionist is usually called in to work out a diet and exercise plan tailored for the patient. The plan may include vitamins to help rebuild the patient's health, special nutritional supplements, and foods carefully designed to provide maximum nutritional value. In a good treatment center, the meals should taste great to encourage patient compliance—this is something parents might want to check out for themselves.

Many patients with eating disorders are also compulsive about exercise, and there may be a temporary prohibition on workouts or certain types of physical activity while the body returns to health. Eventually a common-sense exercise plan can be designed to maintain health without going to extremes.

Psychiatric treatment for OCD, anxiety, depression, and any other mental health issues should be part of the picture once the patient is medically stable. Intensive counseling, including family counseling, is the norm for young patients. In programs geared toward patients for whom an eating disorder is primarily an OCD issue, counseling is usually geared toward first getting the patient to be a partner in her own treatment, and then ending her overvaluation of thinness and control of eating. It may include exposure and response prevention exercises built around food and eating. Patients can also learn about handling their own tendency toward eating disorders in counseling sessions. Counselors can teach strategies for healthy eating and self-monitoring techniques for catching signs of relapse, for example.

Occasional, minor pica does not usually require treatment, unless the material eaten is hazardous. Patients with pica occasionally turn out to have vitamin or mineral deficiencies, so a screen for these problems may be done. In some cases, doctors think these deficiencies may be the cause of pica; in other cases, ingesting unusual items, such as clay, may inhibit vitamin and mineral absorption. Special diets have proven useful in some cases, as have behavior modification techniques. Occasionally, people with pica do need gastrointestinal surgery. Those who eat their hair, for example, may end up having stomach problems caused by formation of a sort of human hairball, known medically as a bezoar.

Medications are often part of eating disorder treatment, including medications normally prescribed to treat OCD and, in some cases, medications to increase a disordered appetite or to treat health conditions that have occurred because of self-starvation, purging, or pica.

Hospitals and treatment centers

There are several situations in which a child with OCD may need to be hospitalized. They include:

- When the child is a danger to himself, either through suicide threats or attempts, or through self-injurious behavior.
- When the child is a danger to others because of aggressive, assaultive behavior or serious threats.
- When the child's behavior cannot be managed safely at home, even with the addition of medication and support services.
- When the child is suffering from severe medication reactions or unusual symptoms that are too difficult medically to handle at home.
- When a child with a seizure disorder in addition to OCD is experiencing severe and medication-resistant seizures.
- When a child with OCD also has an eating disorder that is not responding to traditional treatment.
- When a child with OCD complicated by substance abuse needs intense medical supervision during the detox process.

Of course, children with OCD may also fall victim to disease or injury that's not psychiatric in nature. When these problems require hospitalization, parents should confer with the staff to ensure that their child's diagnosis and current medical treatments are thoroughly understood, and that his needs for medication management, therapy, and special education services can be met in the hospital while he recovers.

If your child is injured due to a suicide attempt, SIB, or drug overdose, go directly to the nearest emergency room. Call your psychiatrist to let him know what's going on, and then stay with your child. Her behaviors may be puzzling to workers in the ER. Sometimes patients who come in with self-inflicted injuries are denigrated or forced to wait longer than others by poorly-educated medical personnel. The presence of a parent who can advocate for proper care should help.

You may have to wait a long time to see someone in the ER, especially if it's a busy weekend night or if most personnel are attending to car accident victims and other life-or-death emergencies. Probably the first person you'll see is an intake worker, who will get your child's identifying and health insurance information. If you need help to control your child in the ER, tell the intake worker or the first security guard you see. Should your child need to be restrained, stay with him to let him know that you'll be there to ensure his safety.

After intake, you should see a triage nurse, who's specially trained to assess the severity of cases presenting at the ER. Let this person know what your greatest concerns are, especially if you feel that your child could be a danger to himself or others. At this point a decision will be made about whether to admit your child immediately.

When you go to the ER, bring any medications, supplements, and herbal remedies that your child uses. If you know or suspect that your child has recently used any illegal drugs or alcohol, let the emergency room personnel know right away. These things affect what medical intervention they can safely use. You may also want to bring a book your child enjoys, a Walkman with tapes of soothing music, some toys, and a change of clothes in case your child needs to be admitted overnight (or longer). If there's no time to collect these items, don't worry—you can have someone else deliver them to you later when the situation stabilizes at the hospital.

Once your child has been admitted to the ER, you'll see a doctor and/or nurses. They may take your child's blood pressure; check his heartbeat; take blood or urine samples to test for drugs, alcohol, infection, medication blood levels, or other factors; and give emergency medical treatment, including medication. Make sure you understand what the effects of any medications will be, especially if your child will be released into your care immediately after treatment, rather than being held for observation.

For mental health crises that do not involve an immediate risk to life, it helps to have a plan worked out in advance. The best place to start is, of course, your child's psychiatrist. Call and ask for an emergency evaluation. If it is after hours or your doctor is unavailable, call your primary care provider, general practitioner, or HMO and ask for an immediate referral. In some cases you may need to take your child to the ER for safety's sake until a doctor can arrive to evaluate your child.

If you reach your doctor, he should make time to see your child immediately if the situation warrants it. If you think you'll need help getting your child to his office, say so—he may be able to send a mental health aide or other staff member to your assistance. If this kind of help is not available through his office, ask your spouse, other relatives, friends, neighbors, or even the police for help. In some areas your county or provincial mental health department may be able to send someone out. If your child is physically difficult to control or at risk for self-harm, the momentary embarrassment you may feel from asking for help will rapidly be overshadowed by the need to ensure her safety.

Some larger cities have a separate "ER alternative" for mental health emergencies. This is a type of facility that should be available to all people with mental illness. The regular ER's parade of accident victims, gruesome injuries, screams, and high drama can be a real horror show for someone suffering from mental distress.

In a mental health triage center, trained personnel are on staff 24 hours a day to deal with crisis situations. Psychiatrists, appropriate medications, and security measures are on hand to meet your needs. Whenever possible, the environment is carefully constructed to be as peaceful, quiet and non-threatening as possible—just the kind of place you would want to be if you were in emotional pain. There may be a play area for younger children.

Usually a triage specialist will meet with you within just a few minutes. As in the ER, the triage nurse will assess your child's condition and start the process of obtaining treatment. Vital sign checks, blood and urine samples, and interviews with the patient are often performed quickly. You may also be interviewed, with your child or separately.

Whether you take your child to your psychiatrist's office, the ER, or a mental health triage center, the criteria for hospital admission will be largely the same. If the patient can be stabilized right there, he may be sent home with you. He may be held for overnight observation, or he may be admitted for short- or long-term treatment.

Parents with HMOs or managed care plans may be required to jump through some hoops to get their child admitted. You will probably need to emphasize, and perhaps even exaggerate, the problems that have culminated in the current emergency. Many parents have reported that it's extremely hard to get their child admitted, even when he is a suicide risk or when the family is in danger from his violent actions. Others note that some facilities release their children far too early, often due less to positive treatment outcomes than to negative news from the family's insurance company.

Hospitals: The good stuff

There are many different types of hospitals for psychiatric care. Most young patients will be admitted to a special psychiatric wing of a local hospital. These adolescent mental health units are usually locked wards, both to protect the patients and prevent escape. They are designed mostly for short-term care, holding patients for observation for a few days or weeks.

Patients in need of long-term hospitalization are usually sent to a stand-alone mental facility. This may be a private facility, a therapeutic residential care facility that specializes in treating mentally ill or emotionally disturbed youth, or a public mental hospital. Generally speaking, public mental hospitals in the US get only the most difficult-to-treat cases, along with uninsured patients. This is not necessarily the case elsewhere in the world, where publicly funded mental health care is available to all citizens.

The type of facility matters far less than the degree to which its program is appropriate for your child. Facilities for children and teens need to have a strong education program to prevent patients from slipping too far behind in school. The staff should be medically savvy, knowledgeable about the latest advances in treatment, and have therapy options that are appropriate for your child's age and needs. For example, facilities that accept very young children should have play therapists on staff, and programs for older children and teens should have considerable resources for treating comorbid drug and alcohol abuse along with psychiatric problems. They should be ready and willing to work closely with parents and other outside helpers. Cleanliness and basic safety are important issues too, as is human decency and kindness.

A lot of the time you have to go with your gut instinct. If the staff members you meet appear to be well trained, competent, and gentle with young people in their care, that's a good sign, as is the presence of a sense of humor and a genuine caring for their patients.

If you have time, talk to your local NAMI chapter or another advocacy group to get other peoples' opinions about the facilities you are considering. If your child is difficult to treat with the usual medications and therapies, you may want to consider a research-oriented hospital, up to and including the special facilities available at the National Institutes of Health in Bethesda, Maryland.

Parents are strongly urged to personally evaluate child and adolescent inpatient psychiatric facilities before their child is in crisis. Programs vary greatly, as does expertise with OCD. Talk to the head of the facility about the typical treatment program for children with your son or daughter's specific diagnosis. Also ask about how you can be part of their program, and how it will involve your child's regular psychiatrist, therapist, outside mental health providers, such as a county social worker, and school personnel.

When your child is in a high-quality hospital or residential care facility, you should feel reasonably comfortable with the care she receives. The environment should be not unlike any other kind of hospital, although it will probably be less sterile and featureless than some. The food may be a drag, as hospital food usually is. Your child will probably chafe at some of the rules, too. Many children's psychiatric units have very strict regulations about appearance, smoking, language, and activities. Teens are very likely to resent being told that they can't wear their favorite heavy metal T-shirt, or that they must hand over jewelry upon admittance. Let them know that these appearance issues are the hospital's thing, not yours, and that they're usually there to protect more sensitive patients from being offended or harmed.

Sarah, mother of 16-year-old Lili, tells her tale:

> *Lili hated her stay in the hospital. They took away her clothes, jewelry, cigarettes, and makeup, and she complained constantly about the rules, the staff, and the food. Only certain types of innocuous pop music were allowed, and she felt that far too much time was occupied with "art therapy" and craft projects.*

She had some learning experiences there too. The youngest child was a psychotic boy about 12 years old who had set someone on fire. Another girl had never come down from an acid trip and walked around asking everyone strange questions. I think one thing that convinced her to try medication was not wanting to be as ill as these kids. Other teens in the hospital were very much like her. One of the girls has remained a friend, which the hospital discouraged. They have both made a good recovery, and I think the bond they forged in the hospital may have helped.

From my point of view, the only benefit was that she was safe when we had been worried about suicide. She was misdiagnosed, mismedicated, and released before this could be discovered because our insurance company refused to pay. It ended up costing us over $7,000 for six days. We are still paying it off three years later.

Ask how the staff deals with infractions of the rules. The regulations may be enforced punitively (not a good thing) or with an effective reward system. Many hospitals use a token economy to reinforce positive behavior on the ward.

When your child is first admitted to a hospital or residential program, you may not be able to see her for a period of time, possibly based on her behavior on the ward. You should be able to meet with the staff during this period, however, and may start planning her treatment and after-care program. Once you do get to visit, be prepared for some ugly words, especially if she was admitted against her will. This oppositional behavior seems to be a part of the adjustment process, and it should pass.

Alternatively, you may be shocked to see your child looking "drugged up." Be sure that you discuss your concerns with the staff, and that any medications given are to treat the condition, not to simply control the patient's behavior. If your child still seems to be in a haze after the first few days, he may be overmedicated. This should be addressed. Ask what medications are being used, at what doses, and talk to your child's regular psychiatrist about them.

If your child is in the hospital for a long time or has been admitted before, she will probably adjust to the routine quite well. You may even find that your visits are less of a special treat than they were at first, as your child eagerly waits to go back to playing or chatting with the other kids. This can be disconcerting for parents, but be assured that regular visits from you are essential to your child's well-being. . .even if she doesn't act like it.

One thing that usually isn't a great idea is visits from your child's friends. Most mental health facilities do not allow these for underage patients, but if yours does, make sure your child and her friends are supervised and that you have control over which friends are allowed in. Supportive friends are the best thing in the world for a child suffering from mental illness. Friends who encourage your child to blame you for his problems, leave the facility, or refuse medication are not. "Friends" who try to sneak in drugs or alcohol for your child are even worse. If you suspect this may be happening, contact the staff immediately.

Your child may be disturbed or frightened by the behavior of some other patients. Most children's psychiatric facilities care for patients with a wide variety of conditions, ranging from eating disorders to active psychosis to neurological problems, such as autism or Tourette's syndrome. Some children will probably be very, very ill. Others will be well on their way to recovery. When you visit, talk to your child about anything he may have seen or heard that bothers him. He may feel uncomfortable bringing up these concerns in group or individual therapy sessions. Information about other mental illnesses or neurological disorders should be able to help him better understand what his fellow patients may be experiencing.

A good hospital is probably the safest possible place for your child to be while in a mental or other type of health crisis. Medication reactions can be carefully observed, therapy can be delivered on a daily basis, and professionals can help families rally around their child's treatment and recovery plan.

Hospitals: The scary stuff

Many of our images of mental hospitals come from old movies like *The Snake Pit*, depictions of past years' horrors in films like *Frances* (the story of actress Frances Farmer), or books by people who suffered in horrid institutions. Today, there are many good hospital programs, and there are still some that verge on the criminal. Danger signs include frequent use of physical restraints and isolation rooms to control "dangerous" patients, a reliance on psychoanalysis as the primary cure for major mental illnesses, lack of knowledge about the most current medications, and poor relationships with family members, schools, and outside care providers.

It appears that some facilities working with young patients still blame parents for their child's mental illness. This attitude can prevent patients from getting proper treatment, and it drives young patients away from the people they need most—those charged with the responsibility to care for them when they leave the hospital.

There's no reason for parents to tolerate hostility from administrators or staff. Of course, none of us are perfect in how we've raised our children, and there are many things we can learn and do to help them more. But suggestions for change within the family can only be listened to in an atmosphere of mutual assistance, in which parents are seen as the greatest source of information, and the greatest resource for helping their child to continue his recovery outside of residential care.

If the facility your child is in can't seem to change its attitude, do what you can to change her location.

Certain treatments used in mental hospitals have gained notoriety. These include electroshock therapy, insulin shock therapy, wet sheet packs, aversives, restraints, and isolation. Any program that relies heavily on these is substandard and should be avoided at all costs. None of these treatments are recommended for use with patients who have OCD.

Debbie, mother of 11-year-old Kristen, had a positive hospital experience:

> *Kristen was hospitalized when she was 10 years old. She was hospitalized for evaluation, and also because her psychiatrist wanted her under the supervision of a doctor while he was trying different medications on her. She had gotten to the point where we could not get her out of the house, and she was having panic attacks about twelve times a day. She was very depressed and was trying to harm herself also.*
>
> *It was very hard on Kristen and myself for her to be in the hospital. But it was helpful because we did find a good combination of medication for her, and they did do family counseling at the time, which was good for the whole family. We like to think of it as a learning experience.*

Growing and changing

No matter what medical care you choose for your child, her needs will change as she gets older and larger. A medication that works at age 12 may not be the best choice when she is 18. As your child becomes a teenager, and especially as she nears adulthood, involve her ever more closely in managing her own medical care. Provide her with accurate information, access to private consultation with her psychiatrist and other professionals, and your support for making informed decisions.

By choosing to treat your child's OCD early, you have made an important step toward easing this illness' impact on her adult life. If she's ready to handle self-care when the time comes, your job will be done.

CHAPTER 6

Other Interventions

BECAUSE OCD IS A NEUROLOGICAL ILLNESS, it has physical roots and symptoms. PANDAS research is uncovering treatments that get to the medical roots of OCD. In the meantime, some patients have also found vitamins or supplements useful, often as an adjunct to medication. This chapter will describe the various approaches available, with special attention to the needs of children and adolescents.

Holistic/alternative treatment systems

In the US, at least one out of three patients relies on "alternative medicine" for some ailments. While there is no secret natural cure for OCD, the holistic approach to patient care used by good alternative medicine practitioners often helps patients maintain optimal general health through adequate diet, stress reduction, and vitamin, mineral, or herbal supplements, if needed. Brief descriptions of the most common alternative medicine systems follow.

Acupuncture

Developed in China, acupuncture is based on the concept of *ch'i*, an energy force that is believed to course through the human body. Acupuncture theory states that if your ch'i is blocked, illness results. Acupuncturists insert tiny needles into the skin to undo these blockages. Modern acupuncturists generally use disposable needles to ensure sterility. Some also employ heat, (noninvasive) lasers, magnetic devices, or electrical stimulation.

You don't have to believe in the *ch'i* concept to enjoy the benefits of acupuncture. Even the alternative medicine skeptics at the National Institutes of Health have been forced to admit that it does seem to have benefits for conditions such as chronic pain, and it works as an adjunct to other methods in the treatment of drug addiction. (In fact, NIH is currently funding several studies on acupuncture.) Western doctors think that the needles influence the body's production of natural opioid chemicals and neurotransmitters.

Reputable research indicates that properly applied acupuncture treatments may help regulate gastrointestinal functions. This may be helpful for people with OCD who experience GI tract difficulties as a result of taking SSRIs. Other studies have indicated (but not proven) that acupuncture may heal nerve damage. If you can find a good acupuncturist, it might be a worthwhile adjunct to other types of medical care.

Acupressure and reflexology are other alternative treatments that borrow much from acupuncture.

Chiropractic

Chiropractors make adjustments to the spine and related body structures. Their work in this area does seem to be useful to some people with back pain.

There is no known benefit from chiropractic treatment for people with OCD. That said, some chiropractors also offer advice on diet, vitamins, and supplements that may be useful.

Naturopathy

Naturopaths are licensed to practice medicine in some countries and in some US states and Canadian provinces. They use the designation ND rather than MD. Naturopaths vary in their personal philosophy about Western medicine. Some will refer patients for ailments they feel are out of their league, others prefer to rely only on nutritional and natural medicine.

For parents and patients who want to try herbal remedies and nutritional interventions, a properly trained naturopath can be a good choice. Be careful whom you choose. In the US, some people calling themselves naturopaths have not completed an accredited program. Properly licensed naturopaths receive medical training roughly comparable to traditional medical school, though with a different emphasis.

For information about finding a licensed naturopath in the US or Canada, contact the American Association of Naturopathic Physicians (on the Web at *http://www.naturopathic.org/*) or the Canadian Naturopathic Association (*http://www.naturopathic.org/canada/Canada.Assoc.List.html*).

Homeopathy

Homeopathy is based on the principle that remedies containing infinitesimal amounts of substances that could cause the medical condition being treated can instead prod the immune system into action against the condition. Homeopathy is a fairly mainstream medical practice in the UK, although repeated studies have not uncovered any reason to believe that it works.[1]

In the US and Canada, homeopathic physicians are not licensed to practice medicine. However, some MDs and NDs do recommend homeopathic treatments, and a few homeopaths are fully licensed practitioners. For information about homeopaths in North America see the National Center for Homeopathy web site at *http://www.homeopathic.org/*.

Although homeopathic remedies can often be purchased at health food stores, responsible practitioners recommend seeing a homeopathic doctor before choosing remedies. The remedies are generally used only as part of an overall treatment plan that may also include diet and stress reduction. Even if the remedies themselves are of no value, as many skeptics believe, the diet and reduced stress part of the program could be beneficial.

Orthomolecular medicine

Orthomolecular medicine largely relies on using vitamins and nutrition to prevent or cure illness. The most famous proponent of orthomolecular medicine was its late founder, Dr. Linus Pauling. Better known for receiving the 1954 Nobel Prize for Chemistry and the 1962 Nobel Prize for Peace, Pauling spent most of his later life studying and publicizing the effects of megadoses of vitamins, particularly vitamin C. Many of Dr. Pauling's more extravagant claims have not been substantiated, but his reputation as a scientist forced the medical establishment to take his ideas seriously.

Some MDs are firm believers in orthomolecular medicine, and Pauling's principles underlie many of the megadose vitamin concoctions found in health food stores. Since large doses of vitamins can have side effects as well as potential benefits, be sure to discuss what you should expect with your doctor if he wants to try an orthomolecular approach. You shouldn't do megadose vitamin therapy without consulting a physician or a competent nutritionist.

Osteopathy

Osteopaths operate somewhat like chiropractors, adjusting the musculoskeletal system to effect improvement. In the UK, licensed osteopaths participate in the National Health scheme. They are licensed to practice medicine in all US states, and use the initials DO (Doctor of Osteopathy) instead of MD.

One area of osteopathy-related treatment, *craniosacral therapy*, is often recommended for children with neurological challenges. Developed by osteopath John Upledger, craniosacral therapy is practiced by trained members of other professions, including some occupational therapists and physical therapists. There are no studies linking this treatment to symptom improvement in people with OCD, however.

Ayurvedic and other traditional medicines

Indigenous peoples everywhere have medical systems based on the use of herbal remedies. Two of these, India's Ayurveda and traditional Chinese medicine, have been systematized and studied to a great extent. The Ayurvedic medicine concept revolves around a life-force called *prana*, while Chinese traditionalists talk about *ch'i*, as mentioned in the previous section on acupuncture.

Ayurvedic practitioners will give you a thorough exam and then tell you which "type" you are in their diagnostic system. Then they'll suggest an appropriate diet, lifestyle adjustments, and probably therapeutic meditation. They may also have various suggestions about cleaning out your digestive tract.

Chinese traditional practitioners take a very similar approach, although their dietary recommendations tend to be less strict than those in a typical Ayurvedic plan.

There is a vast array of Ayurvedic and Chinese herbal remedies available, most of which have not been tested by Western researchers. Some of these concoctions are probably quite effective, while others could be dangerous to your health. If possible, try to find out exactly which herbs are in a potion and check out their effects. For example, the popular Chinese herb Ma Huang is a common ingredient in traditional "nerve tonics." It is also a powerful CNS stimulant, and should be taken with caution.

As far as we can tell from a review of the literature in English, no medical researcher has ever surveyed or studied traditional herbal remedies for OCD, although some people have tried them. It would be an interesting pursuit, and hopefully someone will do so.

Lecithin and inositol

The most common alternative medicine practice these days is taking vitamins or herbal remedies. So far, the only supplement that has actually been studied in relation to obsessive-compulsive symptoms is a carbohydrate called *inositol*, one of the active ingredients in *lecithin*. Clinical studies have indicated that inositol supplements may be helpful for some people with obsessive-compulsive disorder.[2] Other studies have found evidence of benefits for people with depression, panic disorder, and autism.

How might inositol help? It is an ingredient in a chemical process that carries messages for certain neurotransmitters, including serotonin and acetylcholine. It also seems to help serotonin receptors that have stopped working become functional again. It may help repair some types of nerve damage.

Lecithin itself (phosphatidylcholine) is a phospholipid found mostly in high-fat foods. Along with inositol, it contains choline, a substance needed by the brain for processes related to memory, learning, and mental alertness, as well as for the manufacture of cell membranes and the neurotransmitter acetylcholine.

Lecithin supplements are said to improve memory and other brain processes. While it is necessary for normal brain development, claims that lecithin can help people recover lost brain function are unsubstantiated by double-blind studies of patients with Alzheimer's disease. However, it's possible that increased amounts of lecithin may be one of the keys to the success of a special high-fat (ketogenic) diet in some cases of hard-to-treat epilepsy. Some people with less severe epilepsy have also reported a reduced number and severity of seizures from taking lecithin as a supplement. It is possible that extra lecithin might help rebuild damaged myelin protein. So along with the possible benefits of inositol for people with OCD, lecithin itself may be particularly helpful to those who have a seizure disorder as well.

Lecithin is oil-based, so it gets rancid easily. It should be refrigerated. Lecithin capsules are available, but many people prefer the soft lecithin granules. These are a nice addition to fruit-juice smoothies, adding a thicker texture.

St. John's wort and OCD

St. John's wort (*hypericum*) has gone from a little-known European weed to one of the most popular treatments for depression in the US. As soon as it burst into the public eye, people with OCD wondered if it would be effective for them as well.

Unfortunately, early reports indicate that it is not. It appears to have some, but not all, of the properties of two different kinds of antidepressants, the SSRIs and the MAOIs. The latter should make anyone considering giving this supplement to a child pause. MAOIs have a high potential for interacting with other medications, and even with common foods. They are not known for effectiveness when it comes to OCD, either. St. John's wort can also cause greater sensitivity to light.

Some patients with both OCD and depression have noted that their obsessive-compulsive symptoms actually worsened when they took St. John's wort.

Immune system support

For those who have the PANDAS variant of OCD or whose symptoms seem to be made worse by other infections or illnesses, a healthy diet and certain supplements may be helpful.

Vitamin and mineral formulas are often recommended for children with disordered eating habits due to OCD, including those who have been diagnosed with anorexia or bulimia. Because the mineral deficiencies associated with eating disorders can be life-threatening, these patients should take only supplements that have been recommended by a physician as part of their overall treatment plan.

Antioxidants

Antioxidant compounds scavenge the bloodstream for particles called free radicals. Free radicals damage healthy cells and cause inflammation of tissues. Antioxidants are often recommended as general health and immune-system boosters, although those eating a healthy diet normally do not need to take them in supplement form. Antioxidants include the following substances:

- **Beta carotene.** A nutrient related to vitamin A, beta carotene is found in dark green, leafy vegetables and yellow-orange vegetables. It's best to get it through the diet rather than from a supplement.

- **Cat's claw (una de gato, maca, *Untaria tomentosa*).** This is an herbal antioxidant from the Peruvian rainforest. It also appears to have antiviral and anti-inflammatory qualities. It contains plant sterols (compounds related to steroids), among other active ingredients.
- **Coenzyme Q10 (CoQ10, ubiquinone).** CoQ10 is one of the strongest vitamin-like antioxidants available. It takes part in the cellular process that uses fats, sugars, and amino acids to produce the energy molecule ATP. It is said to boost immune-system function and help to heal GI tract problems, including gastric ulcers. It does appear to have some benefit for women with breast cancer (although this claim is based on a very small study), and has been helpful to some children with inborn metabolic disorders, although other claims you may see in magazine articles or on the Internet are as yet unsubstantiated. It is most popular in Japan, where it is widely touted as a cancer preventative.
- **Gingko biloba.** An extract of the gingko tree, Gingko biloba is advertised as an herb to improve memory. There is some clinical evidence for this claim. It is an antioxidant, and is prescribed in Germany for treatment of dementia. It is believed to increase blood flow to the brain. It may help revive sexual response in people taking SSRIs.
- **Glutathione peroxidase.** This is an antioxidant peptide manufactured by the body itself. You need to have enough selenium, vitamin C, and vitamin E to make it. There's no need to supplement directly with glutathione itself.
- **Proanthocyanidins (OPCs, Pycogenol, grapeseed oil).** These are the active ingredients in several naturally occurring antioxidant compounds. Pycogenol is a brand-name formulation derived from maritime pine bark, while grapeseed oil is just what its name indicates. People with neurological disorders have sometimes reported beneficial effects for seizure control, reduced aggression, and improved immune-system function.
- **Selenium.** This works with vitamin E to produce the antioxidant peptide glutathione peroxidase. Selenium deficiency occurs in some people with celiac disease and other autoimmune disorders, so if you or your child experiences GI tract problems, you may want to use a supplement of this mineral, preferably in its easily absorbed chelated form (L-selenomethionane).

- **Vitamin A (retinol).** Vitamin A has antioxidant properties, and helps maintain the mucous lining of the intestines. People with celiac disease have a hard time getting enough vitamin A and often experience a deficiency of this vitamin.
- **Vitamin C (ascorbic acid).** A very powerful antioxidant, studies have shown that C seems to shorten the length of colds and improve the basic health of people with many medical conditions. Vitamin C deficiency, known as scurvy, is mighty rare these days. One population in which it does occur, however, is people who start using megadoses of C and then suddenly stop. The acidic nature of ascorbic acid can also contribute to kidney stones. (The buffered form, calcium ascorbate, is more easily tolerated.) As the cautions mentioned here indicate, megadoses of C shouldn't be taken without consulting your physician first. If you do choose to take large doses of vitamin C, research indicates that you should accompany it with vitamin E.
- **Vitamin E (alpha-tocopherol).** It is believed that vitamin E helps the immune system function properly. People who take neuroleptics, tricyclic antidepressants, or other medications that carry a known risk for tardive dyskinesia should *definitely* take vitamin E supplements. This vitamin appears to protect against and reduce the symptoms of this drug-induced movement disorder.
- **Zinc.** Zinc is an antioxidant mineral. Deficiency occurs in some people with celiac disease, so if your child experiences GI tract problems, you may want to use a supplement of this mineral in its easiest-to-absorb chelated form (zinc aspartate or zinc picolinate).

Vitamin cautions

Vitamins A and D are fat soluble, so they are stored in the body's fat cells for later use. Having a little socked away for a rainy day is probably okay, but if you take too much, you may develop *hypervitaminosis*.

Symptoms of hypervitaminosis A include orange-hued, itchy skin; loss of appetite; increased fatigue; and hard, painful swellings on the arms, legs, or back of the head. Symptoms of hypervitaminosis D include hypercalcemia, osteoporosis, and kidney problems.

Don't overdo it with any fat-soluble vitamin, and also be careful with fish oil supplements, including cod liver oil, which are very high in both vitamins A and D.

Purchase a basic guide to vitamins and minerals that includes information about toxicity symptoms before starting any vitamin-based program. Individuals metabolize vitamins and minerals differently, and some people may be more or less susceptible to potential toxic effects. Along with your doctor's guidance, a good reference book can help you avoid problems.

Also, take vitamin company sales pitches and dosage recommendations with a grain of salt. Consult a physician or a professional nutritionist who does not sell supplements for unbiased, individualized advice.

Minerals

Several minerals are essential for optimal health. Some are also necessary for utilizing certain vitamins. Selenium is listed earlier in this chapter, in the section "Antioxidants." Other important minerals include the following:

- **Calcium.** Calcium is important for the regulation of impulses in the nervous system and for neurotransmitter production. However, excessive levels of calcium (*hypocalcinuria*) can result in stupor.
- **Iron (ferrous sulfate).** Iron deficiency in infants can inhibit mental and motor-skills development, but iron supplements are rarely recommended for children—they can actually cause harm.
- **Magnesium.** This mineral lowers blood pressure, and is important for the regulation of impulses in the nervous system and neurotransmitter production. If you are supplementing with vitamin B6, you will need to take magnesium as well.

Essential fatty acids (EFAs)

The essential fatty acid (EFA) linoleic acid and its derivatives, including gammalinolenic acid (GLA), dihomogamma-linolenic acid (DGLA), and arachidonic acid (AA), are known as the Omega-6 fatty acids. These substances come from animal fats and some plants. Another type of EFA, the Omega-3 fatty acids, are found almost exclusively in fish oils. As the "essential" in their name implies, these substances are needed to build cells and also to support the body's anti-inflammatory response. They are the "good" polyunsaturated fats that improve cardiovascular health when substituted for the "bad" saturated fats.

The heart and blood vessels aren't the only beneficiaries of EFAs, however. People with autoimmune diseases that involve the nervous system say EFAs are very helpful in reducing symptoms, and there is some research to back them up. EFAs appear to help the GI tract resist and repair damage, probably by restoring the lipid cells. Recent research in psychiatry has even found that Omega-3 fatty acids can act as mood stabilizers for some people with bipolar disorders. Researchers believe that a proper balance between Omega-3 and Omega-6 fatty acids is also important for optimal health. No specific benefits have yet been found for people with OCD.

EFAs include the following:

- **Efalex/Efamol.** These are brand-name EFA supplements made by Efamol Neutriceuticals Inc. Efalex was specifically created to treat developmental dyspraxia in the UK, and is widely touted as a supplement for people with ADD or ADHD as well. Efalex contains a mix of Omega-3 fish oil, Omega-6 EPO and thyme oil, and vitamin E. Efamol, marketed as a treatment for PMS, combines EPO; vitamins B6, C, and E; niacin, zinc, and magnesium. Both of these commercial EFA supplements are now available in the US and Canada as well, and can be purchased by mail order. Unlike many supplement manufacturers, Efamol adheres to strict standards and also sponsors reputable research.
- **EicoPro.** Made by Eicotec Inc., this is another brand-name EFA supplement you may hear about. It combines Omega-3 fish oils and Omega-6 linoleic acid. Eicotech is another supplement manufacturer known for its high manufacturing standards.
- **Evening primrose oil (EPO).** One of the best EFA sources around, EPO has become a very popular supplement. Other plants sources for Omega-6 fatty acids include borage oil, flax seed oil, and black current seed oil. The Omega-6 fatty acids in evening primrose oil have been reported to lower the threshold for frontal-lobe seizures, however, so people who have seizures should exercise caution. All are available as gelatin caps.
- **Monolaurin.** Made by the body from lauric acid, this is another medium-chain fatty acid, and is found in abundance in coconuts and some other foods, including human breast milk. It is known to have antibacterial and antiviral properties. Monolaurin may be the active ingredient in colostrum, the "pre-milk" all mammals produce to jump-start a newborn's immune system. Cow colostrum is actually available in supplement form in some areas.

It's great if you can get your EFAs in food. Low-fat may prevent those who are trying to lose weight from getting enough EFAs. Many cold-pressed salad oils, including safflower, sunflower, corn, and canola oils, contain EFAs. When these oils are processed with heat, however, the fatty acids may be changed or destroyed. Oily fish are another great source for EFAs, although again, cooking may be a problem (and not everyone is a sushi fan).

Diabetics may experience adverse effects from an overload of EFAs, and should consult their physician before supplementing with EFA products.

DMG

Dimethylglycine (DMG, calcium pangamate, pangamic acid, vitamin B15) is a naturally occurring amino acid that may help some people attain increased stress tolerance, seizure reduction, and immune-system strengthening. DMG changes the way your body uses folic acid, so you may need to supplement it with that vitamin. Increased hyperactivity may result from a lack of folic acid when taking DMG.

A related product, trimethylglycine (TMG) has recently been introduced. It is available in liquid form.

Both DMG and TMG play roles in the chemical reactions that increase serotonin levels. Those who take medications that affect serotonin should be careful with these supplements.

Herbal antibiotics

Several herbs appear to have antiseptic, antiviral, antifungal, or antibiotic properties. Obviously, if these substances are active, they should be used carefully and sparingly, despite the claims of certain manufacturers who encourage daily use for disease prevention. Those who prefer herbal remedies might want to try cat's claw or grapeseed oil, both mentioned in the section "Antioxidants," earlier in this chapter, or one of the following:

- **Bitter melon (*Momordica charantia*).** An antiviral from the Chinese herbal pharmacopoeia, bitter melon is the plant from which the active ingredient in some protease inhibitors (the powerful drugs used to combat AIDS) is derived.
- **Echinacea.** Another herbal antiseptic, echinacea also dilates blood vessels and is said to have antispasmodic qualities as well.

- **Goldenseal.** Goldenseal is an alkaloid isoquinoline derivative related to the minor opium alkaloids. Its active ingredient, hydrastine, elevates blood pressure. It is a very strong herb with antiseptic properties when taken internally or applied topically in powder or salve form. It acts on the mucous membranes of the GI tract when taken internally.
- **SPV-30.** Derived from the European boxwood tree, this is a fairly new item. It apparently includes some antiviral and steroidal (anti-inflammatory) compounds, and has become very popular among people with AIDS as an alternative to pharmaceutical antivirals.

Sphingolin

Sphingolin is a glandular supplement made from cow spinal-cord myelin, repackaged in pill form. Some practitioners recommend it for children who have tested positive for myelin sheath proteins in the bloodstream. It is used by quite a large number of people with multiple sclerosis and other neurological disorders that cause demyelinization.

There could be a hidden problem with this supplement: it might contain particles that cause the deadly neurological disorder spongiform encephalopathy, otherwise known as "mad cow disease." It is not available in the UK for this very reason—and there's no reason to believe that this disease exists in only in British cows.

Immune-boosting diets

Many popular diet books claim that a particular eating regimen will boost your immune system. Generally speaking, however, these claims have not been proven. A healthy, balanced diet should be sufficient for the average person.

But what about people with known or suspected immune-system dysfunction? Immune-boosting claims have been made (and sometimes substantiated in limited clinical research) for a wide variety of foods, including red wine, tofu, miso (fermented soybean paste), kale, and yams. You might want to research some of these options and incorporate them into your diet plan. As long as these foods are eaten in moderation, they certainly can't hurt.

Probiotics

As the name indicates, probiotics are intended to counteract the harmful effects of antibiotics. As most people who have taken a course of penicillin know, these valuable medications can cause digestive distress as they heal infection. Probiotics are substances that attempt to restore the friendly intestinal cultures that help us digest our food. By replenishing the ranks of friendly bacteria, they keep a lid on unfriendly yeasts, such as *Candida albicans*, that can cause troublesome symptoms.

Commercial probiotic supplements may combine a number of substances, including digestive enzymes as well as helpful bacteria, garlic, and the following:

- **Biotin.** A vitamin in the B family, biotin is normally produced by friendly bacteria in the digestive tract. Replenishing this flora should ensure enough biotin, but some people do choose to take it directly.
- **Caprylic acid.** This fatty acid is said to be active against yeast in the digestive tract. Medium chain triglycerides (MCT oil, also called caprylic/capric triglycerides) is a liquid source of caprylic acid.
- **Garlic.** Garlic is said to be active against yeast in the digestive tract. You can swallow whole cloves raw, or take it in a supplement.
- **Lactobacillus acidophilus, Bifidobacterium bifidum, and Lactobacillus bulgaricus.** These are friendly bacteria familiar to most of us as the "active cultures" found in some yogurts. Yogurt itself is a good probiotic for those who eat dairy products.
- **Soil-based organisms (SBOs).** SBOs are microbes found in organic soils, and are believed to help the body produce important enzymes. Some people believe that modern food-processing techniques have prevented people from ingesting enough, so they take SBO supplements. These are increasingly added to probiotic supplements. No scientific information about their benefits is available at this time.

Stress reduction

One of the most valuable supportive therapies for people with OCD is stress reduction. What works for one person may not for another, but time-tested stress-busters include prayer, meditation, dance, music, and exercise.

Specific forms of meditation are sometimes taught as part of therapy programs. They give patients a silent tool to use when pressure is overwhelming, even at school or at work.

Even very young patients can benefit from stress-reduction techniques, especially relaxation exercises designed for their age level. Simply learning how to count to ten when faced with stress can go a long way.

Young patients should also work with their therapist to identify any rituals that they perform or that get worse when they're faced with stress. They can gradually replace these uncomfortable behaviors with techniques that really work.

Fixing sleep problems

OCD and anxiety can keep children awake for half the night, leading to difficult mornings. It is rare for doctors to recommend sleeping pills for children, as their continued use can lead to dependency. However, if sleeping is a persistent problem you may want to talk to your child's psychiatrist about changing her medications for OCD or other conditions, or about rearranging when she takes them.

For example, some of the antidepressants used to treat OCD tend to be sedating, while others tend to be energizing. If your child takes a stimulant like Ritalin or Adderall, it could also be contributing to sleeplessness. Switching to a different medication, avoiding the use of stimulating medications like Prozac or Adderall in the evening, and taking sedating medications like Paxil or Risperdal in the evening can contribute to improved sleep patterns.

There are also non-medication strategies that can help. Setting a bedtime and a wake-up time and sticking to them is essential, even if there's a big test tomorrow or a rock concert tonight, and even if it's Saturday morning and you want to sleep in. Obviously, this is not going to be a popular point with teenagers, who want to share in the nightlife of their peers, and who delight in lazy weekend mornings. Other advice that applies to anyone who occasionally experiences insomnia includes:

- Avoid unnecessary artificial stimulants and depressants, such as coffee, tea, and alcohol.
- Avoid over-the-counter medications with a stimulating or depressive effect, such as OTC allergy preparations, aspirin with caffeine, No-Doz and other OTC stimulants, and most commercial cough syrups.

- Avoid extremely exciting television programs, music, or games right before bed. Parents can decide when the activity level should start to wind down slowly.
- Use your bed for sleeping only, not for reading, watching television, or playing. This helps associate the concepts of "bed" and "sleep" in your mind.
- Don't just lie there tossing and turning when you can't get to sleep at the proper time. Get out of bed, and do something really, really boring—like housework, or putting together an old jigsaw puzzle.
- Make a relaxing—but time-limited—ritual part of bedtime. For young children this could be a story with mom and some warm milk. Teens might prefer using a computer or reading for twenty minutes at a certain time, followed by brushing teeth, donning pajamas, laying out tomorrow's school clothes, or other end-of-the-day chores. A nice, long bath is another great way to end the day. You may want to vary the bedtime ritual occasionally with kids who have OCD of course, to avoid turning it into a "must-have."
- Add scents to massage oil and rub it into the skin for an extra relaxing effect. Some people find certain scents very soporific, and have added aromatherapy to their relaxation plan.
- Use relaxation audiotapes or background noise machines to help you sleep or return to sleep.
- Try special breathing and muscle relaxation techniques.

Melatonin

Melatonin (MLT) is produced by the pineal gland, and is responsible for helping the body maintain sleep and other biochemical rhythms. Melatonin supplements given about a half hour before bed may be useful for addressing sleep disturbances. The effect may not last, however.

Some studies have found that taking a melatonin supplement on a regular basis can actually make depression worse, so be careful in your use of this supplement. Supplementing directly with any kind of hormone can be problematic in the long run—in some cases the patient's body may respond by producing less of the natural substance.

If you do decide to try melatonin, talk about it with your doctor or psychiatrist, and set up a dosage plan and observation schedule first.

Other sleep supplements

You may be tempted to try "natural" sleep aids. Of the options mentioned here, chamomile is probably the safest and mildest. Be extremely careful to avoid using other central nervous system depressants, including alcohol, at the same time as these substances. Other depressants may potentiate the active ingredients in some of these substances, with possibly dangerous effects.

Indeed, although these herbal potions are not as dangerous as prescription sleeping pills, they are also not inconsequential. It's never a good thing to be dependent on a pill to sleep, and little is known about the long-term effects of herbal sleep aids or their over-the-counter counterparts (Ny-Tol, etc.).

Simply taking a good multivitamin may also help regulate sleep. Vitamins implicated in insomnia and/or hypersomnia include the B vitamins (especially B2 and niacin), potassium, and magnesium. Vitamin B2 helps the body convert the amino acid tryptophan into compounds that raise blood levels of serotonin.

Supplements believed to affect sleep include:

- **5-HTP (5-hydroxytryptophan).** Synthesized from tryptophan, 5-HTP is an even more direct precursor to serotonin. It is available in the US. It appears to help regulate sleep, and to have an antidepressant effect not unlike that of an SSRI. For that reason, do not use this substance if you take any pharmaceutical antidepressant.
- **Black cohosh (*Cimicifuga racemosa*, squaw root).** A nervous system depressant and sedative often used by people with autoimmune conditions for its anti-inflammatory effects. Its active ingredient appears to bind to estrogen receptor sites, so it may cause hormonal changes.
- **Chamomile (*Anthemis nobilis*).** A mild but effective sedative traditionally used to treat sleep disorders or upset stomachs. It is a member of the daisy family, so avoid this herb if you are allergic to its cousin, ragweed.
- **Hops (*Humulus lupulus*).** The herb used to flavor beer. . .and the reason beer makes many people sleepy. It's available in capsules or as a dried herb for use in tea, and works as a gentle sleep aid.
- **Kava-kava (*Piper methysticum*).** A mild sedative herb used for centuries in the South Pacific. It has a slight potential for abuse, although such misuse is rare.

- **Passion flower** (*Passiflora incarnata*). An herb with sedative, antispasmodic, and anti-inflammatory qualities.
- **Skullcap** (*Scutellaria lateriflora*). A medium-strength sedative with anticonvulsive properties. It is found in both European and Ayurvedic herbal remedies. Skullcap has traditionally been used to treat tic disorders and muscle spasms, as well as seizure disorders, insomnia, and anxiety. Other traditional uses include menstrual irregularity and breast pain, indicating that it probably has hormonal effects.
- **Taurine**. Another amino acid that can counteract insomnia. It works by slowing down nerve impulses.
- **Valerian (Valeriana officinalis)**. A strong herbal sedative (and one of the secret ingredients in the soporific liqueur Jagermeister). It should not be given to young children, but it can help teens and adults fight episodic insomnia.
- **Tryptophan**. An amino acid that raises the levels of serotonin in the brain. It's not currently available in the US due to a badly contaminated batch several years ago, but it is sold over the counter in Europe and by prescription in Canada. It appears to help regulate sleep, and to have an antidepressant effect not unlike that of an SSRI. For that reason, do not use this substance if you take any pharmaceutical antidepressant. If you can purchase tryptophan, buy it from a trustworthy source. Take it at bedtime with sweetened milk or fruit juice, and vitamin B6 for maximum effect.

Valerian, kava-kava, passion flower, and skullcap can help ease extreme anxiety as well as insomnia, but their sedating qualities must be taken into account.

Supplement cautions

It's very important to let your doctor know about any supplement your child takes, whether it is vitamin, mineral, or herb. There are many possible interactions between these substances and prescription drugs. Here are just a few that are known at this time:[3]

- Echinacea adds to the hepatotoxic effects of medications, including anabolic steroids, amiodarone, methotrexate, and ketoconazole, increasing the risk of liver failure.

- The antimigraine effects of feverfew may be negated by non-steroidal anti-inflammatory drugs (NSAIDs), including aspirin.
- Feverfew, garlic, Ginko biloba, ginger, and ginseng alter bleeding time, and so should not be used with anticoagulant drugs like warfarin.
- When taken with phenelzine sulfate, ginseng can cause headache, tremor, and mania.
- Ginseng (and other herbs that may affect the hormonal system) may add to or work against the effects of estrogens, corticosteroids, or oral contraceptives.
- St. John's wort (and any other "natural" antidepressant) may add to the effects of prescription antidepressants, increasing the risk of serotonin syndrome.
- Valerian (and any other herbal sedative) should not be used with barbiturates or other prescription sedatives, because the risk of over-sedation, and even coma or death, will increase.
- Kyushin, licorice, plantain, uzara root, hawthorn, and ginseng may interfere with the medical action of digoxin, as well as with digoxin monitoring.
- Evening primrose oil and borage oil may lower the seizure threshold, and so should not be used by people with seizure disorders, or with prescription anticonvulsants.
- The Ayurvedic remedy Shankapulshpi may decrease phenytoin levels as well as diminish drug efficacy.
- Kava-kava can cause coma when combined with alprazolam. It can also damage the liver if used for more than 30 days in a row. It could worsen the effects of other drugs that can harm the liver, including many psychiatric medications.
- Immunostimulants like echinacea and antioxidants should not be given with drugs that suppress the immune system, such as corticosteroids or cyclosporine.
- St. John's wort, saw palmetto, and some other herbs have high levels of tannic acids, which may inhibit iron absorption.
- Karela, ginseng, and some other herbs may affect blood glucose levels, and so should not be used by diabetic patients.

There are surely many more unknown chances for reaction between natural and pharmaceutical remedies.

Desperate to find something that works to ameliorate difficult symptoms, parents and adult patients tend to pile on the interventions. This makes it hard to tell when something really is working—or if it would work without interference from some other remedy!

To get the clearest picture possible of any alternative interventions, you must introduce them independently of each other and of pharmaceuticals or therapeutic interventions. Obviously, this will often be impractical—you wouldn't stop cognitive behavioral therapy to see if inositol might help, for example.

Barring the one-thing-at-a-time scenario, keep careful, daily records of supplements and dietary changes you introduce, when they are given and in what amounts, what brands you use, and any visible effects that you observe. If after four to six weeks you have not seen improvements with a supplement, it's unlikely that it will be of benefit. Dietary changes, bodywork, and other interventions may take much longer to bear fruit.

Self-help for panic attacks

It's not much use to pop a pill when a panic attack strikes. These events are sudden, and usually short-lived. They are also intensely uncomfortable. In fact, the chest pains caused by over-breathing during panic attacks are one of the top causes people show up at emergency rooms in fear that they have suffered a heart attack.

When you feel the early warning signs of panic, try to use the most logical part of your brain to defuse it before it starts. Look objectively at what is frightening you. Most likely, the thing, place, or activity is not really frightening you, it's the "what if" questions about it that you are asking yourself. It's not the escalator, it's your internal question, "What if I fall down on the escalator?" If you can disconnect the what ifs from the reality, the fear level often drops rapidly.

If you can't prevent a panic attack before it starts, there are some tricks that can help you weather it with aplomb. The first impulse most people have during a panic attack is to run. It's important to resist this urge, at least for a little while. It raises your chances of dealing with situation, and of returning to the scene of the attack later on.

Use mental tricks that distract you from thinking of more dire consequences, adding fuel to the fire of panic. Grab hold of something solid, count people or objects nearby, make sure you are breathing from your abdomen instead of taking short panicky breaths. All of these tactics help you stay grounded in reality. Use positive "self-talk" to help you accept the scary symptoms, and to remind yourself that they will soon be gone. Examples of self-talk phrases include:

- "I'm having a panic attack, but it will be over soon."
- "What's bothering me is my reaction, not the actual situation."
- "I can accept this reaction and handle it, and soon I'll feel better."

If you hyperventilate during a panic attack, you may feel sick and lightheaded. Sitting down and lowering your head may help. Breathing into a paper bag will usually keep hyperventilation from getting too bad. If you feel faint due to over-breathing, be sure to sit down. Don't worry; if you do faint, you'll be fine in a minute as long as you're in a safe spot.

You can work with a therapist to use exposure and response prevention techniques for tackling specific panic triggers.

Evaluating alternative interventions

No matter what kind of alternative practitioner or therapy you choose, it's just as important to be a smart consumer in this area as it is with traditional medicine. Unfortunately, it can be more difficult. Medications with approval from the FDA or similar government bodies undergo rigorous testing. Study results and detailed information about these compounds is available in numerous books, online, or directly from manufacturers.

With "natural" remedies, that's not always the case. It seems like every week another paperback book appears making wild claims for a "new" antioxidant compound, herbal medication, or holistic therapy. The online bookstore Amazon.com lists nearly twenty titles about St. John's wort alone! These books—not to mention magazine articles, web sites, and semi-informed friends—sometimes wrap conjecture up in a thin veneer of science. They may reference studies that are misinterpreted, that appeared in disreputable journals, or that were so poorly designed or biased that no journal would publish them.

Supplement salespeople, particularly those who take part in multi-level marketing schemes, seem to have taken lessons from their predecessors from the days of the traveling medicine show. They have little to lose by making outrageous claims for their products, and much to gain financially. Here are just a few unsupported claims found in a single five-minute sweep of supplement-sales sites on the Internet:

- "Glutathione slows the aging clock, prevents disease and increases life."
- "Pycogenol. . . dramatically relieves ADD/ADHD, improves skin smoothness and elasticity, reduces prostate inflammation and other inflammatory conditions, reduces diabetic retinopathy and neuropathy, improves circulation and enhances cell vitality. . ." [and, according to this site, cures almost anything else that might ail you!]
- "Sage and Bee Pollen nourish the brain."
- "Soybean lecithin has been found to clean out veins and arteries—dissolve the gooey sludge cholesterol—and thus increase circulation, relieve heart, vein and artery problems. It has cured many diabetics—cured brain clots, strokes, paralyzed legs, hands, and arms!"

Take the time to browse your local health food or vitamin store's shelves, and you'll probably spot a number of products that are deceptively advertised. Some companies try to deceive you with sound-alike names, packaging that mimics other products, or suggestive names that hint at cures. Other colorful bottles of pills contain substances that can't actually be absorbed by the body in oral form—for example, "DNA" (deoxyribonucleic acid, the building block of human genetic material) graces the shelves of some shops. One site for a manufacturer of this useless supplement claims that "It is the key element in the reprogramming and stimulation of lazy cells to avoid, improve, or correct problems in the respiratory, digestive, nervous, or glandular systems." It also notes that this "DNA" is extracted from fetal cells. Other brands are apparently nothing but capsules of brewer's yeast.

Some other supplements provide end products of internal procedures, such as glutathione, instead of the precursors, such as vitamin E, needed for the body to make a sufficient supply on its own. This approach may not work. When in doubt, consult with your doctor or a competent nutritionist.

How can you assess supplement claims? Start by relying primarily on reputable reference books for your basic information, rather than on advertisements or the popular press. Watch out for any product that salespeople claim will "cure" anything. Supplements and vitamins may enhance health and promote wellness, but they rarely effect cures.

Be wary of universal usefulness claims. The worst offenders in supplement advertising tout their wares as cure-alls for a multitude of unrelated conditions in an effort to make the most sales.

If it's a natural substance but a company claims to be the only one to know the secret of its usefulness, that really doesn't make much sense.

Be especially cautious when sales pitches are written in pseudoscientific language that doesn't hold up under close examination with a dictionary. This is a popular ploy. For example, one product that has occasionally been peddled to parents claims to "support cellular communication through a dietary supplement of monosaccharides needed for glycoconjugate synthesis." Translated into plain English, this product is a sugar pill.

Even when you have seen the science behind a vitamin or supplement treatment, there's still the problem of quality and purity. It's almost impossible for consumers to know for sure that a tablet or powder contains the substances advertised at the strength and purity promised. Whenever possible, do business with reputable manufacturers that back up their products with potency guarantees or standards. In most European countries, potency is governed by government standards; in the US, it's a matter of corporate choice.

"Natural" does not mean "harmless." Vitamins and supplements can have the power to heal and the power to harm. Be sure to work closely with your physician or nutritionist if you're using anything more complex than a daily multivitamin. If you can convince your regular physician to make alternative therapies part of the prescription, you're in luck. Some actively oppose them, and that may force you to find a new doctor.

Whatever you do, don't operate behind your doctor's back in any significant way. If you're philosophically incompatible, you should simply part ways—but you do need a medical expert on your team.

CHAPTER 7

Insurance Issues

MENTAL HEALTH CARE CAN BE DIFFICULT TO GET AND MANAGE. . .not to mention expensive. This chapter will explain how to access the best care through your existing health plan, as well as how to get care if you do not have insurance coverage for mental disorders.

You don't have to have health insurance for this chapter to be useful. We'll also cover private insurance, including health maintenance organizations (HMOs) and other forms of managed care, public health insurance plans, and alternatives to health insurance. We'll describe typical insurance roadblocks, and show you how to get around them. We'll begin by talking about health insurance in the US, but the systems of other English-speaking countries are also addressed.

Because public assistance in the US and some other countries is closely tied to eligibility for public health benefits, we'll also cover Social Security disability income (SSI) and other public benefits that may be available to families with disabled children.

Private insurance: The American way

In the US and other countries where private medical insurance is the norm, the system can be hard to deal with under the best of circumstances. Each insurance company offers multiple plans with various rates and benefits, and there's no central oversight. As a result, a child's OCD diagnosis can come with an unpleasant surprise: needed healthcare services aren't covered, even though you have paid your insurance premiums. Some insurance plans specifically refuse to cover any mental or neurological disorder, and in many cases it's legal for insurers to make that choice.

Other companies cover care for patients with OCD in a substandard way. For example, a company may cover only short-term therapy programs when long-term cognitive behavioral therapy may be needed instead; it may have no qualified "in-plan" practitioners and refuse to make outside referrals; or it may limit your child to a certain number of out-patient visits or inpatient hospital days each year, regardless of what he actually needs.

Making insurance choices

Whenever you are in the position of choosing a new insurance plan, try to find out in advance what its attitude is about treatment for mental illness. You may be surprised at what you learn.

Your best bet is a plan that has an out-of-network clause. These plans allow you to choose your own providers if you can't find the right professional on its list of preferred providers or HMO members. You will generally pay more for out-of-plan visits, but you also won't have to run the referral gauntlet as often. The cost of using these providers regularly, such as for weekly therapy visits, may be more than your budget can bear.

The most difficult companies to deal with are usually those that contract with a so-called "carve-out" for mental health care. These plans do not provide any mental health care themselves, but instead refer patients to outside providers. Sometimes these outside programs are very good. Unfortunately, patients can end up feeling like a ping-pong ball as they are bounced between their major medical carrier and the mental health program. Your insurer or HMO, your medical care facility, and your outside provider may argue with each other about what kind of treatment is needed, who should deliver it, and who will pay for it. Meanwhile, your child may go without appropriate care.

Lin, mother of 9-year-old Bill, puts it this way:

> *When we want to see a regular doctor, we just call and make an appointment. To see a therapist we had to call a special service and talk to a worker. Then they gave us a list of places that were okay to go to. I had to check each one out, and only one clinic had any experience with OCD. Everything turned out all right but it was a lot of extra work.*

One would think that integrated HMOs would do a better job. These are companies that provide both mental and physical care in the same plan, and sometimes at the same site. Some do, but not all. Even within a single company there can be turf wars, payment disputes, and outright denial of services.

If your employer does not offer insurance that covers mental health care, out-of-network providers, or other needed services, take up the issue with the human resources department (or in small companies, the boss). When the cost is spread over a group, these additional benefits may not be very expensive. You can also make a very persuasive case that providing mental health benefits will keep employees on the job more days, as they will be less likely to need hospitalization or long periods off work for their own mental health issues, and they will be less likely to take time off to care for a mentally ill child.

Insurance for families or individuals affected by any long-term disability is very hard to get in the private market (i.e., without going through an employer). It's available, but premium costs can be extraordinarily high. If you are leaving a job that provides you with health insurance for one that does not, pursue a COBRA plan. These plans allow you to continue your coverage for eighteen months after leaving employment. You will pay the full rate, including the contribution previously made by your employer, but it will still be less than what you'd pay as an individual customer. Be sure to apply for SSI (see the "SSI" section, later in this chapter) while using a COBRA plan; it doesn't matter if your child is actually awarded SSI and Medicaid, although that would be nice, but you can keep your COBRA coverage for an extra eleven months if the Social Security Administration determines that your child is disabled.

Maintaining continuous health insurance coverage is critical to prevent being locked out of healthcare by pre-existing conditions. If a COBRA plan is not available, other lower-cost possibilities include group plans offered by trade associations, unions, clubs, and other organizations. You may also want to look into public health insurance options, which are discussed later in this chapter.

For managed care issues, The National Coalition of Mental Health Professionals and Consumers maintains a useful (if opinionated) site at *http://www.NoManagedCare.org*.

Managing "managed care"

Managed care, the dominant trend in today's medical world, ought to be consumer-friendly. In most HMOs and other managed care entities, providers and provider groups earn more if their patients stay healthy. An emphasis on preventative care and timely intervention can definitely benefit the greatest number of patients. People with disabilities, however, may be perceived as obstacles in the way of profits.

There are four basic rules for managing your insurance affairs, whether you're dealing with an HMO, another type of managed care organization, an old-style "fee for service" arrangement, or a public health agency. Following these steps can help you be more secure when dealing with care providers and insurers:

- Make yourself knowledgeable.
- Document everything.
- Make your providers allies.
- Appeal when necessary.

Make yourself knowledgeable

Informed insurance consumers are a rarity. Most people look at the glossy plan brochure and the provider list, but unless something goes wrong, that's about as much as they want to know. For parents of children with OCD, that's not going to be enough. You'll need a copy of the firm's master policy, which specifies what is and isn't covered.

To get this hefty document, call your employer's human resources office (for employer-provided insurance or COBRA plans administered by a former employer) or the insurance company's customer relations office (for health insurance that you buy directly from the insurer). Read it. It will be tough going, but the results will be worthwhile.

If you need help interpreting the master policy, disability advocacy organizations and related sites on the web can help.

Find out in detail what the chain of command is within your provider group and insurer. You'll need to know exactly who to call and what to do if your child needs a referral to a specialist, partial or full hospitalization, or emergency services during a mental health crisis.

Document everything

You will want to keep copies of all your bills, reports, evaluations, test results, and other medical records. You'll also want to keep records of when and how your insurance payments were made. This information will be essential if you have a dispute with your healthcare provider or insurer.

Document personal conversations and phone calls. You needn't tape-record these, although if a dispute has already begun this can be a good idea (make sure to let the other party know that you are recording, if required by law in your area). Simply note the date and time of your call or conversation, the name of the person you spoke with, and what was said or decided. If a service or treatment is promised in a phone conversation, it can be a good idea to send a letter documenting the conversation. For example:

> *Dear Dr. Lawrence:*
>
> *When we spoke on Tuesday, you promised to authorize a referral to Dr. Martin at the University Anxiety Disorders Clinic for my son Jim Johnson's cognitive behavioral therapy program. Please fax a copy of the referral form to me at xxx-xxxx when it is finished. Thanks again for your help.*
>
> *Sincerely,*
>
> *Mark Johnson*

It's especially important to keep referral forms. Most managed care firms send a copy to both the patient and the provider. This document usually has a referral number on it. Be sure to bring your referral form when you first see a new provider. If the provider has not received his or her copy of the form, your copy with its referral number can ensure that you'll still be seen, and that payment can be processed. Without it, you may be turned away.

Make your providers into allies

Money is a motivator for doctors and other healthcare providers, but most of them also care about helping their patients. Your providers are the most powerful allies you have. Give them additional information about OCD if they need it, and make sure they know you and your child's case well. Let them know how important their help is. They have the power to write referrals, to recommend and approve treatments, and to advocate on your behalf within the managed care organization.

Stephanie, mother of 7-year-old Cassidy, tells how her daughter's doctors advocated for treatment:

Thank God for our insurance coverage! I pay ten dollars a visit for up to twenty visits without precertification. Beyond that she will have to be precertified. Our doctors think that will be no problem, as she would likely end up inpatient if she was not seeing them regularly. They think the insurance company will pay for many weekly visits to avoid paying for a day treatment or inpatient program.

Don't rely on your providers completely, however. They have many patients, some of whose needs will likely take precedence over yours. A life-or-death emergency or a large caseload may cause paperwork or meetings on your behalf to be overlooked temporarily or even forgotten.

Another staff member, such as a nurse or office assistant, may be able to keep your provider on track, but you will have to be persistently involved as well. Make sure that you return calls, provide accurate information, and keep the provider's needs in mind. For example, if you have information about a new treatment that you want to give to your doctor, summarize it on one page, and attach the relevant studies or journal articles. The doctor can then quickly scan the basics in her office, and read the rest when time permits.

Appeal

Would you believe that 70 percent of insurance coverage and claims denials are never appealed? It's true. Most healthcare consumers are so discouraged by the initial denial that they don't pursue it further.

However, all insurance companies and managed care entities have an internal appeal process, and it is worth your while to be part of the persistent 30 percent. The appeals process should be explained in the master policy. If it is not, call the insurance company's customer service office or your employer's human resources department for information.

A grievance or appeal is a formal procedure—it is *not* the same thing as a complaint. Companies can ignore complaining letters and calls at their leisure, if they wish to be so callous, as mere complaints do not require a legal response. Grievances and appeals do have legal status, and healthcare consumers are entitled to have such matters addressed. Grievances and appeals should be made in writing, with "grievance" or "appeal" marked clearly at the top of the document. Some companies have special forms that they say you must use, although legally this policy can't be enforced.

When you file a formal grievance or appeal, your managed care entity will convene a committee made up of people not involved in your problem. This committee will meet to consider the matter, usually within 30 days of receiving your written grievance or appeal. Particularly in HMOs, where the committee is usually made up mostly of physicians, your medical arguments may fall upon receptive ears.

It's unlikely that you will be invited to attend your insurance company or HMO appeal. You can send written material to support your appeal, such as medical studies that support your position. It's best if your physician or healthcare provider writes a letter explaining why he supports your request for a specific service.

Some companies have more than one level of grievance resolution, so if you are denied at first, appeal the committee's decision to a higher body. You may have the right to appear in person at this higher-level hearing, to bring an outside representative (such as a disability advocate, outside medical expert, or healthcare lawyer), and to question the medical practitioners involved. In other words, if a second-level procedure is available, it will be more like a trial or arbitration hearing than an informal discussion.

If you are still denied, you may be able to pursue the matter with your state's department of health or insurance commission. If your managed care plan is part of a public insurance program (for example, if you receive state medical benefits and have been required to join an HMO to receive care), you may also have an appeals avenue through a state or county agency, such as your nearest welfare office.

In late 1999, the federal government and several states were considering various proposals to modify the managed care system. Some of these would set up independent review panels to which managed care consumers could send their grievances. Others would permit consumers to sue their HMOs under some circumstances, a practice that usually isn't allowed at this time due to a special federal law that shields HMOs from most patient lawsuits. If you rely on managed care and are having problems, keep abreast of the latest news. If passed, these "patient's bill of rights" laws may help you obtain better healthcare for your child.

Semi-sneaky tips

Some people are better at managing managed care than others. The following suggestions may be a little shady, but they have worked for certain managed care customers:

- Subvert voicemail and phone queues. If you are continually routed into a voicemail system and your calls are never returned, or if you are left on hold forever, don't passively accept it. Start punching buttons when you are stuck in voicemail or on hold, in hope of reaching a real person. If you get an operator, ask for Administration (Claims and Customer Service never seem to have enough people to answer the phone). Nicely ask the operator to transfer you directly to an appropriate person who can help, not to the department in general. The old "Gosh, I just keep getting lost and cut off in your phone system" ploy may do the trick.
- Whenever you speak to someone at your HMO, especially if it's a claims representative, ask for her full name and direct phone number. It will make her feel more accountable for resolving your problem, because she knows you'll call her back directly if she doesn't.
- If you can't get help from a claims or customer service representative, ask for his supervisor. If you're told that she isn't available, get the supervisor's full name, direct phone line, and mailing address. Simply asking for this information sometimes makes missing supervisors magically appear.
- Use humor when you can. It defuses situations that are starting to get ugly, and humanizes you to distant healthcare company employees.
- Be ready to explain why your request is urgent, and do so in terms that non-doctors can understand. For example, receiving a certain treatment now could mean avoiding expensive hospitalization later; that's an argument that even junior assistant accountants comprehend.
- Whatever you do, stay calm. If you yell, you'll probably be dismissed as a loony. That doesn't mean you have to be unemotional. Sometimes you can successfully make a personal appeal. You can act confused instead of angry when you are denied assistance for no good reason. You may also want to make it clear that you're gathering information in a way that indicates legal action—for instance, ask how to spell names and where official documents should be sent.

One bright spot in managed care practices is a move toward integrated case management. Some insurance companies are setting up case management programs that may be able to coordinate care with parents, social welfare agencies, the school system, child protective services, clergy, social workers, and others. This model sometimes includes weekly contact between patient or parent and a permanent case manager. This model should help families dealing with serious mental health or medical needs obtain more consistent care. That will prevent relapses, reduce the number of mental health crises and hospitalizations, and save both insurers and families a great deal of money.

Shana, age 20, has a managed care plan that has not been problematic:

> *I have medical insurance, which covers almost every dollar of my medications and psychiatrist appointments. I pay very little.*

Fighting denial of care

Refusal of appropriate mental health care is the top insurance complaint voiced by parents of children with OCD. You can fight denial of care, but it isn't easy. Begin by asking the insurance company's claims department for a written copy of the denial of coverage or services. Make sure that the reason you were given verbally is also the reason given in this document.

Your next stop is the insurance company's own documents. Somewhere in the fine print of that master policy in your files you should find a provision stating that if any of the company's policies are unenforceable based on state law, they cannot be asserted. Most insurance company claims adjusters know very little about state insurance law. Educate yourself, then educate them.

Now you need to find out what your state says about coverage for mental illness in general, and about OCD in particular. The answer may be found in actual legislation. For example, California state law has specifically declared that as illnesses with organic causes, obsessive-compulsive disorder and many other "mental illnesses" are to be considered medical conditions under the law. Your state may have similar laws or public policies on the books. State mental health parity laws and laws protecting the disabled against discrimination may also have relevance.

Your state's insurance commission—every state has its own, there's no federal insurance commission, even though there are federal laws governing insurers and HMOs—will also have policies about mental health coverage. Remember, actual state law trumps state policy statements every time. If there is a conflict between state and federal law, whichever is more strict prevails.

Your state's National Alliance for the Mentally Ill (NAMI) or OC Foundation chapter will probably already have the information you need on hand, and the national NAMI and OC Foundation offices also collect information on state insurance laws. If no one you call seems to know the status of insurance law and OCD in your state, you'll have to start researching on your own. If you have Internet access, state laws, some public policies, and possibly insurance commission decisions, may be available online. You could also call your state representative's office and ask a staff member to research this issue for you. State insurance commission staff members should also be able to help you.

If you can show your insurance company that it is trying to assert a provision that violates a state or federal law, it should back down and provide treatment. It can be hard for a layperson to craft the sort of legal arguments needed to secure coverage, but advocacy groups may be able to help you write a well-written and persuasive letter of appeal on legal grounds. Some families have even gotten their state representative or a member of Congress to intervene on their behalf, especially if the problem involves a public insurance program or facility.

Formal arbitration is another possibility, although experienced advocates warn that since arbitrators are paid by the healthcare plans, it's a tough arena for consumers. Consumers can't recover their legal expenses in arbitration, and court costs can range upwards of $50,000. Most consumer law cases in the courts are taken by lawyers who work on contingency, meaning that they get paid out of any money they win, so it's hard to secure legal help for arbitration.

Which brings us to the issue of taking your insurance company to court. This is something that you should consider only as a last resort. It's expensive, and it takes so long for a decision to come down and then be implemented that your child is likely to reach adulthood before the process is over. If you have the means and the gumption, don't be dissuaded from making things better for the rest of us. Just don't pin all your hopes on a quick resolution by a judge. If only it were that easy! And remember, as of this writing most HMOs cannot be sued.

Your best bet is to research the reason why your insurance company or provider is denying care, and find persuasive evidence that can change its decision. The next few sections cover three of the most typical reasons for refusal, and offer some suggestions.

Denial for plan limits

If your insurance company only provides treatment for OCD as part of a limited mental health or nervous disorders benefit, you can challenge that limitation. It's easy to show that OCD is biologically based, so you may be able to get out from under the mental health limit altogether. As noted previously, some states have laws that specifically exempt OCD from any insurer's mental health limits.

Sarah, mother of 17-year-old Lili, tells about an insurance disaster:

> *When Lili was admitted to the hospital, we just naturally assumed that it would be paid for. It wasn't. The very day that the hospital found out our insurance company was refusing to pay because it excluded all mental and neurological care, she was suddenly well enough to go home. Because our state permits these kinds of exclusions in individual insurance plans, we were left holding the bill. We refinanced our house to pay the majority of it off, but almost five years later we still owe $175 to a psychiatrist she saw for perhaps ten minutes. You can bet that our next insurance company's literature got a closer inspection.*

One piece of information to gather in advance is how the company treats acquired nervous-system disorders, such as stroke, brain tumors, or traumatic brain injuries. If your insurance covers long-term care for these conditions, most states mandate equal benefits for patients with biologically-based brain disorders.

Incidentally, a neurologist may be your best "witness." Many people with OCD have concrete signs of neurological dysfunction, which can't be written off as simply psychological.

Your child's psychiatrist can also help plead your case by showing the importance of the treatment he has recommended. He can explain its cost-effectiveness by showing the insurance company the financial risk of going without treatment. Hospitalization, for example, is far more expensive than cognitive behavioral therapy, medication, and case management. In fact, OCD is truly one of the most cost-effective psychiatric disorders to manage—when it's done consistently and well.

Unfortunately, notes Mary, mother of 13-year-old Ryan, many insurers just don't get it:

> *We have insurance, but it pays very little (less than 50 percent). We are using an inheritance to pay for sessions.*

Ryan recently had to be admitted to an inpatient program—this might have been avoided with more intensive local services.

Denial for educational services

After blanket denial of coverage or strict limits on mental health care, the second most frequent insurance roadblock is the educational services exclusion. This usually comes into play for services that may also be delivered by school districts, such as speech therapy. Some insurers also try to use this exemption to force schools into paying for day treatment and residential programs for mentally ill children.

In all honesty, when the services provided are medical services, the school district should be able to bill your insurance for them. That's what you paid your premiums for! School districts, state healthcare programs, and the federal government are logical allies in the fight to force insurers to do their share. As long as insurers shirk their duty, families are forced to turn to overworked, under-funded taxpayer programs like Social Security Disability, Medicaid, and public schools.

However, school districts only started to try billing parents' insurance for medical services provided in school settings at the end of the 1990s. Many parents rightfully fear that denial of payment will lead to denial of services by the school district—it is illegal, but lack of funds is one of the most frequent excuses given for refusal of needed special education services. Parents who have been persistent enough to get therapeutic services from both the school district and their insurance company are afraid that their services will be cut in half, not augmented. And since schools and medical facilities generally have very different approaches to therapeutic interventions, this could be detrimental in other ways. For example, the services of a school psychologist with a master's degree may or may not be equal to those of your HMO's psychologist with a PhD and expertise in OCD.

You can sometimes challenge denial of therapeutic services by explaining that therapeutic goals are aimed at permitting essential activities of everyday life, useful not only in school, but for functioning in the larger world. This "essential activities of everyday life" rationale is what people with orthopedic disabilities use to get the therapies they need covered by insurance. In the case of OCD, this might include your child being able to leave the house and attend school, being able to walk without retracing her steps over and over, or being able to eat a normal diet.

It's important to note that schools can be required by special education law to provide certain types of medical and therapeutic services that make it possible for your child to learn. This will be discussed in Chapter 8, *School and Transition*. However, schools are not always the best or most knowledgeable healthcare providers—after all, this is not a school's primary purpose. If you can get your child's school and his healthcare professionals to work together as a team, this will be the best of both worlds.

Denial of "experimental" treatments

All insurance plans bar coverage for experimental treatments. Some do have a "compassionate care" exception, which comes into play when regular treatments have been tried unsuccessfully and the plan's medical advisors agree that the experimental treatment could be workable. This exception is generally available only to people with life-threatening illnesses.

So what do you do to pay for promising new treatments for OCD, such as intravenous immunoglobulin treatments for PANDAS or newly developed medications that aren't on your insurance company's approval list? You either pay out of pocket, or you work closely with your physician to get around the experimental treatment exclusion.

"Creative coding" is the term doctors use to describe billing the insurer or managed care entity for something that's not quite what was actually delivered. For example, a therapist might bill participation in a social skills training group, which the insurance company probably would not pay for, as something else that the insurer will pay for, such as an individual therapy session.

Creative coding is not exactly ethical, and it may not be desirable, either. Providers who do it take tremendous risk, and parents or patients for whom it is done must remember that they can't discuss these services with the rest of their healthcare team for fear of exposing the deception. That said, the practice is becoming increasingly common.

Another option is appealing to your insurer or HMO for special treatment. Your physician may have to prepare a "letter of medical necessity" to support your request—or this task may fall to you. This letter must include:

- The diagnosis for which the service, equipment, or medication is needed.
- The specific symptom or function that the service, equipment, or medication will treat or help with.
- A full description of the service, equipment, or medication, and how it will help the patient.
- If the service, equipment, or medication is new or experimental, evidence (medical studies, journal articles, etc.) to support your request.
- If there are less expensive or traditionally used alternatives to the new or experimental service, equipment, or medication, well-supported reasons that these alternatives are not appropriate for this patient.

Public healthcare in the US

Some US families have an extremely serious health insurance problem: they just can't get any. If this ever-growing group includes you, the primary publicly funded option is Medicaid, with or without a Katie Beckett waiver. The federal government also has the Tricare plan for those in current military service and their dependents and, through the Veterans Administration, coverage for former military personnel.

Medicaid

Medicaid is the federal health insurance program for those who are not senior citizens. It will pay for doctor and hospital bills; six prescription medications per month; physical, occupational, and speech therapy; and adaptive equipment. Medicaid is one of the few insurance plans that will pay for in-home therapy services, therapeutic foster care, partial hospitalization or day treatment, crisis services, and long-term hospitalization or residential care for people with mental illnesses. Although it is excessively bureaucratic, it is, in many ways, superior to private insurance coverage for people who have serious problems with mental illness.

If you are old enough to receive regular Social Security, or if you receive Social Security survivor's benefits, your child should already be eligible for Medicaid. Otherwise, you can get Medicaid coverage for your child by applying for SSI benefits for your child (see the next section) or, in some cases, by qualifying for state health plans for children that are based on Medicaid.

In most states, you can apply for Medicaid through your county disability services department.

There is one more, and drastic, way to get Medicaid: make your child a ward of the state by giving him up to the foster care system. According to a 1999 report from NAMI, about one-fourth of US families whose children are mentally ill have been forced to make this agonizing choice—simply to ensure that their children can be admitted into a publicly funded residential facility, or even just to get them medical and mental health care. This means not only losing physical custody of your child in most cases, but also losing the right to be involved in decisions about his healthcare, education, and living conditions. In almost every case you will retain visitation rights and some role in treatment decisions, unlike parents whose parental rights are terminated by a judge due to abuse or neglect. Transferral of parental rights is done in family court.

SSI

Supplemental Security Income (SSI) is a program that provides a small monthly stipend to disabled people who are unable to support themselves. Disabled children in low-income working families may also be eligible for SSI. Benefits range from around $400 to $500 per month for children or for adults living in another person's household, and over $600 per month for teenagers or adults living independently. This money is to be used only for the direct needs of the disabled individual; it is not family income per se. You will need to keep receipts for all your child-related expenditures.

Disabled adults and children who qualify for SSI automatically qualify for healthcare coverage from Medicaid.

To remain eligible for SSI and Medicaid, your income and assets usually must be limited. You can own a very modest home and car, but you cannot have much in savings. This can force parents desperate for Medicaid coverage for their children to "spend down" their savings and let their careers slide. It's a particularly unfair situation, since in homes where children have mental health problems, stability often depends on parents having enough money saved to permit flexibility during periods of crisis. Current SSI regulations make it very hard for parents to provide a safety net for their families today, or to provide for their child's security as an adult.

To apply for SSI, go to your nearest Social Security office, or call the Social Security hotline at (800) 772-1213 for an eligibility pre-screening. If you are given a green light by the eligibility screener, your next step is to make an initial interview appointment and fill out a Disability Report (Form SSA-3820-BK) for your child. This eleven-page form asks dozens of difficult questions, including information about every physician or clinic that might have medical records or test results for your child, information about his school performance and academic testing, and information about your previous contacts with public health agencies. You'll want to provide copies of as many of your child's mental health records as you can.

If you need help in completing this form (and many families do), a county or school social worker may be able to assist you. Disability advocacy groups may also have staff members or volunteers who can help.

Make sure this form and all of your records are complete when your initial interview takes place. You can be interviewed in person or over the phone. Most experienced applicants say in-person interviews are best, but they aren't always possible. Carefully kept records, including a list of phone numbers and addresses for your doctors and school personnel, are very important if you choose a phone interview.

During the interview, a Social Security representative will go over your child's Disability Report with you. She may ask extra questions. Some of them may seem rather invasive to people who have never applied for any type of government assistance.

In fact, the SSI application process has become increasingly adversarial over the past two decades. You may get the distinct impression that the interviewer thinks you are trying to con them about your child's disability—and your impression may be right. The entire application process usually lasts from three to eight months, sometimes longer. Once your application has been approved, you will receive a check equal to the payments your child would have received from the initial date of application until the approval date. This sum can amount to several thousand dollars, and has helped many families fund things like more secure housing, special tutoring, and expert psychiatric care.

If the Social Security department is not satisfied with the documentation you provide, it may order an Individualized Functional Assessment (IFA), which may mean a review of your medical documentation by Social Security representatives and/or interviews, and observations of your child by a psychiatrist working for Social Security. You have the right to be present for this interview, although parents report that some doctors seem to want to exclude them from the process.

Most applicants for SSI are rejected on their first try. You do have the right to appeal SSI denial, however, and you should, because a high percentage of appeals succeed. If your application for SSI is denied, contact a disability advocacy agency through the National Association of Protection and Advocacy Systems at (202) 408-9514. Publicly funded agencies can help you through the application process, and most can provide legal assistance if you need to appeal.

Additional information about the SSI program is available from the Social Security Advisory Service, a private advocacy group for recipients. It has a special web page on SSI for children with disabilities at *http://www.ssas.com/ssikids.html*.

Frank, father of 9-year-old Lucy, says applying for SSI was well worth the time:

> *Although it was a year before her claim was approved, SSI—and especially Medicaid—has been a real blessing. We have been able to use the money to pay for items Lucy broke during tantrums, as well as for basic needs, and it has helped my wife work about ten fewer hours each week so she can take Lucy to her appointments. It has also been much easier to get decent care for her with Medicaid. Before, we did not have insurance, and the expense for anything but her medication was too high. Now that is free, and she sees a psychiatrist and a therapist regularly.*

The Katie Beckett waiver

SSI is usually an income-dependent program. If you are working and earn more than the regulations allow, your child will not be automatically eligible for SSI. In some cases, family income will reduce the amount of SSI received to as low as one dollar per month, but the beneficiary will still be able to get Medicaid. Other families must apply for a special income-limit waiver called the "Katie Beckett waiver."

The waiver program is named for Katie Beckett, a severely handicapped child whose parents wanted to care for at home. Government regulations would only cover Katie's care in an expensive hospital setting. Her family, which could not bear the full cost of at-home care but had an income too high to qualify for SSI, successfully lobbied for a program that would allow seriously handicapped children to qualify for full Medicaid coverage.

The waiver program is administered at a state level. Some states have severely limited the number of Katie Beckett waivers they will allow. You must apply for SSI and be turned down to qualify. When you are denied SSI, ask for a written proof of denial. Next, contact your county Child and Family Services department and ask for a Medicaid worker. Schedule an appointment with this person to apply for a Katie Beckett waiver.

This appointment will be long, and the questions will be intrusive, so be prepared. You will need copious documentation, including:

- Your SSI rejection letter.
- Your child's birth certificate and Social Security number.
- Proof of income (check stubs or a special form filled out and signed by your employer, and possibly income tax forms).
- Names, addresses, and phone numbers of all physicians who have examined your child.
- Bank account and safety deposit box numbers, and amounts in these accounts.
- List of other assets and their value, including your house and car.
- A DMA6 medical report and a physician referral form signed by the doctor who knows your child best (Child and Family Services will provide you with these forms).

If you have a caseworker with your county's Mental Health offices or an HMO case manager, this person may be able to help you navigate the SSI, Medicaid, and Katie Beckett waiver process.

If you have specific problems with accessing appropriate medical benefits under Medicaid, state health plans, or other public healthcare plans, your caseworker or an advocate from NAMI or similar groups may be able to help. If your problems are of a legal nature, such as outright refusal of services or discrimination, call your state Bar Association and ask for its *pro bono* (free) legal help referral service, or contact the National Association of Protection and Advocacy Systems at (202) 408-9514. You can also consult the Health Law Project at (800) 274-3258.

State and local public health plans

As of this writing, twelve states have a State Children's Insurance Plan (SCHIP) that extends Medicaid benefits to more low-income and disabled children. Fifteen more states have applied to the Federal Department of Health and Human Services to start a SCHIP plan. These plans offer uninsured children the same or similar benefits as Medicaid does. The federal government and child health advocates are pushing to expand the SCHIP program to all 50 states.

Some states also have special state-sponsored insurance pools for people who have been denied insurance due to pre-existing health conditions. At least two—Oregon and Hawaii—have state insurance plans for which all low-income residents are eligible. Others have state insurance plans for children only, such as the Colorado Child Health Plan, Nevada Check Up, and New York's Child Health Plus. Several others have proposed such non-Medicaid plans, including Alabama, Delaware, Iowa, and Kansas.

For updated information about state programs and mental health, see NAMI's special SCHIP web site at *http://www.nami.org/youth/schip.htm*. For state-specific information on both SCHIP and non-Medicaid state plans for children, see the Children's Defense Fund's "Sign Them Up" web site at *http://www.childrensdefense.org/signup/index.html*.

In some areas, city or county health programs that include access to mental health services are available. Most counties in the US fund health clinics that provide low-cost or even free care to low-income residents.

The problem with public health plans

Coverage is a fine thing, but what happens when no one will accept you as a patient? This is the situation faced by millions of Americans who have government-provided healthcare. You may find yourself limited to using county health clinics or public hospitals, or to seeing those private providers who are willing to work for cut-rate fees. Medicaid and its cousins pay healthcare providers less than private insurers do, and there's no law that says a given provider must take patients with public insurance.

This means that facilities may be run-down, understaffed, and hectic. In fact, the emergency rooms of some public hospitals are downright frightening on weekend nights! Familiarize yourself with all of the options covered by your public healthcare plan. You may have more choices than you were initially led to believe. In some cases you may have the option to join one or more HMO plans, receiving the same benefits as non-subsidized HMO members. Check with other recipients or local advocacy groups if you are offered this choice—some of these plans do a good job of caring for disabled clients, while others are not preferable to plain old Medicaid or state healthcare.

Sadly, there is also an "anti-Welfare" attitude abroad among some healthcare workers, who may not know or care what financial and medical troubles drove your family to need public healthcare or income assistance. You shouldn't have to tolerate substandard or unprofessional treatment from providers. If it happens, ask your caseworker about complaint options.

Other public assistance for disabled children

While Canada, all Western European nations, and many other countries provide family support allowances to encourage one parent to stay home with young children, the US government has cut support even to single parents, and provides extraordinarily low allowances when they are available. This policy affects the parents of children with disabilities particularly harshly.

Between the 1950s and 1980s, single, low-income parents of children with disabilities tended to receive Aid to Families with Dependent Children (AFDC, "Welfare") and SSI. When put together, income from these two programs permitted them to eke out a living. While they remained well below the poverty line, they could generally obtain housing and adequate food. For many of these families, the most important benefit of receiving public assistance was access to Medicaid, which is available to AFDC recipients as well as those receiving SSI.

Welfare reform has changed this picture drastically. AFDC has been replaced by the Temporary Assistance for Needy Families (TANF) program, a system of short-term emergency supports. All states have now imposed stringent rules, such as limiting assistance to once in a lifetime, insisting that parents work for their grants, or forcing parents into job-training schemes geared toward a rapid transition to low-wage employment. Although most states have also added childcare services to their offerings to help parents receiving TANF grants transition to the workplace, affordable childcare slots for children and teens with mental illness are almost nonexistent. This leaves even the most determined low-income parent at a severe disadvantage.

Federal law permits exceptions to TANF regulations to be made for some—but not all—parents caring for disabled children, and for parents who are themselves mentally ill. However, caseworkers are responsible for holding down the number of exemptions to 20 percent or less of their clients, even though as many as a third of families on Welfare include either a mother or a child with a serious disability. (See "Recent Studies of AFDC Recipients Estimate Need for Specialized Child Care" at *http://www.welfare-policy.org/childdis.htm* if you'd like to know more.)

If you have OCD or other handicaps yourself and are parenting, TANF may work for you or against you. Some parents who have let their caseworker know about a personal mental problem have been exempted from certain regulations. Others have lost their children to the state. You should see a Welfare rights organization or sympathetic social worker before making the decision to tell. They can help you ensure your children's security by approaching the issue correctly.

You can apply for TANF at your county's Child and Family Services department. The program is primarily for single parents, but two-parent families are eligible in some areas and under some circumstances. The amount of the monthly grant varies. It is determined by the county government, which administers TANF programs at the local level. Grants range from around $150 per month in some rural Southern counties to about $650 per month in expensive cities like San Francisco, where a small supplemental housing benefit is factored into the grant.

You'll need to provide very complete documentation to get and retain benefits on the basis of needing to provide full-time home care for a child. You can expect to have an eligibility review at least every three months, during which all of your documents will be reviewed and you will be re-interviewed. Generally speaking, you cannot have savings or possessions worth over $1,000, although you may own a modest home and car. You may be forced to sell a late-model car and other valuables before you can receive benefits. Your TANF grant may be reduced by the amount of other financial assistance you receive. If you find part-time work, your grant will also be reduced by this amount or a portion thereof—some states do have work incentive programs, however. Court-ordered child-support payments to TANF recipients are paid to the county rather than directly to the parent, and your grant will be debited for these as well.

You may be eligible for Food Stamps, commodities (free food), and other benefits, such as job training, if you receive TANF. People leaving TANF programs may be able to get certain short-term benefits, such as subsidized child care and continued health insurance.

If you need help in obtaining public assistance, contact a local Welfare rights organization or advocacy group, or see the National Welfare Monitoring and Advocacy Partnership (NWMAP) at *http://www.nwmap.org/index.htm* for national information and referrals.

Indirect financial help for your family

In the US, tax deductions have replaced direct financial assistance to the poor in many cases. Since these benefits are provided but once a year, they are less convenient, but families coping with the high cost of caring for a mentally ill child should take advantage of them.

One of the most important federal income tax benefits is the medical deduction. You can write off the direct cost of doctor's visits not covered by health insurance, health insurance co-pays and deductibles, out-of-pocket expenses for medications, travel costs related to medical care, and at least some expenses related to attending medical or disability conferences and classes. Self-employed people can deduct most of their health-insurance premiums as a separate item.

Because medical deductions limit your federal tax liability, they will also reduce your state income taxes, if any (state taxes are usually based on taxable income figures taken from your federal form). Some states have additional tax benefits for the disabled. In Oregon, for example, each disabled child counts as two dependents.

Another important federal tax benefit is the Earned Income Credit (EIC) program. This benefit for the working poor can actually supplement your earnings with a tax rebate, not just a deduction. You can file for EIC on your federal 1040 tax form.

Mortgage interest is also tax deductible, as most people are aware. Since you can usually retain ownership of a home and remain eligible for direct financial assistance, such as SSI, home ownership is particularly attractive to families who are providing care for a child with OCD, especially if the child's symptoms do not respond well to current treatments, and the family must consider being his caregiver into adulthood. Some banks and credit unions have special mortgage programs for low- and moderate-income families. Given the strong financial benefits of home ownership, including the opportunity to keep your housing costs from going up in the future, purchasing a house is very advisable.

Low-income families, including young adults with OCD who rely on SSI or fixed-income trusts, may be able to get additional help in reaching the goal of home ownership from organizations like Habitat for Humanity or Franciscan Enterprises. Mental health advocacy and service organizations have recently begun to push to increase the level of home ownership among mentally ill adults. In some cases, the home can be part of a special trust that provides professional management services, preventing the adult from being conned out of it, selling it, or seriously damaging it during a period of more severe symptoms.

Health Canada

In Canada, the Canada Health Act ensures coverage for all Canadian citizens and for non-citizens who need emergency care. Healthcare regulations are the same nationwide, although providers can be hard to find in the less-populated northern provinces.

John, father of 14-year-old Tori, explains:

> *We live in Canada, near a very large city, Toronto. Even within such a geographical situation there is such little real specialized help for children with OCD. There are some people who are leading the way to better facilities and treatment programs, but so much more needs to be done.*

The government pays for most programs. But if we choose, we have medical insurance that covers a percentage of the cost for private care.

To initiate an evaluation for OCD, parents might go through the school system or talk to their child's pediatrician. Adults would first see their primary care physician. The pediatrician or family doctor would then make a referral to an appropriate specialist.

A wide variety of specialists are available through the Canadian health system, which is called Health Canada/Santé Canada. Many of the best are affiliated with university hospitals. Waiting lists are a reality, but parents report that calls and letters (especially if they come from the pediatrician or family doctor as well as the patient or patient's family) can often open up opportunities more quickly than usual.

If no qualified providers are available in rural areas, public assistance programs may be available to help a patient get expert care in the closest city. This help may include covering transportation costs, housing the child and parent during evaluation and treatment, and providing regular consultations later on with a pediatrician or family doctor who's closer to home. In practice, however, families in rural Canada sometimes have great difficulty in obtaining adequate care for children with mental illness.

Therapeutic services may be delivered in a medical or school setting. There isn't much coordination between schools and Health Canada, according to Canadian parents.

Parents also report that privatization and other changes are starting to limit their access to healthcare. Some families are now carrying private insurance to ensure timely and frequent access to care providers.

Canadians in border areas may wish to consult specialists in the US. Except for rare and pre-approved cases, Health Canada will not cover these visits.

Disability income in Canada

Welfare is available in Canada for people with disabilities, single parents, and unemployed adults with or without children. The amount of the monthly payment is set at the provincial level, and varies from a low of about $580 per month in poor provinces like New Brunswick to around $800 per month in the more expensive provinces of Ontario and British

Columbia. Under the Canadian system, payments to parents caring for children, single or otherwise, are higher than those to disabled adults.

To apply for state benefits, visit your nearest Ministry or Department of Social Services. For disability benefits, regulations vary by state. Typically, you must be 18 years of age or older and have confirmation from a medical practitioner that the impairment exists and will likely continue for at least two years or longer, or that it is likely to continue for at least one year and then reoccur. In addition you must require, as a direct result of severe mental or physical impairment, one of the following:

- Extensive assistance or supervision in order to perform daily living tasks within a reasonable time.
- Unusual and continuous monthly expenditures for transportation, for special diets, or for other unusual but essential and continuous needs.

Also, there are limits on the amount and kinds of savings and other property that a person or family receiving benefits can have.

As in the US, Welfare reform is a growing trend in Canada. Some states have introduced mandatory workfare programs for single adults and for some parents on Welfare. These provisions generally do not apply to people receiving disability benefits, and parents caring for disabled children may be able to have work requirements waived or deferred.

Canadians who are denied benefits or who have other problems with the benefits agency can appeal the decision to an independent tribunal.

Some assistance for people with disabilities may also be available at the federal level, or from First Nations (Native Canadian) agencies.

Indirect financial help in Canada

Other direct and indirect income assistance is available to Canadians, such as subsidized travel and tax benefits. For example, college students with permanent disabilities can have their student loans forgiven, and are also eligible for special grants to pay for hiring a note-taker, for transportation, and for other education-related expenses.

You can get help with medical and disability issues from the support and advocacy organizations listed in Appendix A, *Resources*.

National Health in the UK

The National Health system in Britain and Scotland has undergone tremendous upheaval over the past three decades. All services were once free to UK citizens, while private-pay physicians were strictly for the wealthy. Public services have since been sharply curtailed, and co-pays have been introduced. Nevertheless, services for people with mental illness are probably better now than they were in the past, when institutionalization was the norm.

Parents who want to have a child assessed for OCD may begin with their health visitor, pediatrician, a psychiatrist or psychologist, a Child Development Center, or a local or specialist Child and Family Guidance Clinic. Teenage and adult patients will probably want to access a specialist through their General Practitioner (GP). Referrals to specialists are notoriously difficult to obtain, even for private-pay patients.

Since healthcare practitioners are an important part of the Statement of Special Needs ("Statementing") procedure for getting Early Intervention and special education services, it may be wise to pursue a medical diagnosis and Statementing at the same time.

You can get advice and help from MIND (the National Association for Mental Health), as well as from support and advocacy organizations listed in Appendix A.

Disability income in the UK

In the UK, people with disabilities have access to three major types of direct state benefits. You can apply for these programs at your local Benefits Agency Office.

The Disability Living Allowance (DLA) is for adults or children with a disability. Parents or caregivers can apply on behalf of a child. Payment ranges from 15 to 35 pounds per week. The DLA forms are relatively complex, so find an experienced disability advocate to help you fill them out, if possible. MIND and other mental health advocacy groups have DLA experts on staff, as may your local council.

Parents and others caring for a child who receives DLA can apply for the Attendants Allowance (also called the Carers Allowance) program as well.

Any person over 5 years old who receives DLA can also get a Mobility Allowance, a small sum of money to help them get to appointments, and meet general transportation needs.

Your local council may also have its own benefits scheme. These may be direct payments, such as a supplemental housing benefit, or tax offsets.

Indirect financial help in the UK

A number of supported work schemes are available for people with disabilities and adults receiving other forms of public assistance. In some cases, these programs are mandatory. Your teenage child should start learning about these programs before leaving school.

Teens and young adults attending college or trade school may find themselves in a "Catch 22" situation: on some occasions benefits officers have decided that if they are well enough to go to college, they're well enough to work, and canceled their benefits. You can appeal these and other unfavorable decisions to a Social Security Appeals Tribunal.

Help with disability benefit issues is available from most of the UK groups listed in Appendix A, as well as from the self-help group UK Advocacy Network, (0114) 272-8171.

Disability benefits in the Republic of Ireland

Disability Allowance and Disability Benefit are available in Ireland, but are far from generous. Both are administered via the Department of Social Welfare. Disabled students can continue to receive these benefits while attending third-level courses, although they may lose other types of public assistance, such as Rent Allowance.

Maintenance Grant (a general benefit for poor families) is not affected by these benefits.

Supported work schemes are available, although your earnings may make you lose your disability benefits. The exception is work that your local Welfare officer agrees is "rehabilitative" in nature.

A number of scholarship and grant programs are available to assist students with disabilities in Northern Ireland. An online report at *http://www.ahead.ie/grants/grants.html#toc* offers more information.

Some mental healthcare is available from public or charitable hospitals and clinics in Ireland at low or no cost.

Medicare in Australia

Medicare, the Australian health plan, pays 85 percent of all doctors' fees. It also qualifies Australian citizens for free treatment in any public hospital. Many general practitioners and pediatricians "bulk bill": they charge the government directly for all of their patient visits and let the 15 percent co-payment slide. Specialists usually won't bulk bill. Once a certain cost level has been reached, Medicare pays 100 percent of the bill.

Patients can see the physician of their choice without getting a preliminary referral, but many specialists have long waiting lists.

A number of programs have been set up to identify and help Australian children with disabilities at an early age. Parents say that medical professionals are sometimes less than savvy about neurological disorders in general, but if you can make contact with one who is, services are available.

Kerry, mother of 12-year-old Kim, explains how the system works:

> *In the past, the government used to provide a free screening for all children at age 4, and again at around age 6. This would be conducted in kindergartens, some daycare centers, and in schools. This was mainly a medical screening, but basic developmental and behavioral differences were sometimes picked up at this stage. Nowadays the screening is no longer universal. . . either the parent or teacher/childcare worker has to request it. Many children who would benefit from intervention thus slip through the net.*
>
> *In Australia, some pediatricians specialize in behavioral issues (the specialty of "ambulatory pediatrics"), and at the present time children with neurological issues end up being sent to one of these. Neurologists and psychiatrists are not involved in the care of children, except in cases of clear physical signs (e.g., epilepsy) or adolescent depression.*

Psychologists and nonmedical providers are generally NOT covered by Medicare. However, the school system provides limited services of this sort (free) and the public hospital system is also involved. . . but over-crowded and under-funded.

Services may be delivered in the child's home, in a school, or in a clinical setting. Parents in rural areas may find access to qualified practitioners difficult, although the emergency healthcare system for rural Australia is enviable. In some situations, parents or patients in very rural areas may be able to access professionals for advice or "virtual consultations" over the Internet, telephone, or radio.

Medicaid does not cover some prescription medications, and there is a sliding-scale co-payment for those it does cover.

Disability benefits in Australia

A variety of income support programs is available to Australian citizens, including direct financial assistance for adults with disabilities, parents caring for children with disabilities, single parents, unemployed single adults, youth, and students. Programs related specifically to disabled citizens and their families include:

- Disability Support Pension
- Related Wife Pension
- Sickness Allowance
- Mobility Allowance
- Carer Payment
- Child Disability Allowance

Indirect financial help in Australia

Employment programs for people with disabilities are many and varied, including the Supported Wage System, which brings the earnings of disabled workers in sheltered workshops or other types of supported or low-wage employment closer to the livability range.

Indirect benefits may also be available under the Disability Services Act in areas such as education, work, and recreation.

You can find online information about all of Australia's benefit schemes at the Centrelink web site, *http://www.centrelink.gov.au/*. To apply for benefits or disability services, contact your local Department of Family and Community Services.

You can get help with disability income and health benefit issues from the support and advocacy organizations listed in Appendix A.

Disability help in New Zealand

About 75 percent of all healthcare in New Zealand is publicly funded. Care is delivered through private physicians who accept payment from the public health system. Treatment at public hospitals is fully covered for all New Zealand citizens, and also for Australian and UK citizens living and working in New Zealand.

Healthcare and disability services are both provided through a central Health Authority, which has for the past few years been making special efforts to improve the delivery of mental health, child health, and minority-group care. To start an assessment for OCD, parents should first talk to their child's pediatrician or a family physician about a specialist referral. Self-referral is also possible.

Urban patients may have access to group practices centered on Crown (public) hospitals, which often have excellent specialists. Mäori patients may access healthcare and assessments through medical clinics centered around traditional *iwi* (tribal) structures, if they prefer.

About 40 percent of the population in New Zealand carries private insurance, primarily for hospitalization or long-term geriatric care only. This insurance is helpful when you need elective surgery and want to avoid waiting lists at public hospitals. It is not needed to access speech therapy, occupational therapy, physical therapy, psychiatric care, or other direct health or disability services.

New Zealanders have long complained that waiting lists for assessments and major medical treatments are excessive. Until recently, patients on waiting lists were not given a firm date for their visits, and were expected to be available immediately should an opening occur. A new booking system that is said to be more reliable was instituted in 1998.

Private care options

For patients in need of temporary or permanent residential care, volunteer organizations (particularly churches) are heavily involved in running long-term care facilities in New Zealand. These facilities are usually free of charge to the patient or family, although some are reimbursed by public health.

Privatization is a growing trend in New Zealand. Public hospitals and their allied clinics have been recreated as public-private corporations. However, the government still provides most funding and regulations for healthcare.

Disability income in New Zealand

Direct benefits in New Zealand are similar to those provided in Australia, although the payments have historically been much lower. Domestic Purposes Benefit is for single parents, including those with disabled children. There are also a number of additional services available to the disabled and their caregivers, including training schemes, supported employment, and recreational assistance. The social safety net in New Zealand is currently being revamped, but services for people with disabilities are actually expected to expand.

To apply for benefits or services, contact your local Ministry of Social Welfare office, which runs the Income Support program. If you need help with paperwork or appeals, Beneficiary Advisory Services (*http://canterbury.cyberplace.org.nz/community/bas.html*) in Christchurch provides assistance and advocacy, as do a number of disability advocacy groups, particularly the Disability Information Service (*http://canterbury.cyberplace.co.nz/community/dis.html.*)

Alternatives to insurance

No matter where you live, there are alternatives to expensive medical care. In countries where there is no national health system, those who don't have insurance or whose insurance is inadequate will want to investigate these resources.

In some cases, creative private-pay arrangements may be possible with psychiatrists and other providers. Parents have traded services or products for care, and others have arranged payment plans or reduced fees based on financial need. The larger the provider, the more likely it is to have a system in place for providing income-based fees. The smaller the provider, the more receptive it is likely to be to informal arrangements, including barter.

Hospitals and major clinics usually have social workers on staff who can help you make financial arrangements.

Sources of free or low-cost healthcare or therapeutic services may include:

- Public health clinics, including school-based health clinics
- Public hospitals
- Medical schools and associated teaching hospitals and clinics
- College special education programs (for learning disabilities and cognitive testing, and sometimes for direct help with educational planning and techniques)
- Hospitals and clinics run by religious or charitable orders, such as Lutheran Family Services clinics
- Charitable institutions associated with religious denominations, such as Catholic Charities, the Jewish Aid Society, and the Salvation Army
- The Urban League, which provides counseling services for troubled teens in some cities and can sometimes refer clients for psychiatric care
- The United Way, an umbrella fundraising organization for many programs that can often provide referrals
- Local children's aid associations, such as the Children's Home Society and the Boys and Girls Aid Society
- Grant programs, both public and private

In the UK, special resources outside of National Health include:

- MIND
- The Mental Health Foundation (*http://www.mentalhealth.org.uk/*)
- Community Trust associations, particularly The Zito Trust (0171 240 8422)—see the Mental Health Foundation web site and *http://www.caritasdata.co.uk/indexchr.htm* for lists of many UK trusts related to mental illness, substance abuse, and related issues, including many that focus on particular ethnic or religious communities
- The New Masonic Samaritan Fund (for members and families of Masons)
- Samaritans (0345 909090)

Medical savings accounts

This is a new healthcare payment option in the US that may have benefits for some children and adults with OCD. A medical savings account (MSA) allows families to put away a certain amount of money specifically for healthcare costs. This income will then be exempted from federal (and in some cases, state) income taxes. Unused funds continue to gain tax-free interest. These accounts can be used to pay for insurance deductibles, co-payments, prescriptions, and medical services not covered by insurance.

Families faced with paying out-of-pocket for an expensive residential program or experimental medication might be able to use an MSA to reduce their costs by an impressive percentage. You'll need to check the regulations of the specific MSA plan to see what expenses will qualify.

Help with medications

Low-income patients may be able to get their medications for free by providing documentation to charitable programs run by pharmaceutical companies. In the US, the Pharmaceutical Manufacturers Association publishes a directory of medication assistance programs. Doctors can get a copy of the PMA's official guide by calling (800) PMA-INFO. Alternatively, you or your doctor can call the company that makes your medication directly to find out about its indigent patient program. These programs are listed in Appendix A.

An organization called The Medicine Program ((573) 778-1118, *http://www.themedicineprogram.com*) can help you and your doctor apply to indigent patient programs.

Most of these programs require that you have no insurance coverage for outpatient prescription drugs, that purchasing the medication at its retail price would be a hardship for you due to your income and/or expenses, and that you do not qualify for a government or third-party program that can pay for the prescription.

Doctor's samples

Another source for free medications is your physician's sample cabinet. All you have to do is ask, and hope that the pharmaceutical rep has paid a recent visit. Samples can help tide you over rough financial patches, but you can't rely on getting them monthly.

Mail-order medications

You may be able to reduce the cost of your monthly medication bill by using a mail-order or online pharmacy. These pharmacies can fill your prescription and mail it to you, sometimes at substantial savings. Medications may be available via mail order within your country, or from overseas. The latter option can be surprisingly inexpensive, and may provide you with access to medications that normally would not be available where you live. Some HMOs sponsor their own mail-order services. If you are stationed overseas with the US military, contact your Tricare health benefits representative about mail-order arrangements.

Your doctor may have to fill out some paperwork before you can use mail-order services. As with any other transaction by mail or over the Internet, you'll want to do as much as you can to check out the company's reputation and quality of service before sending money or using your credit card.

Communicating via fax, email, or telephone generally works best with these firms, which can usually send you a three-month supply in each order. If you are doing business with an overseas pharmacy, check Customs regulations that might prohibit you from importing medication before ordering, especially if the drug is not approved for use in your country.

Some mail-order and online pharmacies were initially created to serve the market for AIDS medications, but have since expanded to cover a wide selection. Many will accept health insurance if you have a drug benefit—some will actually cover your medication co-payment as part of the deal.

Mail-order pharmacies that some families have worked with successfully are listed in Appendix A.

Clinical trials

Some patients have received excellent medical care by taking part in clinical trials of new medications or treatments. Others have suffered unpleasant side effects or felt that they were treated like guinea pigs. Before enrolling your child in a clinical trial, make sure that you feel comfortable with the procedure or medication being tested, the professionals conducting the study, and the facility where it will take place. Be as fully informed as possible.

An international listing service for current clinical trials is available at *http://www.centerwatch.com/*. If you don't have web access, contact CenterWatch Inc. at (617) 247-2327.

The OC Foundation sponsors some OCD research projects, and can help you find out about others. You can find information about these at *http://www.ocfoundation.org/ocf1510a.htm*. You may also want to check the web sites of major OCD research centers on a regular basis if taking part in clinical studies appeals to you.

Miscellaneous discounts

Don't forget, children with OCD and sometimes, by extension, their families may be eligible for a variety of discounts and special access programs for the disabled. For example, the US National Parks Service offers a lifelong pass that gives disabled individuals free entry to all national parks, as well as half-price camping privileges. If the recipient is a child, her family also gets the discount. Disneyland, Walt Disney World, and many other theme parks offer special privileges to people with disabilities, such as not having to wait in line for attractions.

There are a number of programs around the world that help disabled people get access to computers and the Internet. One that offers *free* computers is DRAGnet (which can be reached at (715) 322-5103 or *http://www.DRAGnet.org/*).

If your child needs medical care in a location far from home, but you can't afford the cost of a flight or hotel, there are several resources that may be able to help in the US or Canada. See Appendix A for a brief listing.

Similar corporate programs may be available in Europe, Australia, and New Zealand; contact the public relations office of your national airline to find out more. You may also be eligible for an emergency travel grant from a social services agency to cover these needs.

If you would like to learn more about OCD, special education, or other matters related to your child's disability at a state, regional, or national conference, funds may be available through your county mental health or disability office, or through charitable service providers. Talk to your child's caseworker or case manager about "flexible funds" for this and other educational purposes. Some parents have been able to access this type of funding to get special instruction on designing and running home-based cognitive behavioral therapy programs for their child.

Changing the rules

Advocating for changes in the insurance system or your national healthcare system is a big job. Unless you want to make it your life mission, it's probably too big for any one patient or parent. But by working together, individuals can accomplish a lot.

Advocacy organizations can be the point of contact between healthcare consumers, insurers, HMOs, and public health.

In the US, NAMI has been at the forefront of efforts to protect patients and their families by mandating insurance coverage and treatment, but it's an uphill battle.

The Federal Mental Health Parity Act was passed with much fanfare in 1996, and went into effect at the beginning of 1998. Many people now believe that all insurance plans in the US must cover mental health care at the same level as they do physical health care. This is a misconception. This law affects only employer-sponsored group insurance plans that wish to offer mental health coverage. They are not required to do so. Additionally, if such coverage raises the company's premium cost by more than 1 percent, they need not comply with the law. Companies with fewer than fifty employees are also exempted.

The Mental Health Parity Act raises the annual or lifetime cap on mental health care in the plans that it covers, but it does not prevent insurance companies from limiting access or recovering costs in other ways. They may, for example, legally restrict the number of visits you can make to a mental health provider, raise the co-payment required for such visits, or raise your deductible for mental health care.

At the time of this edition, many states have passed their own, more restrictive, mental health parity laws. As noted previously, these laws supersede the federal regulations. Eleven other states have parity laws that are equal to the federal act, and others have less-restrictive parity laws. Of the twelve with tighter restrictions, all of the laws are written in ways that should require coverage for OCD. Colorado, Connecticut, Maine, New Hampshire, Rhode Island, and Texas specifically require coverage for "biologically based" mental illnesses. For parents and patients living in these states, this is a step in the right direction, although it remains to be seen how these laws will be enforced and what steps some insurers may take to evade responsibility.

The University of South Florida maintains an informational web site on state and federal mental health parity research, laws, and proposed laws at *http://www.fmhi.usf.edu/parity/parityhome.html.*

As of this writing, the Mental Health Equitable Treatment Act of 1999 was still making its way through Congress. This law would force insurers to cover major mental illnesses, including OCD, at the same rate as physical disorders. It would also prevent them from limiting outpatient visits and hospital stays when they are needed for effective treatment.

However, insurance is regulated at the state level, so that's where the most effective parity action will take place. There's a need for education, for public advocacy, for legislative action, and in some cases, for legal action. Parents and patients can and should be involved in these efforts.

Parents and patients can make common cause with healthcare providers, many of whom are angry at how their patients with mental illnesses are being mistreated. For example, the Washington, DC-based American Psychological Association (APA) has filed suit against Aetna U.S. Healthcare Inc. and related managed care entities in California, alleging that the company engaged in false advertising when it claimed to offer "prompt, accessible mental health treatment services." The APA later filed similar suits against two other HMOs, alleging that all of these companies put hidden caps on their already limited mental health benefits, disregarded what practitioners had to say about medical treatment of their patients, and deliberately delayed referrals.

As Russ Newman, PhD, JD, executive director for professional practice for the American Psychological Association said in a 1998 press release:

> *Despite the managed care industry's argument to the contrary, it's typically the managed care company that determines and controls the treatment of patients, not the doctor, and the financial bottom-line, not patient need, is usually the controlling factor.*

Of course, parity laws will do little for the increasing number of children and families who are uninsured. That's both an economic issue and a public policy problem, and it will take movement on both of those fronts to effect real change.

All of us—parents, patients, and practitioners—want to see improvements in healthcare and in how it's delivered. By working closely with our allies in the public, private, and volunteer sectors, we can make it happen. Even insurance companies and managed care entities can be brought on board if they're shown the positive benefit of better-functioning patients, who require much less emergency care, fewer hospitalizations, and less expensive medications. Alternative models for delivery of care are evolving, and with hard work these new systems can be both more humane and more cost-efficient.

CHAPTER 8

School and Transition

OBSESSIVE-COMPULSIVE DISORDER can have profound developmental and educational effects on young people. This chapter will cover those effects and discuss ways to handle them, including writing and using a 504 plan or Individual Education Plan (IEP) to help your child achieve his best in school. Parents of pre-kindergarten children will want to consult the "Early Intervention" section of this chapter first.

We'll begin by talking mostly about the US education system and appropriate laws, but education in other English-speaking countries will also be covered.

An IEP can do more than help with your child's K–12 education. Transition services—services that will help your teenager make a smooth transition into higher education or work—must be part of the IEP process as well. Accordingly, this chapter will address transition issues, including IEP-based transition services and finding adult services in the community for young adults.

OCD at school

Most school officials know next to nothing about OCD. They assume it's rare—an issue they'll never be faced with. Some may assume that a child with OCD would not be able to attend school, perhaps even that such children should be institutionalized. You may be told that your child is the first and only person with OCD who has ever graced this school's halls.

Since you now know how prevalent obsessive-compulsive disorder is, you also know that this can't possibly be true.

And since mental illness in children isn't exactly a taboo topic these days, you have to wonder if school officials are deliberately going about their business with blinders on. In any school with 500 students, it's likely that 10 or more will have a serious mental illness, such as OCD, clinical depression, or schizophrenia: that's at least 10 students out of every group of 500 that moves through the school over a period of years—not an insignificant number at all.

In addition, 1997 statistics from the Centers for Disease Control and Prevention revealed that 20 percent of high school students are emotionally upset enough in any given year to consider suicide, and almost 8 percent have made one or more suicide attempts. Some of these troubled youth have a mental illness, and others are reacting (or overreacting) to difficult life events.[1]

Put together the number of children with mental illness and those who are experiencing severe, if transient, emotional distress, and you get a figure that makes you wonder how this population could be overlooked.

Ignorance of mental illness goes beyond the issue of missing its presence in schools. It also prevents children from receiving an adequate education. It causes teachers to punish students for symptoms of their illness, makes kids feel like failures when they can't perform, and creates a rift between schools and parents at a time when they should be uniting to help a child.

Along with ignorance, there is a pervasive fear of mental illness in our society that extends past the schoolroom door. You've probably felt it yourself, and you've no doubt seen it in the reactions of some friends and relatives when they learned of your child's diagnosis. This fear causes many schools to "push out" affected children by denying them special education services, denigrating them and their families, refusing to create support systems that might make education easier, and doing anything within their power to move them into another setting. . .*any* other setting, even sitting at home on the couch without a diploma and with little hope of decent employment.

Indeed, the results of this fear and ignorance are tragic. In 1999, the US Department of Education released its annual report on special education. This document trumpeted the excellent news that thanks to new laws, parental efforts, and better teaching methods, 31 percent more students with disabilities are now receiving high school diplomas. Buried in this report was the sad news that this trend does not yet extend to children with "emotional disturbances," the special education category that includes major mental illnesses. According to the DOE, an outrageous *55 percent* of emotionally disturbed children leave school without earning a diploma. They also fail more courses, earn lower GPAs, miss more school, and are held back more often than students with other types of disabilities.[2]

That's a shameful record—one that must be changed. Children with mental retardation, children whose physical disabilities confine them to wheelchairs, and those with other health problems are making great strides in accessing an education. This wasn't always the case. These changes have only come about through the efforts of dedicated parents and education researchers, working in concert with teachers, school administrators, and lawmakers to revamp school programs for the disabled. A similar effort is now underway for students with mental and neurological problems, and parents and caring professionals are duty-bound to be a part of it.

Parents can do three things to dispel ignorance and fear of OCD in schools. They can:

- Communicate with their child's school about the diagnosis. The potential stigma of labeling a child as having obsessive-compulsive disorder is far less serious than what will happen if the school labels the same child as having a behavior problem or as a lazy student who refuses to do his work.
- Use the special education laws to put supports into place for children with OCD at school.
- Educate the educators: provide reading material about OCD, and be available to teachers, counselors, and administrators who want to know more.

Special school problems

Certain school problems are common for kids with OCD. These include symptoms that are likely to impact schoolwork, issues of transitioning back into school after hospitalization, the use of medications at school, and teasing and bullying.

Most adults can visualize how OCD might affect them at work. The same issues that impact adult performance on the job can make school more difficult for children with OCD. Perhaps the most important aspect of OCD for students is its capacity to distract them from the task at hand. Obsessive thoughts and the need to perform ritual behaviors take time away from paying attention in class and completing schoolwork. If a teacher hasn't been informed about the child's diagnosis, they might think the child is daydreaming or willfully ignoring her homework, when she is instead fighting hard to stay focused.

Seventeen-year-old Patty explains how OCD affects her at school:

> *I do okay, although the fact that my mind wanders constantly makes it difficult to concentrate on work. I also become nervous around other people, and find it hard to be comfortable around my friends.*

Medication and CBT can reduce OCD's ability to distract, but until they take effect (and for those students who do not respond to these interventions), classroom modifications can help. Eliminating unnecessary distractions is an important step, especially for students with OCD who are extremely sensitive to noise, smells, and visual clutter. These students may find that working in a resource room, quiet library, or individual study carrel is a good idea when they are having trouble concentrating. Classrooms can be designed to minimize sensory overload.

Eighteen-year-old Beth, a recent high school graduate with OCD, has found the illness irritating:

> *The only challenge that I have experienced with school is paying attention, as well as taking tests. My mind tends to wander and focus on my obsessions and compulsions, and it's hard to concentrate during tests because one of my compulsions involves looking at certain people, so I'm constantly looking up and down. It's very distracting.*

Some students with OCD find transitions during the school day especially difficult. These kids may do their best work when the number of classroom and personnel changes is limited, either by being in an inclusive special education classroom or by spending longer blocks of time in the same classroom. Alternatively, they may need extra time to get from class to class.

Perfectionism is a serious problem for many people with OCD. In school this might lead to excellent performance, and to problems at other times. For example, grade school children with OCD often find handwriting and drawing intensely frustrating due to perfectionism. They may try to get letters, numbers, and drawings absolutely perfect, to the point of writing, erasing, and rewriting figures over and over. Even simple math assignments can become torturous as they check and re-check their answers, and attempt to make their numbers perfectly shaped and lined up on the page.

Parents and teachers can work together on strategies. For instance, they can spell out specific standards of quality so that students don't set their own bar too high, allow students to prepare assignments on a typewriter or computer rather than by hand, permit checking math homework answers once (and only once) with a calculator, and shorten assignments if needed. Many students with OCD are able to let go of perfectionist goals when working within time limits, especially if there are limits attached to each item rather than an entire set of items.

E. J., age 19 and a college freshman, has used self-imposed time limits when her symptoms get worse:

> *My OCD got much worse during my first semester at college. I had to learn to compensate for my symptoms by not taking as many notes because of a writing compulsion. Academic pressures were very stressful; I was a very good student to begin with, so luckily my grades had some room to drop. I got through only with God's help!*

Perfectionism and stress have both harassed 16-year-old Amy:

> *Large tests and especially pop quizzes aggravate my symptoms tremendously, and school serves as the main trigger for my obsessions. I am a straight-A student, and my largest fear is failing. I did not suffer social pressures, but academic pressures push me to the breaking point.*

Procrastination is sometimes the result of perfectionism. Students with OCD may start a school project over and over, throwing away half-finished versions or ruminating endlessly over what they should do. As the deadline gets closer, anxiety increases and may reach paralyzing intensity. The result is work left undone, despite the fact that thinking and worrying about the project has occupied far more hours of time than would have been needed to complete it.

Like students with ADD/ADHD, kids with OCD can almost always benefit from general instruction in study and schoolwork skills, including systems for conceiving and completing projects that are most likely to be stymied by procrastination, such as essays, reports, and science projects. Successful strategies used by some students include breaking up large projects into small, manageable tasks, each with its own deadline; learning formulas that, if followed, will always turn out a serviceable essay or report; using an assignment or agenda book that teachers and parents check each day; using visual organizing systems, such as color-coded folders or sticky notes, to keep assignments organized and on time; and setting a specific amount of time aside daily for schoolwork. Of course, parents should provide a good environment for studying at home and ensure that extracurricular activities, medical appointments, and family activities do not disrupt a child's regular study sessions.

Kids with OCD may benefit from working with a tutor on certain types of subjects or projects. The tutor could be an adult volunteer or resource room teacher, but many students have had equally good results from working with a peer or slightly older student whose study skills are particularly good. Tutors should pay special attention not to just helping with a problem topic or project, but to imparting general guidelines and ideas about studying and doing schoolwork.

There are several OCD symptoms that school-age patients find particularly distracting. These include:

- Compulsions to count words as they are being said or while reading
- Compulsions to count other items in the classroom
- Compulsions to smell, touch, or look at other students
- Obsessions with "good" or "bad" numbers that cause students to avoid certain math problems, pages in books, or sentences with that number of words
- Obsessions with making things turn out even, which can wreak havoc on mathematics skills, reading, and drawing
- Compulsions to read each word or number perfectly or follow steps with precision, causing students to start over again if they make even small errors
- Compulsion to reread due to doubt that the first reading was done properly; compulsion to rewrite due to similar perfectionism or other obsessions
- Compulsions to repeat words, numbers, or phrases to oneself, making the child slow to answer questions or process information
- Contamination fears involving school bathrooms or classroom surfaces that other children have touched
- Overwhelming topic obsessions that make other subjects of little interest
- Specific rituals that are time consuming, such as hand washing or checking rituals, or that cause severe anxiety if they are not carried out
- Anxiety that is disguised as vague illness, such as stomachaches

- Memory problems that are sometimes associated with OCD
- Social phobia that limits interaction with other students, making group projects, oral reports, and other types of schoolwork extremely stressful
- For those students with a comorbid diagnosis of Tourette's syndrome or a tic disorder, physical or vocal tics that are hard to suppress in the classroom

Nine-year-old Ian tells how a topic obsession was disruptive in school:

> *When I was 6, everything I did had to do with squids. I would look at a certain book that had pictures of squids in it in our class, and count the legs. Some of the pictures were not right: they had fourteen or fifteen legs instead of ten. That made me mad and I wanted to talk about it a lot. People did not understand why I cared.*

Each child's OCD symptoms are different, and their response to interventions will differ as well. For that reason, there's no single school program that has proven success with all students who have the illness. Since children aren't always forthcoming about their symptoms, you may have to ask lots of questions before you get to the root of the problem.

Raegan, age 18, offers one of her school-related symptoms as an example:

> *My grades slipped in eighth grade because I wouldn't use my old textbooks. I was afraid my textbooks carried diseases, since other students had used them years before I did.*

Teachers and parents should craft accommodations or modifications by first observing the behavior or talking to the child about internal thought processes, and then brainstorming several possible solutions. You may have to try a few before finding a workable accommodation. Often the child or teen already knows some strategies that work, and simply needs your approval to put them in place.

Teachers and parents can find a huge list of specific ideas for accommodations and modifications in the book *Teaching the Tiger*, which is listed in Appendix A, *Resources*. This practical volume is highly recommended for anyone planning an education program for a child with OCD, Tourette's syndrome, and/or ADHD. It includes hundreds of invaluable classroom ideas, organizational hints, and ideas for writing IEP goals and 504 plans.

Programs designed to meet an individual student's needs must be flexible, due to the waxing and waning nature of OCD symptoms. Students with OCD may have long periods during which their symptoms are minimal. Teachers can take advantage of these periods to help them make up missed assignments or move ahead rapidly, leaving room to relax a bit during periods when symptoms are more severe. Accommodations that are no longer needed can be suspended until symptoms flare up again.

Cindy, mother of 10-year-old Brett, works closely with school personnel to handle sporadic symptoms:

> *I was fortunate to have a teacher last year who kept in constant contact with me. I also worked with the school nurse. The three of us have a system worked out to keep Brett in school. He is very good at hiding his anxiety by creating a sickness. Basically, once I assured them that it was okay not to give in to him, they were comfortable with keeping him in school. They would also call me and let me know when he was having a bad day and what the possible triggers were.*
>
> *As for the social aspect, the other children often taunted him because he has a severe fear of storms and would become extremely upset. It is not something easy to explain to a group of 10-year-olds. Many times I thought maybe he would be better in a private school with smaller classes, but we are going to keep him in public school and do our best to give him the skills to deal with this.*

Some children with OCD may become aggressive due to OCD-related anxiety and frustration, which can trigger rages. Children who experience these difficulties, even if behavior problems have so far occurred only at home, should always have a behavior plan in place at school that can be followed in case of an incident. Parents can let teachers know about any triggers and warning signs that they have discovered, helping teachers intervene early and prevent problems when possible. For more information about the issue of OCD and school violence, see the section "School behavior and school violence," later in this chapter.

From hospital to school

Imagine how it must feel to be sent to a hospital for a period of a couple weeks, months, or even years, then dropped back into your old school as if nothing had happened. If the hospital was a psychiatric facility, you may not want to talk to your friends about it. You may be embarrassed. Your medications may make you feel different. Everything probably seems very strange.

And yet we expect children and teens to handle this sudden transition with little support other than encouraging words.

It's best to make the transition from hospital to school a gradual one, starting with a few days or weeks of homebound instruction, then going back to school in a resource room (perhaps with "pull-outs" for some inclusion activities), half-days at school, or an intermediate period in day treatment. Making a slow transition improves your child's chances for successful reintegration. Think of a best-case scenario and one or more fallback positions, just in case.

As soon as you begin planning a hospitalization, or when your child enters the hospital in a crisis situation, start planning for this transition. Communication is the key. As discussed in the section "Hospital-based education" later in this chapter, the school and the hospital must be talking to each other (and to you) from the start. Ask the professionals working with your child in the hospital what they would recommend. They have seen many children your child's age, and may have some good ideas.

Identify one person at your child's school—a teacher, counselor, school psychologist, or perhaps an administrator—who can be in charge of the transition back to school. If you have to personally explain the situation to too many people, it's likely that someone will be missed, or that someone will miss out on important information. It's better to have someone at the school who is fully informed. Preferably this person will be someone in whom your child can confide if problems crop up.

Make sure that both you and your child's school are fully informed about any medications he may be taking, how they should be administered, and side effects that school personnel should watch out for. You may also need to adjust the school program to fit new knowledge about your child, or the effects of medication (such as cognitive dulling, sleepiness, or agitation).

Medications at school

Many children and teens with OCD can take all their medications at home, and this is the best way to avoid school medication problems. Generally speaking, kids prefer not to take medicine at school. Some will need to take daytime doses, though, and these will have to be administered at school.

In any school there are many, many children who have daily medication needs, ranging from Ritalin to asthma inhalers. Your child will not be seen as unusual if he needs to take a pill every day. . .in fact, he'll probably have to wait in line.

On the other hand, schools these days are very uptight about student drug use. Anti-drug policies usually include prescription medications and over-the-counter drugs, such as aspirin, as well as illicit drugs. Make sure you have a copy of your child's school's policy on using prescription and non-prescription medications at school to avoid problems. It is very rare for even a teenager to be allowed to self-administer medication at school. The usual exceptions to this rule are medications to treat life-threatening symptoms that could emerge suddenly, such as emergency asthma inhalers or an anaphylactic shock kit for students with severe allergies. Medications other than these must usually be kept and administered by a school employee.

Medications should be properly stored. The pill bottle's label or pharmacy insert should tell you if a medication needs refrigeration or should simply be stored away from light or heat. For safety's sake, medications should be kept in a locked drawer or cabinet. This will prevent them from misuse, abuse, and theft. Ask to see where your child's medications will be kept.

If your school has an on-site health clinic or nurse's office, that's probably the best place for your child to get and take his medication. If it does not, someone who is neither licensed nor trained in how to handle medication-related problems will give out medications. This is a major problem for many families whose children need to take medication at school. School secretaries and teachers are frequently pressed into the role of pill-pushers, and it's rarely one that they relish. (Incidentally, in hospitals and nursing homes, a Certified Medication Aide [CMA] license is the minimum qualification required to give medications to patients.)

If your child takes medication daily, make sure there is some sort of checklist used to monitor compliance. The person in charge should actually *see* the child take the medication, not hand it out and let the child walk away. It may be necessary to check the child's mouth to make sure the pills were swallowed. Ask to see the medication compliance checklist at least once a semester, and talk to your child about whether he is getting his medications regularly.

Emergency or "as-needed" psychiatric medications are problematic for schools. Unless they have a medical person on staff, they will naturally be unsure of when to allow their use. If your doctor prescribes this kind of medication for your child, the pill bottle should say "use as needed" or "prn" (from the Latin from the Latin *pro re nata*, as circumstances dictate). Ask your physician to write a brief statement about when school personnel should give the medication out. Alternatively, you could write this statement yourself. Older children and teens should know the symptoms that these drugs can help with and be able to ask for them independently. The medications most commonly prescribed in this way are tranquilizers and other antianxiety drugs. When used properly, they can be very helpful.

Students may be prescribed medications by a psychiatrist working at the school, with parental permission. Occasionally someone without a license to practice medicine, such as a psychologist or school counselor, may tell parents that their child should take a certain medication. In either case, parents have the right to refuse medication for their child, and to ask for a second opinion.

Teasing and bullying

While some teens with OCD are very adept at hiding their problems, others are not, and younger children's difficulties are typically noticed by classmates. Like pack animals, children have a tendency to pick on anyone perceived as weak or different. However, whether teasing and bullying actually occurs, as well as its degree of severity, depends less on the children involved than on the adults in charge.

Some schools have not yet caught on to the idea that children should not be permitted to treat other children in ways that we would not allow adults to treat each other. An employee who calls coworkers names, steals their possessions, threatens them, or actually harms them physically would be disciplined or fired, whether the employee is 16 or 40. That person might even be sued for creating a hostile workplace environment. For those students who are forced to run a daily gauntlet of humiliations, school is truly a hostile environment.

Learning appropriate social behavior starts in the preschool years, and should require declining amounts of adult supervision and intervention as children get older. If your child is taunted by others on the playground, in the lunchroom, or worse yet, in the classroom, teachers and other school personnel probably know—and have either chosen to do nothing, or are unsure of what to do. As a society, we can't dismiss cruel behavior by saying "kids will be kids." Nobody wins when teasing and bullying are permitted. Not only are the victims harmed in enduring ways, the victimizers lose a chance to learn the social skills they will need to be desirable members of the community as adults.

There's no way to make kids like each other, of course, but adults do have the power to enforce codes of conduct, including rules against teasing, name-calling, and bullying. These rules should apply to all students, and in all school-related situations. Adults have more power over student behavior than they assume, even at the high school level. They model appropriate or inappropriate behavior, set up most official social interactions between students, and are charged with monitoring unofficial interactions on the school grounds. When adults abdicate this responsibility, children with OCD tend to be among those who suffer most.

That's not to say that children with OCD are always innocent victims. Some do have behaviors that annoy other students, such as compulsions to touch or kiss their classmates. It's not realistic to expect other children to ignore behavior that parents and teachers would also find annoying. When these behaviors emerge, seek targeted treatment for them and use a behavior plan to create workable interim solutions that keep the rest of the class comfortable and that do not punish the student with OCD for something he can't help at this time.

Taking a "zero tolerance" position on teasing and bullying is only a start toward creating a positive school environment, one that not only reduces unwanted conduct, but rewards tolerance, caring, and cooperation. There are many steps schools can take to celebrate and include students of different abilities, talents, and backgrounds. School programs that emphasize respect for others and non-violent conflict resolution can go a long way toward preventing teasing and bullying, especially when they are implemented from the earliest grades onward. Teachers and school administrators need to keep their eyes on the environment at their school, including social and racial stratification, attitudes toward disabilities and other differences, and official responses to students who complain of being teased or bullied. Proactive planning can reduce such problems, and rapid and consistent response is needed when they do occur.

Support for students with OCD

In the US, discriminating against the disabled is illegal in almost every setting, including schools. Federal law also specifically mandates that all children receive a free and appropriate education (referred to in special education circles as "FAPE"), regardless of disability. That means providing free-of-charge special education programs, speech therapy, occupational therapy, physical therapy, psychiatric services, and other interventions that can help the child learn.

Several laws protect your child's access to an education. These include:

- Section 504 of the Rehabilitation Act of 1973
- Individuals with Disabilities Education Act (IDEA)
- Americans with Disabilities Act (ADA)
- Other state and federal laws concerning disability rights and special education

504 plans

At the very least, your child should have in place a 504 plan—an agreement between the child's family and the school about accommodations that can help him attend school successfully. Section 504 of the Rehabilitation Act of 1973, one of the very first laws mandating educational help for students with disabilities, lays out the regulations for such plans, hence the name. A 504 plan can be written mostly by a team made up of the parents and teachers or school administrators, with minimal involvement by the school district's administrators. It is a simpler and less detailed process than writing an IEP, but it also doesn't cover as many contingencies.

Unlike special education eligibility, Section 504 eligibility is not based on having a certain type of disability. Instead, it is based on the following:

- Having a physical or mental impairment that substantially limits a major life activity, such as learning. Note that in contrast to IDEA regulations, learning is not the only activity that applies: 504 plans can cover other major life activities, such as breathing, walking, and socialization.
- Having a record of such impairment, such as a medical diagnosis.
- Being regarded as having such impairment.

A 504 plan is a good idea even if your child has never had an academic or behavior problem in school. The nature of OCD dictates that new symptoms could emerge at any time and have unexpected effects on school performance. Your child's 504 plan can determine procedures such as:

- Who will give out medication and where it will be stored
- How communication between home and school will transpire
- What organization systems will be used for homework and books
- What exemptions are necessary, such as those from timed tests
- What to do if your child has a difficult behavior episode at school

Children and teens with OCD are prone to the occasional meltdown, and this is one area in which a 504 plan shines. Episodes of anxiety, rage, or unusual behavior may occur in response to stress, fear, teasing, illness, missed medications, or simply out of the blue. You can develop a response in advance and put it in place via a 504 plan. It can include procedures for giving emergency medication, calling for outside help, and keeping the child and others safe until that help arrives. Without advance planning, it's easy for a bad day to turn into a crisis.

If you apply for 504 status and are still denied services, appeal this decision to your school district's 504 compliance officer. If that doesn't produce results, contact your state's Office of Civil Rights. If your child has been diagnosed with OCD, he should not be denied this limited protection under any circumstances—a 504 plan is the very least for which any child with a health impairment qualifies. Even students with mild ADHD or occasional asthma attacks qualify for assistance under a 504 plan.

Some special education advocates recommend that parents request a 504 evaluation at the same time that they start the IEP process. This can mean asking the 504 compliance officer to attend your IEP meetings. It may confuse your district because it isn't a common practice, but it will save time in obtaining some services and accommodations if services are denied under IDEA and the parents have to appeal.

Because most 504 plans are fairly uncomplicated documents, you may be tempted to simply set up an informal agreement with your child's school instead. Don't do it. Informal agreements only work as long as the people involved stay the same, and as long as everyone chooses to honor them. If your school gets a new principal or your child's teacher decides to change plans in midstream, you'll be right back where you started. With a 504 plan, you have a document that mandates access to needed services. If your school or district decides not to follow it, you can appeal directly to your district's 504 compliance officer and/or your state office of civil rights.

IDEA and special education

Special education has been revolutionized by IDEA, a set of comprehensive rules and regulations that was most recently revised and expanded in 1997. IDEA's mission is to ensure that all children get an adequate education, regardless of disabilities or special needs. This includes children with OCD and other mental or neurological problems.

The special education process starts with evaluation. In most areas, a committee of specialists, called the eligibility committee, multidisciplinary team (M-team), child study team, or another similar name, determines eligibility. As the parent, you should have input during this eligibility process. You may be asked to fill out forms, and you can also request a personal interview with the team and submit information, such as medical evaluations, to help it make a decision.

The eligibility committee will decide if your child has a condition that qualifies him for special education services. Exact language differs between states, but typical qualifying categories include:

- Autistic
- Hearing impaired (deaf)
- Visually impaired
- Both hearing impaired and visually impaired (deaf-blind)
- Speech and language impaired
- Mentally retarded/developmentally delayed
- Multi-handicapped
- Severely orthopedically impaired
- Other health impaired (OHI)
- Seriously emotionally disturbed (SED)
- Severely and profoundly disabled

- Specific learning disability
- Traumatic brain injury

Check your state's special education regulations for the list of labels used in your state.

Most children and teens with OCD receiving special education services are classified under the OHI or SED labels. An SED designation is often required to access day treatment or residential slots; on the other hand, this label may prevent your child from being admitted to some alternative school programs without a fight.

The condition that causes the most impairment in school-related activities will usually be called the primary handicapping condition, and any others that co-exist with it will be called secondary handicapping conditions. For example, a child with OCD and dyslexia might be qualified for special education under the primary condition SED, with specific learning disability as a secondary label.

Although the eligibility committee will take your child's medical diagnosis and the opinions of Early Intervention evaluators into account when they make their determination, qualifying categories are defined by each school district or state Department of Education in terms of education, not medicine. If your child has an OCD diagnosis from a psychiatrist, neurologist, or other physician, the committee can still decide that your child does not meet the educational definition of SED or another label. This means that either the committee feels your child does not need special services to take advantage of educational opportunities, or that the committee is unwilling to offer your child needed services. Technically, a medical diagnosis of OCD should automatically qualify a child for the label OHI, even if his illness is currently controlled via medication or his symptoms are not prominent.

You have the right to appeal the eligibility team's decision about your child's educational label or any other issue. If its decision prevents your child from receiving special education eligibility or needed services, you should do so. It is helpful to prepare a detailed list of ways your child's problems impact his ability to be educated without the added help of special education services.

The Individualized Education Plan (IEP)

When completed, your child's special education evaluation will be the basis of a document that will soon become your close companion: your child's Individualized Education Plan (IEP). The IEP describes your child's strengths and weaknesses, sets educational goals and objectives for her, and details how these can be met within the context of the school system. Unlike the IFSP, a similar kind of plan used in Early Intervention programs for preschool children (see the section "Early ntervention," later in this chapter), the IEP is almost entirely about what will happen within school walls. Unless the IEP team agrees to include it, it will not mandate services from outside programs, services provided by parents, or services provided to parents.

The IEP is created during one or more IEP team meetings. The IEP team has a minimum of three members: a representative of the school district, a teacher, and a parent. The district may send more than one representative, and parents may (at their child's peril) choose not to attend. If your child has more than one teacher, or if direct service providers, such as her therapist, would like to attend, they can all be present. If it is your child's first IEP and first assessment, one team member is required by federal law to have experience with and knowledge of the child's suspected or known disabilities. You may want to check this person's credentials in advance. "Specialists" employed by some school districts can have as little as one college psychology course, or even no qualifications other than the title itself.

Both parents should participate in the IEP process, if possible, even if they do not live together. Parents can also bring anyone else they would like: a relative or friend, an after-school caretaker, a mental health advocate, or a lawyer, for example. This person may act as an outside expert, or may simply offer moral support or take notes so that you can participate more freely.

The child himself can also be at the IEP meeting if the parents would like—however, it's a good idea to bring a baby-sitter for a young child, to avoid disruptions. You want to be able to give the IEP process your full attention, and that's hard if you're also trying to keep a child out of trouble. Most young children find IEP meetings rather boring.

Older teens and self-advocacy

Districts are trying to involve middle school and high school students in the IEP process more often, and this is probably a good trend. Discuss the meeting with your older child and elicit her suggestions in advance. Some adolescents prefer to write up their suggestions rather than (or in addition to) attending the meeting. As with young children, bring someone to take care of your child if she tends to be disruptive, and bring a book or game in case the meeting gets boring. It's not beneficial to force an unwilling child to take part in the meeting.

Recently parents of older teens in special education have reported a disturbing new trend: school districts that try to circumvent IDEA by making teens "self-advocates" at the age of 18, regardless of their ability to make wise choices, and regardless of their parents' wishes. If parents agree—and *only* if parents agree—any child in special education who has reached age 18 can take full control of all further contacts with the school district. Needless to say, this is often a very unwise thing to agree to. In most cases, the outcome has been that the child immediately leaves school and loses all services.

If your district tries this ploy, there is a way back in. As an adult self-advocate, your child can appoint another person to advocate for her. That person can (and should) be you, or if you prefer, a professional advocate.

Remember that unless you decline it, special education services continue until at least the age of 21, or until the attainment of a regular high school diploma (not a GED or IEP diploma).

Building an IEP

Usually the IEP meeting is held at a school or a district office. However, you can request another location for the meeting if it is necessary—for example, if your child is on homebound instruction, or has severe behavior problems that make caring for him away from the controlled environment of home at that time impossible. The meeting date and time must be convenient to you (and, of course, to the other team members).

Your first IEP meeting should begin with a presentation of your child's strengths and weaknesses. This may be merely a form listing test scores and milestones, or it can include reports from observations by team members—including you. You can use this time to tell the team a little more about your child, her likes and dislikes, her abilities, and the worries that have brought you all together for this meeting. Even if you're repeating information that the team members already know, this kind of storytelling helps other team members see your child as a person rather than just another case. You'll want to keep it brief, though, so you may want to use a short outline and even practice in advance. Five or ten minutes seems about right, although you may find that you need more time. If you can keep your written description to one or two pages, that would be good.

This kind of information may also be entered on an evaluation or record summary form.

The IEP itself has two important parts: the cover sheet, usually called the *accommodations page*, and the *goals and objectives pages*. Your district may have its own bureaucratic names for these pages, such as a "G3" or "eval sheet." If team members start throwing around terms you don't understand, be sure to speak up! If the wrong forms are filled out, or if important paperwork is left undone, you may not have an acceptable IEP at the end of the meeting.

Accommodations

Parents tend to focus on the goals and objectives pages, and often overlook the accommodations page. That's a mistake. The goals and objectives are all about what your child will do, and if they are not accomplished, there's no one who can truly be held accountable but your child. The accommodations page is about what the school district will do to help make your child able to meet those goals: what services it will provide or pay for, what kind of classroom setting your child will be in, and any other special education help that the district promises to provide.

The accommodations page is where the district's promises are made, so watch out: saying that your child will do something costs the district nothing, but promising that the district will do something has a price tag attached. Be prepared to hear phrases like "I don't want to commit the district to that" over and over—and to methodically show that the accommodations you're asking for are the only way the goals and objectives the team wants to set can be met.

District representatives tend to see their role in the IEP meeting as being the gatekeeper. They may interpret this as spending as little money as possible, or, on the other hand, as ensuring that children are matched with services that meet their needs, depending on the person, the district, and the situation. Most struggle to balance these goals for the benefit of each child and the district's resources. As your child's advocate, your job is to persuade the representative to tip the scales in your child's favor.

Accommodations that your child may need include:

- A specific type of classroom.
- A provision of other types of environments, such as a resource room setting for certain subjects, mainstreaming for other subjects, or an area for time-outs or self-calming.
- A set procedure for allowing the child to take a "self time-out" when overwhelmed, angry, or especially symptomatic. For example, your child might quietly show a green card to the teacher, who could send him on his way to a quiet area (the school nurse's office or the school library, for example) for a predetermined length of time with a nod of her head.
- A reduced number of required courses for graduation.
- Class schedules adapted to the child's ability to concentrate and stay alert, especially during times of acute stress (such as just after release from the hospital) and during medication changes.
- Specific learning materials or methods.
- Accommodations for testing, such as untimed tests, extended test-taking times, exemption from certain types of tests, or oral exams (this is an especially good idea for students who have hand tremor due to medication or problems writing due to perfectionism).
- Grade arrangements that take into account assignments and school days missed due to symptoms or to hospitalization. These might include estimating semester grades based only on the work that was completed; offering the option of an "incomplete" grade to allow the student to finish the course when well; or basing grades on some combination of class participation when present, work completed, and a special oral exam.
- A personal educational assistant, aide, or "shadow"—either a monitoring aide who simply helps with behavior control, or an inclusion or instructional aide.
- Other classroom equipment needed to help your child learn if he has auditory processing or learning disabilities, such as a microphone or sound field system, a slanted work surface, or pencils with an orthopedic grip.
- Preparation and implementation of a behavior plan.

The cover page should also summarize any therapeutic services your child will receive, including by whom, where, and how frequently they will be delivered.

The accommodations page should not already be filled out when the IEP meeting begins, as your child's individual goals and objectives should dictate what accommodations will be needed.

Goals and objectives

Goals and objectives in the IEP should be as specific as possible. Often each team member will come to the IEP meeting with a list, hopefully with each goal already broken down into steps. This saves a lot of time, and allows everyone to concentrate on the pros and cons of their ideas, rather than having to actually come up with the ideas themselves at the meeting. You may choose to meet one-on-one with these team members to talk over IEP ideas before the big meeting.

There is a tendency for the IEP of a child with OCD to look more like a behavior plan than an education plan. Goals like "Armando will comply with his teacher's instructions nine times out of ten" are fairly typical—and almost useless. They specify that the student—and the student alone—will do something that has obviously been difficult in the past. For behavior improvements to occur, teachers and parents need to know why misbehavior has happened in the past. This is where a well-researched, well-written behavior plan (see "School behavior and school violence" later in this chapter) should come into play.

Appropriate behavior goals for the IEP can be tied to what you've learned from analyzing the child's problem behaviors, and how the behavior plan addresses them. These two documents can work together. For example, if Armando has often been noncompliant in the past due to having little knowledge of how to get appropriate attention from his teacher or his peers, a better set of goals might be "Armando will identify three appropriate ways to get his teacher's attention," and "Armando will be able to identify appropriate and inappropriate times to seek his peers' attention." Other behavior goals might include: "Armando will find three unobtrusive ways to deal with physical compulsions that could be disruptive," "Armando will take a self time-out for five to ten minutes when he is feeling overwhelmed," and "Armando will learn to use two stress-reduction strategies when he is becoming irritated or angry at school."

Although these behavior goals still seem to be all about what the student will do, fulfilling these goals will really require the active participation of teachers and other professionals. Armando is not going to learn these strategies for improving his behavior by osmosis—someone is going to have to teach him, work with him to improve his skills, and reinforce him when he gets it right. To as great an extent as possible, you want to spell out just how that will be done, and by whom, in the IEP and/or the behavior plan.

These goals also have the advantage of being measurable, permitting you to hold teachers accountable for meeting them. When it's time for an IEP review, you can find out which three strategies Armando is using to get the teacher's attention, and find out if doing so has reduced inappropriate attention-getting behaviors.

Academic goals on IEPs are controversial. Schools do not want to guarantee that a student will learn certain material; they usually don't even want to promise that they'll try to teach it. And if most of your child's academic skills are age-appropriate or even superior, it is very hard to have anything written into the IEP about maintaining or developing these skills further. Special education services are about addressing deficits, say the educators. (One exception to this rule is the state of Massachusetts, which has regulations requiring school districts to "maximize the potential" of disabled students.)

In reality, the student's achievement is not to be compared against the average or that of other students, but against his own ability as measured by past performance or ability testing. If there is a measurable and significant discrepancy between ability and achievement, you have room to ask for academic goals on the IEP. This is frequently the case for students with OCD: related traits such as perfectionism and anxiety-derived procrastination can stymie even brilliant students.

Parents also know from experience that any gifts or islands of competence their child has are essential to his emotional well-being and educational success. Parents and experienced, caring teachers can often show the rest of the team why IEP goals based on strengths can be as important as those based on deficits or discrepancies. For example, your daughter may excel in reading and music. Just as schools often claim that sports programs keep some at-risk kids in school, enhanced opportunities to pursue her special interests may motivate your daughter to attend classes regularly and keep up her GPA. . .especially if you can take a page from the football team's book and tie her ability to participate in a desired activity, such as band or chorus, to maintaining passing grades. As every parent knows, the carrot is often mightier than the stick!

Generally speaking, children in special education programs should be educated to the same standards as all other students whenever that is possible. They should work with the same curriculum and objectives, although specific requirements can be adjusted to fit the child. For example, if third graders in your district are normally required to present a ten-minute oral report about state history, a child with medication-induced fatigue might be allowed to present a shorter oral report, to have her written report read out loud by a helper, or to present her report in two parts.

As a parent, you'll want to talk to your child's teacher about the academic curriculum in use in your child's school and in the district itself. Make sure that your child is being instructed in the skills, concepts, and facts needed to proceed in school. If you live in one of the many states that is introducing competency standards for all students, make sure that your child (and all children in special education) are not exempted from the same expectations. If your state has set the goal of having all children reading at grade level by fifth grade, for example, your child should be held to the same standard—and offered the special education assistance she may need to achieve it.

In some states, children are required to meet certain benchmark standards to move on to the next grade level, to complete high school, or to earn a type of diploma that qualifies them to attend state colleges. You may be able to include a provision in your child's IEP regarding how standardized achievement tests of this type will be handled. This may range from exempting the child from the testing requirement to insisting that the school provide extra academic help and/or test-taking accommodations to allow the student an equal chance of doing well on the test.

Children with OCD come in all sizes, from slow to average to gifted. A good IEP doesn't dumb down classes or take away the joy of achieving something difficult, it just ensures that a child with disabilities gets an equal shot. The IEP can provide flexibility while maintaining appropriate academic standards by permitting your child to audit some courses before taking them for credit, and arranging in advance to use correspondence courses, distance learning (courses taken over the Internet), or independent study to fill in gaps created by hospitalization or flare-ups of OCD symptoms.

Another important set of IEP goals concern socialization. Again, you may be told that this is not part of education. However, the school's task is preparing your child to function in the working world, and book learning alone will not help unless he has also mastered the give and take of social interaction. The best place for children to learn appropriate social skills is in supervised activities with peers, and most schools make a plethora of these available to their students. This makes school an especially appropriate arena for children to work on socialization.

Social skills are used during the school day in classroom conversation, in the lunchroom and library, and in school-sponsored activities, such as student clubs or arts groups. Social skill instruction may be provided in any of these settings, in targeted classroom exercises on social skills, or through non-affiliated community programs. You can write supports into an IEP that will help your child succeed in school social activities despite her illness.

Some schools have introduced social skills groups or peer mentoring programs for students who need extra help in socialization. Often these pair younger students with older students, under the guidance and supervision of adults. The older student can show younger kids the ropes, help integrate them into school and after-school activities, and encourage them to feel like they belong. For children entering a new school, returning to school after a long period of hospitalization or homebound education, or suffering from social phobia, peer mentoring and social skills groups can be fabulous.

Signing the IEP. . .or not

When the IEP is complete, the accommodations page will include a list of each promise, information about where and when it will be met, and the name of the person responsible for delivering or ensuring delivery. If the complete IEP is acceptable to everyone present, this is probably also where all team members will sign on the dotted line.

You do not have to sign the IEP if it is not acceptable. This fact can't be emphasized enough! If the meeting has ended and you don't feel comfortable with the IEP as it is, you have the right to take home the current document and think about it (or discuss it with your spouse or an advocate) before you sign. You also have the right to set another IEP meeting, and another, and another, until it is completed to your liking. Don't hinder the process unnecessarily, of course, but also don't let yourself be steam-rolled by the district. The IEP is about your child's needs, not the district's needs.

Needless to say, you should never sign a blank or unfinished IEP—it's a bit like signing a blank check. Certain school districts ask IEP meeting participants to sign an approval sheet before even talking about the IEP. Others are in the habit of taking notes for a prospective IEP and asking parents to sign an approval form at the end of the meeting, even though the goals, objectives, and accommodations have not been entered on an actual IEP form. This is not okay. If they insist that you sign a piece of paper, make sure to add next to your name that you are signing because you were present, but that you have not agreed to a final document.

If your child already has an IEP in place from the previous year, this IEP will stay in place until the new one is finalized and signed. If your child does not, you may need to come to a partial agreement with the district while the IEP is worked out.

If the process has become contentious, be sure to bring an advocate to the next meeting. A good advocate can help smooth out the bumps in the IEP process while preserving your child's access to a free and appropriate education.

Placement decisions

Two factors govern the choice of school for your child: the most appropriate educational program, and the least restrictive environment (LRE). For most children with OCD, the least restrictive environment is their neighborhood school, or one very much like it that happens to have an especially good teacher or support services.

This is called inclusion, full integration, or mainstreaming. Inclusion is usually the best strategy for children and teenagers with OCD, as long as the school is willing to accommodate your child's special needs with a 504 plan and/or IEP.

Over and over, parents interviewed for this book stressed the importance of teacher and classroom flexibility in the face of this unpredictable illness, preferably coupled with clear expectations.

Debbie, mother of 11-year-old Kristen, explains:

> *We have found that it is hard for Kristen to sit still due to intrusive thoughts. When she is having a stressful period, we have talked with her teachers and arranged to have her workload decreased. An environment*

where Kristen knows what is expected of her is the best. If the teacher goes back and forth on expectations or does not explain what is required of her, it can cause great anxiety.

Characteristics of successful inclusive classrooms include:

- Caring, informed personnel
- Adequate ratio of children to classroom personnel
- Frequent and productive communication between classroom personnel, specialists, and parents
- Appropriate teaching materials
- Individualized educational programming for each child with a disability
- Encouraged interaction between children with disabilities and their non-disabled peers
- Consistent expectations regarding behavior and academic work, with flexibility built in to allow for changes in the child's psychiatric symptoms and needs

Full inclusion is not a magical solution to school problems. Too often schools use the concept of full inclusion as a way to deny special education services to the students who need them. That's why many classroom teachers dread having children with mental or physical disabilities in their classes—it's not that they're callous or think these kids don't deserve an equal education, it's that they are not given any additional resources to work with them. Imagine yourself teaching a class of thirty junior high students in which two or three have ADHD, one has autism, and another has OCD. Without help from classroom aides and specialists, administrative support, well-written IEPs, and the resources to help each child meet his goals, your job would be a nightmare.

Parents play a key role in making sure their children are properly served in an inclusive setting. Teachers love parents who go to bat with the administration or district to get needed classroom help.

Perhaps the best advice that successful students with OCD and their parents can offer is that the people and atmosphere of a school count the most, and that one program does not fit all. Some students desire the anonymity and lower social pressure of large public schools, while others thrive in small classes with lots of personal attention. The best school environment is very much an individual thing.

Special classrooms

Some children will not be able to handle the noise, confusion, and demands of a traditional school program. Some troubled schools are, in turn, barely capable of meeting the needs of average students, much less those with special needs. There should be a range of placements available, from staying in the neighborhood school but spending part or all of the day in a resource room or special education classroom, to learning at home with one-on-one instruction, or day treatment or residential placement.

Some children will need a special classroom for only part of the day. Perhaps they need special help with math or reading, or maybe their obsessions and compulsions tend to worsen as the day wears on. A "resource room" can be part of the solution. This is a space in the school where kids can get help from a special education teacher to meet their individual needs.

If you walk into a typical resource room, you'll usually see several activities going on. At one table a group of children are working together on reading skills, in another corner of the room a student with Tourette's syndrome whose tics are flaring up is taking a "time-out" from his regular classroom, and at a third table a speech therapist is doing one-on-one work with a child who stutters. A child whose medication makes him sleepy might be napping, while another group of kids works on special math software on the room's computers.

Each of these children is in the resource room for only part of the day, either for a scheduled visit with a specialist (such as the speech therapist) or on an as-needed basis due to symptoms. When children use a resource room for certain types of work, that's called a pull-out. The rest of the day these kids are in either a regular class or a special education class. Well-run resource rooms act as a safe haven within a busy school.

For those students who do need a full-day special education program, there are many types of self-contained special classrooms. Children with OCD are most likely to be sent to a behavioral classroom, where their classmates will be other children whose disabilities impact behavior.

Most of these classrooms use some variation of the behavior modification approach. Many use a level system, in which children start with no privileges at all and earn each privilege by meeting behavior goals. As their behavior improves (or declines), they work their way through levels that might be numbered or given the name of a color. A child on green level, for instance, would be performing optimally and able to have recess time, eat lunch with peers, and perhaps have a special treat at the end of the week. A child on blue level would be performing badly, confined to the classroom for recess and lunch, and unable to have cookies with the green level guys on Friday.

Level systems and behavior modification techniques work very well for children who are deliberately misbehaving, perhaps as a result of learning poor behavior at home. Level systems do *not* work well with children whose behaviors are due to neurological dysfunction. These kids may simply feel humiliated when symptom exacerbations prevent them from reaching behavior goals. Their teachers may also be mystified when techniques that worked so well when the child's illness was well controlled on medication suddenly become useless as the medication no longer works.

Despite the drawbacks of the level system/behavior modification approach, some behavioral classrooms are excellent learning environments for kids with OCD. They are usually small (no more than fifteen children, sometimes as few as six), they often have aides and support staff in place to meet the children's needs, and they are headed by teachers with training and, hopefully, expertise in working with kids who have special needs.

Lin, mother of 9-year-old Bill, says:

> *Bill was put in a special education class this spring. We objected at first when the school talked about putting him there, but it has been for the best. He is learning much more, and his teacher is much more understanding. She has a strict rule about teasing—it is not allowed at all. This has made school less stressful, so he is happy to go now.*

The curriculum in a behavioral class should be identical to that used in regular classrooms, with adaptations as needed for each student. Many of these classes mix students who are in several grades, however, and it takes a skilled teacher to ensure that each child learns what he needs to know.

In most school districts, behavioral classes are seen as a short-term placement—like a boot-camp class for kids who behave badly. For children with OCD whose symptoms are severe, this view is neither realistic nor wise. If a particular behavioral class is working well for your child, see what you can do to hold onto that placement.

Some school districts do have special classes for "seriously emotionally disturbed" students. Unfortunately, many of these classes also use level system/behavior modification techniques exclusively, without the level of therapeutic support that most of the kids they serve really need. If your child is offered placement in a classroom that *does* happen to have a good therapeutic support program, grab it!

Most districts have special classes for children with moderate to severe developmental delays (mental retardation, autism, etc.). In small districts, this may be the only special education classroom available. Such a placement might seem like a terrible idea for your child—and it might well be a mistake. However, if the classroom happens to have a very good teacher and other needed supports will be available to your child, it could be worth considering. There may a be a stigma attached for your child, of course. . .especially if the class is in his neighborhood school and neighbor kids will know that he has been put in the "retarded kids class." Many of these classes are actually quite good, with a caring and individualized approach that some of the behavioral classes would do well to emulate. For some kids with OCD, especially the very youngest students, there will be times that being the "smart kid" in a developmental delay class is a great solution to a difficult education problem.

The law mandates that children be educated in the most inclusive environment possible, and that's an important value. However, recognizing that the best environment for an individual child may not always be fully inclusive is of equal importance.

Parents must also remember that the school's classrooms, computers, and books are often of secondary importance when compared to the value of caring teachers and administrators. If your child has an ally in his school—a favorite teacher, a super counselor, a teacher's aide who bends over backwards to help her—that person can often do more to help her get through school than the best-designed special education program. Parents should try to identify and develop allies for their children within their school, wherever they are placed.

Alternative school

For some students with OCD, alternative schools (including the charter schools that are springing up in some parts of the country) offer the best mix of high academic expectations, strong behavioral supports, and flexibility. Of course, that depends on the alternative school program itself. Large urban districts may offer all sorts of public alternative schools, ranging from special schools for at-risk/gang-affected youth, to arts magnet schools. Small, rural districts may have no choices at all. Suburban areas may have only alternative schools that emphasize behavior modification rather than academics, and with little regard for these children's actual needs or abilities, they often use these schools as a dumping ground for problem students.

If your district does offer alternative programs, be sure to look before you leap. Visit the site with your child, and ask for a guided tour. If your child can get a chance to talk to other kids about the school, that usually helps (assuming that these peers don't hate their school). Sit in on a typical class. If you can, talk to other parents whose children attend the school, and meet the actual teachers whom your child would be working with. Make sure you feel comfortable with the alternative school's philosophy, methods, and objectives.

Take your time; if your child has had difficulty handling school in the past, you don't want to set him up for additional failure by making a hasty decision. Finding the right fit will make school success more likely.

Alternative schools and, in most cases, charter schools will still need to abide by your child's IEP. Often these schools are much more flexible, but occasionally they have been set up with a very specific program in mind, such as a levels-based behavior modification system or an arts-centered program designed for self-directed learners. If you sense that the alternative school is rigid in its format, make sure that format is already a good fit for your child. Like a regular public school that has a one-size-fits-all mentality, alternative schools with a specific mission are unlikely to change their approach, even to meet your child's IEP objectives.

Diagnostic classroom

If your child's diagnosis is still not set in stone, your district might suggest placement in a diagnostic classroom. This classroom might be a joint project of the school district and a regional medical center or medical school.

Diagnostic classrooms are used for long-term medical or psychiatric observation and evaluation of children whose behavior and abilities don't seem to fit the profile of any typical diagnosis. This is not a permanent placement, but if your child's case is especially unusual she may stay in the diagnostic classroom for quite some time.

A well-run diagnostic classroom offers your family a unique opportunity to have your child seen at length by experts, and to try new medications, therapies, and other treatments in a medically savvy setting. Make sure that the classroom staff and doctors involve your whole family in the diagnostic and treatment process. Parents report that some diagnostic classrooms are so patient-centered that they forget to talk to parents after the initial interview process.

Special schools

There are very few special public schools for children with mental illness. Some private schools serve "emotionally troubled" youth, who may or may not have an actual clinical diagnosis. Some of these special schools are excellent, and some are not.

Many districts contract with private schools that work with certain types of students. For example, they might contract with a private school that uses the Orton-Gillingham method to teach students with dyslexia, or with a private school that specializes in educating deaf and blind students.

One would expect a special school for mentally ill children to have a psychiatrist and therapists on staff, and to do some form of milieu therapy (see Chapter 4, *Therapeutic Interventions*) in addition to academic work. For children with OCD, most contract programs involve day treatment centers. If the district sends your child to a special school or day treatment center, it will pay the full costs. You will not be required to pay tuition or additional fees.

Day treatment centers for children are for those with very difficult behaviors—such as self-injurious or aggressive behavior—that make even a self-contained special education classroom inappropriate. They may be attached to or affiliated with a residential school or hospital. At the end of the school day, children in day treatment go home to their families.

Good day treatment centers provide medical and psychiatric support, specially trained staff, a very secure environment, and intensive intervention. However, many specialize in the treatment of behavior disorders (such as behavior problems that occur as a result of child abuse), and may not have a full understanding of OCD.

The other problem with many current day treatment programs is that they tend to be conceived as short-term interventions. Slots may be limited to one school year, or even to as little as three months. Students cycle in and out, and staff turnover may also be high. Since most children with OCD do not deal well with constant upheaval, this can present a problem. Your child may also be in class with children whose behaviors are even more unmanageable than her own.

As with any other placement, be sure to tour the facility, meet the staff, and ask lots of questions before you agree to a day treatment placement.

Residential schools

In some cases, residential programs are your only option. If you live in a small, rural school district, there simply may be no appropriate placement available—assuming that homebound instruction would not be appropriate for your child or your family situation. If your child is dangerously self-abusive or actively suicidal, residential settings may be able to offer a safer setting than your home. Unlike hospital inpatient programs, they usually include a strong educational component, not just psychiatric treatment.

Residential schools offer educational programming and 24-hour care for the child. If your school district asks to send your child to a residential program, the district will pay her tuition and all associated costs. Of course, you also have the option to choose a residential program for your child and pay for it yourself, if you have the financial means.

The best residential programs have staff with a strong medical/psychiatric background, a high level of employee retention, and a commitment to communicating and working with students' families. As with any other type of school program, you'll want to proceed with caution. Visit the campus, observe a classroom, see the living quarters, talk to staff and (if possible) students, and try to talk to other parents whose children have attended the school. No place is perfect, but some residential schools have deservedly bad reputations.

If your child needs a residential setting, security is probably a major concern. Make sure security measures are more than adequate to prevent students from self-harm, assault, and running away. Also find out how they manage difficult behaviors. Schools that rely on isolation rooms, restraints, or excessive medication should be avoided at all costs.

You'll also want to know about how the residential program handles returning to the community—whether it prepares your child for coming home and going back to his former school after he stabilizes, or simply moves him into a less restrictive residential setting. Some children with very complicated psychiatric problems leave residential schools for a therapeutic group home rather than return to the family home, either as a permanent placement or a transitional measure.

Hospital-based education

If your child needs to be an inpatient in a psychiatric hospital (or in a regular hospital, if he has a medical problem in addition to OCD) for more than a week or so, you'll need to ensure that his education is continued. Most child and adolescent psychiatric wards don't exactly excel in this department, though. With the trend toward short hospitalizations in crises only, there's barely time to find out what the student should be working on, much less to devise a program of instruction.

Instead, adolescents who have spent time as inpatients report that much of their daily schoolwork consisted of art projects, lessons copied out of workbooks, and perhaps current affairs discussions. Often, of course, that's all a kid in psychiatric crisis can handle.

If your child is going to have a planned hospitalization, contact the hospital program and find out who's in charge of communicating with patients' schools. There may be a formal school-hospital liaison. Make sure this person is in contact with your child's teacher (or in the case of a high school student who has many teachers, a homeroom teacher, school counselor, or other person who can be a go-between) before your child's scheduled entry date, and that they have set up an educational program in advance. This might include providing lesson plans and reading lists, sending your child's homework assignments to the hospital, and returning graded papers to you.

If the hospitalization is sudden, you will probably need to act as the go-between yourself. Call your child's teacher or teachers and make arrangements for what they feel would be appropriate work to complete during her illness. Before her release, make plans for what she should be doing at home while she recuperates, or how she should segue back into school. You can then make arrangements with hospital staff to ensure that she has the tools and time that she needs to do the work. Staff can also let you know if the teacher's plans are too ambitious, and can provide medical documentation for reducing or even eliminating schoolwork for a while if needed.

Homebound instruction

Homebound instruction is considered the most restrictive school environment, because it involves sending someone to teach your child individually. However, children may prefer homebound instruction to attending a special school or entering a residential program because it keeps them in the company of their parents and siblings, even though it does restrict their ability to interact with peers.

John, father of 14-year-old Tori, says homebound instruction is their only solution for now:

> *Tori has not been able to attend school for the past two years. The regular school system is a very difficult place for a child with OCD, especially when it is complicated by Asperger's syndrome. Tori placed high, perfectionist academic goals on herself, but they were unrealistic when she had attention and written work difficulties. The social aspect of school became intolerable as she reached higher grades. She does best with home instruction, one on one, with most of the learning verbal.*

Homebound instruction can be delivered in person, via correspondence courses or distance learning arrangements, or through any combination of methods. If your child is in high school, you'll probably need to make sure his homebound program will help him meet the requirements for graduation. This may mean having the instructor follow specific lesson plans, use certain textbooks, or help your child complete required projects.

You should also meet privately with the homebound instructor to explain your child's symptoms, go over her IEP, and talk about grading arrangements.

Although homebound instruction sounds ideal for students with severe OCD, therapists and many parents note that the reality is often not so rosy.

Mary, mother of 13-year-old Ryan, reports:

> *Ryan is currently on homebound status. My son has not coped well with schooling. It is even hard for him to have a teacher come to our home for instruction. He thinks the teacher brings in germs and contaminates the house.*

Homebound instruction is usually available for only a few hours each week, and can reinforce avoidance and other OCD-related symptoms (if therapy to combat them is not taking place at the same time).

Homeschooling

Educating your children at home is legal in most US states. Each state has its own regulations about who can homeschool, what (if anything) must be taught, and how (or if) children's educational achievements will be tested. If your state mandates standardized testing for homeschooled students, exceptions to the testing requirements for disabled children are usually not written into the law. You will want to be very careful about doing baseline testing, and about documenting any reasons why your child may not do well on required standardized tests, or why he may have regressed due to his illness or medication.

Eligible homeschooled children are entitled to Early Intervention and special education services. These services may be delivered in the child's home, at a neutral site, or in a nearby school or clinic. This means that even if you choose to teach your child at home, you can still have an IEP with the school district that provides your child with speech therapy, counseling, and other needed services. Homeschoolers can choose to take part in extracurricular activities at their neighborhood public school, and may even be able to take some classes at school (advanced math, for example) while doing the bulk of their schoolwork at home.

Some districts have programs that help homeschooling parents create good programs for children with disabilities, while others go out of their way to make it difficult.

When home learning opportunities are well planned, it isn't necessary for children to spend an eight-hour day doing schoolwork. Consider how much of a typical school day is taken up with lunch, recess, waiting for the teacher's help, filling out ditto sheets, and other relatively non-academic activities, and it's easy to see that just a couple hours of structured learning activities each day with one-on-one attention could provide equal educational benefits. Add in unstructured learning opportunities, like impromptu math lessons while measuring ingredients in the kitchen, and the school day at home looks rather inviting. For children whose attention problems or uncontrolled OCD symptoms make attending school for long periods too difficult, homeschooling offers an especially flexible option.

It's important to set up socialization opportunities if you are homeschooling, because as with homebound instruction, social avoidance and other OCD-related symptoms may otherwise be reinforced. Many homeschooling families share teaching duties with other parents, bringing several children together for certain lessons or activities.

If you are forced to homeschool your child because your district cannot or will not provide a free and appropriate education program, you may be eligible to be paid to teach your child. This option has worked for parents in very rural areas, as well as for some in districts that could not provide a safe setting for a child with assaultive behaviors.

Stephanie, mother of 8-year-old Cassidy, feels that homeschooling has been a positive choice for her daughter, who has several comorbid diagnoses:

> *We homeschool, and Cass tests three to five grade levels above in every area except spelling and listening, both areas she struggles with—and even with those, she tests at grade level. She loves homeschooling and participates in many outside activities, including art, musical theater, and judo. She is not always able to participate in those classes, as sometimes she just is too "off" to handle them. She loves to ride horses in the summer, but is as happy walking one in a field as she is actually riding them. We hope to move next year so we can have our own horses for her.*
>
> *We make learning a part of life. . . so to us, school is our world, not always a sit-down lesson at the table. Even her therapist, who was very wary of homeschooling when we first met him, has told me he would never want her schooling changed, that she does better than she could possibly do anywhere else, and is very happy. I have found that her homeschooling friends are much nicer to her than their traditionally schooled counterparts.*

Homeschooling is not for everyone, even if you can get help from other parents who are in the same boat. Parents are a child's first teacher, but they're not always the best teachers for all topics. There's also the issue of burnout. Parents don't like to bring it up, but spending all day, every day, with a child who has OCD can be exhausting. There are many parents who send their child off to school each day knowing that he will learn little, but also knowing that getting a break will make it possible for the parent to help him after school. You don't have to feel badly if you are not emotionally or financially able to homeschool your child.

If you do homeschool, decide in advance whether your child work toward a high school diploma (this is possible if you use certain homeschool curricula), a GED, or a portfolio of work. Experienced homeschooling parents can help you consider your options, and can be contacted through local groups or online.

Private schools

As noted earlier in this chapter, school districts sometimes contract with private schools and programs to provide services that they do not. These programs are usually not religious in nature (there are a few exceptions, such as residential programs that are affiliated with a religious denomination), and they must be willing to comply with district regulations.

Sometimes parents opt for private school placement directly, at their own cost. Perhaps daily religious instruction is very important to them, or their child's siblings already attend a private school. Luckily, choosing a private school does not automatically disqualify their child from publicly funded Early Intervention and special education services.

In a few areas, parents may be able to use school vouchers to lower the cost of private schools, making educational options more accessible. Depending on local regulations (and on the mood of the courts) these options may include parochial schools.

When looking at private school programs, give them the same level of scrutiny that you would subject a public program to. The private school that served your other children well may be horribly wrong for a child with OCD. Educational programming for children with mental illness requires a certain level of knowledge and flexibility that not all schools have, public or private. You can advocate until you're blue in the face, but in the end, private schools do not have to work with your child.

Seventeen-year-old Emma, who has since transferred to a different private school, explains:

> *Last year I went to an all-girls, private Anglican school. My teachers found it amusing to tell me how dumb I was, even though I have a higher-than-average IQ. It made me very depressed.*

To receive public special education services, you must have your child evaluated and qualified within the public system. Then you'll use an IFSP or IEP to determine which services will be delivered, where they will be delivered, and by whom.

Delivery of public services in a parochial school can get sticky, depending on your state or local district. Some districts are so cautious about maintaining separation of church and state that if several children in a parochial school need speech therapy, they will send a "speech van" to park outside the school to have children receive speech therapy in the van rather than allowing a public employee to help children inside the walls of a parochial school. Other districts have no qualms about sending employees to private school sites.

Unlike a public school, your private school itself will not be required to fulfill any academic promises made in an IEP. The IEP is a contract between you and the school district only. However, enlightened private schools that wish to better serve students with disabilities are well aware of how valuable the ideas in a well-written IEP can be. Some private schools encourage their teachers to attend IEP meetings as a guest of the child's parents. In some cases, these representatives have been treated as full team members, able to help determine meeting agendas and propose IEP goals.

Private schools that accept any form of public funding may be subject to additional regulations. Most are also subject to the Americans with Disabilities Act, which may prevent a school from discriminating against your child due to his disability. However, unlike Section 504 and IDEA, it will not give you tools to require the school to do anything specific to help him learn.

Let the setting fit the child

In between the placement options presented in this chapter are combination settings created to meet a student's specific needs. For example, one student might be able to handle a half-day inclusion program in the morning, then have home-based instruction for other subjects in the afternoon. Another child might be placed in a special class for everything but art and music.

The setting(s) listed in your child's IEP should be reviewed every year (or more often, upon your request) to ensure that the educational program is still meeting his needs, and that he is still in the least restrictive setting.

The current movement in US schools is toward full inclusion whenever possible. Although this is the best choice for the majority of students with OCD, sometimes it is not appropriate. If a setting is proposed by the district, be open-minded enough to check it out, but don't say yes unless you're sure it's right. Inquire about supports, such as personal or classroom aides, who can be added to make inclusive settings more realistic.

It's important to remember that because your child's symptoms may wax and wane drastically, a school setting that once worked well may not work forever. Even though you may want your child to finish high school on time, take college prep courses, or be in a special magnet program, she may not be able to handle it. At the same time, be a fierce advocate for allowing your child to get an education. Far too many kids with OCD are pushed out or sent to get a GED or an IEP diploma, when with appropriate support they could have made it through.

GED programs

Because of the high drop-out rate among children with mental illness, and because of many school districts' unwillingness to serve these children, there is a possibility that your child may end up pursuing a General Equivalency Diploma (GED) rather than a regular high school diploma. The GED is earned by passing a test. The test includes a short essay and addresses a variety of topics. In most states, you must be 16 to take the GED.

If the school district forces your child out of school, the very least you should receive is assistance for helping her pass the exam. This might mean homebound instruction focusing on skills needed to pass the GED, an alternative school program that has earning a GED as its goal, or study materials. There are books, videos, and software programs available to help people study for the GED.

Frankly, the GED is not a difficult test. If your child has successfully completed junior high and can apply a simple formula for writing a short essay, he can probably already pass it.

A GED is legally equal to a high school diploma. You can get a job or attend any community college or trade school program with a GED. If your child wants to pursue a degree at a four-year college, he will probably be able to get in with a GED if he meets the school's other requirements, such as having an adequate score on college placement exams like the SAT and ACT. His chances of admission will be best if he can document his abilities through writing a persuasive admissions essay and building a portfolio of work. He may also want to complete a year or two of community college before applying, as this will be the best possible indicator of his ability to handle college-level work.

Monitoring school progress

Once you have an educational program in place, your next job is playing spy and enforcer. You can't rely totally on the school or school district to monitor your child's progress or ensure compliance with his IEP. Keep a copy of this document and other important notes on hand, and check them against any communications notebooks, progress reports, report cards, and assignments that come home from the school.

Of course you'll want to attend all official meetings, but make a point of just dropping by occasionally on the pretext of bringing your child her coat or having paperwork due at the school office. If you can volunteer an hour a week or so in the school (not necessarily in your child's classroom), that's even better.

If the school is not complying with the IEP, start by talking to the teacher, and work your way up. Most compliance problems can be addressed at the classroom level.

It can be especially difficult to monitor the delivery of therapy and other pull-out services. It seems like a relatively simple task, but parents across the country report that their school district refuses to provide any type of checklist that lets parents see if their child is receiving the services listed in the IEP.

Another problematic area is the administration of medication at school. Some parents have reported refusal to deliver medication at the appointed time, mysteriously missing pills (especially Ritalin and other amphetamines), and missed or mistaken doses. Most self-contained classrooms have many children who take scheduled medications, and they tend to have processes in place. The worst medication problems seem to occur in full-inclusion settings, especially if the student is not capable of monitoring medication delivery himself. You may need to insist on a daily checklist and increase your own monitoring efforts.

If your IEP includes academic goals, see if there are standardized ways to monitor progress (grades aren't always enough). Too often, parents are told that their child is participating well and learning, and then they discover that he has not gained new skills, or has regressed, when an objective measure is used. Ask that your child be tested every year, if possible. You are entitled to the results of any standardized tests your child may take. Check the scores to make sure your child is progressing.

Many parents have found that their children are actually regressing due to inadequate classroom support or curricula. Lack of progress or regression both give you firm grounds for demanding that your child's academic needs be included in the IEP. Several parents report that one of the best ways to get the rest of your IEP team to understand the problem is by using visual aids, such as charts. If you aren't an artistic whiz, there are software programs that can make simple graphs from your numbers.

Taking on the school system

If your child's school persistently refuses to comply with her IEP, what can you do? A lot—the IEP is a type of legal contract, although far too many schools treat it like a nuisance that they can ignore at their leisure. Your options include:

- Sitting back and letting it happen (obviously not recommended)
- Advocating for your child within the classroom and the IEP process
- Bringing in an expert to help you advocate for your child
- Requesting a due process hearing
- Filing a complaint with your state department of education
- Organizing with other parents to advocate for a group of students with similar problems
- Working with other advocates at a legislative level
- Going to court

While some schools and school districts have a well-deserved reputation for venality, most are simply hamstrung by low budgets and lack of knowledge. These are areas in which an informed parent can make a difference. You can provide the teacher and administrators with information about educational possibilities, and you can let them know that their resource problems are something to take up with government funding sources, not something to unfairly penalize children with.

Remember that as a full member of the IEP team, you have the power to call an IEP meeting whenever one is needed. This will bring together all of the team members to review the document and compare its requirements with what your child is receiving.

There are times when you will need to bring in an expert. Special educational advocates and self-styled IEP experts are available all over the country. Some of these people work for disability advocacy organizations or disability law firms. Others are freelance practitioners. Some are parents of children with disabilities who have turned their avocation into a vocation.

You will probably have to pay for expert services, unless they are available through your local NAMI chapter or another parent group. Expert services can include researching programs available in your area, connecting you with appropriate resources, helping you write a better IEP, and advocating for your child at IEP meetings and due process hearings.

Due process

The words "due process" make schools very nervous. This term refers to the processes to which a child and his family are supposed to have access while being evaluated for special education or provided with special education services. If you or the school has requested that your child be evaluated for special education services, whether or not he has been approved, you are entitled to due process.

When parents start talking about due process, they're usually referring to a due process hearing: an internal appeals procedure used by school districts to determine whether or not procedures have been handled properly. Due process hearings hinge on whether the district has followed federal and state-mandated procedures for evaluating a child for special education and setting up a program for that child. Violations can include small things, like notifying parents of a meeting over the phone rather in writing; or major issues, like using untrained or incompetent personnel to evaluate children, or deliberately denying needed services to save money.

Issues that tend to end up in due process include disagreements over evaluations or educational labels, provision of inadequate therapeutic services, placement in inappropriate educational settings, noncompliance with the IEP, lack of extended school year services when appropriate, and poor transition planning.

Obviously, every due process case is unique. Each state also has its own due process system. Regulations that all these systems have in common are:

- Parents must initiate a due process hearing in writing.
- The hearing must take place in a timely fashion.

- Hearings are presided over by an impartial person who does not work for the district.
- Children have the right to stay in the current placement until after the hearing (this is called the "stay put" rule).
- Parents can attend due process hearings and advocate for their child.
- Parents can hire an educational advocate or lawyer to represent them at the due process hearing.
- If the parents use a lawyer and they win, they are entitled to have their legal fees paid by the district.

Due process hearings resemble a court hearing before a judge. Both sides will be asked to argue their case and present evidence on their behalf. Both sides can call on experts or submit documents to buttress their statements. However, experienced advocates know that despite the veneer of impartiality, if it comes down to your word against the district's on educational or placement issues, the district will probably have an edge.

Some districts offer arbitration or mediation, which are not as formal as due process hearings. In an arbitration hearing, both parties agree in advance to comply with the arbitrator's ruling. You can't recover your legal fees in arbitration, and your rights are not spelled out in the law. Be very cautious before agreeing to waive your right to a due process hearing in favor of mediation.

However, you can try mediation *without* waiving your right to due process while you're waiting for your due process hearing date to come up. If mediation works, you're done; if it doesn't, you can continue with the due process proceeding.

Section 504 actions

You can bypass the cumbersome due process procedure if your child has a 504 plan rather than or in addition to an IEP. Assuming that the school and then the district 504 compliance officer do not respond to your written complaints, take your case directly to your state Office of Civil Rights. This office is responsible for enforcing the Rehabilitation Act.

The state Office of Civil Rights is also charged with enforcing the Americans with Disabilities Act (see the section "The ADA and the schools," later in this chapter).

Public advocacy

If your child is denied special education services, you'll soon find that you have a lot of company. Some problems in special education are systemic. Parents in several states have banded together effectively to get better services for their children. The National Alliance for the Mentally Ill (NAMI) is just one of several national organizations that are actively trying to secure improvements in special education. (See Appendix A for a list of helpful groups.)

You may choose to form your own organization, join an existing group covering childhood mental health issues, or work with a larger group of special education parents. You may also find allies in teacher's unions and organizations, the PTA and other parents associations, and elsewhere in your community.

Parents can personally help improve school funding for special education by lobbying their local school board or state legislature. They can help press for and help write laws that require adequate support for these students, and for others in the special education system.

If you're not the kind of person who enjoys conflict, advocacy and due process can be very draining. School district lawyers count on endless meetings, criticism of your parenting skills, and constant references to their superior knowledge to wear down your defenses. You must always stay on guard, and yet be open to logical compromises and the possibility of beneficial alliances. It's not easy, but it's necessary.

Going to court

Due process is bad enough. Going to court is absolutely, positively your last recourse. It's something you do only when nothing else works, not even marching on a school board meeting with a bunch of disgruntled parents.

Going to court is time-consuming, exhausting, and expensive. The outcome is uncertain, and while the case drags on, your child may be languishing in an inappropriate setting. But if you've exhausted every other avenue, it may just have to happen.

Most special education court cases involve school districts that have lost a due process hearing and yet persist in denying the services mandated for a child. A 1994 case, *W. B. v. Matula*, also established the right of parents to sue a school on constitutional grounds. The parent of a grade-schooler, who was eventually diagnosed with multiple neurological disabilities, took her district to court over violation of her child's due process rights and under the Fourteenth Amendment of the Constitution, which entitles all citizens to equal protection under the law. To the consternation of school districts everywhere, she won her case, which included a substantial financial judgment (she used the money to pay her massive legal bills and to get her son an appropriate education).

Since the Matula case, school districts have been put on notice that parents of special-needs children can successfully pursue them beyond the due process hearing. Besides the grounds used in the Matula case, parents may be able to ask the courts for redress under state education laws, or even contract law. There are few legal precedents as of yet, but the number of successful legal challenges is growing. Court battles are underway in almost every state over unavailable, inadequate, or even harmful special education services.

The ADA and schools

The Americans with Disabilities Act is a pioneering civil rights law. Patterned on civil rights laws that bar discrimination based on race, ethnicity, or gender, the ADA mandates access to all public and most private facilities for disabled citizens. It's usually invoked to make sure people with physical disabilities have access to wheelchair ramps, elevators, grab bars, and other aids to using public or private accommodations. It also prevents handicapped people from most forms of job discrimination.

Many people do not know that people with mental illnesses are included in the federal definition of disabled, and are therefore eligible for protection under the ADA.

In schools, the ADA does more than force the district to install handicapped-accessible restrooms and wheelchair ramps for physical access. It mandates that children with disabilities have the right to be involved in all school activities, not just classroom-based educational activities. This includes band, chess club, chorus, sports, camping trips, field trips, and any other activities of interest to your child that are school-sponsored or school-affiliated.

If your child will need accommodations or support to take advantage of these activities, the IEP is where these should be listed. If you do not have an IEP, a 504 plan can be used.

If your child's behavior is actually dangerous to himself or others, that's another issue. . .but under the ADA, the school cannot discriminate based simply on his diagnosis or on assumptions they might have about his behavior.

Education in Canada

The Canadian special education process is very similar to that used in the US. Provincial guidelines are set by the national Ministry of Education and governed by the Education Act. However, most educational decisions are made at the regional, district, or school level. Children between the ages of 6 and 22 who have OCD should qualify for special education assistance under the Targeted Behavior Program (TBP).

Special education evaluations are done by a team that may include a school district psychologist, a behavior specialist, a special education teacher, other school or district personnel, and, in some cases, a parent, although inviting parents to participate is not required by law.

The evaluation is used as a basis for an IEP. Almost identical to the American document of the same name, the IEP is usually updated yearly, or more frequently if needed. A formal review is required every three years.

Rae, mother of 13-year-old D'Arcy, has learned the ins and outs of Canada's school system:

> *We have IEPs, but they don't have quite the same clout here that they appear to have under the US legislation. What you have to trumpet here is the legal requirement, under Human Rights legislation, that disability be "accommodated." For us, the school counselor is being very helpful, as is the district behavior specialist. I'm doing some research at the moment on the actual legal requirements so that I know just how much I can demand. I've found the most effective resource is to be a pleasant, informed, persistent, somewhat annoying pest.*

Placement options for Canadian students with OCD range from home-based instruction to full inclusion. Partial inclusion is increasingly common, as is supported mainstreaming. Students from rural or poorly served areas may be sent to a residential school, or funding may be provided for room and board to allow the student to attend a day program outside of his home area.

If disputes arise between the school or the district and the parents, there is a School Division Decision Review Process available for adjudicating them. The concept known as due process in the US is usually referred to as "fundamental justice" in Canada.

Education in the UK

When a child in the UK is judged eligible for special education services, he is said to be "statemented." This term refers to an IEP-like document called a Statement of Special Educational Needs, or Record of Needs. This document is developed at the council level by the Local Educational Authority (LEA), and lists the services that a child needs. Usually, the team that creates the statement includes an educational psychologist, a teacher, and the parents. It may also include the family's health visitor or other personnel, such as a psychiatrist or child development specialist. Each child's statement is reviewed and updated annually. Disability advocates strongly urge parents to get expert help with the statementing process.

Your LEA can limit services according to its budget, even if those services are listed as necessary on your child's statement. Service availability varies widely between LEAs. Some therapeutic services that would be delivered by schools in the US, such as psychiatric care and therapy, may be made available through National Health instead.

School placements in the UK run the gamut from residential schools to specialist schools to full inclusion in mainstream schools. There are more residential options available than in the US system due to the English tradition of public schools. (American readers may be confused by this term: in the UK, public schools are privately owned and run; schools run by the LEAs are called government schools.)

Schools working with statemented students operate under a government Code of Practice that is analogous to, but much weaker than, IDEA in the US. Parents and disability advocates can insist that LEAs follow this code when devising programs for statemented students, and have access to a formal appeals process.

The UK government has recently taken steps toward improving Early Intervention offerings. Currently, EI services are not mandated by law, although they are available in many areas.

Parents report that homeschooling a child with a disability is particularly hard in some parts of the UK. Regular inspection by an Educational Welfare Officer is required, and some of these bureaucrats are not very knowledgeable about mental health issues. Parents should be prepared to provide detailed documentation of what they are teaching, and of how well their child is progressing.

Education in Australia

Australia's system is paradoxically looser and yet more accommodating to students with disabilities of all sorts. There is only a thin legal framework for the provision of special education services, but in the urban areas where most Australians live, these services are apparently no harder to obtain than they are in the UK.

Early Intervention services are readily available in urban areas for children ages 6 and under. To obtain an EI evaluation, parents should contact the Specialist Children's Services Team at their local Department of Human Services.

Placement options for older children include residential schools (including placement in residential schools located in the UK, for some students), Special Schools for children with moderate to severe developmental delay or severe behavior disorders, special classrooms for disabled children within regular schools, and the full range of mainstreaming options. "Mix and match" placements that allow students to be mainstreamed for just part of the day are still rare, however. For students in rural areas, there is a Traveling Teacher service that can provide special education services and consultation to children learning in "outback" schools or at home.

Australia has federal special education regulations, but each state's Department of Education, Training, and Employment (DETS, formerly the Department of Education and Children's Services) is more important. Each DETS provides information, parent services, assistive technology, augmentative communication, special curricula, and many more services for students with disabilities. Individual school districts and schools themselves may also apply different rules or offer special programs.

Kerry, mother of 12-year-old Kim, put it this way:

> *We don't have anything like IEPs, and I think that there are some cultural factors involved in the way disability is approached here. I've been trying to put my finger on just what it is. . . . I think it has to do with the fact that Australian society is less "harsh" than American society. There's a bit more sense of cooperation and caring for the underdog. People don't talk as much about "rights," don't sue each other very often, etc. (though it is happening more). Perhaps there has been less need to label kids because there is somewhat less of a tendency to isolate and discriminate.*
>
> *I'm not saying that there aren't huge problems for kids with differences, especially subtle differences that aren't at all obvious; however, I think that people here tend to expect to talk things through with schools and teachers and make informal arrangements. There's an expectation of reasonableness, in many cases. I get to know teachers on a personal level and explain about Kim's differences. On the one hand we have less bureaucratization of services and more individual innovation; on the other hand, we have fewer services altogether.*

Education in New Zealand

Students who qualify for special education services in New Zealand are called "section nined" (old terminology) or "qualified for the Ongoing Resourcing Scheme" (ORS). ORS qualification is currently reserved for those children whose impairment is judged to be "high" or "very high," with the most resources going to the latter group. As of this writing, special education services for Early Childhood centers and home-based programs are not funded. Nevertheless, special arrangements have to provide services to some young children with disabilities in a clinical setting or in home-based programs.

The Ministry of Education sets qualifying guidelines for Early Childhood and school-age special education services.

Recent news reports indicate that limited local resources and a move to push for full inclusion under the Special Education 2000 program has eliminated many special education resources that were once available in New Zealand's schools. According to New Zealand parents, mentally ill children were never particularly well served by the system anyway. There is a corresponding move to community-based services for children and adults with mental illness that advocates hope will eventually fill in the gaps, but as of yet, services are neither widespread nor easy to obtain.

School placements include a few special schools, attached special education units within regular schools, and a range of inclusion options in mainstream settings. Some students are in residential settings. Under Special Education 2000, many more schools will have an arrangement similar to a resource room rather than self-contained special education units.

School behavior and school violence

Due to recent episodes of violence, many US schools are taking a hard line on verbal threats, aggressive or assaultive behavior, and even on the presence of students with behavioral, emotional, or neurological disorders in schools. In some cases, this campaign has crossed over from prudent caution to violating the rights of special education students. For example, some districts have announced that all assaults (a category that includes hitting, biting, and even playground pushing) will result in police being called to actually arrest the student. Students have been suspended or threatened with expulsion for angrily saying things like "I wish this school would burn down," or for threatening the school bully with a stick hastily grabbed off the ground.

According to IDEA, students with disabilities are subject to discipline for infractions of school rules just like all other students—unless the problem is a result of the disability. For example, it would be unfair to suspend a child with Tourette's syndrome for having a spitting tic, even though spitting would normally be a rule violation. Likewise, it would be wrong to expel or arrest a student with OCD if he has a rage episode as a result of his illness.

At the same time, schools do have a duty to protect other students, faculty, and staff. Case law has upheld the idea that if a student cannot be safely maintained in a less restrictive setting, the district has the right to place the student in a more restrictive setting. The devil is in the details, of course. Parents in these situations find that they carry the burden of proving that the district did not do all it could to keep the student in the least restrictive setting.

If you or the school suspects that your child's misbehavior is the result of her disability, work with the school for a *functional behavior assessment* (FBA) and a *functional intervention plan* (FIP). The FBA should include:

- A clear description of the problem behavior, including the pattern or sequence of behavior observed
- Time and place when the behavior occurs (setting and antecedents)
- The current consequences attached to the behavior
- A hypothesis about the cause and effect of the behavior
- Direct observation data

The functional intervention plan should derive from the functional behavior assessment, and consist of guidelines for modifying the student's environment to eliminate or improve behavior, as well as ideas for teaching the student positive alternative behavior. Creating a workable plan may require trying on several hypotheses about the behavior, and then testing different interventions. This procedure should be followed whenever a special education student has a long-lasting behavior problem, or if he has any behavior problem that puts him at danger for suspension, expulsion, or arrest.

For example, for the situation cited earlier, in which a child has a spitting tic, the plan could include several ideas for handling the problem. The child could go to the bathroom to spit, use a trash can, or spit into a handkerchief. Adults could see if stress increases the frequency and then reduce stress, or try a different medication for tic reduction. For the child who rages, the functional behavior assessment could be used to find out if there is an environmental trigger, and the functional intervention plan could provide ways to prevent the behavior. These might include removing the environmental trigger, designating a safe place for the child to go when he feels the warning signs of impending rage, training personnel in safe restraint techniques, or providing emergency medication.

Parents of a child who is sometimes aggressive, assaultive, or even just plain hateful often secretly worry that he could turn his rage on others, with serious or even deadly results. Considering the rash of school killings in the late 1990s, this is a logical worry. After fourteen students and one teacher were killed by a pair of gun-toting students at Columbine High School in Littleton, Colorado, the press and legislative arenas were filled with calls to remove "problem students" from schools. Parents of teens with OCD were especially alarmed by the news that one of the students involved, Eric Harris, had previously been prescribed Luvox. This medication is frequently used to treat OCD, and some newspapers speculated that Harris suffered from the disorder. Suddenly all the reassurances parents had been given about teenagers with OCD never acting on violent obsessions seemed like cruel lies.

Eric Harris committed suicide, his parents are not talking to the press, and his psychiatric records have never been released. He may have had OCD, but he surely also had other, very serious psychiatric problems. He was not taking Luvox when the crime was committed; he may in fact have never taken the medication, despite being given a prescription. He was never offered any other treatment for OCD, such as cognitive behavioral therapy. In fact, a look at facts about teens guilty of school shootings who were supposedly under the care of a psychiatrist reveals that their care was generally cursory—perhaps a single visit and a quickly discarded prescription, as was apparently the case with Kip Kinkel in Oregon, as well as with Harris. Some may have been misdiagnosed or mismedicated; for example, given SSRIs when they actually suffered from bipolar disorder, possibly causing mania or psychosis to emerge. The vast majority had never gotten any substantive help for their psychiatric or emotional problems.

Responsible parents can do much to ensure that their child does not become the perpetrator of such crimes. Almost every teen involved in a school killing has had several traits in common. They have been very depressed, usually suicidal; and they have had easy access to weapons, little parental oversight, and no special program of supports at school. Most had been the victims of teasing and mistreatment at school, with no intervention from school administrators. For example, Michael Carneal, the 14-year-old who shot classmates in ultra-conservative West Paducah, Kentucky, had been labeled a homosexual in the school newspaper. He had been the butt of jokes for many years before he allegedly "snapped" and became violent. He had actually been exhibiting psychotic behavior since eighth grade, but had not received any help. Carneal, who pled guilty though mentally ill, has since been variously diagnosed with a cyclic mood disorder and schizotypal personality disorder.

If you are reading this book, you are the kind of involved, informed parent who will make sure that weapons are not easily available to your child, who will ensure that he is under proper medical care, and who will see to it that your child's school is part of the solution to his problems, not a problem itself.

If your child develops a fascination with weapons and violence, you must intervene immediately. Although intrusive violent thoughts are relatively common in OCD, overpowering guilt normally accompanies them. On the off-chance that your child might prove the exception to the rule, however, don't wait to get help if it is needed—call on all possible resources in his school and in the community.

Suspension and expulsion

Some students with OCD will break school rules, and not necessarily as a result of their illness. When they do so, they must pay the price. However, if a student covered by an IEP is suspended for more than ten days in one school year or is expelled, the district is responsible for finding an appropriate alternative educational setting immediately, and for continuing to implement the IEP. Suspension of a disabled student for more than ten days requires parental permission or a court order. The district is also required to do a functional behavior assessment and create a functional intervention plan if this has not already been done, or to take a new look at the existing plan in light of the incident.

Suspensions of longer than ten days constitute a change of placement, and that means that an IEP meeting must be called immediately. IDEA does not spell out exactly how this procedure should work, so districts may not have a plan in place to deal with emergency placements. Parents have reported that many school districts respond by putting the student on homebound instruction until a new placement can be found. This may or may not be acceptable. Delivery of therapeutic services may be a problem on homebound instruction. Parents will probably have to get involved to prevent the search process from dragging on too long.

For the purpose of these protections, the category of disabled students includes not only those with a special education IEP or other formal agreement with the district, but also those students whose parents have requested a special education assessment or written a letter of concern about the child to school personnel (if the parent is illiterate or cannot write, a verbal inquiry will suffice) before the incident occurred. It also includes students whose behavior and performance should have indicated a disability to any objective observer, and children about whom district personnel have expressed concern before the incident.

Expulsion is an even more serious matter. Parents must be informed in writing about the district's intention to seek expulsion, and this document must include clear reasons for this action, evidence, and information about the child's procedural rights. There must be an assessment before expulsion can take place, and parents must also be informed about this in writing. Only if all safeguards are provided and all procedures are followed can a disabled student be expelled.

Expulsion for a disabled student does not mean the same thing as it does for a garden-variety miscreant, who may simply be kicked out to rot in front of the TV at home. It's more like a forced change of placement. By expelling the student, the district has determined that the current placement is not working. It must then find an appropriate placement, which means revisiting the IEP.

As a result of school violence, several states and the federal government are considering laws that would mandate the arrest and incarceration (pending a hearing before a judge) of any child who brings a gun to school. Under current circumstances, this seems like a logical response. If your child is ever in this situation, you should be able to use this opportunity to get him into a diversion program with psychiatric support. Unfortunately, some of the proposed laws go far beyond suspending IDEA for students with guns, and may represent a serious threat to special education services for a wider group who pose little if any risk to others.

Extended school year services

If your child needs to have a consistent educational and therapeutic program year round, most school districts will provide services during summer vacations and other long breaks only if you can document his need for extended school year (ESY) services. This action requires special attention to monitoring how your child copes with breaks in the school routine. Teachers and your child's psychiatrist or therapist can help you gather the evidence you need to show that your child loses skills or regresses behaviorally after being out of school for more than a weekend. During breaks from school, keep your own log of behaviors and regressions, if any.

Some parents have also been able to qualify their children for ESY services by showing that services can be made available during the summer that satisfy parts of the IEP not addressed adequately during the school year. For example, a student might be able to get ESY funding approved for a special summer program geared toward teaching social skills or independent living skills.

Early Intervention

It is very rare for a child to be diagnosed with OCD as a preschooler, although patients have been identified as young as age two-and-a-half. If your child falls into this category, or if she has another disabling condition that emerges in early childhood, she should be eligible for Early Intervention (EI) services.

EI service offerings vary widely according to where you live. They should, however, be determined by the child's needs, not just by what happens to be available or customary in your area. Evaluation is the first, and sometimes most important, service provided through EI programs. Once an evaluation has been carried out, if your child is found to have OCD or another disability, an Individual Family Service Plan (IFSP) is developed. The IFSP spells out the needs of the child and the family, and the services that will be provided to meet those needs.

The Individual Family Service Plan

This document should be created at a meeting to which you will be invited to attend and contribute. Although it's a good idea for both parents and practitioners to write down their ideas for goals and interventions in advance, the IFSP itself should not be written in advance and simply handed to the parents to sign.

The cover page of the IFSP summarizes what's known about the child and his diagnosis, and lists the team members present at the IFSP meeting. It also lists the services to be provided, and how, where, and by whom they will be provided. Further details about these services are entered on goals and objectives pages later in the IFSP. Accordingly, the cover page should be mostly blank until the goals and objectives pages have been filled out.

Goals and objectives will be developed by the team at the IFSP meeting. They can be written to cover any area in which your child has a deficit, including cognition, behavior, coping strategies, fine and gross motor development, communication, social skills, and self-help skills. Goals should be finite, observable items rather than general concepts. For example, "Kim will learn to use counting to ten and deep breathing as a response to frustration," is a workable goal, while "Kim will learn to deal with frustration," is not.

One or more pages of the IFSP describe your child's evaluation. These pages should cover medical information, psychiatric diagnoses, and the results of hearing, vision, and developmental screenings, if any.

The IFSP can also include services needed by the whole family to help you care for your child. For example, these services might include parent education classes, the services of a cognitive behavior therapist who can provide parent training in CBT techniques, psychiatric consultation, and assistance in finding and accessing community resources.

The goals set in your child's IFSP will dictate what kind of setting services should be delivered in. Typical EI settings include:

- **Home-based services.** For very young children, home-based services often make the most sense. Home-based programs may include direct therapeutic and educational services, training and supervision for parents and volunteers working with the child, assistance with medical procedures, and care needed to allow education to take place.
- **Direct services.** This category includes all types of professional services, such as psychological therapy, that are delivered in a school setting (but not as part of the preschool program itself), in a clinic, or in other settings outside the home. For example, the IFSP might specify that your child is to receive 45 minutes of play therapy twice a week at a nearby university clinic. These services may be delivered by professionals or facilities under contract with Early Intervention, or by practitioners working directly for the EI program.
- **School-based services.** This category includes all services delivered as part of a public or private preschool program, at the school site. Therapeutic services may be integrated into a special or typical preschool program, or may be delivered as pull-out services, for which your child leaves the class for one-on-one or small-group work.

A primarily home-based program goes the furthest to build a strong relationship between the child and his parents. It takes place in a familiar, non-distracting environment that has probably already been made appropriate for the child's sensory and safety needs. It eliminates lost time and problems related to transporting a preschool child to school (many EI programs actually bus infants and toddlers across town). It also provides the best stage for intensive, one-on-one intervention, such as devising cognitive behavioral therapy plans targeted to a child's symptoms and delivered as part of her daily activities.

Unfortunately, it is very difficult to get approval for a home-based schooling program. One tool that may help you win this battle is a thorough and accurate financial appraisal that compares the cost of an intensive home-based program in the early years to twelve years of residential or private placement. If your child has been diagnosed with OCD at this early of an age, it is likely that his symptoms are already very severe. That makes early, intensive intervention the most cost-effective solution, no matter how you cut it.

Early Intervention classrooms

A preschool setting with other children is often considered the best placement for a young child with a psychiatric condition, because it provides the child with the greatest number of opportunities to relate to others, play, and learn. Spending time with other children in a structured setting can be very beneficial for developing social skills. However, attention must be paid to your child's special needs, deficits, strengths, and so on—just any preschool class won't do.

EI preschools come in four major flavors:

- **Regular preschool classroom, with or without special support.** Also called a *full integration* setting or *mainstreaming*, this might be a Head Start or similar preschool classroom. Your child would attend preschool with therapeutic services, classroom adaptations, and personal support, such as an aide, as needed. These services, adaptations, and supports must be written into the IFSP.
- **Supported integrated preschool classroom.** Also called a *reverse integration* setting, because it's the non-disabled students who are integrated into a special program rather than the other way around. This is a specially created preschool setting that brings together a small group of

children with disabilities and children without disabilities. Therapeutic services, classroom adaptations, and personal support are provided to each child with a disability as per his IFSP. Children in a supported integrated classroom may have a variety of different disabilities, such as autism, Down's syndrome, or mental illness.

- **Special preschool classroom.** This is a specially created preschool setting for children with disabilities only. The children may have a mix of various physical or emotional disabilities, or a mix of different behavior disorders only. The classroom may be part of a larger school with other types of classrooms.
- **Special preschool.** This is an entire preschool program created specifically to work with children who have disabilities. It may be within a larger school program that also educates school-age children. It may be owned and run by a public school district, or it may be a private school that contracts with the Early Intervention program to provide services. If it is private, EI and/or the school district should pay the full cost of tuition if it is judged to be the most appropriate setting for your child.

There are positive aspects to each of these typical settings. For children who can handle full, supported inclusion in a regular preschool classroom, there are ample opportunities to model the behavior of less-challenged peers.

Supported integrated classrooms offer similar benefits, with a daily program and structure that's more geared toward the child with special needs.

Special classrooms and schools generally have the most services, but provide few opportunities to interact with non-disabled peers. Your child's needs, abilities, and difficulties will dictate the right placement, as there is no workable one-size-fits-all approach.

Why school matters so much

School is your child's work, the most important thing he does outside of his relationships with family members. It is preparation for the rest of his life. And although many young people are not developmentally or emotionally ready for all of the challenges of school, it is a legal responsibility as well as a societal one.

One of the most devastating effects of childhood-onset OCD is the disruption of a child's education. It can affect your child's prospects for higher education and employment, and his ability to function in the community as an adult. This is especially true when the onset of severe symptoms is sudden. The patient feels intense self-doubt, anxiety, and shame when he is unable to handle something that other kids seem to tackle with ease, and that was once a source of personal pride.

School failure and dropping out of school can be predictors for serious trouble in adult life. . .but only if the problem is not solved. There are so many options for young people with OCD that an inability to manage traditional schooling should not be a barrier to learning. Parents and their allies at school may have to be more creative and flexible than they have ever been before, but the outcome will be worth it.

Transition to adulthood

The period of transition that begins around age 15 can be a minefield for young people with OCD. School starts getting serious, as college and careers become less of an abstract proposition. Grades matter, missing school can have a major impact, the social scene becomes more cliquish, and the pressures of teenage romantic and sexual yearnings add stress.

It's during this very period of high anxiety that parents and teenagers take crucial steps toward becoming independent of each other. Of course, the presence of OCD in the equation adds an extra element of trouble. Transition planning is the formal name given to preparing your child for adulthood. There are two kinds of transition planning: a formal process that will be part of your child's IEP and will concentrate on school and employment issues, and a family process that covers legal, financial, and personal concerns.

For most students, high school graduation marks a jumping-off point: some go straight to work, some to apprenticeships, some to community college or tradeschool, and some to college. But there's nothing magical about the number 18. When your child reaches the age of legal majority, he may still need your assistance. How much help he'll need will depend entirely on the severity of his symptoms, and on how well you have been able to plan for the future.

Within the special education system, transition planning should begin by age 13 or 14, when your child's peers are beginning to gain basic work skills and amass credits toward high school graduation. Special education students also have a right to be prepared for graduation, higher education, and work in ways that fit their needs. For many, extra support will be needed.

Your teenager's transition plan should address high school graduation, higher education, and work skills and opportunities. It may also include preparing the young adult to apply for public assistance, supported housing, and other necessary benefits; helping her learn how to self-manage medical and psychiatric care; and instructing her in life skills such as budgeting, banking, driving, and cooking.

A high school student's IEP must include an area for transition planning. Because this is an area that has received little emphasis in the past, you may need to keep the IEP team on track. Make sure your child's transition plan involves all relevant life areas, not just education.

Preparing for work

Preparing for the world of work means gaining appropriate basic skills, such as typing, filing, driving, filling out forms, writing business letters, using tools, or cooking. These skills may be gained in school-based vocational/technical classes, in classes taken at a community college or vocational school while the student is still in high school, in a union- or employer-sponsored apprenticeship program, via job shadowing arrangements or internships, or on the job. Vocational planning is mandatory for special education students in the US by age 16, and should start much earlier.

Transition-to-work services may include moving into the public Vocational Rehabilitation system, which trains and places adults with disabilities into jobs. However, in many states the Vocational Rehabilitation system is severely overloaded, with waiting periods for placement ranging from three months to five or more years. Typical opportunities range from sheltered workshop jobs (splitting kindling wood, sorting recyclables, light assembly work) under direct supervision, to supported placement in the community as grocery clerks, office helpers, chip-fabrication plant workers, and the like. Often the person works with a job coach—a person who helps them handle workplace stresses and learn work skills. In some cases, the job coach actually comes to work with the person for a while.

School districts may sponsor their own supported work opportunities for special education students, such as learning how to run an espresso coffee cart or working in a student-run horticultural business. Many schools have vocational programs that give students a chance to have a mentor in their chosen field, possibly including actual work experience with local employers. Not all vocational programs are for low-wage or "blue-collar" jobs. Vocational options in some urban districts include health and biotechnology careers, computing, and the fine arts.

Some public and private agencies may also be able to help with job training and placement. These include your state employment department; the Opportunities Industrialization Commission (OIC); the Private Industry Council (PIC); and job placement services operated by Goodwill Industries, St. Vincent de Paul, and similar service organizations, for people with disabilities.

All students with disabilities should receive appropriate vocational counseling, including aptitude testing, discussion of their interests and abilities, and information about different employment possibilities. Parents need to ensure that capable students are not shunted into dead-end positions that will leave them financially vulnerable as adults.

Graduation

Most students with OCD are headed for a regular high school diploma. This usually requires passing a certain number of specified courses. If the student needs changes in the graduation requirements—for example, if your child has been unable to develop proficiency in a foreign language due to cognitive deficits caused by medication, or if he was hospitalized during a required course and needs a waiver—now is the time to arrange for these changes.

Some students will need extra coursework to make it through high school, such as special instruction in keyboarding or study skills. These abilities will also help with higher education or work later on, and you can make them part of your child's transition plan.

Some students will need more than the usual four years to complete diploma requirements. This can be a problem—most teens have a strong desire to graduate with their class. It is sometimes possible for a student who is still short some requirements for graduation to participate in the commencement ceremony with her class, if a plan has been made to remedy the deficits over the next few months.

Some students will not be able to earn a regular diploma. They may choose (or be forced) to pursue a GED, as noted earlier in this chapter. A special form of certification called an *IEP diploma* is also available. If a student earns an IEP diploma, it means she has completed all the objectives set out in her IEP for graduation. This option is usually reserved for students who are unable to master high school level work, such as students with severe mental retardation. However, it could be the route to a creative graduation option for your child.

Students who are headed for college may want or need to go beyond the basic high school diploma. If your state has a special diploma for advanced students, such as Oregon's Certificate of Advanced Mastery or New York's Regents Diploma, check early on about any accommodations that may be needed for the examination or portfolio process. Some states (including Oregon, as of this writing, but not New York) have refused to permit accommodations. This is patently illegal, and will surely be successfully challenged. If you don't want to be the one to bring a lawsuit, ask instead for special tutoring in advance of the test.

In the UK, Australia, New Zealand, and Ireland, special help may be available to help teens pass their level exams, including modified exams in some cases. Talk to your LEA or education department for more information about options in your area.

Higher education

If your child has been evaluated and judged eligible for special education services, the school district's responsibility for his education does not end with the GED or high school diploma. Students planning to attend trade school, a two-year community college program, or a four-year college program need information far in advance about which high school courses will be required for entry. This is especially important for those students with disabilities who carry a lighter course load, as they may need to make up some credits in summer school or via correspondence courses.

Transition programs should address the move from high school to higher education with specific assistance, including financial help if needed, not just vague words about college counseling services. Disabled students are eligible for publicly funded education and/or services until age 22 if needed. In some cases this assistance includes tuition; in all cases it should include setting up mentoring and counseling services in advance at the student's new school. Special education services and help for students with learning disabilities are available on campus and in dorms at many colleges.

It's against the law to deny admission to a student just because he has a disability, but other college admission criteria generally must be met. Public universities and community colleges may waive some admission criteria for disabled students on a case-by-case basis if the student can show that he is capable of college-level work. Standardized test requirements might also be set aside if high school grades or the student's work portfolio look good.

Schools that normally require all freshmen to live on campus may waive this requirement for a student with special needs. If living at home is not an option, a group home or supervised apartment near campus might be. Before your child leaves for college in another city, make sure that you have secured safe and appropriate housing, and found competent local professionals to provide ongoing care. You'll also want to work out a crisis plan with your child, just in case things go wrong. She will want to know who to call and where to go. The freshman year of college is a very common time for symptoms to flare up. The stress, missed sleep, and attractions of newfound freedom (such as drug and alcohol use) all play a role.

Healthcare

Family therapy can be very useful for helping teens and parents balance issues of healthcare and independence. The ultimate goal should be ensuring that your teenager is well-informed about his diagnosis and treatment options, and capable of self-care by young adulthood.

Parents need to start teaching their children as early as possible about using public transportation or driving, picking up prescriptions and reading their labels, making and keeping medical appointments, paying medical bills, and knowing where to go for help.

Some adults are never able to handle all of these tasks adequately, even though they may be perfectly competent in other areas of their life. These individuals will need support to help them get appropriate medical care. Case management services (see the next section) can help, but a personal aide or a self-care advocate may be even better.

You'll also need to identify adult healthcare providers in advance as your child nears the end of adolescence. Young women will need to see a gynecologist, for example, and both boys and girls will be leaving their pediatrician for a general practitioner.

If there will be changes in how your child's healthcare is paid for—for example, if she will be transitioning from private health insurance to Medicaid—you may have to prospect for knowledgeable doctors in an unfamiliar medical bureaucracy.

Hopefully, you've been providing your child with reminders all along about symptom triggers and "early warning signs" that should send him in search of help. You might want to go over this information more formally with your teenager and his psychiatrist at this time. Sometimes getting the word from a doctor is more effective than parental advice, which many teens simply blow off as nagging.

Case management

You may continue to act as your adult child's informal case manager for many years, or you may wish to give this job to a professional. Case management services can encompass arranging for healthcare, connecting the client with community services, a certain amount of financial management (such as being the client's payee for SSI), and more.

Case managers can be hired privately, found within government mental health or community services departments, or accessed through advocacy agencies for the mentally ill. Some health insurance plans provide case management services as part of their behavioral health package, including coordinating outside services as well as managing the patient's medical needs.

Sarah, mother of 17-year-old Lili, found a good case manager through a county program:

> *What we opted for was the services of a caseworker with our county's Mental Health Department. He will continue to be a resource person for Lili as she transitions to adulthood.*
>
> *He signed her up for a supplemental mental health insurance program available through the state that will cover any needs that fall outside of our insurance plan, like mental health inpatient care or extra*

therapy sessions. When she reaches the age of 18 she'll be eligible for subsidized health insurance from the state, based on her own income from work. She has already submitted the paperwork for this insurance.

Especially for young women

By the time transition planning comes around, your daughter has weathered the worst storms of puberty. She has probably noticed if her symptoms change significantly before, during, or after her monthly period. It's important for her to understand that patterns she observes now will change as she continues to mature.

With luck, any monthly symptom changes will become less prominent. However, changes in her hormonal balance due to birth control medication or pregnancy can cause symptoms to flare. If your daughter is a teenager, it may seem too early to discuss how her illness might impact birth control and pregnancy, but it definitely isn't. Women may be unable to take their regular medication while pregnant or trying to get pregnant. Emphasize the need for your daughter to work closely with her psychiatrist, gynecologist, and/or obstetrician during her child-bearing years.

OCD on the job

Few career options are off-limits to people with OCD. In fact, the only door that is specifically barred is the US military. Current regulations prohibit anyone who has ever taken a psychiatric drug from enlisting. This includes all of the medications used to treat OCD. For a teenager or adult who has never taken medication, the diagnosis itself may not preclude enlistment if he can pass the preliminary mental health screening.

There is ample reason to believe that people who took psychiatric medications as children or teens have entered the military, with varying degrees of success. Whether they did not divulge their medication use when enlisting, or whether the officers in charge simply chose to ignore this one "blemish" in an otherwise promising candidate, is an open question. With Ritalin and Prozac now topping the list of childhood prescriptions, it does seem likely that the military will have to take a second look at this policy to keep its ranks filled. Should the draft be reinstated, the ban will almost certainly have to be lifted.

Other careers involving firearms could also be off-limits, including work as a police officer or armed security guard. That's because under some gun control laws, a person who has been found mentally ill by a court or who has a "history of mental illness" is legally prohibited from purchasing or being licensed to carry a gun. Most police departments also do mental health screening of applicants. A person whose OCD is well controlled by medication could probably pass one of these, however.

For most adults with OCD, the big work issue is whether to tell employers or coworkers about having OCD. Some feel that their employers might see them as unworthy of responsibility or promotion, or that there will be worries about how their mental health could affect company operations. Although it's illegal to discriminate on the basis of mental illness, most adults with OCD have personal experiences with job discrimination, or know someone else who has. Their reticence is natural.

If your child's symptoms are well controlled, there's probably no reason for him to tell, unless it is required by company policy. People who need to take a pre-employment drug screen, or whose jobs require regular screening for drugs, will need to inform the tester about prescription medications they take. In most circumstances this information is not shared with the employer.

If your child occasionally has breakthrough symptoms, she may want to consider confiding in one key person at work. Surprisingly, that person may not be her direct supervisor. The personnel department might be a better choice. She could ask that a letter be placed in her personnel file outlining her diagnosis and any accommodations she might need should her symptoms worsen.

If she does have a sympathetic boss, urge your child to approach the topic with caution. She might try making a joking reference to the illness ("I think I'm having one of my OCD moments," for instance) to break the ice. Some adults have simply left their medication in plain view one day—another conversation opener.

Adults with OCD who feel secure in their ability to manage on the job are often comfortable about addressing the issue forthrightly and openly. It would be wonderful if more people could do so.

You can get more information about the legal rights of disabled people on the job—including tips for approaching employers—from the Job

Assistance Network (which can be reached at (800) ADA-WORK) or the US Department of Justice Hotline (which can be reached at (800) 514-0301).

Public assistance

Although the majority of young people with OCD will be able to support themselves as adults, some will have severe symptoms that do not respond to current medications or to CBT. Others will have periods of severe symptoms, and will need temporary financial help.

This is exactly what public assistance programs were designed to do, and no one affected by severe OCD should feel embarrassed about asking for financial help if it's needed. SSI and similar programs are discussed in Chapter 7, *Insurance Issues*.

Housing

Some disabled people in the US are eligible for financial assistance with housing, and for housing preference programs through Housing and Urban Development (HUD) programs, such as the Section 8 grant program. Section 8 is especially flexible, because the monthly grant can be used to reduce the cost of housing found on the open market, not just in a housing project or other government-owned building. Some charitable organizations and churches also manage low-income housing projects or voucher programs, and may have preferential treatment for people with disabilities.

Subsidized housing ranges from adult foster homes with full-time staff on up to private apartments with no onsite support. The wait for housing can be long (three years or more for Section 8 vouchers), so it's important to apply before there's a pressing need. This may mean applying while a teenager is still in high school.

Some subsidized housing is substandard, especially in urban areas where the supply of low-cost units is tight. You'll need to pay special attention to security concerns, such as locking doors and windows, having a personal telephone in case of emergencies, and for a person who may be particularly vulnerable to crime, the safety of the surrounding neighborhood. Some older housing projects and residential hotels are also very dirty, and may not have fully functional plumbing, lighting, and heating. Landlords can be made responsible for bringing units up to code, but they may not respond until the tenant's family or a social services agency gets involved.

Group homes that stress independent living, including self-managed group homes or co-ops, are also options. Some of these programs may be covered by long-term care insurance, health insurance, funds placed in a trust, or monthly payments made by you or your adult child. Your local NAMI chapter may have information about special housing options for adults with mental illness, or you can check with a public or private social services agency. A number of innovative housing options are starting to spring up, including subsidized apartment buildings where each tenant has a maximum of personal autonomy despite having on-site medical management staff, therapy groups, Alcoholics Anonymous and Narcotics Anonymous meetings, and the like.

Young adults with severe symptoms, particularly those who have tendencies towards hoarding, may need services to maintain themselves in a regular apartment or home rather than a special housing arrangement. These are usually less expensive to boot, and may be available through government or private social services. Options include housekeeping assistance, self-care help, medication and case management, and special transportation arrangements to help the person handle shopping, medical appointments, and recreation needs.

There is a growing trend toward helping disabled adults purchase their own homes. Sometimes grants are available for down payment assistance, along with special loan programs, trust arrangements, and home buying and home ownership training.

In Canada, the UK, Ireland, Australia, and New Zealand, your local housing authority or council housing office can help you get on the waiting list, and inform you of any preference programs for the disabled and their carers that might move you up the queue faster. Charitable agencies and churches may also have low-income housing programs.

Legal and financial planning

If you or a grandparent plan to help your child financially, before or after death, you'll have to make special arrangements. Because of the laws surrounding public disability benefits—benefits your adult child could need if his symptoms require hospitalization or prevent him from working—inheriting money could end up being a terrible burden rather than a safety net.

Guardianship

When your child's eighteenth birthday occurs, you will no longer have the same legal control over him, unless you've made prior arrangements. If your 18-year-old is still unable to safely care for himself, or if he becomes so at any time in the future, you will need to go to court to obtain legal guardianship.

In most US states there are three types of guardianship: full, limited, and temporary. Full guardianship is just what it sounds like: full authority over all decisions in the person's life. Limited guardians have authority only in certain areas where the court recognizes the need for oversight. In your child's case, these areas might include medical care, housing, or entering into financial contracts. Temporary guardianship is limited to a short period of time (usually 30 days) and for a specific purpose. You might be appointed as your adult child's temporary guardian when he is hospitalized. Conversely, the court might appoint someone else as his temporary guardian.

There are other forms of legal status that you or another responsible person might want to hold for an adult child with a mental illness. These include power of attorney and medical power of attorney status.

Your will

Even if you and your child are both young, you should have a will to protect your estate. It doesn't matter if you don't have much to leave. Even furniture, an old car, or a modest home can have tremendous value to an adult whose earning power could be limited by illness.

You'll want to consult a lawyer who understands disability/inheritance issues. She can help you write a will that protects your child's interests and helps him retain eligibility for needs-based services.

Generally speaking, you don't want to leave money or property to your child with OCD. Instead, you can make a Special Needs Trust part of your will. These trusts can make funds or real property (such as a home) available to an adult with a disability. Formally established in the US by the Omnibus Budget Reconciliation Act, Special Needs Trusts are set up to keep the recipient eligible for government assistance, publicly funded health insurance, and subsidized housing if needed.

Money held in trust can be used to pay for items other than food, clothing, and shelter, such as education, phone bills, and recreation, without reducing benefits. If these funds are used for food, clothing, or shelter, a limited amount can be deducted from the SSI check.

Another financial instrument that benefits adults with special needs is the Pooled Trust, in which several parents and perhaps other entities (such as a social services organization or charity) combine their resources. A Pooled Trust might be used to fund a group home, for example.

You can set up your estate to fund a Special Needs trust at your death, or during your lifetime you can set up an Irrevocable Special Needs Trust. It is also possible to purchase certain types of annuities, such as life insurance policies, and earmark the proceeds for a trust to be set up in the future.

You'll need to consult a financial planner and/or a lawyer with experience in working on disability issues to set up a trust. Special Needs Trusts require a trustee other than the recipient to be in charge. This trustee might be a sibling, another relative, a trusted friend, or a professional trust manager. For adults with mental illness, it's crucial that the trust administrator be someone who understands how the money should be used. You don't want it to be frittered away on whims, or worse yet, on substance abuse. Neither would you want the trust manager to use funds to keep your adult child in a hospital when she could safely be living in the community. The trust manager may need to be instructed to pay bills directly from the trust, and never to give funds directly to your adult child. Either the trust manager or a co-trustee should have full understanding of your adult child's needs, and how they might be met in the most inclusive, community-based way.

Letter of intent

A letter of intent is not a *legal* document, but it's an important one when it comes to how your child's affairs will be handled after you're gone. The letter of intent can serve as your voice to guide future caretakers, should you ever be out of the picture. It should be written as though intended for someone who knows nothing about your child or family, and stored with your will and other legal documents.

The letter of intent should include at least four sections:

- **General information.** This section should include such things as your child's full name, date of birth, Social Security number, address, blood type, religion, and citizenship status. It should also include a list of all known family members and any non-relatives (such as a family friend, clergy member, or caseworker) who can provide advice and help to a caretaker.
- **Medical history and care.** In this section, list all of your child's diagnoses, with a brief explanation of the symptoms of each that a caretaker might need to be aware of. List any hospitalizations and surgeries your child has had. Include complete contact information for all doctors involved in your child's care, as well as dentists and therapists, and provide insurance information.
- **Goals.** This is a section to work out with your child. It should state what his preferences are for his living situation, daily activities, diet, social activities and hobbies, religious observance, etc. Should your child be unable to communicate his needs for any reason, this section will help guide his care.
- **Legal information.** List all assets, including bank accounts, annuities, property, life insurance policies, stocks, trusts, and safe-deposit boxes, in this section. It should also include contact information for any financial advisor who handles your finances or assets held in trust for your child.

Overcoming OCD's challenges

In the presence of good medical and family support, life after high school is actually easier for most people who were diagnosed with OCD during childhood or adolescence. There is more room for choice and flexibility in adult pursuits, including college and work.

Shana, a 20-year-old community college student with OCD, agrees:

> *I find it easier being in college than it was for me in high school. I can leave if my anxiety starts to flare up, unlike high school, where I had to stay at all times. Now I cope fairly well with pressures at school.*

When you hear about adults with OCD who are confined to their homes by fear, impoverished due to an inability to work, or in emotional pain from uncontrolled symptoms, it may make you worry about your child's future. Know that by ensuring that your child received an early diagnosis and treatment, you have done your best to ensure a good outcome for his adult life. A good education and proper transition planning will build a strong foundation for coping with OCD, and with all the usual challenges and joys of adult life.

APPENDIX A

Resources

THIS APPENDIX LISTS ASSESSMENT TOOLS, support and advocacy organizations, books, online resources, and other items of interest to people who want to know more about OCD.

Diagnostic tools

Children's Yale-Brown Obsessive Compulsive Scale

See Appendix B, *Children's Yale-Brown Obsessive Compulsive Scale*.

Florida Obsessive-Compulsive Inventory (FOCI)

http://www.ocfoundation.org/ocf1070a.htm

This interactive online version rates OCD severity based on a list of common symptoms.

University of Hamburg Obsession-Compulsion Inventory Screening Form

http://www.geocities.com/~john_papproth/examples/ocd.html

Online interactive version of a commonly used screening questionnaire for OCD.

Yale-Brown Obsessive Compulsive Scale

http://www.gethelp-online.com/ybocs[expln.html

The YBOCS questionnaire for adults allows quick rating of OCD severity. This online version is interactive.

Treatment

The following items are print and online sources of information on OCD treatment. See also the sections "Books about OCD," "Online OCD resources," "General medical information," and "Information about medications," later in this appendix, or contact one of the groups listed in the section "Advocacy and support organizations."

Books

Beck, Aaron T., Gary Emery (Contributor), and Ruth L. Greenberg. *Anxiety Disorders and Phobias: A Cognitive Perspective.* Reprint edition. New York, NY: Basic Books, 1990.

Beck, Aaron T. and S. Judith. *Cognitive Therapy: Basics and Beyond.* New York, NY: Guilford Press, 1995.

Clark, David M. and Christopher G. Fairburn, editors. *Science and Practice of Cognitive Behaviour Therapy.* Oxford: Oxford University Press, 1996.

March, John, MD and Karen Mulle. *How I Ran OCD Off My Land: A Guide to Cognitive-Behavioral Psychotherapy for Children and Adolescents with Obsessive-Compulsive Disorder.* OC Foundation, 1994. (see "Advocacy and support organizations" later in this appendix) Therapy protocol for use with children. Designed for professionals, but has also been successfully used by families who do not have access to a trained CBT therapist.

March, John, MD and Karen Mulle. *OCD in Children and Adolescents: A Cognitive-Behavioral Treatment Manual.* New York, NY: Guilford Press, 1998.

Reinecke, Mark A., Frank M. Dattilio, and Arthur Freeman, editors. *Cognitive Therapy With Children and Adolescents: A Casebook for Clinical Practice.* New York, NY: Guilford Press, 1996.

Wells, Adrian. *Cognitive Therapy of Anxiety Disorders: A Practice Manual and Conceptual Guide.* West Sussex, UK: John Wiley & Son Ltd., 1997.

Other resources

G.O.A.L. (Giving Obsessive-Compulsives Another Lifestyle) video and manual available through the OC Foundation (see "Advocacy and support organizations" later in this appendix).

"Practice Parameters for the Assessment and Treatment of Children and Adolescents with Obsessive-Compulsive Disorder." *Journal of the American Academy of Child and Adolescent Psychiatry,* 37, no. 10 suppl. (1998): 27S-45S. This supplement lays out currently accepted treatments for OCD in children and teens. Meant for doctors, but of interest to parents as well.

CBT for OCD

http://www2.mc.duke.edu/depts/psychiatry/pcaad/abstracts/cbtocd.htm

Excellent online introduction to the use of cognitive behavioral therapy techniques used to treat OCD.

Advocacy and support organizations

Federation of Families for Children's Mental Health

1021 Prince Street
Alexandria, VA 22314-2971
(703) 684-7710
Fax (703) 836-1040
http://www.ffcmh.org/

A group for families, especially low-income families, who are caring for a child with a mental illness.

National Alliance for the Mentally Ill (NAMI)
200 N. Glebe Road, Suite 1015
Arlington, VA 22203-3754
(703) 524-7600
Fax (703) 524-9094
TDD (703) 516-7227
(800) 950-NAMI (Helpline)
http://www.nami.org

NAMI is the largest organization for mentally ill people and their families in the US. It has state and local chapters around the country, sponsors legislation, advocates for mentally ill people, and provides excellent information via its web site and publications.

Obsessive-Compulsive and Spectrum Disorders Association (OCSDA)
18653 Ventura Boulevard, Suite 414
Tarzana, CA 91356
(818) 990-4830
Fax (818) 760-3784
Jill@ocsda.org
http://www.ocdhelp.org/

Obsessive-Compulsive Foundation Inc. (OC Foundation)
337 Knotch Hill Road
North Branford, CT 06471
(203) 315-2190
info@ocfoundation.org
http://www.ocfoundation.org/

Obsessive Compulsive Information Center
Madison Institute of Medicine
7617 Mineral Point Road, Suite 300
Madison, WI 53717
(608) 827-2470
Fax (608) 827-2479
http://www.miminc.org/

Canada

Canadian Mental Health Association
2160 Yonge Street, 3rd Floor
Toronto, Ontario M4S 2Z3
(416) 484-7750
Fax (416) 484-4617
cmhanat@interlog.com
http://www.cmha.ca/

Integrated Network of Disability Information and Education
info@indie.ca
http://www.indie.ca/

Ontario Obsessive Compulsive Disorder Network
PO Box 151
Markham, Ontario L3P 3J7
(905) 472-0494
Fax (905) 472-4473
oocdn@interhop.net

UK

First Steps to Freedom
7 Avon Court, School Lane
Kenilworth, Warwickshire CV8 2GX
01926 851 608 (helpline, open 10 am to 10 pm)
Fax 0870 164 0567
http://www.firststeps.demon.co.uk/

National Alliance of the Relatives of the Mentally Ill (NARMI)
Tydehams Oaks
Tydehams, Newbury
Berkshire RG14 6JT
(01635) 551923

Northern Ireland Association for Mental Health
80 University St.
Belfast BT7 1HE
(01232) 328474

SANE
2nd Floor
Worthington House
199-205 Old Marylebone Rd.
London NW1 5QP
(0171) 724 6520 (office)
National Helpline 0345 678000 (daily from 2 pm until midnight)

Young Minds
102-108 Clerkenwell Road, 2nd Floor
London EC1M 5SA
(0171) 336 8445 (office)
(0345) 626376 (Parents Information Service hotline)

Ireland

Mental Health Association of Ireland
Mensana House, 6 Adelaide Street
Dun Laoghaire, Co. Dublin, Ireland
(01) 284-1166 Fax (01) 284-1736
http://www.mensana.org/

Recovery Inc.
PO Box 2210
Dublin 8, Ireland
(01) 453-5633
http://www.mensana.org/Alliance/RecoveryInc.htm

Australia

Association of Relatives and Friends of the Mentally Ill (ARAFMI)
http://www.span.com.au/mhrc/arafmi.html

ARAFMI has chapters in most Australian states.

Obsessive Compulsive Disorders Support Group, Inc.
1 Richmond Road
Keswick, SA 5035
(08) 8221-5166
Fax (08) 8221-5159
http://www.span.com.au/mhrc/obsessive.html

SANE Australia
PO Box 226
South Melbourne, Vic. 3065
(61) 3 9682 5933
Fax (61) 3 9682 5944
sane@sane.org
http://www.vicnet.net.au/~sane/

New Zealand

Richmond Fellowship
249 Madras Street, Level 3
Christchurch, N.Z.
(64) 3 365-3211
Fax (64) 3 365-3905
national@richmond.org.nz
http://www.richmondnz.org/

Books about OCD

Baer, Lee, PhD. *Getting Control: Overcoming Your Obsessions and Compulsions*. Boston, MA: Little, Brown and Co., 1991. Dr. Baer provides another behavior-therapy-based model for tackling OCD, as well as solid information on diagnosis. Written as an adult self-help book, but may help some teenagers and parents as well.

Foster, Connie. *Polly's Magic Games: A Child's View of Obsessive-Compulsive Disorder.* Ellsworth, ME: Dilligaf Publishing, 1994. A book about OCD for younger children, in the form of stories they can understand and share.

Hyman, Bruce and Cherry Pendrick. *The OCD Workbook: Your Guide to Breaking Free from Obsessive-Compulsive Disorder.* Oakland, CA: New Harbinger Publications,

1999. A well-written CBT self-help manual for adults, could be used by older teens and adapted for use with younger children.

Jenike M. A., Dr. Michael L. Baer, and W. E. Minichiello, eds. *Obsessive-Compulsive Disorders: Practical Management.* Chicago, IL: Mosby Books, 1998. This is the definitive guide to OCD treatment for doctors, and may also be useful for families. The chapters by Dr. John March, Dan Geller, and Barbara Coffey cover childhood OCD issues specifically.

Osborn, Ian. *Tormenting Thoughts and Secret Rituals: The Hidden Epidemic of Obsessive Compulsive Disorder.* New York, NY: Pantheon Books, 1998. Who would have thought a book about OCD could be entertaining as well as informative? Osborn offers up medical fact, hundreds of years of history, and personal observations.

Rapoport, Judith L., MD. *The Boy Who Couldn't Stop Washing: The Experience and Treatment of Obsessive-Compulsive Disorder.* New York, NY: Signet, 1991. A classic introduction to OCD. Includes some case studies involving children and teenagers, and a particularly good section on spiritual help for people with scrupulosity from both Catholic and Jewish perspectives.

Rapoport, Judith L., MD, editor. *Obsessive Compulsive Disorders in Children and Adolescents.* Washington, DC: American Psychiatric Press Inc., 1989. Although it is somewhat out of date, this book brings together quite a bit of data from medical research on childhood-onset OCD. Geared toward professionals rather than parents or patients.

Schwartz, Jeffrey M., MD and Beverly Beyette. *Brain Lock: Free Yourself from Obsessive-Compulsive Behavior.* New York, NY: Regan Books, 1996. Dr. Schwartz's book offers a four-step model for dealing with OCD symptoms. Written as an adult self-help book, but may help some teenagers and parents as well.

Spencer, Terry. *Kissing Doorknobs.* New York, NY: Delacorte Press, 1998. A teen novel about OCD—solid information and a really good story, too.

Summers, Marc, and Eric Hollander. *Everything in its Place: My Trials and Triumphs With Obsessive-Compulsive Disorder.* Los Angeles, CA: Jeremy P. Tarcher, 1999. Nickelodeon TV host Summers is a familiar face to most kids, and his story is inspirational.

Online OCD resources

See also other sections in this appendix for online resources related to specific issues that impact children with OCD, and for sites belonging to OCD support and advocacy groups.

OCD-L

OCD-L-request@VM.MARIST.EDU

To subscribe, send email to *listserv@VM.MARIST.EDU* with the message body "subscribe ocd-l."

OCD-L is probably the largest OCD-related discussion group on the Internet. Members include adults and some teens with OCD, as well as family members and excellent medical professionals. Moderated by Chris Vertullo.

see p.13 for another website

OCD Online
http://www.ocdonline.com

Managed by Dr. Steven Phillipson of the Center for Cognitive Behavioral Psychotherapy in New York. Includes a good overview of CBT, articles, and links.

ocdteen list
http://www.angelfire.com/il/TeenOCD/

This online discussion group is sponsored by the Obsessive Compulsive and Spectrum Disorders Association (OCSDA). It is open to teenagers and young adults with OCD (pre-teens ages 10 to 13 are welcome with parental supervision), monitored by adults, and includes Dr. Jim Hatton and others who offer expert advice. Contact moderator Kelly at *kelly@ocsda.org* for more information.

To subscribe, see the web site or send email to *ocdteen-subscribe@egroups.com*

OCSDA chat room (live chat)
http://www.ocdhelp.org/chat.html

Treatment and research centers

This is by no means a complete list of treatment and research centers that work with children and teens who have OCD—just a short compilation of some of the best-known facilities in North America. Unfortunately for Southerners and Midwesterners, most are clustered on either the east or west coast. (Incidentally, the OCSDA maintains a very complete list of providers in California at *http://www.ocdhelp.org/doctors.html*.)

If you don't see a convenient center listed, call a national OCD organization for a local referral, or check the medical listings in your local phone book for clinics that specialize in anxiety disorders and/or cognitive behavioral therapy.

The OC Foundation maintains a regularly updated list of OCD-related studies that are seeking research subjects. This is an avenue that can sometimes provide diagnostic and/or treatment help at no cost to you. See the web site at *http://www.ocfoundation.org/ocf1510a.htm* for more information.

An international listing service for current clinical trials is available at *http://www.centerwatch.com/*. If you don't have Web access, contact:

CenterWatch Inc.
581 Boylston Street, Suite 200
Boston, MA 02116
Fax (617) 247-2535
Phone (617) 247-2327

If more than one person in your family has OCD, you might be eligible for genetic screening and related medical services through the two colleges working on this project: the University of Chicago and University of Michigan. For more information see its web site at *http://www-psy.bsd.uchicago.edu/~student/ocd.html*.

If you need help getting to a treatment center or need a place to stay while in treatment, one of the following organizations may be able to help:

AirCare Alliance
(800) 296-1217 (referrals for TWA Operations Liftoff and AirLifeLine)

AirLifeLine
(916) 429-2166 or (800) 446-1231

Continental Care Force
(713) 261-6626

Corporate Angel
(914) 328-1313 (arranges flights on corporate jets for patients)

Miles for Kids in Need
(817) 963-8118

National Association of Hospitality Houses
(800) 524-9730

Wings of Freedom
(504) 857-0727 (negotiates with commercial airlines for low-cost tickets)

US facilities

California

Alphabet Soup Center
Call the OCSDA at (818) 990-4830 for more information.

Anxiety and Mood Disorder Clinic
California Pacific Medical Center
2340 Clay Sreet, Suite 716
San Francisco, CA 94120
(415) 923-3297

Anxiety and Panic Disorder Clinic of Santa Barbara
115 W. Arrellaga Street
Santa Barbara, CA 93101
(805) 962-2869
Fax (805) 962-2406

Center For Anxiety & Stress
University Town Center
4350 Executive Drive, Suite 204
San Diego, CA 92121
(619) 458-1066
(619) 543-0510

Center For Anxiety Management
1100 Glendon Avenue, Suite 1601
Los Angeles, CA 90024
(310) 208-4077

Center For Cognitive Therapy
9565 Wilshire Boulevard, Suite 520
Beverly Hills, CA 90210
(213) 651-1199
Pager (800) 233-7231 ext. 98779

Center For Cognitive Therapy
1101 Dove Street, Suite 240
Newport Beach, CA 92660
(714) 646-3390
Fax (714) 955-2044

Center For Cognitive Therapy
5435 College Avenue, Suite 108
Oakland, CA 94618-1502
(510) 652-4455 ext. 12

OCD Research Unit Clinic
Department Of Psychiatry
Stanford University School Of Medicine
401 Quarry Road
Stanford, CA 94305
(415) 723-5154

The San Diego Regional Program For Obsessive-Compulsive Disorders And Trichotillomania
4510 Executive Drive, Suite 203
San Diego, CA 92121
(619) 457-8428
Fax (619) 536-1802

Jeffrey M. Schwartz, MD
12304 Santa Monica Boulevard, Suite 210
Los Angeles, CA 90025
(310) 392-4044

UCLA Obsessive Compulsive Program
Child and Adolescent OCD Program
760 Westwood Plaza
Los Angeles, CA 90024
(310) 794-7305
http://www.npi.ucla.edu/anxiety/OCD/default.htm

Contact Karron Maidment, RN, to get involved with UCLA's program.

UCSD School of Medicine
Department of Psychiatry
La Jolla, CA 92093-0804
(619) 543-6270
Contact Dr. Neal R. Swerdlow

Connecticut

Yale Child Study Center
230 S. Frontage Road
New Haven, CT 06520-7900
(203) 785-2513
http://info.med.yale.edu/chldstdy/

Florida

OCD Resource Center of South FLorida
3475 Sheridan Street, Suite 310
Hollywood, FL 33021
(954) 962-6662
FAX (954) 962-6164
http://www.ocdhelp.com/

Directed by Bruce Hyman, PhD, LCSW, co-author of *The OCD Workbook.*

Maryland

Johns Hopkins Anxiety Disorders Clinic
Johns Hopkins Hospital
600 N. Wolfe Street, Meyer 1–115
Baltimore, MD 21287
(410) 955-6111
http://www.med.jhu.edu/anxietyclinic/index.html

National Institutes of Mental Health (NIMH)
Biological Psychiatry Branch
Building 10, Room 3N212
9000 Rockville Pike
Bethesda, MD 20892
(301) 496-6827
Fax (301) 402-0052

NIMH Patient Recruitment and Referral Service
(800) 411-1222
prcc@cc.nih.gov

Massachusetts

OCD Clinic and Research Unit
Massachusetts General Hospital East
Department of Psychiatry
Building 149, 13th Street
Charlestown, MA 02129
(617) 724-6146

MGH also has clinics focused on trichotillomania, Tourette's syndrome, and other OCD-related conditions.

OCD Institute
McLean Hospital
115 Mill Street
Belmont, MA 02178
(617) 855-3279

The OCD Institute is one of only two world-class residential programs in the US that specializes in stabilization and treatment for difficult OCD cases. Directed by Dr. Michael Jenike, it has seventeen beds for residential care, as well as fifteen slots for intensive outpatient care. Contact Diane Baney, RN, at the Institute for information about the program and admissions.

Michigan

Obsessive-Compulsive Disorder Clinical Research Program
Department of Psychiatry and Behavioral Neurosciences
Wayne State University School of Medicine
Detroit, MI 48207
(313) 577-7853
(888) DMC-PSYC (toll-free triage line)
http://neuron.med.wayne.edu/OCD/

Missouri

Anxiety Disorders Center
St. Louis Behavioral Medicine Institute
1121 Maclind Avenue
St. Louis, MO 63104
(314) 534-0200

New Hampshire

Hampstead Hospital
218 East Road
Hampstead, NH 03841
(603) 329-5311 ext. 3226

Offers residential and day treatment programs.

New York

Anxiety Disorders Clinic
New York State Psychiatric Institute
Columbia-Presbyterian Medical Center
1051 Riverside Drive
New York, NY 10032
(212) 543-5367
http://www.nyspi.cpmc.columbia.edu/nyspi/pidpt_t.htm#Anxiety

The NYSPI Anxiety Disorders Clinic has programs for Spanish-speaking patients in addition to the usual offerings in English.

Compulsive, Impulsive and Anxiety Disorders Program
Mount Sinai Medical Center
Box 1230
1 Gustave Levy Place
New York, NY 10029
(212) 241-8185

North Carolina

Duke University Program in Child and Adolescent Anxiety Disorder (PCAAD)
Civitan Bldg., Room 269
Durham, NC 27708
(919) 684-4950
http://www2.mc.duke.edu/depts/psychiatry/pcaad/welcome.htm

Dr. John March, author of *How I Ran OCD Off My Land*, heads Duke's OCD program.

Pennsylvania

Center for the Treatment and Study of Anxiety
MCP Hahnemann University
Conference Center
3200 Henry Avenue
Philadelphia, PA 19129
(215) 842-4010
Fax (215) 843-7054
http://www.auhs.edu/medschool/ctsa/ctsahome.html

CTSA has special programs for people with trichotillomania, social phobia, and other anxiety disorders, as well as for OCD.

Western Psychiatric Institute and Clinic
University of Pittsburgh Medical Center
Department of Psychiatry, University of Pittsburgh
3811 O'Hara Street
Pittsburgh, PA 15213
(412) 624-2100

Options include a partial hospitalization program for OCD treatment.

Canadian facilities

Anxiety Disorders Clinic
Clarke Institute of Psychiatry
250 College Street
Toronto, Ontario M5T 1R8
(416) 979-6819
http://www.clarkeinst.on.ca/programs
http://www.clarke-inst.on.ca/services/anxietydisordersclinic.html

TTH Tourette Syndrome Clinic
The Toronto Hospital, Western Division
399 Bathurst Street
Toronto, Ontario M5T 2S8
(416) 603-5794
Fax (416) 603-5292
http://www.uhealthnet.on.ca/tsclinic/

Dr. Paul Sandor's program at TTH is highly recommended to patients with Tourette's syndrome in addition to OCD.

Information about related disorders

These resources cover OCD subtypes, specific OCD symptoms, and related disorders.

For general information on childhood psychiatric disorders and learning disabilities, see:

Hollowell, Dr. Edward. *When You Worry About the Child You Love: Emotional and Learning Problems in Children*. New York, NY: Simon & Schuster, 1996.

ADD/ADHD

Books

Hollowell, Dr. Edward. *Driven to Distraction: Recognizing and Coping With Attention Deficit Disorder from Childhood Through Adulthood.* Reading, MA: Addison-Wesley, 1994. The classic book on ADD/ADHD.

Hollowell, Edward, MD, and John Ratey. *Answers To Distraction.* New York, NY: Bantam Books, 1996. A companion to Dr. Hallowell's *Driven To Distraction*, this book provides behavior management and learning strategies to help the ADD/ADHD child.

Organizations

ADDnet UK
addnet@web-tv.co.uk
http://www.web-tv.co.uk/abusnet.html
44 (0) 181 269-1400 or 44 (0) 181 516-1413

Children and Adults with Attention Deficit Disorder, national office (CHADD)
8181 Professional Place, Suite 201
Landover, MD 20785
(301) 306-7070
Fax (301) 306-7090
http://www.chadd.org/

Anxiety disorders

Books

March, John. Editor. *Anxiety Disorders in Children and Adolescents.* New York, NY: Guilford Press, 1999.

Hallowell, Edward, MD. *Worry: Controlling It and Using It Wisely.* New York, NY: Ballantine Books, 1998.

Online resources

The Anxiety-Panic Internet Resource (tAPir)
http://www.algy.com/anxiety/index.shtml

The Anxiety Network/La Red de la Ansiedad
http://www.anxietynetwork.com/

Organizations

Anxiety Disorders Association of America
6000 Executive Boulevard, Suite 513
Rockville, MD 20852
(301) 231-9350

Autistic spectrum disorders

Waltz, Mitzi. *Pervasive Developmental Disorders: Finding a Diagnosis and Getting Help.* Sebastopol, CA: O'Reilly & Associates, 1999. *http://www.patientcenters.com/autism.*

Body dysmorphic disorder

Books

Phillips, Katherine, A. *The Broken Mirror: Understanding and Treating Body Dysmorphic Disorder.* Oxford: Oxford University Press, 1996.

Online resources

BDD (Body Dysmorphic Disorder) list
http://www.onelist.com/subscribe/BDD

Moderated by Emma Broughton (*emmab@netspace.net.au*); open only to people with BDD.

Eating disorders

Online resources

Eating Disorders Shared Awareness (EDSA)
http://www.eating-disorder.com/

This site includes links to US and Canadian support and informational sites on anorexia and bulimia.

Organizations

BODYWHYS
c/o PO Box 105
Blackrock, Dublin 7
Ireland
http://www.mensana.org/Alliance/BODYWHYS.htm

Eating Disorders Association
Wenson House, 1st Floor
103 Prince of Wales Road
Norwich NR1 1DW UK
(0160) 362-1414
eda@netcom.co.uk
http://www.gurney.org.uk/eda/

Hoarding/cluttering

Hoarding/Clutter list
http://www.onelist.com/subscribe/H-C

An Internet mailing list for people with OCD who are hoarders or clutterers, and want support from others with this symptom as they try to dig their way out. Medical advice provided by Jim Claiborn, PhD.

For more information, contact moderator Paula Kotakis at *disi@igc.org*, or subscribe through the web site.

Hypochondria

Cantor, Carla. *Phantom Illness: Recognizing, Understanding and Overcoming Hypochondria*. New York, NY: Houghton Mifflin Co., 1997.

Learning disabilities

LDOnLine: Learning Disabilities Information
http://www.LDOnline.com/

Scrupulosity

Books

Ciarrochi, Rev. Joseph W. *The Doubting Disease: Help for Scrupulosity and Religious Compulsions*. Mahwah, NJ: Paulist Press, 1995.

Online resources

Obsessions, Compulsions, and the Christian
http://www.epigee.org/ocd/ocdchristian.html

Organizations

Scrupulous Anonymous
c/o Rev. Thomas M. Santa
One Ligouri Drive
Liguori, MO 63057-9999
(314) 464-2500

Self-injurious behavior

Books

Favazza, Armando R. *Bodies Under Siege: Self Mutilation and Body Modification in Culture and Psychiatry.* Second edition. Baltimore, MD: Johns Hopkins University Press, 1996. Interesting look at SIB and cultural factors.

Levenkron, Steven. *Cutting: Understanding & Overcoming Self-Mutilation.* New York, NY: W. W. Norton and Co., 1998. Good for information about the practice and prevalence of self-injurious behavior, although its interpretation of the behavior and treatment recommendations are almost purely psychological, and therefore of little use to people with OCD and SIB.

Strong, Marilee. *A Bright Red Scream: Self-Mutilation and the Language of Pain.* New York, NY: Penguin USA, 1998.

Online Resources

Bodies-Under-Siege mailing list
http://www.palace.net/~llama/psych/busfaq.html

Bodies-Under-Siege is an online support group for people with self-injurious behavior. May not be appropriate for all teens with SIB, but some may find this therapeutic. To subscribe, send email to *majordomo@majordomo.pobox.com* with the message body: subscribe bus.

Secret Shame
http://www.palace.net/~llama/psych/injury.html

A web site about self-injury, offering information and support to people with SIB and their families.

Sensory integration dysfunction

Books

Kranowitz, Carol Stock. *The Out-Of-Sync Child: Recognizing and Coping with Sensory Integration Dysfunction.* New York, NY: Perigee, 1998.

Organizations

Sensory Integration International (SII)
1602 Cabrillo Ave.
Torrance, CA 90501
(310) 320-9986
Fax (310) 320-9934
http://home.earthlink.net/~sensoryint/

Referrals to SII-qualified occupational therapists, books, and other materials for sensory integration.

Sleep problems

Durand, V. M. *Sleep Better: A Guide to Improving Sleep for Children with Special Needs.* Baltimore, MD: Paul H. Brookes Publishing Co., 1998. Step-by-step instructions for improving sleep for children with special needs.

Substance abuse

Online resources

Adolescent Substance Abuse and Recovery Resources
http://www.winternet.com/~webpage/adolrecovery.html

Includes links to AA, NA, and many other groups that can help young people stop using drugs and alcohol.

Dual Diagnosis web site
http://www.monumental.com/arcturus/dd/ddhome.htm

ocd-plus-twelvesteps
http://www.onelist.com/subscribe.cgi/ocd-plus-twelvesteps

A mailing list for people with OCD who are over 21, and who are also using a 12-step program, such as NA or AA, to help with recovery from substance abuse. For more information, contact Sheryl at *sherylp@writeme.com*. To subscribe, see the web site or send email to *ocd-plus-twelvesteps-subscribe@onelist.com*.

Organizations

Canadian Centre on Substance Abuse
75 Albert Street, Suite 300
Ottawa, ON K1P 5E7
Canada
(613) 235-4048
Fax (613) 235-8101
http://www.ccsa.ca/default.htm

Drugline Ltd.
9A Brockley Cross
Brockley, London SE4 2AB
UK
(0181) 692-4975

Tourette's syndrome

Books

Haerle, Tracy, editor. *Children With Tourette Syndrome: A Parent's Guide*. Rockville, MD: Woodbine House, 1992.

Leckman, James F., and Donald J. Cohen. *Tourette's Syndrome: Tics, Obsessions, Compulsions: Developmental Psychopathology and Clinical Care*. New York, NY: John Wiley & Sons, 1999.

Online Resources

Sunrise Tourette
http://igc.topica.com/lists/sunrise-tourette

An online mailing list for parents of children with Tourette's syndrome/adults with Tourette's syndrome. There are many families on this very active list who are also affected by OCD and other neurological disorders. To subscribe, send a blank email message to: *sunrise-tourette-subscribe@igc.topica.com*.

Tourette Syndrome "Plus"
http://www.tourettesyndrome.net/

A very good site covering issues associated with having Tourette's syndrome with one or more comorbid disorders, such as OCD.

Organizations

Tourette Syndrome Association
42-40 Bell Boulevard
Bayside, NY 11361-2820
(718) 224-2999
tourette@ix.netcom.com
http://neuro-www2.mgh.harvard.edu/TSA/tsamain.nclk

Trichotillomania

Online resources

Amanda's Trichotillomania Guide
http://home.intekom.com/jly2/

Organizations

Trichotillomania Learning Center
1215 Mission Street, Suite 2
Santa Cruz, CA 95060
(408) 457-1004
trichster@aol.com

Special-needs parenting

Books

Duke, Marshall P., Stephen Nowicki, Jr., and Elisabeth A. Martin. *Teaching Your Child the Language of Social Success*. Atlanta, GA: Peachtree Publishers Ltd., 1996.

Greene, Ross. *The Explosive Child: A New Approach for Understanding and Parenting Easily Frustrated, "Chronically Inflexible" Children*. New York, NY: HarperCollins, 1998. The title says it all: this may be the best book on raising a child with a "difficult" temperament. Full of parent-tested strategies for defusing behavior problems.

Greenspan, Dr. Stanley I., with Jacqueline Salmon. *The Challenging Child*. Reading, MA: Addison-Wesley, 1995. Greenspan explains why some kids have a "challenging" temperament, and offers excellent ideas for turning down the volume of outbursts, anxiety, and other behavior problems.

Greenspan, Dr. Stanley I., and Serena Wieder, with Robin Simons. *The Child with Special Needs*. Reading, MA: Addison-Wesley, 1998. This book concentrates on working with developmentally or emotionally challenged children from infancy through school age. Highly recommended, especially if your child has an additional diagnosis of PDD/autism, ADHD, etc.

Greenspan, Dr. Stanley I., with Jacqueline Salmon. *Playground Politics: Understanding the Emotional Life of Your School-Age Child*. Reading, MA: Addison-Wesley, 1993. Help for parents with children who "don't fit in."

Kurcinka, Mary Sheedy. *Raising Your Spirited Child*. New York, NY: HarperPerennial, 1991. Covers handling sensory defensiveness and other contributors to "spirited" behavior.

Marsh, Diane T., Rex M. Dickens, and E. Fuller Torrey. *How To Cope With Mental Illness in Your Family: A Self-Care Guide for Siblings, Offspring, and Parents*. New York, NY: Putnam Publishing Group, 1998.

Meyer, Donald, editor. *Uncommon Fathers: Reflections on Raising a Child With a Disability*. Rockville, MD: Woodbine House, 1995.

Naseef, Robert A. *Special Children, Challenged Parents: The Struggles and Rewards of Raising a Child with a Disability*. New York, NY: Birch Lane Press, 1997.

Osman, Betty B. *No One to Play With: The Social Side of Learning Disabilities.* New York, NY: Random House, 1982.

Phelan, Thomas W. *1-2-3 Magic: Effective Discipline for Children 2-12.* Glen Ellyn, IL: Child Management Inc, 1996. Phelan has devised a workable system for managing behavior without getting physical, especially for strong-willed kids. Many parents swear by it. Also available on tape.

Wollis, Rebecca and Agnes Hatfield. *When Someone You Love Has a Mental Illness: A Handbook for Family, Friends, and Caregivers.* Los Angeles, CA: J.P. Tarcher, 1992.

Other resources

Budman, Cathy, MD, and Ruth Dowling Bruun, MD. "Tourette Syndrome and Repeated Anger Generated Episodes (RAGE)." (pamphlet) Bayside, NY: Tourette Syndrome Association, 1998.

Dowling Bruun, Ruth, MD, et al., "Problem Behaviors and Tourette's Syndrome." (pamphlet) Bayside, NY: Tourette Syndrome Association, 1993. Distributed by TSA (see "Tourette's syndrome" section earlier in this appendix).

OCD and relationships list

Moderated by Emma—send an email message to *emmab@netspace.net.au* to join. Open to people with OCD only.

"Bending the Rules: A Guide for Parents of Troubled Children" (1996)

Michael McDonald Productions
19582 Ventura Boulevard
Tarzana, CA 91356
(818) 881-3211
Fax (818) 881-7250

Made by the Southern California chapter of the Tourette's Syndrome Association, this is an excellent video on handling problem behaviors driven by brain dysfunction.

Education and transition planning

Books

Anderson, Winifred, Stephen Chitwood, and Dierdre Hayden. *Negotiating the Special Education Maze: A Guide for Parents and Teachers, Second Edition.* Rockville, MD: Woodbine House, 1997.

Coyne Cutler, Barbara. *You, Your Child, and "Special" Education: A Guide to Making the System Work.* Baltimore, MD: Paul H. Brookes Publishing Co., 1993. An uppity guide to fighting the system on your child's behalf.

Dornbush, Marilyn P. and Sheryl K. Pruitt. *Teaching the Tiger: A Handbook for Individuals Involved in the Education of Students With Attention Deficit Disorders, Tourette Syndrome, or Obsessive Compulsive Disorder.* Duarte, CA: Hope Press, 1995. This is a wonderful book, full of practical suggestions, organizing aids, and ideas for teachers, parents, and students about handling OCD symptoms in the classroom.

McLoughlin, Cavin S., editor, et al. *Getting Employed, Staying Employed: Job Development and Training for Persons with Severe Handicaps.* Baltimore, MD: Paul H. Brookes, 1994.

Online resources

Advocating for the Child

http://www.crosswinds.net/washington-dc/~advocate/

Maintained by the mother of neurologically challenged children, this site is an all-purpose guide to advocating for your child's educational rights in the US. Information-rich, with great links and lots of inspiration.

OCD and Homeschooling list

http://www.onelist.com/subscribe/ocdandhomeschooling

For more information, contact moderator Louis Harkins at *louisharkins_6@hotmail.com*. To subscribe, see the web site.

OCD and Parenting

http://www.onelist.com/subscribe/ocdandparenting

Excellent, very busy mailing list for parents of children with OCD. For more information, contact moderator Louis Harkins at *louisharkins_4@hotmail.com*. To subscribe, see the web site.

OCD-FAMILY list

A list for family and friends of people with OCD only (not for OCD sufferers themselves). To subscribe, send email to monitor Kelly at *mantia@iglou.com*.

OCD-SSI (Social Security Disability) list

http://www.onelist.com/subscribe/OCD-SSI

For more information, contact monitor Paula Kotakis at *disi@igc.org*. To subscribe, see the web site.

Private, moderated, confidential mailing list open only to members of the OCD-L list who are current or past recipients, or are thinking about applying for benefits. Could be a good resource for parents looking at SSI for a child or as part of a teenager's transition plan.

The Special Ed Advocate/Wrightslaw

http://www.wrightslaw.com

This is the place to find the actual text of special education laws, information on the latest court battles, and answers to your special education questions.

Special Education and Disabilities Resources

http://www.educ.drake.edu/rc/sp_ed_top.html

US information and links on special education law, assistive technology, and related topics.

Healthcare and insurance

Books

Beckett, Julie. *Health Care Financing: A Guide for Families*. To order, contact: the National Maternal and Child Health Resource Center, Law Building, University of Iowa, Iowa City, IA 52242, (319) 335-9073. This overview of the healthcare financing system includes advocacy strategies for families, and information about public health insurance in the US.

How to Get Quality Care for a Child with Special Health Needs: A Guide to Health Services and How to Pay for Them. To order, contact: The Disability Bookshop, PO Box 129, Vancouver, WA 98666-0129, (206) 694-2462 or (800) 637-2256.

Larson, Georgianna, and Judith Kahn. *Special Needs/Special Solutions: How to Get Quality Care for a Child with Special Health Needs*. St. Paul, MN: Life Line Press, 1991.

Neville, Kathy. *Strategic Insurance Negotiation: An Introduction to Basic Skills for Families and Community Mental Health Workers* (pamphlet). To order, contact: CAPP/NPRC Project, Federation for Children with Special Needs, 95 Berkeley Street, Suite 104, Boston, MA 02116. Single copies available at no cost.

Organizations

Association for the Care of Children's Health
ACCH Publications
19 Mantua Road
Mt. Royal, NJ 08061
(609) 224-1742
http://www.acch.org/

This group offers a variety of publications on child healthcare, including guides to prepare a child for the hospital and many items for parents of special-needs children.

Association of Maternal and Child Health Programs (AMCHP)
1350 Connecticut Avenue NW, Suite 803
Washington, DC 20036
(202) 775-0436

Call AMCHP to locate your state's Children with Special Health Care Needs Program (CSHCN).

National Association of Insurance Commissioners (NAIC)
444 National Capitol Street NW, Suite 309
Washington, DC 20001
(202) 624-7790

Call NAIC to locate your state insurance commissioner, who can tell you about health insurance regulations in your state regarding PDDs.

General medical information

Medscape

http://www.medscape.com

Searchable, online index to hundreds of medical journals. Many articles are available in full, others as abstracts only.

PubMed

http://www.ncbi.nlm.nih.gov/PubMed/

Free interface for searching the MEDLINE medical database, which can help you find out about studies, medications, and more.

Information about medications

There are a number of books available that list side effects, cautions, and more regarding medications. The biggest and best is the *Physicians Desk Reference* (PDR), but its price is well out of the average parent's league. You may be able to find a used but recent copy at a good price.

If your child is allergic to food dyes—or to corn, wheat, and other materials used as "fillers" in pills—you should consult directly with the manufacturer of any medications he takes.

Books

The British National Formulary (BNF). British Medical Association and the Royal Pharmaceutical Society of Great Britain, 1998. The standard reference for prescribing and dispensing drugs in the UK, updated twice yearly.

Preston, John D., John H. O'Neal and Mary C. Talaga. *Consumer's Guide to Psychiatric Drugs*. Oakland, CA: New Harbinger Publications, 1998.

Silverman, Harold M. editor, et al. *The Pill Book, Eighth Edition*. New York, NY: Bantam Books, 1998. A basic paperback guide to the most commonly used medications in the US.

Sullivan, Donald. *The American Pharmaceutical Association's Guide to Prescription Drugs*. New York, NY: Signet, 1998.

Wilens, Timothy E., MD. *Straight Talk About Psychiatric Medications for Kids*. New York, NY: Guilford Press, 1998.

Online resources

Canadian Drug Product Database

http://www.hc-sc.gc.ca/hpb-dgps/therapeut/htmleng/dpd.html

Dr. Bob's Psychopharmacology Tips

http://uhs.bsd.uchicago.edu/dr-bob/tips/

Excellent information on psychiatric drugs, including the MAOI dietary restrictions and common SSRI interactions.

Federal Drug Administration (FDA)
http://www.fda.gov/cder/drug.htm

Official US information on new drugs and generic versions of old drugs, FDA warnings and recalls, etc.

The Internet Drug List
http://www.rxlist.com/

MedEc Interactive/PDR.net
http://www.pdr.net/consumer

This medical information site includes a link to a Web-accessible version of the PDR.

Pharmaceutical Information Network
http://pharminfo.com/

PharmWeb
http://www.pharmweb.net/

The Royal Pharmaceutical Society's Technical Information Center
http://www.rpsgb.org.uk/300.htm

There is a nominal fee for use of the RPS database, but one might be able to have it waived.

RXmed
http://www.rxmed.com/

Medication assistance programs

The following corporate programs can help some patients get their medications at reduced or no cost (as explained in Chapter 7, *Insurance Issues*):

Pharmaceutical Company	Phone Number
3M Pharmaceuticals	(800) 328-0255
Allergan Prescription	(800) 347-4500
ALZA Pharmaceuticals	(415) 962-4243
Amgen	(800) 272-9376
AstraZeneca	(800) 456-3669
Berlex	(800) 423-7539
Boehringer Ingelheim	(203) 798-4131
Bristol-Myers Squibb	(800) 736-0003
Burroughs Wellcome	(800) 722-9294
Ciba-Geigy Patient Support Program	(800) 257-3273 or (908) 277-5849
Eli Lilly	(317) 276-2950
Genentech	(800) 879-4747
GlaxoWellcome	(888) 825-5249
Hoechst-Roussel	(800) 776-5463

Pharmaceutical Company	Phone Number
Hoffman-La Rouche	(800) 526-6367
ICI-Stuart	(302) 886-2231
Immunex Corp.	(800) 321-4669
Janssen	(800) 253-3682
Johnson & Johnson	(800) 447-3437
Knoll	(800) 526-0710
Lederle	(800) 526-7870
Lilly Cares Program	(800) 545-6962
Marion Merrell Dow	(800) 362-7466
Ortho-McNeil Pharmaceuticals	(800) 682-6532
Merck Human Health	(800) 672-6372
Miles	(800) 998-9180
Ortho-McNeil Pharmaceuticals	(800) 682-6532
Parke-Davis	(202) 540-2000
Pfizer Indigent Patient Program	(800) 646-4455
Pharmacia	(800) 795-9759
Procter & Gamble	(800) 448-4878
Rhône-Poulenc Rorer	(610) 454-8298
Roche Labs	(800) 285-4484
Roxane Labs	(800) 274-8651
Sandoz	(800) 937-6673
Sanofi Winthrop	(800) 446-6267
Schering Labs	(800) 521-7157
Searle	(800) 542-2526
Serono	(617) 982-9000
SmithKline Access To Care Program	(800) 546-0420 (patient requests) (215) 751-5722 (physician requests)
Solvay Patient Assistance Program	(800) 788-9277
Survanta Lifeline	(800) 922-3255
Syntex Labs	(800) 822-8255
Upjohn Co.	(800) 242-7014
Wyeth-Ayerst	(703) 706-5933

Mail-order pharmacies

CanadaRx

http://www.canadarx.net/

This is a consortium of Canadian pharmacies set up specifically to provide discounted prescriptions to US customers, although Canadians and others can use the service as well. Mail-order arrangements must be made over the Net, or directly through one of the consortium members (their addresses are available on the web site).

Continental Pharmacy
PO Box 94863
Cleveland, OH 44101-4863
Phone (216) 459-2010 or (800) 677-4323
Fax (216) 459-2004

DrugPlace.com
2201 W. Sample Road, Bldg. 9, Suite 1-A
Pompano Beach, FL 33073
Phone (954) 969-1230 or (800) 881-6325
Fax (800) 881-6990
cust-svc@drugplace.com
http://www.drugplace.com/

Farmacia Rex S.R.L.
Cordoba 2401
Esq. Azcuénaga 1120
Buenos Aires, Argentina
Phone (54-1) 961-0338
Fax (54-1) 962-0153
http://www.todoservicio.com.ar/farmacia.rex/rexmenu.htm

Greatly discounted prices, and they mail anywhere.

GlobalRx
4024 Carrington Lane
Efland, NC 27243
Phone (919) 304-4278 or (800) 526-6447
Fax (919) 304-4405
info@aidsdrugs.com
http://globalrx.com/

Masters Marketing Company, Ltd.
Masters House
5 Sandridge Close
Harrow, Middlesex HA1 1TW
UK
Phone (011) 44-181-424-9400
Fax (011) 44-81-427-1994
mmc@mastersinc.com
http://business.fortunecity.com/ingram/858/

Carries a limited selection of European pharmaceuticals, as well as a few American-made drugs, including Prozac.

Peoples Pharmacy
http://www.peoplesrx.com/

Based in Austin, Texas, this chain provides Net-only mail-order service, and can compound medications as well.

Pharmacy Direct
3 Coal Street
Silverwater, NSW 2128
Australia
Phone (02) 9648-8888 or (1300) 656-245
Fax (02) 9648-8999 or (1300) 656-329
pharmacy@pharmacydirect.com.au
http://www.pharmacydirect.com.au/home.htm

You must have a prescription from an Australian doctor to use this mail-order service.

The Pharmacy Shop (also known as Drugs By Mail)
5007 N. Central
Phoenix, AZ 85012
Phone (602) 274-9956 or (800) 775-6888
Fax (602) 241-0104
sales@drugsbymail.com
http://www.pharmacyshop.com/ or *http://www.drugsbymail.com/*

This online pharmacy waives your co-payment on prescriptions covered by insurance.

Stadtlanders Pharmacy
600 Penn Center Boulevard
Pittsburgh, PA 15235-5810
(800) 238-7828
enroll@stadtlander.com
http://stadtlander.com/

Stadtlanders Pharmacy has a stellar reputation in the disability community.

Usave Pharmacy (also known as No Frills Pharmacy)
1510 Harlan Dr.
Bellevue, NE 68005
Phone (800) 485-7423
Fax (402) 682-9899
refill@nofrillspharmacy.com
http://www.nofrillspharmacy.com/

Victoria Apotheke (Victoria Pharmacy)
Bahnhofstrasse 71
Postfach CH-8021
Zurich, Switzerland
Fax (01) 221-2322 (Europe) or (011) 411-221-2322 (US)
Phone (01) 211-2432 (Europe) or (011) 411-211-2432 (US)
victoriaapotheke@access.ch
http://www.access.ch/victoria_pharmacy

Public mental health agencies

United States

Alabama

Department of Mental Health and Mental Retardation
RSA Union
100 N. Union Street
PO Box 30140
Montgomery, AL 36130-1410
(334) 242-3417
Fax (334) 242-0684
http://www.asc.edu/archives/agencies/mental.html

Alaska

Alaska Division of Mental Health and Developmental Disabilities
50 Main Street, Room 214
PO Box 110620
Juneau, AK 99811-0620
(907) 465-3370
Fax (907) 465-2668
TDD/TTY (907) 465-2225
http://www.hss.state.ak.us/dmhdd/

Arizona

Arizona Department of Health Services
Behavioral Health Services
2122 E. Highland
Phoenix, AZ 85016
(602) 381-8999
Fax (602) 553-9140
http://www.hs.state.az.us/bhs/home.htm

Arkansas

Department of Human Services
PO Box 3781
7th & Main Streets
Little Rock, AR 72203
(501) 682-6708

Colorado

Mental Health Services
3824 W. Princeton Circle
Denver, CO 80236
(303) 866-7400
Fax (303) 866-7428
http://www.cdhs.state.co.us/ohr/mhs/index.html

District of Columbia

DC Commission on Mental Health Services
Child Youth Services Administration
2700 Martin Luther King Avenue SE
St. Elizabeth's Hospital, L Bldg.
Washington, DC 20032
(202) 373-7225

Florida

Children's Medical Services (CMS)
Department of Health and Rehabilitative Services
1311 Winewood Boulevard
Building 5, Room 215
Tallahassee, FL 32301
(904) 488-4257
http://www.doh.state.fl.us/

Georgia

Department of Human Resources
878 Peachtree Street NE, Room 706
Atlanta, GA 30309
(404) 894-6670

Hawaii

Department of Human Services
1000 Bishop Street, No. 615
Honolulu, HI 96813
(808) 548-4769

Idaho

Department of Health and Welfare
450 W. State Street
Boise, ID 83720-0036
(208) 334-5500
http://www.state.id.us/dhw/hwgd_www/home.html

Illinois

Department of Mental Health and Developmental Disabilities
402 Stratten Office Building
Springfield, IL 62706
(217) 782-7395

Indiana

Department of Mental Health
117 E. Washington Street
Indianapolis, IN 46204-3647

Iowa

Department of Human Services
Hoover Building, 5th Floor
Des Moines, IN 50310
(515) 278-2502

Kansas

Child & Adolescent Mental Health Programs
506 N. State Office Building
Topeka, KS 66612
(913) 296-1808

Kentucky

Department of Mental Health and Mental Retardation Services
275 E. Main Street, 1st Floor East
Frankfort, KY 40621
(502) 564-7610

Louisiana

Department of Health and Human Resources
PO Box 4049
655 N. 5th Street
Baton Rouge, LA 70821
(504) 342-2548

Maine

Department of Mental Health and Mental Retardation
411 State Officers Building
Station 40
Augusta, ME 04333
(207) 289-4223

Maryland

Department of Health and Mental Hygiene
201 W. Preston Street
O'Connor Building, 4th Floor
Baltimore, MD 21201
(410) 225-5600

Massachusetts

Department of Mental Health
24 Farnsworth Street
Boston, MA 02210
(617) 727-5600

Minnesota

Children's Mental Health
Minnesota Department of Human Services
444 Lafayette Road
St. Paul, MN 55155
(651) 297-5242

Minnesota Children with Special Health Needs
717 Delaware Street SE
PO Box 9441
Minneapolis, MN 55440-9441
(612) 676-5150 or (800) 728-5420
Fax (612) 676-5442
mcshn@kids.health.state.mn.us
http://www.health.state.mn.us/divs/fh/mcshn/mcshn.html

Mississippi

Department of Mental Health
1101 Robert E. Lee Building
239 N. Lamar Street
Jackson, MS 39201
(601) 359-1288
http://www.dmh.state.ms.us

Missouri

Department of Mental Health
1706 East Elm Street
PO Box 687
Jefferson City, MO 65102
(573) 751-3070 or (800) 364-9687
dmhmail@mail.state.mo.us
http://www.modmh.state.mo.us

Montana

Department of Public Health and Social Services
PO Box 4210
111 Sanders, Room 202
Helena, MT 59604
(406) 444-2995
http://www.dphhs.state.mt.us/

Nebraska

Nebraska Health and Human Services
Office of Community Mental Health
PO Box 95007
Lincoln, NE 68509
(402) 471-2330
http://www.hhs.state.ne.us/beh/behindex.htm

Nevada

Department of Human Resources
State Capitol Complex
505 E. King Street
Carson City, NV 98710
(702) 687-4440

New Hampshire

Division of Mental Health and Developmental Services
Department of Health and Welfare
State Office Park South
105 Pleasant Street
Concord, NH 03301
(603) 271-5013

New Jersey

Services for Children With Special Health Care Needs
New Jersey Department of Health and Senior Services
PO Box 364
Trenton, NJ 08625
(609) 984-0755
http://www.state.nj.us/health/fhs/schome.htm

New Mexico

Department of Health and the Environment
1190 St. Francis Drive
Santa Fe, NM 87503
(505) 827-2707

New York

New York State Office of Mental Health
44 Holland Street
Albany, NY 12229
(518) 473-3456
http://www.omh.state.ny.us/

North Carolina

Department of Human Resources
620 N. West Street
PO Box 26053
Raleigh, NC 27611
(919) 733-6566

North Dakota

Department of Human Services
State Capitol Building
Bismarck, ND 58505
(701) 224-2970
http://notes.state.nd.us/dhs/dhsweb.nsf

Ohio

Ohio Department of Mental Health
State Office Tower
30 E. Broad Street, 8th Floor
Columbus, OH 43266-0315
(614) 466-1483
http://www.mh.state.oh.us/

Oklahoma

Oklahoma Department of Mental Health and Substance Abuse Services
1200 NE 13th Street
PO Box 53277
Oklahoma City, OK 73152-3277
(405) 522-3908
http://www.odmhsas.org/

Oregon

Office of Mental Health Services
Department of Human Resources
2575 Bittern Streer NE
Salem, OR 97310
(503) 975-9700
http://omhs.mhd.hr.state.or.us/

Pennsylvania

Special Kids Network
Pennsylvania Department of Health
PO Box 90
Harrisburg, PA 17108
(800) 986-4550
http://www.health.state.pa.us/php/special.htm

Rhode Island

Department of Mental Health, Retardation, and Hospitals
Aime J. Forand Building
600 New London Avenue
Cranston, RI 02920
(401) 464-3234

South Carolina

Department of Mental Health
2414 Bull Street, Room 304
Columbia, SC 29201
(803) 734-7859

South Dakota

Developmental Disabilities and Mental Health
700 N. Illinois Street
Pierre, SD 57501
(605) 733-3438

Tennessee

Department of Mental Health and Mental Retardation
Andrew Johnson Tower, 11th Floor
710 James Robertson Pkwy.
Nashville, TN 37243-0675
(615) 532-6500

Texas

Department of Mental Health and Mental Retardation
Box 12668
Capitol Station
Austin, TX 78711
(512) 465-4657

Utah

State Division of Mental Health
Department of Human Services
120 N. 200 W., Room 415
Salt Lake City, UT 84145
(801) 538-4270
http://www.hsmh.state.ut.us/

Vermont

Department of Developmental and Mental Health Services
103 S. Main Street
Weeks Building
Waterbury, VT 05671-1601
(802) 241-2609
http://www.state.vt.us/dmh/

Virginia

Department of Mental Health, Mental Retardation, and Substance Abuse Services
PO Box 1797
Richmond, VA 23214
(804) 786-0992

Washington

Mental Health Division
Health and Rehabilitative Services Administration
PO Box 1788, OB-42C
Olympia, WA 98504
(800) 446-0259
http://www.wa.gov/dshs/hrsa/hrsa2hp.html

West Virginia

Department of Health and Human Resources
1800 Washington Street E.
Charleston, WV 25305
(304) 348-0627

Wisconsin

Bureau of Community Mental Health
Department of Health and Family Services
1 W. Wilson Street, Room 433
PO Box 7851
Madison, WI 53707
(608) 261-6746
Fax (608) 261-6748
http://www.dhfs.state.wi.us/mentalhealth/index.htm

Canada

British Columbia

British Columbia Ministry of Health
Parliament Buildings
Victoria, B.C. V8V 1X4
(250) 952-1742 or (800) 465-4911
http://www.hlth.gov.bc.ca/

Manitoba

Manitoba Health
Legislative Building
Winnipeg, Man. R3C 0V8
http://www.gov.mb.ca/health/

New Brunswick

New Brunswick Health and Community Services
PO Box 5100
Fredericton, N.B. E3B 5G8
(506) 453-2536
Fax (506) 444-4697
http://www.gov.nb.ca/hcs/

Newfoundland and Labrador

Newfoundland Department of Health and Community Services
Division of Family and Rehabilitative Services
Confederation Building, West Block
PO Box 8700
St. John's, N.F. A1B 4J6
(709) 729-5153
Fax (709) 729-0583
http://www.gov.nf.ca/health/

Nova Scotia

Nova Scotia Department of Health
PO Box 488
Halifax, N.S. B3J 2R8
(902) 424-5886 or (800) 565-3611
http://www.gov.ns.ca/health/

Prince Edward Island

Prince Edward Island Health and Social Services
Second Floor, Jones Building
11 Kent Street
PO Box 2000
Charlottetown, P.E.I. C1A 7N8
(902) 368-4900
Fax (902) 368-4969
http://www.gov.pe.ca/hss/index.asp

Québec

Québec Ministére de la Santé et Services Sociaux
1075 Chemin Sainte-Foy, R.-C.
Québec, Québec G1S 2M1
(418) 643-3380 or (800) 707-3380
Fax (418) 644-4574
http://www.msss.gouv.qc.ca/

Saskatchewan

Saskatchewan Health
T.C. Douglas Building
3475 Albert Street
Regina, Sas. S4S 6X6
(306) 787-3475
Fax (306) 787-3761
http://www.gov.sk.ca/health/

UK

People in England, Scotland, Wales, and Northern Ireland usually need to be referred to a specialist at a clinic or hospital by their general practitioner.

The National Health Service Confederation
http://www.nahat.net/gateway.htm

This site lists all local NHS authorities and boards, as well as specific sites for health-care (including mental health services).

Ireland

Eastern Health Board
Dr. Stephens Hospital
Dublin 8
(679) 0700

Midland Health Board
Arden Road
Tullamore, County Offaly
(0506) 21868

North Eastern Health Board
Kells, County Meath
(046) 40341
http://www.nehb.ie/

North Western Health Board
Manorhamilton, County Leitrim
(072) 55123
Fax (072) 20431
http://www.nwhb.ie/

Southern Health Board
Wilton Road
County Cork
(021) 545011
Fax (021) 545748
http://www.shb.ie/

Western Health Board
Merlin Park Regional Hospital
Galway
(091) 751131

Australia

Australian Capitol Territory

Commonwealth Department of Health and Family Services
Child Health and Development Service
Weingarth Street at Blackwood Terrace
Holder, A.C.T. 2611
(02) 6205-1277

New South Wales

Commonwealth Department of Health and Family Services
1 Oxford Street
Darlinghurst, N.S.W.
(02) 9263-3555 or (800) 048-998
http://www.health.nsw.gov.au/

Northern Territory

Northern Territory Health Services
PO Box 40596
Casuarina, N.T. 0811
(08) 8999-2400
Fax (08) 8999-2700
http://www.nt.gov.au/nths/

Queensland

Commonwealth Department of Health and Family Services
340 Adelaide
Brisbane, Qld.
(07) 3360-2555

South Australia

Commonwealth Department of Health and Family Services
55 Currie Street
Adelaide, S.A. 5000
(08) 8237-6111
Fax (08) 8237-8000

Tasmania

Commonwealth Department of Health and Community Services
Child and Family Services
4 Farley Street
Glenorchy, Tasmania
(03) 6233-2921

Victoria

Department of Health and Family Services
Disability Programs
Casselden Place
2 Lonsdale Street
G.P.O. Box 9848
Melbourne, Vic. 3001
(03) 9285-8888

Western Australia

Department of Health and Family Services
Central Park, 12th Floor
152 St. George Terrace
Perth, W.A. 6000
(08) 9346-5111 or (800) 198-008
Fax (08) 9346-5222
http://www.public.health.wa.gov.au/

New Zealand

New Zealand Ministry of Health
133 Molesworth Street
PO Box 5013
Wellington, N.Z.
(04) 496-2000
Fax (04) 496-2340
http://www.moh.govt.nz/

APPENDIX B

Children's Yale-Brown Obsessive Compulsive Scale

BETTER KNOWN AS THE CY-BOCS, the Children's Yale-Brown Obsessive Compulsive Scale is designed to measure the severity of obsessive-compulsive behaviors in children. In the US, it is the main tool used for assessing children's symptoms. Older teenagers may be better assessed by using the Yale-Brown Obsessive Compulsive Scale for adults.

The CY-BOCS is reprinted here in its entirety by permission of its copyright holder, Wayne K. Goodman, MD. It is to be used as a research tool for clinical purposes only, and to help parents better understand the OCD assessment process. Professionals who wish to use the CY-BOCS must order copies from Dr. Goodman. Copies cost $1.00 each, and should be ordered directly from:

Wayne K. Goodman, MD
c/o Tomasina Gray
University of Florida, College of Medicine
Department of Psychiatry
100 Newell Drive, Bldg. 59, Suite L4-100
Gainesville, FL 32611

Children's Yale-Brown Obsessive Compulsive Scale (CY-BOCS)

Developed by:

Wayne K. Goodman, MD
Department of Psychiatry, University of Florida College of Medicine
Steven A. Rasmussen, MD
Department of Psychiatry, Johns Hopkins University School of Medicine
Mark A. Riddle, MD
Department of Psychiatry, Brown University School of Medicine
Lawrence H. Price, MD
Department of Psychiatry, Yale University School of Medicine
Judith L. Rapoport, MD
Child Psychiatric Branch, National Institute of Mental Health

General instructions

Overview

This scale is designed to rate the severity of obsessive and compulsive symptoms in children, ages 6 to 17 years. In general, the ratings depend on the child's and parent's report; however, the final rating is based on the clinical judgment of the interviewer. Rate the characteristics of each item during the prior week up until and including the time of the interview. Scores should reflect the average (mean) occurrence of each item for the entire week, unless specified otherwise.

Informants

Ideally, information should be obtained by interviewing: 1) the parent(s) or guardian alone, 2) the child alone and 3) the child and parent(s) together (to clarify differences). The preferred order for the interviews may vary depending on the age and developmental level of the child or adolescent. Information from each of these interviews should then be combined to inform the scoring of each item. Consistent reporting can be ensured by having the same informant present for the rating session.

Definitions

Before proceeding with the questions, define "obsessions" and "compulsions" for the child and primary caretaker as follows:

- "Obsessions are thoughts, ideas, or pictures that keep coming into your mind even though you do not want them to. They may be unpleasant, silly, or embarrassing."

  "An example of an obsession is: the repeated thought that germs or dirt are harming you or other people, or that something unpleasant may happen to you or someone special to you. These are thoughts that keep coming back, over and over again."
- "Compulsions are things that you feel you have to do although you may know that they do not make sense. Sometimes, you may try to stop from doing them but this might not be possible. You might feel worried or angry or frustrated until you have finished what you have to do."

  "An example of a compulsion is: the need to wash your hands over and over again even though they are not really dirty, or the need to count up to a certain number while you do certain things."
- "Do you have any questions about what these words called compulsions and obsessions mean?"

Symptom specificity

The rater must determine that reported behaviors are true obsessions or compulsions and not other symptoms, such as phobias or anxious worries. The differential diagnosis between certain complex motor tics and certain compulsions (e.g. touching or tapping) may be difficult or impossible. In such cases it is particularly important to provide explicit descriptions of the target symptoms and to be consistent in including or excluding these symptoms in subsequent ratings. Separate assessment of tic severity with a tic rating instrument may be necessary in such cases.

Some of the items listed on the CY-BOCS Symptom Checklist, such as trichotillomania, are currently classified in the DSM-III as symptoms of an Impulse Control Disorder.

Items marked "*" in the Symptom Checklist may not be obsessions or compulsions.

Procedure

This scale is designed to be used by a clinician in a semi-structured interview format. After reviewing with the child and parent(s) the definitions of obsessions and compulsions, inquire about specific compulsions and complete the CY-BOCS Compulsions Checklist on page 355. Then complete the Target Symptom List for Compulsions on page 357. Next, inquire about and note questions 6 through 10 starting on page 357, repeat the above procedure for obsessions: review definitions, complete the Obsessions Checklist on this page, complete the Target Symptoms List for obsessions on page 353, and inquire about and rate questions 1 through 5 starting on the same page.

Finally, inquire about and rate questions 11 through 19 starting on page 360. Scoring can be recorded on the scoring sheet on page 363. All ratings should be in whole integers.

Scoring

All 19 items are rated, but only items 1–10 are used to determine the total score. The total CY-BOCS score is the sum of items 1–10, whereas the obsession and compulsion subtotals are the sums of items 1–5 and 6–10, respectively. Items 1B and 6B are not being used in the scoring.

Items 17 (global severity) and 18 (global improvement) are adapted from the Clinical Global Impression Scale (Guy, W., 1976) to provide measures of overall functional impairment associated with the presence of obsessive-compulsive symptoms.

CY-BOCS Obsessions Checklist

Check all that apply, but clearly mark the principal symptoms with a "P". (Items marked "*" may or may not be OCD phenomena.)

Name: ______________________ Date: __________

Current	**Past**	
Contamination Obsessions		
		Concern with dirt, germs, certain illnesses (e.g., AIDS)
		Concern or disgust with bodily waste or secretions (e.g., urine, feces, saliva)
		Excessive concern with environmental contaminants (e.g., asbestos, radiation, toxic waste)
		Excessive concern about household items (e.g., cleaners, solvents)

Current	Past	
Contamination Obsessions (continued)		
		Excessive concern about animals/insects
		Excessively bothered by sticky substances or residues
		Concerned will get ill because of contaminant
		Concerned will get others ill by spreading contaminant (aggressive)
		No concern with consequences of contamination other than how it might feel*
		Other (describe):
Aggressive Obsessions		
		Fear might harm self
		Fear might harm others
		Fear harm will come to self
		Fear harm will come to others because something child did or did not do
		Violent or horrific images
		Fear of blurting out obscenities or insults
		Fear of doing something else embarrassing*
		Fear will act on unwanted impulses (e.g., to stab a family member)
		Fear will steal things
		Fear will be responsible for something else terrible happening (e.g., fire, burglary, flood)
		Other (describe):
Sexual Obsessions		
		Are you having any sexual thoughts? If yes, are they routine or are they repetitive thoughts that you would rather not have or that you find disturbing? If yes, are they:
		Forbidden or perverse sexual thoughts, images, impulses
		Content involves homosexuality*
		Sexual behavior towards others (aggressive)*
		Other (describe):
Hoarding/Saving Obsessions		
		Fear of losing things
Magical Thought/Superstitious Obsessions		
		Lucky/unlucky numbers
		Other (describe):
Somatic Obsessions		
		Excessive concern with illness or disease*
		Excessive concern with body part or aspect of appearance (e.g., dysmorphophobia)*
Religious Obsessions		
		Excessive concern or fear of offending religious objects (God)
		Excessive concern with right/wrong, morality
		Other (describe):

Current	Past	
Miscellaneous Obsessions		
		Need to know or remember
		Fear of saying certain things
		Fear of not saying just the right thing
		Intrusive (non-violent) images
		Intrusive sounds, words, music, or numbers
		Other (describe):

Target symptom list for obsessions

Obsessions

(Describe, listing by order of severity.)

1. ______________________________
2. ______________________________
3. ______________________________
4. ______________________________

Avoidance

(Describe any avoidance behavior associated with obsessions; e.g., child AVOIDS putting clothes away to prevent thoughts.)

____

____

Questions on obsessions (items 1–5)

"I am now going to ask you questions about the thoughts you cannot stop thinking about."

1. Time occupied by obsessive thoughts

How much time do you spend thinking about these things?

(When obsessions occur as brief, intermittent intrusions, it may be impossible to assess time occupied by them in terms of total hours. In such cases, estimate time by determining how frequently they occur. Consider both the number of times the intrusions occur and how many hours of the day are affected.)

How frequently do these thoughts occur?

(Be sure to exclude ruminations and preoccupations which, unlike obsessions, are ego-syntonic and rational [but exaggerated].)

0—None	
1—Mild	Less than 1 hr/day or occasional intrusion
2—Moderate	1 to 3 hrs/day or frequent intrusion
3—Severe	Greater than 3 and up to 8 hrs/day or very frequent intrusion
4—Extreme	Greater than 8 hrs/day or near constant intrusion

1B. Obsession-free interval (not included in total score)

On the average, what is the longest amount of time each day that you are not bothered by the obsessive thoughts?

0—None	
1—Mild	Long symptom-free intervals or more than 8 consecutive hrs/day symptom-free
2—Moderate	Moderately long symptom-free intervals or more than 3 and up to 8 consecutive hrs/day symptom-free
3—Severe	Brief symptom-free intervals or from 1 to 3 consecutive hrs/day symptom-free
4—Extreme	Less than 1 consecutive hr/day symptom-free

2. Interference due to obsessive thoughts

How much do these thoughts get in the way of school or doing things with friends? Is there anything that you don't do because of them?

(If currently not in school, determine how much performance would be affected if patient were in school.)

0—None	
1—Mild	Slight interference with school or social activities, but overall performance not impaired
2—Moderate	Definite interference with social or school performance, but still manageable
3—Severe	Causes substantial impairment in school or social performance
4—Extreme	Incapacitating

3. Distress associated with obsessive thoughts

How much do these thoughts bother or upset you?

(Only rate anxiety/frustration that seems triggered by obsessions, not generalized anxiety or anxiety associated with other symptoms.)

0—None	
1—Mild	Infrequent, and not too disturbing
2—Moderate	Frequent, and disturbing, but still manageable
3—Severe	Very frequent, and very disturbing
4—Extreme	Near constant, and disabling distress/frustration

4. Resistance against obsessions

How hard do you try to stop the thoughts or ignore them?

(Only rate effort made to resist, not success or failure in actually controlling the obsessions. How much patient resists the obsessions may or may not correlate with their ability to control them. Note that this item does not directly measure the severity of the intrusive thoughts; rather it rates a manifestation of health, i.e., the effort the patient makes to counteract the obsessions. Thus, the more the patient tries to resist, the less impaired is this aspect of his/her functioning. If the obsessions are minimal, the patient may not feel the need to resist them. In such cases, a rating of "0" should be given.)

0—None	Makes an effort to always resist or symptoms so minimal doesn't need to actively resist
1—Mild	Tries to resist most of the time
2—Moderate	Makes some effort to resist
3—Severe	Yields to all obsessions without attempting to control them, but does so with some reluctance
4—Extreme	Completely and willingly yields to all obsessions

5. Degree of control over obsessive thoughts

When you try to fight the thoughts, can you beat them?

How much control do you have over the thoughts?

(In contrast to the preceding item on resistance, the ability of the patient to control his/her obsessions is more closely related to the severity of the intrusive thoughts.)

0—Complete Control	
1—Much Control	Usually able to stop or divert obsessions with some effort and concentration
2—Moderate	Sometimes able to stop or divert obsessions
3—Severe	Rarely successful in stopping obsessions, can only divert attention with difficulty
4—Extreme	Experienced as completely involuntary, rarely able to even momentarily divert thinking

CY-BOCS Compulsions Checklist

Check all that apply, but clearly mark the principal symptoms with a "P". (Items marked "*" may or may not be compulsions.)

Current	Past	
Washing/Cleaning Compulsions		
		Excessive or ritualized handwashing
		Excessive or ritualized showering, bathing, toothbrushing, grooming, or toilet routine
		Excessive cleaning of items (e.g., personal clothes or important items)
		Other measures to prevent or remove contact with contaminants
		Other (describe):
Checking Compulsions		
		Checking locks, toys, school books/items, etc.
		Checking associated with getting washed, dressed, or undressed
		Checking that did not/will not harm others
		Checking that did not/will not harm self
		Checking that nothing terrible did/will happen

Current	Past	
Checking Compulsions (*continued*)		
		Checking that did not make mistake
		Checking tied to somatic obsessions
		Other (describe):
Repeating Compulsions		
		Rereading, erasing, or rewriting
		Need to repeat routine activities (e.g., in/out door, up/down from chair)
		Other (Describe):
Counting Compulsions		
		Objects, certain numbers, words, etc.
		Describe:
Ordering/Arranging Compulsions		
		Need for symmetry or evening up (e.g., lining items up a certain way or arranging personal items in specific patterns)
		Describe:
Hoarding/Saving Compulsions		
		(Distinguish from hobbies and concern with objects of monetary or sentimental value.)
		Difficulty throwing things away, saving bits of paper, string, etc.
		Other (describe):
Excessive Magical Games/Superstitious Behaviors		
		Distinguish from age-appropriate magical games. (e.g., array of behavior, such as stepping over certain spots on a floor, touching an object/self a certain number of times as a routine game to avoid something bad from happening)
		Describe:
Rituals Involving Other Persons		
		The need to involve another person (usually a parent) in ritual (e.g., asking a parent to repeatedly answer the same questions, making parents perform certain meal time rituals involving specific utensils*)
		Describe:
Miscellaneous Compulsions		
		Mental rituals (other than counting)
		Need to tell, ask, confess
		Measures (not checking) to prevent harm to self
		Measures (not checking) to prevent harm to others
		Measures (not checking) to prevent terrible consequences
		Ritualized eating behaviors*
		Excessive list making*
		Need to touch, tap, rub
		Need to do things (e.g. touch or arrange) until it *feels* just right*
		Rituals involving blinking or staring
		Trichotillomania (hair pulling)*

Current	Past	
Miscellaneous Compulsions (*continued*)		
		Other self-damaging or self-mutilating behavior* Other (describe):

Target symptom list for compulsions

Compulsions

(Describe, listing by order of severity.)

1. ______________________________
2. ______________________________
3. ______________________________
4. ______________________________

Avoidance

(Describe any avoidance behavior associated with compulsions; e.g., child AVOIDS putting clothes away to prevent start of counting behavior.)

____

____

Questions on compulsions (items 6–10)

"I am now going to ask you questions about the habits you can't stop."

6. *Time spent performing compulsive behaviors*

How much time do you spend doing these things?

How much longer than most people does it take to complete your usual daily activities because of the habits?

(When compulsions occur as brief, intermittent behaviors, it may be impossible to assess time spent performing them in terms of total hours. In such cases, estimate time by determining how frequently they are performed. Consider both the number of times compulsions are performed and how many hours of the day are affected.)

How often do you do these habits?

(In most cases compulsions are observable behaviors [e.g., handwashing], but there are instances in which compulsions are not observable [e.g., silent checking].)

0—None	
1—Mild	Spends less than 1 hr/day performing compulsions or occasional performance of compulsive behaviors
2—Moderate	Spends from 1 to 3 hrs/day performing compulsions or frequent performance of compulsive behaviors
3—Severe	Spends more than 3 and up to 8 hrs/day performing compulsions or very frequent performance of compulsive behaviors
4—Extreme	Spends more than 8 hrs/day performing compulsions or near constant performance of compulsive behaviors

6B. Compulsion-free interval (not included in total score)

How long can you go without performing compulsive behavior?

(If necessary, ask "What is the longest block of time in which (your habits) compulsions are absent?")

0—No Symptoms	
1—Mild	Long symptom-free interval or more than 8 consecutive hrs/day symptom-free
2—Moderate	Moderately long symptom-free or more than 3 and up to 8 consecutive hrs/day symptom-free
3—Severe	Short symptom-free interval or from 1 to 3 consecutive hrs/day symptom-free
4—Extreme	Less than 1 consecutive hr/day symptom-free

7. Interference due to compulsive behaviors

How much do these habits get in the way of school or doing things with friends?

Is there anything you don't do because of them?

(If currently not in school, determine how much performance would be affected if patient were in school.)

0—None	
1—Mild	Slight interference with social or school activities, but overall performance not impaired
2—Moderate	Definite interference with social or school performance, but still manageable
3—Severe	Causes substantial impairment in social or school performance
4—Extreme	Incapacitating

8. Distress associated with compulsive behavior

How would you feel if prevented from carrying out your habits?

How upset would you become?

(Rate degree of distress/frustration patient would experience if performance of the compulsion were suddenly interrupted without reassurance offered. In most, but not all cases, performing compulsions reduces anxiety/frustration.)

How upset do you get while carrying out your habits until you are satisfied?

0—None	
1—Mild	Only slightly anxious/frustrated if compulsions prevented; only slight anxiety/frustration during performance of compulsions
2—Moderate	Reports that anxiety/frustration would mount but remain manageable if compulsions prevented; anxiety/frustration increases but remains manageable during performance of compulsions
3—Severe	Prominent and very disturbing increase in anxiety/frustration if compulsions interrupted; prominent and very disturbing increase in anxiety/frustration during performance of compulsions
4—Extreme	Incapacitating anxiety/frustration from any intervention aimed at modifying activity; incapacitating anxiety/frustration develops during performance of compulsions.

9. Resistance against compulsions

How much do you try to fight the habits?

(Only rate effort made to resist, not success or failure in actually controlling the compulsions. How much the patient resists the compulsions may or may not correlate with his/her ability to control them. Note that this item does not directly measure the severity of the compulsions, rather it rates a manifestation of health, i.e., the effort the patient makes to counteract the compulsions. Thus, the more the patient tries to resist, the less impaired is this aspect of his/her functioning. If the compulsions are minimal, the patient may not feel the need to resist them. In such cases, a rating of "0" should be given.)

0—None	Makes an effort to always resist or symptoms so minimal doesn't need to actively resist
1—Mild	Tries to resist most of the time
2—Moderate	Makes some effort to resist
3—Severe	Yields to almost all compulsions without attempting to control them, but does so with some reluctance
4—Extreme	Completely and willingly yields to all compulsions

10. Degree of control over compulsive behavior

How strong is the feeling that you have to carry out the habit(s)?

When you try to fight them what happens?

(For the advanced child ask):

How much control do you have over the habits?

(In contrast to the preceding item on resistance, the ability of the patient to control his/her compulsions is closely related to the severity of the compulsions.)

0—Complete Control	
1—Much Control	Experiences pressure to perform the behavior, but usually able to exercise voluntary control over it
2—Moderate Control	Strong pressure to perform behavior, can control it only with difficulty
3—Little Control	Very strong drive to perform behavior, must be carried to completion, can only delay with difficulty
4—No Control	Drive to perform behavior experienced as completely involuntary and overpowering, rarely able to even momentarily delay activity

11. Insight into compulsive behavior

Do you think your concerns or behaviors are reasonable? (Pause)

What do you think would happen if you did not perform the compulsion(s)?

Are you convinced something would really happen?

(Rate patient's insight into the senselessness or excessiveness of his/her obsession(s) or compulsion(s) based on beliefs expressed at the time of the interview.)

0—None	Excellent insight, fully rational
1—Mild	Good insight, readily acknowledges absurdity or excessiveness of thoughts or behaviors but does not seem completely convinced that there isn't something besides anxiety to be concerned about (i.e., has lingering doubts)
2—Moderate	Fair insight, reluctantly admits thoughts or behavior seem unreasonable or excessive, but wavers; may have some unrealistic fears, but no fixed convictions
3—Severe	Poor insight, maintains that thoughts or behaviors are not reasonable or excessive, but wavers; may have some unrealistic fears, but acknowledges validity of contrary evidence (i.e., overvalued ideas present)
4—Extreme	Lacks insight, delusional, definitely convinced that concerns and behaviors are reasonable, unresponsive to contrary evidence

12. Avoidance

Have you been avoiding doing anything, going any place, or being with anyone because of your obsessional thoughts or out of concern you will perform compulsions? (If yes, then ask):

How much do you avoid? (Note what is avoided on symptom list.)

(Rate degree to which patient deliberately tries to avoid things. Sometimes compulsions are designed to "avoid" contact with something that the patient fears. For example, excessive washing of fruits and vegetables to remove "germs" would be designated as a compulsion not as an avoidant behavior. If the patient stopped eating fruits and vegetables, this would then constitute avoidance.)

0—None	
1—Mild	Minimal avoidance
2—Moderate	Some avoidance clearly present
3—Severe	Much avoidance; avoidance prominent
4—Extreme	Very extensive avoidance, patient does almost everything he/she can to avoid triggering symptoms

13. Degree of indecisiveness

Do you have trouble making decisions about little things that other people might not think twice about (e.g., what clothes to put on in the morning, which brand of cereal to buy)?

(Exclude difficulty making decisions which reflect ruminative thinking. Ambivalence concerning rationally-based difficult choices should also be excluded.)

0—None	
1—Mild	Some trouble making decisions about minor things
2—Moderate	Freely reports significant trouble making decisions that others would not think twice about
3—Severe	Continual weighing of pros and cons about nonessentials
4—Extreme	Unable to make any decisions, disabling

14. Overvalued sense of responsibility

Do you feel responsible for what you do and what effect this has on things?

Do you blame yourself for the things that are not within your control?

(Distinguish from normal feelings of responsibility, feelings of worthlessness, and pathological guilt. A guilt-ridden person experiences him/herself or his/her actions as bad or evil.)

0—None	
1—Mild	Only mentioned on questioning, slight sense of over-responsibility
2—Moderate	Ideas stated spontaneously, clearly present, patient experiences significant sense of over-responsibility for events outside his/her reasonable control
3—Severe	Ideas prominent and pervasive, deeply concerned he/she is responsible for events clearly outside his/her control, self-blaming far-fetched and nearly irrational
4—Extreme	Delusional sense of responsibility (e.g., if an earthquake occurs 3,000 miles away patient blames themselves because they didn't perform their compulsions)

15. Pervasive slowness/disturbance of intertia

Do you have difficulty starting or finishing tasks?

Do many routine activities take longer than they should?

(Distinguish from psychomotor retardation secondary to depression. Rate increased time spent performing routine activities even when specific obsessions cannot be identified.)

0—None	
1—Mild	Occasional delay in starting or finishing tasks/activities
2—Moderate	Frequent prolongation of routine activities but tasks usually completed, frequently late
3—Severe	Pervasive and marked difficulty initiating and completing routine tasks, usually late
4—Extreme	Unable to start or complete routine tasks without full assistance

16. Pathological doubting

When you complete an activity do you doubt whether you performed it correctly?

Do you doubt whether you did it at all?

When carrying out routine activities do you find that you don't trust your senses (i.e., what you see, hear, or touch)?

0—None	
1—Mild	Only mentioned on questioning, slight pathological doubt, examples given may be within normal range
2—Moderate	Ideas stated spontaneously, clearly present and apparent in some of patient behaviors, patient bothered by significant pathological doubt; some effect on performance but still manageable

3—Severe	Uncertainty about perceptions or memory prominent, pathological doubt frequently affects performance
4—Extreme	Uncertainty about perceptions constantly present; pathological doubt substantially affects almost all activities, incapacitating (e.g., patient states "my mind doesn't trust what my eyes see")

17. Global severity

Interviewers judgment of the overall severity of the patient's illness.

Rated from 0 (no illness) to 6 (most severe patient seen).

(Consider the degrees of distress reported by the patient, the symptoms observed, the functional impairment reported. Your judgment is required both in averaging this data as well as weighing the reliability or accuracy of the data obtained. This judgment is based on information obtained during the interview.)

0—No illness	
1—Slight	Illness slight, doubtful, or transient; no functional impairment
2—Mild	Little functional impairment
3—Moderate	Functions with effort
4—Moderate–Severe	Limited functioning
5—Severe	Functions mainly with assistance
6—Extremely Severe	Completely nonfunctional

18. Global improvement

Rate total overall improvement present SINCE THE INITIAL RATING whether or not, in your judgment, it is due to drug treatment.

0	Very much worse
1	Much worse
2	Minimally worse
3	No change
4	Minimally improved
5	Much improved
6	Very much improved

19. Reliability

Rate the overall reliability of the rating scores obtained. Factors that may affect reliability include the patient's cooperativeness and his/her natural ability to communicate. The type and severity of obsessive-compulsive symptoms present may interfere with the patient's concentration, attention, or freedom to speak spontaneously (e.g., the content of some obsessions may cause the patient to choose his/her words very carefully).

0—Excellent	No reason to suspect data unreliable
1—Good	Factor(s) present that may adversely affect reliability
2—Fair	Factor(s) present that definitely reduce reliability
3—Poor	Very low reliability

Children's Yale-Brown Obsessive Compulsive Scale (3/1/90)

CY-BOCS total (add items 1–10): ____________________

Patient name: ____________________ Date: __________

Patient ID: ____________________ Rater: __________

	None	Mild	Moderate	Severe	Extreme		
1. Time spent on obsessions	0	1	2	3	4		
2. Interference from obsessions	0	1	2	3	4		
3. Distress of obsessions	0	1	2	3	4		
4. Resistance	0	1	2	3	4		
5. Control over obsessions	0	1	2	3	4		
6. Time spent on compulsions	0	1	2	3	4		
7. Interference from compulsions	0	1	2	3	4		
8. Distress from compulsions	0	1	2	3	4		
9. Resistance	0	1	2	3	4		
10. Control over compulsions	0	1	2	3	4		
11. Insight into o-c symptoms	0	1	2	3	4		
12. Avoidance	0	1	2	3	4		
13. Indecisiveness	0	1	2	3	4		
14. Pathologic responsibility	0	1	2	3	4		
15. Slowness	0	1	2	3	4		
16. Pathological doubting	0	1	2	3	4		
17. Global severity	0	1	2	3	4	5	6
18. Global improvement	0	1	2	3	4	5	6
19. Reliability	0	1	2	3			

Notes

Chapter 1: *Introduction to OCD*

1. Nigel Hymas, "The Neurology of Obsessive-Compulsive Disorder," *CNS Spectrums* (July 1998): *http://www.cme-reviews.com/CNS798_Hymas.html*.
2. Judith L. Rapoport, MD, et al., "Quantitative Brain Magnetic Resonance Imaging in Attention-Deficit Hyperactivity Disorder," *Archives of General Psychiatry* 53 (1996): 607–16.
3. E. H. Aylward, et al., "Basal Ganglia Volumes and White Matter Hyperintensities in Bipolar Disorder," *American Journal of Psychiatry* 151 (1994): 687–93.
4. Arline Kaplan, "Imaging Studies Provide Insights into Neurobiology of Bipolar Disorders," *Bipolar Disorders Letter* (Feb 1998): *http://www.mhsource.com/bipolar/bp9802image.html*.
5. J. T. Nigg, and H. H. Goldsmith, "Genetics of Personality Disorders: Perspectives From Personality and Psychopathology Research," *Psychology Bulletin* 115, no. 3 (May 1994): 346–80.
6. K. P. Lesch, et al., "Association of Anxiety-Related Traits with a Polymorphism in the Serotonin Transporter Gene Regulatory Region," *Science* 274 (1996): 1527–31.
7. Maria Karayiorgou, et al., "Genotype Determining Low Catechol-O-methyltransferase Activity as a Risk Factor for Obsessive-Compulsive Disorder," *Proceedings of the National Academy of Sciences* 94 (Apr 1997): 4572–5.
8. J. T. Walkup, et al., "Family Study and Segregation Analysis of Tourette Syndrome: Evidence for a Mixed Model of Inheritance," *American Journal of Human Genetics* 59 (1996): 684.
9. Ed Cook, et al., "Evidence of Linkage between the Serotonin Transporter and Autistic Disorder," *Molecular Psychiatry* 2, no. 3 (May 1997): 247–50.
10. D. A. Collier, et al., "A Novel Functional Polymorphism within the Promoter of the Serotonin Transporter Gene: Possible Role in Susceptibility to Affective Disorders," *Molecular Psychiatry 1*, no. 6 (Dec 1996): 453–60.
11. International Molecular Genetic Study of Autism Consortium, "A Full Genome Screen for Autism with Evidence for Linkage to a Region on Chromosome 7q," *Human Molecular Genetics* 7, no. 3 (Mar 1998): 571–8.
12. P. Bolton and P. Griffiths, "Association of Tuberous Sclerosis of Temporal Lobes with Autism and Atypical Autism," *Lancet* 349 (Dec 1997): 392–5.
13. Susan Swedo, MD, Henrietta Leonard, MD, et al., "Identification of Children with Pediatric Autoimmune Neuropsychiatric Disorders Associated with Streptococcal Infections by a Marker Associated with Rheumatic Fever," *American Journal of Psychiatry* 154, no.1 (1997): 110–2.

14. T. K. Murphy, W. K. Goodman, et al., "B-Lymphocyte Antigen D8/17: A Peripheral Marker for Childhood-Onset Obsessive-Compulsive Disorder and Tourette's Syndrome?" *American Journal of Psychiatry* 154, no. 3 (1997): 402–7.
15. A. J. Allan, MD, "Group A Streptococcal Infections and Childhood Neuropsychiatric Disorders—Relationships and Therapeutic Implications," *CNS Drugs* 8 (Oct 1997): 267–75.
16. Eric Hollander, et al., "Repetitive Behaviors and D8/17 Positivity," (letter) *American Journal of Psychiatry* 154 (1997): 1630.

Chapter 2: *Diagnosis*

1. Lawrence Scahill, et al., "Children's Yale-Brown Obsessive Compulsive Scale: Reliability and Validity," *Journal of the American Academy of Child and Adolescent Psychiatry* 36, no. 6 (1997): 844–52.
2. L. Bellodi, et al., "Psychiatric Disorders in the Families of Patients with Obsessive-Compulsive Disorder," *Psychiatry Research* 42 (1992): 11–20.
3. M. C. Lenane, et al., "Psychiatric Disorders in First Degree Relatives of Children and Adolescents with Obsessive-Compulsive Disorder," *Journal of the American Academy of Child and Adolescent Psychiatry* 29 (1990): 407–12.
4. D. L. Pauls, et al., "A Family Study of Obsessive-Compulsive Disorder," *American Journal of Psychiatry* 152, no. 1 (1995): 76–84.
5. Ligouri Publications, "Alphonsus Ligouri, Founder of the Redemptorists Community," *http://www.clonard.com/globalh.htm*.
6. Michael A. Jenike, MD, et al., *Obsessive-Compulsive Disorders: Practical Management, Third Edition* (Mineola, NY: Mosby-Year Book Inc., 1998).
7. Gavin Wilson, "Anorexia Kills Elderly Men, Records Suggest," *UBC Reports* (9 Jan 1997): *http://publicaffairs.ubc.ca/reports/97ja9/anorexia.html*.
8. Dara Gruen, "Anorexia Nervosa and Bulimia Nervosa: Forms of Obsessive-Compulsive Disorder?" *Perspectives In Psychology*, 1999: *http://dolphin.upenn.edu/~upsych/journal/gruen.html*.
9. Mae S. Sokol, MD and N. S. Gray, "Case Study: An Infection-Triggered, Autoimmune Subtype of Anorexia Nervosa," *Journal of the American Academy of Child and Adolescent Psychiatry 36* (1997): 1128–33.
10. Brian Fallon and Carla Cantor, *Phantom Illness: Shattering the Myths of Hypochondria* (New York, NY: Houghton Mifflin, 1996).
11. Steven Phillipson and Robert K. Stewart, Jr., "A Rose By Any Other Name," *Obsessive-Compulsive Newsletter* (June 1996): 2–3, *http://www.ocdonline.com/articlephillipson4.htm*.
12. Frederick I. Penzel, PhD, "Body Dysmorphic Disorder: Recognition and Treatment," *Medscape Mental Health* 2, no. 1 (1997): *http://www.medscape.com/Medscape/psychiatry/journal/1997/v02.n01/mh8.penzel/mh8.penzel.html*.
13. David H. Barlow, "Anxiety Disorders, Comorbid Substance Abuse, and Benzodiazepine Discontinuation: Implications for Treatment," National Institute on Drug Abuse: *http://165.112.78.61/pdf/monographs/monograph172/033-051_Barlow.pdf*.
14. Kate Carey, "Challenges in Assessing Substance Use Patterns in Persons with Comorbid Mental and Addictive Disorders," National Institute on Drug Abuse: *http://165.112.78.61/pdf/monographs/monograph172/016-032_Carey.pdf*.

15. V. B. Brown, et al., "The Dual Crisis: Mental Illness and Substance Abuse," *American Psychologist* 44 (1989): 565–9.
16. Barlow, ibid.
17. P. Bolton and P. Griffiths, "Association of Tuberous Sclerosis of Temporal Lobes with Autism and Atypical Autism," *Lancet* 349 (Dec 1997): 392–5.

Chapter 5: *Medical Interventions*

1. J. Jay Fruehling, "OCD Medication: Children—What Parents Should Know," Obsessive-Compulsive Foundation: *http://www.ocfoundation.org/ocf1060a.htm.*
2. Fruehling, Ibid.
3. Wayne K. Goodman, MD, keynote address at the 1997 Obsessive-Compulsive Foundation.
4. B. E. Lippitz, P. Mindus, B. A. Meyerson, et al., "Lesion Topography and Outcome After Thermocapsulotomy or Gamma Knife Capsulotomy for Obsessive-Compulsive Disorder: Relevance of the Right Hemisphere," *Neurosurgery* 44 (1999): 452–8.
5. Leslie Packer, PhD, "Rage Attacks," (1999): *http://www.tourettesyndrome.net/TouretteSyndrome_Plus/NoFrames/rage.htm.*
6. Vijendra K. Singh, MD, S. X. Lin, and V. C. Yang, "Serological Association of Measles Virus and Human Herpesvirus-6 with Brain Autoantibodies in Autism," *Clinical Immunology and Immunopathology* 89, no. 1 (Oct 1998): 105–8.

Chapter 6: *Other Interventions*

1. "Homeopathy: A Position Statement by the National Council Against Health Fraud," National Council Against Health Fraud (Loma Linda, CA, 1994): *http://www.skeptic.com/03.1.jarvis-homeo.html.*
2. M. Fux, J. Levine, A. Aviv, R. H. Belmaker, " Inositol Treatment of Obsessive Compulsive Disorder," *American Journal of Psychiatry* 153 (1996): 1219–21.
3. Lucinda G. Miller, "Herbal Medicinals: Selected Clinical Considerations Focusing on Known or Potential Drug-Herb Interactions," *Archives of Internal Medicine* (9 Nov 1998); and other sources.

Chapter 8: *School and Transition*

1. Laura Kann, et al., "National Youth Risk Behavior Surveillance," Division of Adolescent and School Health, Centers for Disease Control and Prevention (1997): *http://www.cdc.gov/epo/mmwr/preview/mmwrhtml/00054432.htm* (summary).
2. "Twentieth Annual Report to Congress on the Implementation of the Individuals with Disabilities Education Act," Office of Special Education and Rehabilitation, US Department of Education (12 Mar 1999): *http://www.ed.gov/offices/OSERS/OSEP/OSEP98AnlRpt/.*

Index

B

C

D

E

F

G

H

J

K

L

M

N

O

P

R

S

T

U

V

W

X

Y

Z

About the Author

Mitzi Waltz has been an author, journalist, and editor for more than a decade, covering topics from computers to health care. She has experienced the effects of childhood-onset obsessive-compulsive disorder first hand, both as a patient and as a parent. She has also been heavily involved in support and advocacy work for special-needs children within the medical, insurance, and education systems.

"Obsessive-compulsive disorder is one of the most common neuropsychiatric conditions affecting young people, but many still suffer by going without diagnosis and treatment. Parents may not know where to turn for help, and teachers and other helping professionals may not have the answers. This book was written to provide a thorough grounding in the latest medical information about OCD, and to offer help and hope to children and teens in need and their families."

Ms. Waltz has also authored *Pervasive Developmental Disorders: Finding a Diagnosis and Getting Help* and *Bipolar Disorders: A Guide to Helping Children and Adolescents* for O'Reilly's Patient-Centered Guides series, among other books.

Colophon

Patient-Centered Guides are about the experience of illness. They contain personal stories as well as a combination of practical and medical information. The faces on the covers of our Guides reflect the human side of the information we offer.

Edie Freedman designed the cover of *Obsessive-Compulsive Disorder: Help for Children and Adolescents,* using Adobe Photoshop 5.0 and QuarkXPress 3.32 with Berkeley fonts from Bitstream. The cover photo is from Rubberball Productions and is used by permission. Emma Colby prepared the cover mechanical.

Alicia Cech designed the interior layout for the book, based on a series design by Nancy Priest and Edie Freedman. The interior fonts are Berkeley and Franklin Gothic. Mike Sierra prepared the text using FrameMaker 5.5.6.

The book was copyedited by Sarah Jane Shangraw and proofread by Ann Schirmer. Darren Kelly and Claire Cloutier conducted quality assurance checks. Judy Hoer wrote the index. The illustrations that appear in this book were produced by Robert Romano and Rhon Porter using Macromedia Freehand 8 and Adobe Photoshop 5.0. Interior composition was done by Ann Schirmer and Sarah Jane Shangraw.

117 simply discussing fears + worries without gaining tools can increase severity of OCD.

Patient-Centered Guides™

Questions Answered
Experiences Shared

We are committed to empowering individuals to evolve into informed consumers armed with the latest information and heartfelt support for their journey.

When your life is turned upside down, your need for information is great. You have to make critical medical decisions, often with what seems little to go on. Plus you have to break the news to family, quiet your own fears, cope with symptoms or treatment side effects, figure out how you're going to pay for things, and sometimes still get to work or get dinner on the table.

Patient-Centered Guides provide authoritative information for intelligent information seekers who want to become advocates of their own health. They cover the whole impact of illness on your life. In each book, there's a mix of:

- **Medical background for treatment decisions**
  We can give you information that can help you to intelligently work with your doctor to come to a decision. We start from the viewpoint that modern medicine has much to offer and also discuss complementary treatments. Where there are treatment controversies we present differing points of view.

- **Practical information**
  Once you've decided what to do about your illness, you still have to deal with treatments and changes to your life. We cover day-to-day practicalities, such as those you'd hear from a good nurse or a knowledgeable support group.

- **Emotional support**
  It's normal to have strong reactions to a condition that threatens your life or changes how you live. It's normal that the whole family is affected. We cover issues like the shock of diagnosis, living with uncertainty, and communicating with loved ones.

Each book also contains stories from both patients and doctors — medical "frequent flyers" who share, in their own words, the lessons and strategies they have learned when maneuvering through the often complicated maze of medical information that's available.

We provide information online, including updated listings of the resources that appear in this book. This is freely available for you to print out and copy to share with others, as long as you retain the copyright notice on the print-outs.

http://www.patientcenters.com

Other Books in the Series

Childhood Cancer

A Parent's Guide to Solid Tumor Cancers

By Nancy Keene

ISBN 1-56592-531-9, Paperback, 6"x 9", 544 pages, $24.95

"I recommend [this book] most highly for those in need of high-level, helpful knowledge that will empower and help parents and caregivers to cope."

—Mark Greenberg, MD, Professor of Pediatrics, University of Toronto

Pervasive Developmental Disorders

Finding a Diagnosis and Getting Help

By Mitzi Waltz

ISBN 1-56592-530-0, Paperback, 6" x 9", 592 pages, $24.95

"Mitzi Waltz's book provides clear, informative, and comprehensive information on every relevant aspect of PDD. Her in-depth discussion will help parents and professionals develop a clear understanding of the issues and, consequently, they will be able to make informed decisions about various interventions. A job well done!"

—Dr. Stephen M. Edelson, Director, Center for the Study of Autism, Salem, Oregon

Your Child in the Hospital

A Practical Guide for Parents, Second Edition

By Nancy Keene and Rachel Prentice

ISBN 1-56592-573-4, Paperback, 5" x 8", 176 pages, $11.95

"When your child is ill or injured, the hospital setting can be overwhelming. Here is a terrific 'road map' to help keep families 'on track.'"

—James B. Fahner, MD, Division Chief, Pediatric Hematology/Oncology, DeVos Children's Hospital, Grand Rapids, Michigan

Choosing a Wheelchair

A Guide for Optimal Independence

By Gary Karp

ISBN 1-56592-411-8, Paperback, 5" x 8", 192 pages, $9.95

"I love the idea of putting knowledge often possessed only by professionals into the hands of new consumers. Gary Karp has done it. This book will empower people with disabilities to make informed equipment choices."

—Barry Corbet, Editor, New Mobility Magazine

Patient-Centered Guides

Published by O'Reilly & Associates, Inc.

Our products are available at a bookstore near you.

For information: 800-998-9938 • 707-829-0515 • info@oreilly.com

101 Morris Street • Sebastopol • CA • 95472-9902

Life on Wheels

For the Active Wheelchair User

By Gary Karp

ISBN 1-56592-253-0, Paperback, 6" x 9", 576 pages, $24.95

"Gary Karp's *Life On Wheels* is a super book. If you use a wheelchair, you cannot do without it. It is THE wheelchair-user reference book."

—Hugh Gregory Gallagher, Author,
FDR's Splendid Deception

Cancer Clinical Trials

Experimental Treatments and How They Can Help You

By Robert Finn

ISBN 1-56592-566-1, Paperback, 5" x 8", 216 pages, $14.95

"I highly recommend this book as a first step in what will be for many a difficult, but crucially important, part of their struggle to beat their cancer."

—From the foreword by Robert Bazell, Chief Science Correspondent for NBC News and Author,
Her-2: The Making of Herceptin, a Revolutionary Treatment for Breast Cancer

Hydrocephalus

A Guide for Patients, Families & Friends

By Chuck Toporek and Kellie Robinson

ISBN 1-56592-410-X, Paperback, 6" x 9", 384 pages, $19.95

"Toporek, a medical editor, and wife Robinson, a writer and hydrocephalus patient, fill a void of information on hydrocephalus (water on the brain) for the lay reader. Highly recommended for public and academic libraries."

—Library Journal

"In this book, the authors have provided a wonderful entry into the world of hydrocephalus to begin to remedy the neglect of this important condition. We are immensely grateful to them for their groundbreaking effort."

—Peter M. Black, MD, PhD, Franc D. Ingraham Professor of Neurosurgery, Harvard Medical School, Neurosurgeon-in-Chief, Brigham and Women's Hospital, Children's Hospital, Boston, Massachusetts

Patient-Centered Guides

Published by O'Reilly & Associates, Inc.

Our products are available at a bookstore near you.

For information: **800-998-9938 • 707-829-0515 • info@oreilly.com**

101 Morris Street • Sebastopol • CA • 95472-9902

Bipolar Disorders

A Guide to Helping Children & Adolescents

By Mitzi Waltz

ISBN 1-56592-656-0, Paperback, 6" x 9", 450 pages, $24.95

"As bipolar disorders are becoming more commonly diagnosed in children and adolescents, a readable, informative guide for these youths and their families is certainly needed. This book certainly fits the bill. It covers all of the major topics that are of greatest importance to guide parents and families on the topic of pediatric bipolarity ..."

—Robert L. Findling, MD, Director, Division of Child and Adolescent Psychiatry, Co-director, Stanley Clinical Research Center, Case Western Reserve University/University Hospitals of Cleveland

Childhood Leukemia

A Guide for Families, Friends, and Caregiver, 2nd Edition

By Nancy Keene

ISBN 1-56592-632-3, Paperback, 6" x 9", $24.95, 564 pages

"What's so compelling about Childhood Leukemia *is the amount of useful medical information and practical advice it contains. Keene avoids jargon and lays out what's needed to deal with the medical system."*

—The Washington Post

Adolescent Drug & Alcohol Abuse:

How to Spot It, Stop It, and Get Help for Your Family

By Nikki Babbit

ISBN 1-56592-755-9, Paperback, 6"x9", 304 pages

"The clear, concise, and practical information, backed up by personal stories from people who have been through these problems with their own children or clients, will have readers keeping this book within easy reach for use on a regular basis."

—James F. Crowley, MA
President, Community Intervention, Inc.
Author, Alliance for Change:
A Plan for Community Action on Adolescent Drug Abuse

Patient-Centered Guides

Published by O'Reilly & Associates, Inc.

Our products are available at a bookstore near you.

For information: 800-998-9938 • 707-829-0515 • info@oreilly.com

101 Morris Street • Sebastopol • CA • 95472-9902